"FIDELMANIA!"
THE SISTER FIDELMA PHENOMENON
LIVRES HEBDO, PARIS
6 MAY 2006

THE
SISTER FIDELMA
COMPENDIUM

THE SISTER FIDELMA COMPENDIUM

A READER'S GUIDE TO THE SISTER FIDELMA MYSTERIES OF PETER TREMAYNE

ERIC MÜLLER

EDITED BY
DAVID ROBERT WOOTEN

THE INTERNATIONAL SISTER FIDELMA SOCIETY

CRITICAL ACCLAIM FOR
FIDELMA AND TREMAYNE

FIDELMANIA – The Sister Fidelma Phenomenon
Livres Hebdo, Paris, 6 May 2006

Sister Fidelma is listed No 9 in the Top 10 Literary Nuns
The Guardian, 28 February 2009

Winner of
Prix Historia du Roman Policier Historique 2010
(*Historia* Prize of an historical crime novel in 2010)

A National Treasure!
Alan Kelly, TD, Irish Minister for the Environment, 2014

The Best of the Best in Medieval Mysteries
Booklist, Journal of the American Library Association, June 2014

**Dans le genre trés couru de polar médiéval, Peter
Tremayne tint la corde!**
(In the genre of medieval mysteries, Peter Tremayne is the leader!)
L'Express, Paris, July 2006

**Crime literature at its finest... the author ensures a reading
pleasure far outside mainstream thrillers... Tremayne
proves again he belongs on the Crime Writers Throne of
Great Britain."**
Susann Fleischer, *Literatseitschift für Deutschland*, December 2016

**Tremayne's Celtic thrillers have now reached cult status
worldwide**
BuchMarkt, Germany, 2018

This is historical crime fiction at its best.
The Belfast News Letter

The most authentically detailed medieval mystery series
currently being published.
Booklist, Journal of the American Library Association

[Fidelma]... cannot be categorized as just genre fiction. It is
literature. We can compare it to Umberto Eco's *The Name
of the Rose.*
Lucha Crovi, *La Libertà*, Italy, 2006

Title: The Sister Fidelma Compendium
Subtitle: A Reader's Guide to the Sister Fidelma Mysteries of Peter Tremayne
Editor: David Robert Wooten

For information about special discounts for bulk purchases, as well as information about reproducing selections from this book, please contact david@sisterfidelma.com.

Published by Gryfons Publishers for:
The International Sister Fidelma Society
PMB 312
1818 North Taylor Street, Suite B
Little Rock, Arkansas 72207 USA

First Edition, 2022

978 0 9654 2208 6

First published in the United States of America

Front and back cover artwork © Michael Walsh Photography, used with permission
Frontspiece and cover illustrations of Sister Fidelma by Eric Müller, © The International Sister Fidelma Society
Cover and content design and layout by David Robert Wooten

Details on membership in
The International Sister Fidelma Society
may be found online at **www.sisterfidelma.com**

FOR PETER

A KINDRED SPIRIT AMONGST A DEARTH OF THE SAME

AITHNÍONN CIARÓG CIARÓG EILE

WRITERS AREN'T PEOPLE, EXACTLY.
OR, IF THEY'RE ANY GOOD,
THEY'RE A WHOLE LOT OF PEOPLE
TRYING SO HARD TO BE
ONE PERSON.

F. SCOTT FITZGERALD

Contents

MÓR Í AN FHIRRINNE, AGUS BUAIDHFE SÍ
TRUTH IS GREAT AND WILL PREVAIL

– Brehon Morann

Foreword

In 1993, when I wrote the first Sister Fidelma short mystery stories, I knew that I was describing a world that few readers would have knowledge of outside of the Celtic Studies departments of universities. I was depicting 7th century Ireland, its laws, social system, and its fascinating history. The next year, I found myself commissioned by Jane Morpeth (1954-2021), the gifted and capable editor of Headline Publishing, to write the first of the Sister Fidelma novels. I was not expecting that the result of their publication would ignite such fascination from so many countries.

Before long, questions about the background of the stories were flooding in from enthusiastic readers.

David Robert Wooten, a graduate of North Carolina University, and executive director of the American College of Heraldry and editor of its own journal, *The Armigers' News* (est. 1996), had been in contact with me before on Irish historical matters. He proposed a Sister Fidelma website to answer some of the questions. The excited response to it inspired the launch The International Sister Fidelma Society with its thrice-yearly journal *The Brehon*.

Over the years I have watched with amazement as the Society grew thanks to David's passion and the enthusiasm of the Society's members. It took on its own life. This is now reflected in this tremendous and exciting volume that he has put together.

Although he has claimed that this is "my baby," that it is not so. Without his unflagging enthusiasm, his persuasion of many distinguished experts, authors, and those who just love the mysteries to participate, the Society would not have existed. And, by the same logic, neither would this educational and exciting volume. For here, in this volume, is the answer to the background to the series, its settings and its characters.

My job was writing fiction; murder mysteries that were derived from historical fact set in real places and in the appropriate historical reality of the period. In spite of being a relatively unknown world, enthusiasts wanted to know more about it. Their letters to the Society, from many parts of the world, Germany to Japan, and from the United States to the Czech Republic, often drew forth various academic experts in the field to come forward. Many of the contributions in this volume expand and explain the places and the times. In making this happen, David deserves the highest praise as not only a literary detective but an historical educator. He has created, in this volume, what is an essential adjunct to the stories.

This tome is not only about the facts of the "Sister Fidelma Age and Culture," but will help the discerning reader — or even those who just enjoy following the adventures — in navigating the travels and travails of Fidelma of Cashel with her faithful companion, Brother Eadulf of Seaxmund's Ham, of the South Folk of East Anglia.

— *Peter Tremayne*

Introduction

For true Fidelmaniacs, a book such as this is long overdue, and its pages will doubtless be quickly dog-eared by both longtime and newly-initiated readers of Sister Fidelma and her mysterious-murder tales. Ideally this will serve as both reference and tribute to an author whose works are universally read (in a plethora of languages) and loved.

It is the editor's hope that this work will sit table-side, bedside, wherever-side the reader chooses to devour the dozens of Sister Fidelma novels and short stories penned by one of the world's leading Irish historiographers – ever at-the-ready should some question arise.

To this day, many people do not readily associate the name "Peter Tremayne" with his non-fiction alter-ego, Peter Berresford Ellis. Oft is the time that, as Director of The International Sister Fidelma Society, I receive correspondence from readers (or, on occasion, "academics") unaware of this fact, pointing out what they believe to be inaccuracies or anachronisms in the novels and stories (the more common of these often make their way into our website's FAQs page). In most cases, the aforementioned "academics" haven't the bona fides to challenge any of Peter's assertions, let alone with the haughty attitude that usually accompanies such messages.

And, more often than not, they will suggest that Peter Tremayne brush up on the works of Peter Berresford Ellis for a better understanding of Irish history and culture. With a smile on my face I am all too pleased to inform them that these two separate individuals actually inhabit the same encyclopædic brain (non-schizophrenically, of course), and so they should rest assured that what appears in Mr. Tremayne's novels runs along the same lines of fact as appear in Mr. Ellis's many works of non-fiction.

A couple of minor "housekeeping" points on the contents herein before we begin...

Many of the chapters are either gleaned in whole or in part from articles, essays, and other sources with similar subjects, but with additional (but not differing or "conflicting") facts. Many such instances occur in the Frequently Asked Questions chapter. Thus, reading both sections together will prove a more "cumulative" resource than either alone.

The other minor issue is one which grammarians on either side of "the pond" may or may not take issue. Contributors to this book are Irish, English, and even American. And to paraphrase George Bernard Shaw, such contributors are "peoples separated by a common language (and – quite often – spelling)." So, rather than "Anglicize" or "Americanize" all of the text, each chapter has been left in its "native" English (save for all of the Irish, Latin, Greek, and other words Peter may toss in from time to time, as he is wont to do).

So, please forgive any rebounding from "civilisation" to "civilization," and back again. I choose not to retype words into other authors' keyboards. I believe the reader can well-discern the meaning of a given "English" word, no matter the spelling.

One final word of advice – depending on what century this book lands in your hands, the internet may be an antiquarian idea itself, with all knowledge being constantly piped directly into humans' brains via some system as yet uninvented... that we know of. To those of us who love to leaf through the pages of REAL books, especially old ones, for that wonderful feel and bibliosmia you get when walking into an antique bookstore, such an "innovation" would be a sad day indeed.

So, some how, some way, at some point (soon), we invite the reader to visit the website of The International Sister Fidelma Society at **sisterfidelma.com**. Therein you will find EVEN MORE information, updated far more often than is possible with revised editions of this text. And I would certainly encourage you to join the Society (provided we're still – hopefully – around, in one form or another), as all Fidelmaniacs should definitely avail themselves of the benefits exclusive to members.

Ideally this reference tool will help sharpen your plow/plough as you voraciously till the fields of Fidelma's "mysterious" adventures. ***Léamh Sona! (Happy Reading!)***

– David Robert Wooten

The Sister Fidelma Phenomenon

It is unique that a series of crime thrillers could achieve such international popularity these days without having, so far, a media involvement in promoting them to the public. There have been neither movies nor television series of the Sister Fidelma Mysteries that have brought these books to public attention. The books were originally published both in the UK and USA without fanfares, without any promotion or hype that is often attendant on other books that publishers think is in a class by themselves. Indeed, the books appeared on what publishers call their "backing list."

But, over the years, their popularity has spread, and they have appeared in numerous translations in many countries. The critical praise they have received, their still growing following, as witnessed by The International Sister Fidelma Society, founded five years ago, has been because they are superb stories, set in a unique period and culture, and told by a master craftsman. Like only a handful of writers before him, Peter Tremayne has taken the historical crime thriller to the level of literature.

When the first Sister Fidelma Mystery was published in 1994, many critics recognised that the event was something unusual in mystery fiction. As historical mysteries they were associated in some critics' minds at the time with the series made famous by BBC television, the Brother Cadfael Mysteries of Ellis Peters (Edith Pargetter – 1913-95). Critics from the London *Evening Standard* and others felt that Fidelma was to be the successor to Brother Cadfael. The *Oxford Times* called her a "Brother Cadfael on the distaff side."

What the early critics overlooked was that the Sister Fidelma books were not mediaeval church mysteries but were set in a period eight centuries before the setting of the Cadfael books. The setting of 7th century Ireland, its culture, its law system, the conflict of its native social philosophies and the incoming Roman Christian ethics, again single the series put as unique. Fidelma is an advocate of the ancient Irish law system and has to act according to those laws. Before the books appeared, few people outside of university Celtic Studies Departments had even heard of the Brehon Law system, which had finally been destroyed in the 17th century. They had no idea of the rich culture of Ireland of this period that, in Europe was said to be the "Dark Ages" but in Ireland was the "Age of Golden Enlightenment." These books have changed that lack of knowledge.

Only a few critics initially challenged the authenticity of the background of the books through their own ignorance of Irish culture and the period. They leapt in with their criticism without realising that the author was also a published expert in Celtic Studies. So, they soon fell silent as scholars of the period were united in their praise of the veracity of the background and the law system.

While the comparison with Brother Cadfael was clearly meant as high praise, nevertheless, the Sister Fidelma Mysteries are in a class of their own. As the critic, anthologist and editor, Mike Ashley, has written in his *Encyclopaedia of Modern Crime Fiction*, no other writer has written in this area. The Sister Fidelma Mysteries are unique. As the critic of *The Belfast Telegraph* wrote: "This is masterly storytelling from an author who breathes fascinating life into the world he is writing about."

Some of the Sister Fidelma Mysteries have been read on Irish and Canadian radio and one novel has been dramatised on German radio, a dramatisation now available on commercial CD from Audio Verlag of Berlin. It is astonishing to reflect that even without this sort of profile, the books are selling in more languages than most mystery series that do have such media promotional backing.

Well might the Irish literary world claim that Sister Fidelma is Ireland's most famous fictional detective.

– Maurice McCann
Féile Fidelma 2006 program booklet

FIDELMANIA!

t was not until 2004 that France discovered the Sister Fidelma Mysteries, when Editions 10/18 published the first title to appear in French. In May 2014, they published the 23rd title in the series, having – amazingly – sometimes published as many as three new titles a year in order to catch up with the demand for the books.

The reaction from French readers was immediate, and two of the titles were selected as Grand Livres de Mois (Book of the Month) Club choices in 2005. Peter was invited to Paris to do some supporting publicity for the books.

The main French book journal *Livres Hebdo* (May 13, 2006) coined the word "Fidelmania" to describe the demand, while a French journal specialising in crime fiction simply described the phenomenon under the headline: *Soeur Fidelma – Superstar!*

While a comparative late-comer to Fidelma's World, there seems no stopping the "Fidelmania," and *The Dove of Death* is due for publication in 2015. The prestigious French history magazine *Historia* awarded Peter the Prix Historia du Roman Policier Histoique in December 2010, for *Maitre des âmes (Master of Souls)* as the best historical mystery novel of 2010.

But France is not the only country to acknowledge the Fidelma "phenomenon."

In London, Professor James Mullen, top literary critic of *The Guardian* newspaper, declared (February 28, 2009) Sister Fidelma was Number 9 in his "top ten" literary nuns. The list was impressive, for Peter was preceded by Chaucer (Prioress), Shakespeare (Isabella), Alexander Pope (Elissa), Samuel Richardson (Bold Nun), Daniel Defoe (Suzanne Simonin), Matthew Lewis (Bleeding Nun), Chateaubriand (Amélie), Charlotte Brontë (Ghostly Nun), **Peter Tremayne (Sister Fidelma)**, and making number ten was Muriel Spark (Abbess of Crewe). Now that's some list to be in!

Italian critic Luca Crovi agreed: "Fidelma... cannot be categorized as just genre fiction. It is literature. We can compare it to Umberto Eco's *The Name of the Rose.*"

"No one can make the seventh century come so alive as Tremayne,"

3

said *Library Journal* in the USA.

"There is an ever-growing mass of ardent admirers of Sister Fidelma worldwide... the series has become highly popular across the globe," observed the UK's *Book and Magazine Collector*.

"The most authentically detailed medieval mystery series currently being published," declared *Booklist, the Journal of the American Library Association*.

To sum it all up, *Publishers Weekly*, simply said that Fidelma was "A heroine for any age."

– *Livres Hebdo*, Paris
6 May 2006

Was Fidelma a Real historical Person?

One of the most regular inquiries that the Society receives is "was Fidelma a real person?" We could respond placing the question in the same category as the many millions who ask, "was Sherlock Holmes a real person?" The answer, of course, is that Fidelma is a literary creation like Holmes or other famous fictional detectives such as Hercules Poirot, Miss Maple, Philip Marlow, Sam Spade, Charlie Chan, Father Brown, and so on.

Fidelma is the literary creation of Peter Tremayne.

But wait there is more to this than meets the eye. *Booklist*, the journal of the American Library Association, said of the Fidelma series: "The most authentically detailed medieval mystery series currently being published." How authentically detailed? Are Fidelma and her family based on any 7th century Irish historical characters?

FIDELMA

Image Courtesy De Leeskamer: Graphic Novel adaptation of Absolution By Murder

As we know, Peter Tremayne is the pseudonym of an historian with degrees in Celtic Studies. We know that his 7th century Irish background is always accurate and that he places Fidelma firmly as the daughter of Failbhe Flann, King of Muman (modern Munster) from AD 628 – AD 637/639. He was a member of the Eóghanacht dynasty. Peter opts to use AD 637 as the year of Fidelma's birth, making Fidelma 27 years old when we meet her in the first novel *Absolution by Murder* (1994). This was set against the famous Synod of Whitby (*Stroneshalh*) in AD 664.

As the daughter of Failbhe Flann, she was sister to Failbhe's sons Fogartach and Colgú. Fogartach was eldest but, under the electoral Brehon system, he was not elected by the *derbhfine* to become king. Succession was not by primogeniture and the family council (usually of three generations from the last known head of the family) had to meet and elect the person they thought best qualified to be the next head of the family from King, Princes, or other nobility.

So Fogartach was not qualified. However, one of Fogartach's descendants, Tnúgthal, is listed as the king who died AD 820. This is not entirely supported by reference in the annals or chronicles.

It was Failbhe Flann's second son, Colgú, who becomes King of Muman in AD 665/6 – as mentioned in *Suffer Little Children*. Colgú (we know it's spoilers for avid readers of the series so far) marries and has a son called Nad Fraích. Nad Fraích does not become King after his father but has progeny who eventually emerge as Kings of Muman in the 9th and 10th centuries. The last was Fer Graid mac Clérig (AD 856-961). Two years after he died, the Dál gCais, or Uí Fidgente, seized the Muman throne and produced the famous Brían Bóruma (Bórú), who went on to seize the High Kingship. Brían became one of the famous High Kings of all Ireland. He was killed in his tent by the retreating Danes in his moment of victory at the Battle of Clontarf in AD 1014.

This is a page from the Lebor na hUidre (Book of the Dun Cow) *11th century copy which shows a passage from the story 'The Táin Bó Cualigne' in which the prophetess Fidelma warns Queen Medb about her ambitions on the eve of war with Ulaidh.*

Fidelma's brother Colgú frequently appears in the series and, indeed, her brother Fogartach's has also been mentioned. Both brothers are mentioned in the Irish annals and chronicles. But does Fidelma ever get an historical mention?

The name Fedelm and Feidhelm, which today is more popularly rendered Fidelma, the form Peter uses, was a frequently used Irish name of the period in both feminine and masculine forms. The masculine forms, Feidelimid and Feidhlimidh, often occur as the name of several Eóghanacht Kings of Muman.

In Irish mythology the female form also occurs several times. We have a Fidelma as the prophetess who warns Queen Medb (Maeve) of Connacht against her ambition that leads to the war against the Ulaidh (Ulster men). This is in the great saga *The Táin Bó Cualigne* regarded

WAS FIDELMA A REAL HISTORICAL PERSON?

as the Irish equivalent of the Greek *Illiad*. Another Fidelma is a goddess of the *Sidh Druimm* – Ridge of the Otherworld – which became Cashel. She appears in *Shenchas Faghbhála Caisil andso sis agus Beanndacht* (The Finding of Cashel). It is another great myth tale to which Peter Tremayne expounds in *Sister Fidelma's Cashel: The Early Kings of Munster and their Capital*, which this Society published in 2008. This Fidelma is thereby the central to the story of the foundation of Cashel as the principal fortress of the Eóghanacht King of Muman (Munster) Conall Corc said to have ruled in the 3rd century.

Although not of Muman, there was Fidelma Noíchrothach – Fidelma "the nine times beautiful," a daughter of Con-chobhar mac Nessa of Ulaidh – who was one of the famous female warriors in Irish mythology. She abandons her husband Cairbre Nia Fer, who is eventually slain by the warrior Cú Chulainn at Battle of Ros na Rígh, and elopes with Conall Cearnach, the famous hero and warrior in the Ulster

Peter addressed attendees of the first Féile Fidelma at Emly in 2006

Cycle of tales. He is foster brother of Cú Chulainn, who is often his companion in adventure.

Of course, aside from myths, there are several Fidelma's in early history. Seathrún Céitinn's famous *Foras Freasa ar Éirinn's* refers to Fidelma of Laigin who bears twins with her husband Eochaidh. But one of the twins, Aodhan, was kidnapped and the other, Brandubh, went into exile in Alba with his father. The twins grow to manhood and find themselves fighting against each other for the throne of Laigin in the 6th century. Certainly, there was Eochaidh whose son Brandubh became King of Laigin. There were Feidlimid (males) in his ancestry including Feidlimid, son of Eanna Cennsalach, who is the progenitor of the Uí Cennsalach dynasty, enemies of the Eóghanacht appearing several times in Peter's books. Brandubh is recorded in the chronicles for his defeat of the High King Aed mac Ainmuirach who is killed at the battle of Dun Bolg in AD 598.

There are six saints at this time named Fidelma but only five saints are accorded a "name day" January 11, August 3, October 30, December 9, and December 13, Three more Feidlimid are noted but accorded masculine status (August 9, 28, and December 29). The most popular of these saints was the daughter of the High King Laoghaire, converted by St. Patrick. She was sister to St. Eithne who shares her saint's day.

So, can we now identify Fidelma of Cashel in the records?

We enter some confusion here as it seems that King Failbhe Flann had two daughters. Fidelma, as we know her, or Fedelm, as daughter of Failbe Flann is referenced in the *Fragmentary Irish Annals*. There are eight recorded in the *Ban Shencus* (History of Women) a surviving manuscript is one credited to Gilla Mo Dutú (*Ua Casaide*) of the abbey of Daimh Inis (Devenish) in 1147. Starting in early times, this history is records leading women up to 1193. Scholars have remarked that this work is not all encompassing as many prominent women, recorded in the annals and chronicles, are omitted. Of the eight Fidelmas, unfortunately, there is nothing to specifically record them as the daughter of Failbhe Flann.

The *Ban Shencus* does refer to a daughter of Failbhe Flann. However, she is listed as Failind as the wife of Mael Ochtraig, a prince of the Déisi who died in AD 645. It is confusing that there is also a Fail-ind listed as a princess of the Déisi, who was the mother of Eithne, wife of the legendary Oengus, King of Cashel c.

Intrepid "mountaineers" climb to Knockgraffon during the 2017 Féile Fidelma – Knockgraffon was the main Eóghanacht fortress until they moved to Cashel in the 3rd century AD

AD 490.

As the Eóghanacht are portrayed in Peter's books as not being on good terms with their sovereign kings at Cashel, which is an accurate reflection, perhaps we could nudge Peter to mention how Fidelma saw her elder sister. If Mael Ochtraig died in AD 465 he would have to assume that Fidelma was eight years old at that time and so her sister Failind would be eight or ten years older.

However, as we have mention of Faelinn also as a religieuse, we are left in confusion. Failind might well be a female variation of Fáelán (meaning wolf) of which there were 14 saints of that name,

Peter has chosen to start the life of Fidelma after the death of her father. This is the daughter he places in the religious. Hence, when we first meet our heroine, she is Sister Fidelma of Cill Dara. Might it be that, when Fidelma enters the religious, it is at the instigation of Abbot Laisran, her cousin? This is for the sake of security, as her cousins, having become Kings after her father's death, were not welcoming to either her nor her brother Colgú. But referring to the *Ban Shencus*, could it be that her widowed elder sister Failind was already in an abbey? However, Fidelma left the abbey of Cill Dara and eventually the religious to become her brother's legal adviser. The rest is "history" in his series.

Failbe Flann, son of Aedo Dubh, ruled from Cashel for ten years, but was he a good king? Some scribes do not think so.

He had succeeded his cousin Cathal mac Aedo Fhaind Carthrach when he died in AD 628. But the interesting point is that Failbhe Flann's brother had been king before and ruled from Cashel AD 619-622. Although he ruled for a short time, it was obvious that Fingen left a reputation behind which Fidelma's father did not match. One bard wrote:

> *To be without Fingen, to be without Mór*
> *To Cashel is a cause of grief;*
> *It is as if there were no king*
> *If Failbhe Flann is to be king,*

Fingen (AD 571-622) was certainly generally praised and recorded by the bards:

> *Fingen, the fierce, the active,*
> *Reckless, intrepid to the last,*
> *Kind and gentle towards women*
> *Alas! In bonds held fast.*

The *Annals of Tighnernach* say:

> *Muman*
> *In the time of Fingen mac Aedo*
> *Its store houses were full*
> *Its homesteads were fruitful.*

Mór, a feminine name meaning tall or great in this instance, was, it seems, the most popular name in Ireland in this period. Mór was daughter of Áed Bennan, who was King, became wife to Fingen. She bore him a son, Sechnussach, although she is not recorded as the mother of Maenach d. 662 who was a cousin Fidelma hated. The story of Mór became intertwined with that of the sovereignty goddess. Either Mór was his queen or, more likely, this is a symbolic reference to Mór the female goddess for whom Muman took its name.

However, if Failbhe had been such a bad ruler it is strange he would have lasted so long. He was 9th in line from Fiachu Muilleathan and 58th in line from the legendary Eber Finn, son of Milidh (Golamh) Milidh of Spain.

We know the family are known as the Eóghanacht and that the various branches of this family came to rule all Munster. The Eóghanacht (dynasty of the yews) dominated the kingdoms and territories of southern Ireland from the 5th to 12th centuries. So, who was the Eóghan who was the progenitor of the family?

This was the great legendary King of Muman (Munster) also known as Mag Nuadat, Eóghan Mór.

It is pointed out that the Eóghanacht descend from sons of Eóghan son of Ailill Olomm. A few generations on, it was Conall Corc mac Luigthig, who was advised by the goddess – Fedelm or Fidelma – with a vision of a yew bush on the rock which now bears the name Cashel. Their kingdom spread with alliances with the Ciarraige (Kerry) and Osraige (Ossory) and the Déisi Muman. The stories surrounding these early characters are a mixture of genuine history and symbolic fiction.

The Petrie Crown (c.100 BC – 200 AD) – discovered in Co Cork – named after its former owner, Irish antiquarian George Petrie. Part of an elaborate horned head-dress, this exquisite piece of pagan goldsmithery was created in the La Tene style, using repoussé embossing and cloisonné enameling, derived from Etruscan and Greek forms.

It is with Fiachu Muillearthan that most scholars agree that the Eóghanacht emerged from mythology into history. It was said battle took place with Fiachu's victory at Domhire Damgaire ("the hill of the oxen") in AD 250. Today this is now called Knocklong and told in the story *Forbais Dromma Damgaire* (The Siege of Knocklong).

The location comes back into history in AD 650, during Fidelma's childhood, when Dioma, prince of the Dál gCais (Uí Fidgente) defeated an army from Connacht when they attempted to bring the area under Dioma is claimed a co-ruler with Dioma son of Ronan, is referred to in *Foras ar Feasa* by Ceitinn but not as a Dalcassian prince while Cuan was mentioned as ruler of the Uí Fidgente. In *Collectaries de Rebur Hibernicus*. Peter has admitted that the King Lists, while basically consistent, have so many twists and turns in them. He acknowledges that he has been basically guided by *Irish Kings and High Kings*, by John Francis Byrne, 1973. Dr Byrne was Professor of Early Irish History at University College Dublin. Professor Byrne was Professor of Early History at University College, Dublin.

Anyway, Peter has made the life of Fidelma firmly anchored in her country's background for the period. Her family, her education, the historical events, the law system she is an advocate of and the decisions she makes are all embedded in reality. This is why Peter has attracted so many academic fans as well as general readers and why so many leading professors of early Irish history have accepted, as invited guests over the years of the Féile Fidelma, to come along to endorse the background by their talks.

– *The Brehon*, XXI, 1, January 2022

THE SISTER FIDELMA COMPENDIUM

Who Was Fidelma's Father?

While Fidelma's father, Failbhe Flann, was dead by the time her adventures began, he is often referred to, and remembered fondly by Fidelma, in some of the stories. We know that he was a King of Muman (Munster) reigning at Cashel and that he had died when Fidelma was a few years old. Her mother died from postnatal complications following her birth. Therefore, her memories of her father are dim. So, do we know anything else about him?

He is certainly referred to several times in the ancient annals and chronicles.

He was the younger son of Aed Dubh, an Eóghanacht noble who was a direct descendant of Feidlimid (the masculine form of Fidelma), the son of the first Christian King of Cashel Oengus mac Nad Froích died c. AD 490-491. Aed Dubh had two sons – Fíngen and Failbhe Flann.

Fíngen mac Aedo Duib succeeded a cousin also called Feidlimid, son of Coipre Cromm; but here the chronicles have some confusion by placing three other rulers between Feidlimid and Fíngen. Whether this indicated some contention between three rivals is uncertain. However, the chroniclers say that, on his succession, Failbhe Flann's elder brother ruled from Cashel, peacefully and well, until he died in AD 619. At the time Fíngen's father-in-law, Aed Bennán, was the ruler of the Eóghanacht of Locha Léin, was very powerful in the west of the kingdom, and supported his son-in-law. The Annals of Inishfallen remember Fíngen in this fashion:

In Muma Re linn Fíngen mac Aedha
Robdar lána a cuiledha
Robdar torrtighe a treba

Muman In the time of Fíngen mac Aedo
The storehouses were full
The homesteads were fruitful

Such an entry indicates it was a peaceful and prosperous time.
For nearly a decade, until AD 628, the kingship went to another

cousin, Cathal, before Failbhe Flann (sometimes given as Fland) mac Aedo Duib became installed as King of Muman in Cashel. Now the name Flann means "red," and usually "blood red," and this applied to the colour of his hair. Fidelma is always described as having long red tresses and the name means "of the smooth hair." It was a distinction of the Eóghanacht's to have red or deep black (Dub) hair, and we find many Eóghanacht with the nickname either Flann or Dub.

We are not sure what age Failbhe Flann was when he came to power. Judging the age of his elder brother and his father, we can assume he was already about 30 years old or more.

During his reign he had two sons. One was Fogartach, who more or less vanished in obscurity. The other son became the well known (to readers of Fidelma) Colgú, And, of course, Fidelma herself, was born sometime in November, AD 637. This would make her two years old when her father, Failbhe Flann died.

Now when Failbhe Flann was inaugurated on The Rock of Cashel in AD 628, he immediately found himself under attack. The old enemies of the Eóghanacht, the Uí Fidgente had joined the Déisi Becc or Deisi Tuisceart, claiming themselves as the Dál gCais rightful rulers of Muman. They had tried to control the territory of northern Muman (Tuadh Mhumhain – today remembered as Thomond). Cashel had clearly extended its rule over the rebellious northern part of the territory during a previous attempt to break away. But the very year that Failbhe Flann was made King in Cashel, violence again threatened the kingdom.

Guaire Aidne mac Colmán had succeeded his father as King of Connacht in AD 627. Guaire was persuaded to take up the cause of the would-be Dál gCais and decided to march an army into northern Muman in the year AD 628 to join the rebels of Muman.

Failbhe Flann marched his army northwest immediately to counter him. The clash was recorded as the Battle of Carn Feradaig in the Ballyhoura Hills (Cahermarry, Limerick). It was a decisive victory for the King of Cashel, as he not only put the King of Connacht to flight but, in the ensuing battle, one of Guaire's most experienced warriors, and a close relative, Conall of the Uí Maine, was killed. Guaire was to die in AD 633. A border was established between the Déisi who had settled in northern Munster and those who settled in Connacht. The rebellious Uí Fidgente and Déisi were quickly pacified, and peace was ensured for the rest of Failbhe's reign. The story is recorded in the Annals of Inisfallen.

However, this was not the only battle that Failbhe Flann found himself fighting. The second battle was in alliance with a friend and not in defence of his kingdom. This was the Battle of Ath Goan, on the western plain of the Life (River Liffey) and was fought in AD 636, according to the Annals of Tigernach. Dates either side of this year are given by other annals but Daniel P. McCarthy in *Chronology of the Irish Annals* (Royal Irish Academy, 1998), with its extensive checking and dating comparisons, is what I shall follow.

The High King Domhnall mac Aed (d. AD 642) had led an army into neighbouring Laigin because of the refusal of the provincial king Crimthann mac Aedo, to deliver due tribute. It seems that it was decided that Crimthann had to be deposed. A young noble, Fáelán mac Colmán, had emerged into history in AD 628 as a skilled warrior who had slain in combat another influential noble, Crúnmael Bog Luath of the Uí Cheinnselaigh.

Fáelán was ambitious but he did not want to see Laigin being devastated by the policies of Crimthann. However, the Laigin King had power. He was the son of Aed Dibchine, who had also been King of Laigin. Their connections were powerful, which allowed them to be strong enough to stand up even against the High King and reject the imposition of the famous *boruma* (cattle tribute).

In AD 633 Fáelán sought an alliance with Failbhe Flann of Cashel. Also joining Fáelán was the father of his wife, Sarnat; a noble called Conell Guthbinn who was also well connected.

The armies clashed at the ford of Goan (Ath Goan) and Crimthann was slain in the ensuing battle. Some of the chroniclers said that Failbhe Flann was so rich that he also paid the *boruma* tribute to the High King Domhnall on behalf of his ally, Fáelán, the new King of Laigin. It may have involved Laigin paying Cashel some form of tribute in exchange. Some say that it was just a boast to exert Cashel authority over Laigin. Chroniclers give Fáelán some 30 years as King and record him dying in AD 666.

Apart from these two battles, the reign of Failbhe Flann seemed relatively peaceful.

Fidelma's father appears in one other record, and one, if there is a germ of truth in it, may have accounted for some of Fidelma's scepticism about members of the religious. It is recorded in *Vita Sancti Machoemoci Pulchorii Abbatis*, also referred to in the Annals of the Four Masters, the Calendar of Oengus, and the Martyrology of Donegal.

It seemed that during Failbhe Flann's reign, a young religious came to Muman. He was son of an artisan named Beoan, but little is known of his given name. He simply became "My Fair Youth;"' that is, Mo Chaem Óg, or Pulcherius. He decided to set up his own abbey at a place which became known as Liathmochaemog – *liath* means a grey place and it

These are the remains of the early medieval church at Liathmore. This was the community founded by St Mochaemog (Mo Chaem Ó,g sometimes called Pulcherius) d. AD 655 who argued with Fidelma's father King Failbhe Flann and cursed him for refusing to allow the 'saint' to have these same fields to build his community.
Image: IrishStones.org

was perhaps this is because it was a place surrounded by marshes.

Today it is called Liathmore. There are still remains of the religious settlement founded by him. To get there you have to go north on

Here one can see the foundation base of what was a 9th century Round Tower, built to protect the religious from Viking raids. At the right is the smaller early medieval chapel. Image: Ireland ByWays

the R639 from Littleton. From Cashel it is about 20 miles. The easiest route is to go north on the M8, take the left turn at Junction 6, onto the N62 signpost to Thurles but turn fairly immediately on the R629 to Littleton. Beyond that there is a track on the right to a farm and signs to the churches at Liathmore. But beware! To cross to the remains, you need both a stout heart and sturdy rubber boots.

There are two churches. The smaller one is early medieval and the larger one is late medieval. There is also the base of what was a 9th century Round Tower. The ruins have some intriguing surviving carvings including sheela-na-gigs.

So how does Failbhe Flann come into this story? Well, it just so happened that Mo Chaem Óg had chosen to set up his community on one of the favourite grazing lands for the King's horses. So, when the keeper of Failbhe Flann's horses arrived for the summer grazing, Mo Chaem Óg and his followers chased them away. The keeper of horses reported as much to Failbhe who promptly sent his steward to inform Mo Chaem Óg that he was trespassing. The arrogant young man hot-footed it south to Cashel and instead of trying to negotiate permission and seek an alternative spot, he simply demanded that the King hand over the land. When Failbhe Flann refused, the young man cursed him and forewarned his eyesight would fail unless he did what he was told, and his authority came from God.

According to the chroniclers, Failbhe Flann's eyesight did begin to fail.

Mo Chaem Óg died in AD 655. In spite of his argument with the King he had remained in possession of the land whose buildings you can still see today. This land passed to his community. Interestingly the "saint" and his family are often associated with cures relating to eyesight. We are told St Ita even cursed the saint's own eyesight when he was a baby.

Failbhe Flann certainly is recorded as suffering some eyesight disability and perhaps this led to his death in AD 639.

– *Tom Dudley*
The Brehon, XV, 1, January 2016

THE SISTER FIDELMA COMPENDIUM

The History we Weren't Told

When I was at junior school in the 1950s I enjoyed history and, at the time, didn't give much thought to why it was so anglocentric – and even "anglo" is a bit dubious as, apart from Alfred the Great and Harold II, I don't recall learning about any other Anglo – Saxons. It was the usual history – William the Conqueror, Stephen and Matilda's civil war, Edward I vs Robert the Bruce, Wars of the Roses, etc. etc. At least a bit of Scottish history crept into the syllabus, but not much. Precious little Welsh history. And as for Irish history – I confess, I don't recall that we had any. Did we learn about King John becoming Lord of Ireland? I don't think so. Did we learn about Oliver Cromwell's genocidal onslaught of the Irish? I'm sure we didn't. Did we learn about... well, I could go on.

No, we didn't.

We didn't when I moved on to grammar school, either, but by then I'd come to realize that the education system at that time told you very little about the history of the British Isles, let alone about the rest of the world.

Another aside, if I may. In 1956 my Dad gave me a copy of *Whittaker's Almanack*. I believe it's still published. It was an annual compendium of more information than you could ever want to know. I consumed it and in particular the various lists and charts. I soon realized I was a listaholic. Lists fascinate me because it's a good way to present information in an orderly fashion and it helps you understand things methodically.

Amongst the lists were the Kings and Queens of England and for once it started at Egbert rather than William the Conqueror. It also included the Kings and Queens of Scotland, though for some reason started at Malcolm III. It even had a few Princes of Wales but only a few, going back to one or other of the Llewellyns. But there were no rulers of Ireland, which puzzled me, because I'd already heard of Brian Boru. What struck me about the *Whittaker's* listing was the gaps. Why did the Scottish list start at Malcolm III? Who were the other two? Where was Macbeth? Why did the Princes of Wales list only start in the 1200s? Why did the king-list of England start with Egbert? Where did he come from?

It was this more than anything else that started me to research. I became obsessed with producing lists of rulers, not only fleshing out the Scottish and Welsh listings, but moving on to France and Spain and Russia and ancient Egypt, and ancient China – you get the picture.

But Ireland was different, and difficult. No matter how I researched back in the late 1950s, hardly any reference book I came across gave any information at all on early Irish history. Not even the *Encyclopædia Britannica* which was the best I could come across in my local library.

Over time I moved on, moved house several times, changed schools, went to work, began writing – other things filled my mind. But my interest in history never went away, and I still wanted to know about the histories we weren't told.

So, it was a delight when, in 1977, I discovered the historical mysteries of Ellis Peters, telling of Brother Cadfael. I confess it did pass through my mind at one point whether Ellis Peters was a pseudonym of a certain Peter Berresford Ellis. He soon told me that it wasn't! But I went in search of other historical mysteries. So, my story reaches 1992, thirty-six years after seeing that *Whittaker's Almanack* that set fire to my enquiring mind. And over thirty years ago, almost as long. By then I'd already had several anthologies published and had become friends with Nick Robinson who had not long set up his own Robinson Publishing, and I was contributing to his *Mammoth Book* line. Over lunch one day I mentioned my interest in historical mysteries. Nick already knew of the popularity of the Brother Cadfael books, so he commissioned me to compile a *Mammoth Book of Historical Whodunnits*.

I wrote to Peter, and he told me he'd been thinking about writing stories about a young female *dálaigh*, which meant nothing to me, but I was keen to see what he would produce. When I received that story, "The High King's Sword," I was fascinated-well, I don't think "fascinated" goes far enough. The title mentioned "High King" and it immediately took me back over thirty years because I had endeavoured to find a list of the Irish High Kings without success.

The story did not disappoint, and I was delighted to publish it in my anthology which came out in October 1993. I hadn't realized at the time that somehow my simple request had kickstarted something in Peter's mind, because at the same time as my anthology appeared so did others with Sister Fidelma stories – "Hemlock at Vespers" *in*

THE HISTORY WE WEREN'T TOLD

Midwinter Mysteries 3, "Murder in Repose" in *Great Irish Detective Stories* and "Murder by Miracle" in *Constable New Crime 2*. It was as if something had been moved off the bottom of a shelf and a whole pile of stories had come tumbling down.

I like to think it was me who pulled that something off the shelf and began the avalanche, and I continue to be amazed that the avalanche has yet to settle. It was immensely satisfying, not just because here was a wonderful new character in a very special setting, with a whole different world about her. It meant that as I read these stories and novels the world of ancient Ireland opened up for me, something that I had longed to find over thirty years before and which I now found totally absorbing and highly rewarding.

Sister Fidelma reveals a world that was never taught in school – I suspect it still isn't – and throws a very different light on how we should perceive the so-called Dark Ages. It might have been the Dark Ages in Britain – well, certainly in England, a nation which at times

I think has yet to emerge fully from the Dark Ages – but it certainly wasn't the Dark Ages in Ireland. Here was a land at the very western end of the known world that was full of learning, treated women equally, and with a mastery of law and art. I think the Fidelma books should be required reading in schools so that our understanding of our history isn't so anglocentric and we see it in perspective and in depth. And if only he'd written them in the late 1950s – I mean, after all he was fifteen or sixteen then!-it would have saved me all that anguish trying to research ancient Ireland. Thank goodness he got round to it in the end.

– Mike Ashley
The Brehon, XX, 1, January 2021

Mike Ashley (b. 1948) is an internationally known editor, anthologist, bibliographer, and writer. He was a winner of an Edgar Allan Poe Award from The Mystery Writers of America, Members with long memories may recall that Mike contributed an article to the very first edition of The Brehon *(February 2002, Vol 1, No 1) having published the first Sister Fidelma short story in his anthology,* The Mammoth Book of Historical Whodunits, *on October 23, 1993. The volume had a foreword from Ellis Peters, famed author of the Brother Cadfael series. In fact, there is a mystery here for Peter had written four Sister Fidelma* short stories and all four were published from different publishers at the same time. 'The High King's Sword' made an immediate impression inspiring Headline to launch the bestselling Fidelma Mystery series as novels and, of course, the story itself was being picked up in many languages before going into the very first Fidelma Collection of short stories in Hemlock at Vespers (1999).

We should say that Mike was not only one of the first editors to recognise Fidelma but to recognise Peter's awesome short story writing talent. Over the years he bought no less than 21 short stories from Peter and not just Fidelma mysteries. Peter has now published over 100 short stories, as his phenomenal story telling talent was recognised by many anthologists and editors such as Stephen Jones, Peter Haining, Maxim Jakubowski, Anne Perry, Martin H. Greenberg, Michael Kurland, Charles Grant, as well as various magazines such as the Ellery Queen Mystery Magazine, the world's most famous mystery and crime magazine.

Why Fidelma is Not a Nun:
A Review of Fidelma's Character

Many years ago a book critic, who was sadly imbued with a modern view of the medieval western religious way of life, and who probably had not really read the Fidelma series as carefully as they should, described Fidelma "as a sexually active nun" (*Books Ireland*, September, 2004). At no time was Fidelma a "nun," which is a woman under certain religious vows, usually those of poverty, chastity and obedience living in an enclosed community.

The rôle of a "nun" certainly does not describe Fidelma's position or, indeed, most women in the early Irish Christian churches. It is essential to remember that we are talking about 7th century Ireland which had only been converted to Christianity two centuries earlier and many isolated areas (as in *Valley of the Shadow*) were still pagan.

Yet even when the country was fully Christianised, there was no enforced rule of celibacy, not even in the Roman church. Celibacy among the religious in the Roman churches was not widely enforced until the 11th century and even then it was not generally accepted. Men and women in religious life, until the edicts of Leo IX and his successors, such as Urban II, who actually ordered the wives of priests and religious to be abducted ass sold as slaves for Papal funds. Previously they had been free to form relationships in the same manner as did any other members of society.

So how could we describe Fidelma? This was a problem for me from the outset of the stories, although I had no concept of how internationally popular and what a long life the stories would have.

Could Fidelma have been called a *caillech*, a veiled woman in the religious? That would be an Irish equivalent for nun. I could also have described her as a *derbsiur*, a woman living in a religious community. Being in a religious house, the English form of address would have to be "Sister." While she was in the religious, I had to use that title because, in the early days, her rôle as a lawyer, a *dálaigh*, might have required too much explanation. But I was also looking for a reference that English readers might recognise but that would not be as specific as the word "nun."

As readers know, I chose – from the term religious (plural). The singular word religieuse (female), attested in the English language *OED* (*Oxford English Dictionary*), from 1796, and the term religieux (masculine) entered English according to the *OED*, in 1654. Both originally came from Latin via Norman French.

This choice appeared to annoy a few readers, who thought they knew their etymologies better and thereby claimed that I was throwing in French words instead of good old Anglo-Saxon words. I'd lay a pound to a penny these readers would be hard pressed to find "good old Anglo-Saxon" equivalents in popular use in the 7th century as most of the religious words of that period were being adopted from Latin anyway. They also failed to realise that the Irish were not speaking Anglo-Saxon.

Nun, of course, came from Late Latin, the feminine of *nonnus/ nonna*, a term for an elderly, respected person, perhaps derived from children's speech. Of course, *nana* and *nonno* are still affectionate terms for grandmother and grandfather in modern Italian.

Perhaps the best way to understand Fidelma and her position in society in 7th century Ireland is to sketch the biographical facts that have been recounted in the series.

Fidelma was the daughter of historic Failbe Flann mac Aedo Duibh, who had become King of Muman (Munster) in AD 628. Fidelma had two elder brothers, Fogartach and Colgú. She was born in AD 637 and obviously the youngest child as we are told that her mother dies in childbirth or soon afterwards her birth. Now her father is given two dates of death in the annals, that of AD 637 and AD 639. She seems to have some "ghost" memories of her father. Were they actually learned memories or genuine baby memories? If her date of birth is correct, then AD 639 is a better choice as the date of her father's death. In the January 2016, issue of *The Brehon*, there was an excellent article about the life of Failbe Flann.

On their father's death, the children of Failbe Flann were sent to fosterage according to the ancient educational tradition. A cousin of Failbe Flann succeeded to the throne of the kingdom. Cuan mac Amalgado, of the Eóghanacht Áine, lasted only a year or so on the throne. Then Máenach mac Fíngín ruled from AD 641 until AD 662, during most of Fidelma's early life. We learn from the short stories that she dislikes Máenach for his unsupportive treatment of her and her siblings. Máenach was the son of Fíngín, Failbe's elder brother. He was certainly a selfish ruler, and nothing is noted by the chroniclers in praise of the twenty years he held the throne in Cashel.

After his death, Fidelma's distant cousin, Cathal Cú-cen-máthair of the Eóghanacht Áine, becomes king and it was then that Colgú, Fidelma's brother, becomes his *tánaiste* or heir apparent. That was when her relationship with Cashel improved. When Cathal was dying from the Yellow Plague in AD 665, the year after she had attended the Synod of Whitby, had met Brother Eadulf and gone to Rome, she was invited to Cashel to carry out another mission. When Cathal died during this period, her brother Colgú succeeded as King. She then made Cashel her base, having left the religious community she was in. This is background to *Suffer Little Children*.

Fidelma was not brought up in any close or loving family atmosphere as both parents dead. Not much is known of her eldest brother, Fogartach, except that he married, and his son eventually became King of Muman. However, Fidelma seems to have a sibling's closeness with her other brother Colgú who shares her fiery red hair and temper. They frequently clash but always respect and love one another. However, Fidelma's childhood seems to have been a lonely one.

Her early education was at a community on Inis Cealtra, an island in Lough Derg, first founded as a religious site by St Colmcille and developed as a famous school of learning by St Caimin, who died cc. AD 644-652. Her tutor there was Brother Ruadán. In AD 664, returning from her mission to Rome, she finds her old tutor in the Abbey of Bobbium (Bobbio) in northern Italy and hears he is ill. She travels through the Trebbia Valley to the abbey to find he is dying. This is told in *Behold A Pale Horse*. His death is the result of murder and a conspiracy which she unravels.

At Inis Cealtra she has a close companion called Liadin who is also her *anam chara*, or soul friend, which is the early Irish Christian concept as opposed to the idea of a priest hearing confessions. There was no confession to a priest, but soul friends discussed and helped one another. When Liadin reached the age of maturity she had married a Gaulish warrior, serving the chieftain of the Uí Drona clan in the kingdom of Laigin (Leinster). Years later Fidelma is called to defend Liadin who is charged with murdering both her husband and her son. The story is told in "At the Tent of Holofernes" (in *Hemlock At Vespers*).

It was at Inis Cealtra that Fidelma began to receive lessons in *troid sciathagid*, battle through defence, the technique of unarmed combat, which is first mentioned in *Shroud for the Archbishop*, chapter 13. She explained to Eadulf that it was taught to Irish missionaries, or potential missionaries, as a means of defending themselves without recourse to weapons. However, references in ancient texts indicated that it was unarmed combat form used by warriors in pre-Christian times.

At the end of her basic schooling, Fidelma is accepted into Brehon Morann's famous law school in the vicinity of Tara, the seat of the High Kings. She shows an extraordinary aptitude for law and solving riddles. There are some stories that tell of her adventures while learning her profession, stories like "The Comb Bag," "Sanctuary," "Catspaw," "The Copyist" and "The Lair of the White Fox." We find that during this time, she emotionally falls for a smooth talking, handsome member of the High King's élite bodyguard – the Fianna. His name is Cian. He ends their relationship and leaves Fidelma for another woman. This has a profound effect on the young Fidelma and hardens her attitude and suspicion of men.

In fact, it is not until she meets up again with Cian in *Act of Mercy* and is able to lay his "ghost" to rest. She realises that Cian's attitude to life was shallow and how he behaved to her was something to be pitied for.

As she approaches an end to her studies and is about to achieve the second highest degree the law college can bestow (*Anruth*), she is faced with choices for her future career. Brehon Morann wants her to continue studying to take the highest degree of *Ollamh*. This word still survives as the modern Irish word for "professor." However, she wants to be an "active" lawyer rather than teach law. She is now qualified to practice as a *dálaigh* but to do so she would be leaving Brehon Morann's school without a patron and without a reputation to attract patronage. Building up a reputation as a lawyer required time. Her cousin, Máenach, is still King in Cashel at this time but she realises it was no use looking to him for patronage. She finds herself on her own.

It is another cousin, Abbot Laisran of Darú (Durrow) who suggests that the Abbey of Bridgit of Kildare, might have an opening for her. The abbess is looking for someone to act as legal advisor. Kildare, like many religious institutions, is a *conhospitae* or mixed house. Abbot Laisran offers to recommend her.

Fidelma's main commitment is to law. But she is knowledgeable in many areas including the New Faith. Ireland has been Christian for a little over two hundred years. Fidelma is of a sceptical nature, while accepting the Christianity; she is in no way a devout practitioner. There are still many areas in Ireland which still follow the old pre-Christian ways as well as several differing schools of the New Faith. She is hesitant about joining any religious institution. For her, truth and justice – as epitomised in the ancient laws – is her religion. She takes a long time before being persuaded to accept Abbot Lauran's suggestion.

There is a class of short stories collected in the two volumes *Hemlock at Vespers* and *Whispers of the Dead*, showing her in a solitary role, building up her reputation as a lawyer. She is consulted when the High King's sword of office is stolen. Her reputation becomes such that she is sent to advise the Irish delegation at the Synod of Whitby where she meets and is attracted to Brother Eadulf.

Brother Eadulf is a convert to Christianity from Seaxmund's Ham, in the land of the South Folk in the kingdom of the East Angles. (Modern day Saxmundham, Suffolk, East Anglia). He was the youthful hereditary *gerefa* or magistrate of his people. He has been converted by an Irish missionary, studied in Ireland at the famous medical school at Tuaim Brecain and then in Rome and decided to follow the Roman interpretation of the New Faith. Their meeting is told in *Absolution By Murder*. Their friendship is further enhanced when they both find themselves in Rome – *Shroud for the Archbishop*. The story follows on from *Absolution*. There is an initial "spark" between Fidelma and Eadulf when they meet in *Absolution By Murder*, Fidelma, however, is suspicious of her feelings. That it why it takes several books before there is a real development in their relationship.

While we are told that Eadulf did not complete his medical studies, or qualify, he has learnt enough to be of intrinsic help to Fidelma in her various investigations. Also, in spite of several critics referring to him as Fidelma's "Watson," Eadulf is not there just to show how brilliant Fidelma is. As an hereditary *gerefa,* or lawgiver, of his people, he can combine his intellectual skills with equal facility. In fact, in *Valley of the Shadow* he is able to swot up enough Irish law to defined Fidelma when she is charged with murder. He is his own person; a brilliant foil for Fidelma at times and not merely an appendage in the modern "sidekick" concept of which Watson is now a stereotype.

At the end of *Shroud for the Archbishop*, Fidelma and Eadulf part in Rome, still friends only, and it is on the way home that Fidelma's is shipwrecked and finds her old teacher at Bobbio – *Behold A Pale Horse*.

When Fidelma returns to Ireland she encounters a mystery at

the abbey of Brigit of Cill Dara (Kildare) where conspiracy, theft and murder, involves the new Abbess Ita. Having revealed the abbess's culpability, Fidelma leaves the abbey in disillusionment to make her own way based on her increasing reputation in law.

It is at that point that the dying King of Muman, Cathal, asks her to undertake an investigation of the murder of a scholar in *Suffer Little Children*. At this time, her brother is now heir apparent to the kingship. By the end of the story Cathal is dead and her brother is king.

In the next book *The Subtle Serpent*, Fidelma is reunited with Eadulf. He was sent as an envoy to the chief bishop of Muman, Segdae, by the new Archbishop of Canterbury. Theodore. But Eadulf has fallen into the hands of the enemies of Cashel and Fidelma is instrumental in his rescue and resolving a murder and conspiracy at the Abbey of the Three Wells.

Colgú finds work for his sister as his legal representative and her reputation grows while she still finds herself at odds with resolving her feelings for Eadulf. There is a conflict in their relationship. Finally, Eadulf leaves Cashel for Canterbury while she joins a pilgrim voyage (*Act of Mercy*) where she meets her old lover Cian and begins to resolves her feelings. Against this background, there is a murder among the pilgrims and suspicion is on her former lover Cian. At the end of that story she finds that Eadulf has been taken captive in Laighin accused of rape and murder. She hastens back to Ireland and, in *Our Lady of Death*, to defend him and is successful.

She decides to join him in continuing his journey to Canterbury, but they are shipwrecked on the shores of Dyfed and asked to resolve a mystery where an entire monastic community has vanished. This is in *Smoke in the Wind*. Eventually arriving in Canterbury, resolving a mystery there ("The Lost Eagle"), they hastened to Eadulf's home among the East Angles (*The Haunted Abbot*). They have decided to swop vows and contract a traditional Irish trial marriage for a year and a day. At the end of that story, Fidelma reveals that she is pregnant and wants to return to Muman. Eadulf goes with her.

As we have discussed, there is no such specific rule against married religious at this time, neither in the Western "Celtic," Eastern "Orthodox" or even the Roman churches. Nevertheless, there are groups who are propagating the concept of celibacy and Fidelma and Eadulf do cross paths with many of their advocates.

Over the next months, she represents legal matters for her brother and for Abbot Segdae the chief bishop of Muman. The period after Al-chú's birth is a tough one for her and she has what, in modern terms, is called post natal depression. It takes the kidnapping of Alchú, *The Leper's Bell*, and the efforts of both Fidelma and Eadulf to track the culprit down and get their son returned, that brings her out of her depression. She is aware of her lack of motherliness but eventually takes on the role which Eadulf seems to enjoy more. The nurturing of their son has fallen mainly to Eadulf.

When the trial marriage of a year and a day are up, Fidelma and Eadulf are due to be formally be married at Cashel. This is recounted in *A Prayer for the Damned*. Many dignitaries attend and it is only a matter of religious extremism and murder that puts the ceremony on hold until the end of the story.

In *Council of the Cursed* Fidelma and Eadulf find themselves as legal advisors to the Irish delegation at the great Council of Autun, Burgundy, in AD 670. It is a council that was far more damaging to the "Celtic Church" concepts than Whitby. Naturally murder and conspiracy is prevalent. On the journey back, their ship is attacked, and they are wrecked in Brittany, in the area of Morbihan, where there is involvement in the murderous dynastic squabbles of the Breton kings. This is in *The Dove of Death*.

This does not end the tension between Fidelma and Eadulf. Readers should have realised by now that Fidelma is no longer interested in being "*Sister* Fidelma." She even aspires to be Chief Brehon of her brother's kingdom. Eadulf is more committed to the religious life than she is. There is a conflict and at the start of *Chalice of Blood* they have separated because of this issue. King Colgú attempts to bring them together again as he realises not only are they good for each other but a formidable combination at the resolving of mysteries. He orders them to join forces again to solve a locked room mystery of a well-known scholar, killed in his cell in the Abbey of Lios Mór. They do so and are rejoined again.

While a compromise is reached about their differing ambitions, Fidelma has left the religious "but not the religion," as she assured Abbot Ségdae. Not having succeeded in being elected as Chief Brehon, Fidelma continues in her role as her brother's personal legal advisor and is often sought to resolve and even judge legal matters. Her reputation is such that even the High King, and the Chief Brehon of the Five Kingdoms, consults her, such as in the *Dancing With Demons*. Eadulf accepts not only her position but his own role playing an important part in her investigations. He now accepts that Fidelma's over riding interest is law not religious. However, it is pointed out from time to time that Fidelma's reputation has been build up as *'Sister* Fidelma" and so that epithet will stick with her. But careful readers will have noted the subtle change in terminology. She is now Fidelma *of* Cashel, denoting her relationship to the Eóghanacht royal family.

What we are dealing with here is not a person whose life is one dimensional but who has travelled through several changes, while keeping to her essential personality, through the many books that comprise the series to date.

Apart from one or two stories, the locations are wide and varied. Travel is an essential feature of the stories whether within Munster (Muman) or beyond its borders – stories occur in Northumbria, in what is now Wales, Brittany, Burgundy, northern Italy and Rome. Fidelma is an expert horsewoman and usually travels on her Camargue Pony (an ancient European breed) whose name is Aonbharr, after the horse of the Sea God Manannán Mac Lir. Aonbharr was given to her by her brother, Colgú, who bought it from a Gaulish merchant. In contrast to Fidelma, Eadulf is not a lover of horses and often complains when he has to travel by horseback.

Fidelma is now an expert at unarmed combat. She is as quick tempered as she is quick witted and analytical. She does not tolerate fools gladly, nor people who are arrogant and disrespectful. But neither is she overbearing and arrogant herself. She has a deep knowledge of many matters and, as well as law; she is well read in Latin, with a little Greek and Hebrew as well as her native Irish (and knows the *bérla na filed,* the language of the poets with its Ogam alphabet). She also speaks a little Anglo-Saxon and Brythonic Celtic which encompasses Gaulish and eventually developed into what we know today as Welsh, Cornish, and Breton.

Eadulf's knowledge of the healing arts (the medical practices of the time), gained by his initial study at Tuaim Brecain, is often helpful in many of the stories. He is highly intelligent and in one story, while Fidelma has been imprisoned, he is able to "swot" up the necessary Brehon Law to argue for her freedom. Eadulf has a sense of law being raised as a hereditary *gerefa* (lawgiver) of his own people.

He goes to pains to point out that he is an Angle (not a Saxon) and still has some of the fears of the pre-Christian gods and goddesses of his own people with which he was brought up until his teenage. He speaks his own language as well as Irish (as he studied in Ireland), Latin of Church missionaries, some Greek, Hebrew and Brythonic Celtic.

He is not so "fiery tempered" as Fidelma, slow to anger, and considerate. In all, he is a softer, gentler person. Hence, when Fidelma suffers her post traumatic stress, it is a period when Eadulf steps forward to take care of the nurturing of their son, Alchú. Later, he overcomes his dislike of riding to accept the charge of going on the morning horse ride with his son. Having converted from paganism to Christianity, Eadulf is more emotionally reflective in his analysis of religion and still retains many superstitions of his pagan upbringing as opposed to Fidelma's more intellectual analysis.

They are complementary characters, each bringing their intellect and skills to the mysteries. I confess, I wince whenever I see the "Holmes and Watson" comparison.

So, I hope that I have tried to persuade those who have a modern view of the medieval church, why they should not dismiss Fidelma as a nun.

– Peter Tremayne
Program booklet from Féile Fidelma 2017

THE SISTER FIDELMA COMPENDIUM

ᘃhence Cometh Brother Eaðulf?

Peter Tremayne's appearance at the Felixstowe Book Festival in Suffolk (Suffolk being the land of the South Folk of East Anglia) in June 2011, he chose to speak about Fidelma's companion Brother Eadulf.

Peter Tremayne speaking at Felixstowe:

So exactly how did Eadulf of Saxmundham became involved as companion to Fidelma of Cashel, Co. Tipperary, the heroine detective of The Sister Fidelma Mysteries? The background of the series is 7th century Irish law and culture, although eight of the novels are located outside of Ireland. So how and why does Eadulf of Saxmund's Ham, in the land of the South Folk, of the kingdom of the East Angles, enter these stories?

In attempting to introduce readers to an entirely unfamiliar society – unfamiliar outside Celtic Studies departments of universities, I basically needed a means to explain the cultural problems; I had to create a character through which explanations could be made avoiding textual lectures. After all is said and done, these are murder mysteries; entertainments, although the Celtic scholar/historian in me refused to be anachronistic. So was Brother Eadulf's appearance a purely random choice?

I needed to have a character who could ask questions, to receive explanations without heavy lectures. I also needed a helper for Fidelma ... but I certainly did not want a Holmes-Watson relationship. I wanted someone who, while a completely different character, was their own person, who would act as a foil, if you like, and able to bring other talents to the stories. It should not be just someone who is there to show how brilliant the detective was, like Watson is to Holmes or Hasting is to Hercules Poirot.

Image Courtesy De Leeskamer: Graphic Novel adaptation of Absolution By Murder

While I felt this character should not be Irish, he had to have some knowledge of Ireland otherwise more problems would arise than be resolved. So what better place than an area I knew and that had been converted to Christianity by Irish missionaries in the 7th century – the kingdom of the East Angles. I discussed my reasons with a cousin, Dave Peppiatt, who was headmaster of a local school not far up the coast from here (Gorleston-on-Sea). It was Dave who suggested Saxmundham – a place where Dorothy and I sometimes used to stop off on our way to visit him and his family. Although Dave died in December 2010, he lived to see the success of his suggestion. Therefore, Eadulf and his place of origin were not randomly chosen.

Let's look at Eadulf's early years and his society. He had been born at a time when the East Angles had not been fully converted. Early surviving chronicles and annals are not always precise on dates. I have accepted a dating system which modern scholarship agrees by computer comparisons with available texts.

In my chronology, Eadulf had been born AD 635. He had grown up by the banks of the Fromus, a tributary of the Alde, that passes through the Ham or place or Seaxmund. Eadulf might not have known that Fromus bears the name given it by the original Celtic inhabitants of the area meaning the "brisk water." Eadulf was set to become hereditary *gerefa* or magistrate of his village as his father had been before him. So, he knew and understood something of Anglo-Saxon Law. His early youth was as a pagan believing in the gods and goddesses that we still commemorate today in the names of the days of the week – Tyr's day, Woden's day, Thor's day, Freya's day.

From the Venerable Bede, writing in the 8th century – we accept that it was Felix of Burgundy, sometimes called Felix of Dunwich, who converted East Anglia to Christianity. However, Bede's text has not been read carefully enough.

Felix, we are told, was sent by Honorius, archbishop of Canterbury, to King Sigebert of the East Angles. Honorius was the last of the Gregorian mission. Sigebert did not become King until 634 and he was already a Christian. Bede, in fact, knew well that much of the principal work of conversion had already been done before Felix arrived and by the Irish.

In fact, one of Bede's quoted sources was *Vita Sancti Fursei*, a 7th century Latin mss – copies still exist in the Bibliothèque Royale de Belgique. Fursa was proselytising East Anglia in AD 625.

Who was this Fursa? Literary folk should know this saint as he is even mentioned in James Joyce's novel *Ulysses*. Mervyn Wall (1908-

1997) wrote two novels about him back in the 1940s. Wall, a Dubliner, wrote about the misadventures of Fursa – *The Unfortunate Fursey* (1946) and *The Return of Fursey* (1948).

Fursa was born in AD 595, the eldest of three brothers, Fursa, Foillan and Ultan. They were sons of a noble called Fintan and his wife, Gelgeis, who was a daughter of a King of Connacht, called Aed mac Echach. Aed died in AD 577.

Fursa and his brothers studied at Clonfert in Galway, an abbey founded by the famous St Brendan the Voyager. You may recall that the adventurer Tim Severin, inspired by the surviving 12th century text about Brendan's voyage, built a replica of a 6th century Irish ship and sailed it to America in 1976/77 to show that Brendan could have actually made that famous voyage. Fursa and his brothers studied under the abbot Senach Garbh mac Buidhi who died in AD 621.

So Fursa, Foillan and Ultan brought Christianity to the early 7th century East Anglia. King Raedwald had been converted while on a visit to Kent, and died in the very year Fursa, his brothers and their followers arrived. Was it Raedwald or his son Eorpwald who invited them? Eorpwald was also a Christian and it is recorded that the Irish were allowed to set up an abbey in AD 630 in a long abandoned Roman fort which is Burgh (Burra) Castle six kilometres west of Great Yarmouth on the east bank of the River Waveney. Now Waveney is a good Anglo-Saxon word for a "quaking river" but it is interesting that, on Roman maps, it is called Gariannonum in which is seen the original Celtic name "babbling river" – same concept, different languages?

Eorpwald was assassinated in AD 632 apparently by a family member named Ricberht, who Bede says was a pagan. By the way, Raedwald, Eorpwald and Ricberht are all contenders for being the king buried at Sutton Hoo.

Ricberht was soon removed from power. And the saintly Sigebert, already a Christian, became King and welcomed Felix to East Anglia sometime after 634. So, the Irish missionaries had been at work for nearly ten years before then.

Fursa eventually left his brother Foillan as abbot in Burgh Castle and went to the Frankish kingdom of Neustria (modern day Belgian) to continue his work. By AD 638 Sigebert had decided to abdicate and retire to a monastery. His brother Egric then became King. Disaster came in AD 641 when the Angles of Mercia, who were still pagan, invaded East Anglia. My character Eadulf, by the way, was seven or eight about this time. And his younger brother, named after the new King, Egric, had just been born. Sigebert came out of his monastery to help King Egric defend the kingdom, but they were both killed in battle.

During invasion of the pagans of Mercia in AD 641, the abbey at Burgh Castle was sacked and many of the converts were taken as slaves. Foillan and Ultan managed to escape and raise enough ransom to get some of their followers released. They then fled to Neustria (Belgium). When they reached there, they found their brother Fursa had already died. Foillan was later killed by bandits while journeying through a forest. Ultan, the survivor, went to live at the mixed abbey of Gertrude of Nivelles (Nivel) where it is recorded, he taught music and the singing of psalms to the community.

In the following few years, two Kings of the East Angles, Anna and Athelhere, were killed fighting the pagan Mercians, both seemed to be Christian. Now there is some argument whether Burgh Castle and an abbey called Cnobheresburg was one and the same place. Bede reports King Anna who endowed this abbey around AD 651 and later chronicles started to associate it with Fursa's name. But Fursa was, of course, no longer in East Anglia. Significantly other Irish names begin to appear such as Dícuil and Gobán. The latter is recorded as being killed in AD 670.

Athelwold became King of East Anglia in AD 655 and the Mercians were driven out. Rendlesham, north of Ipswich, once more became the royal centre, near Sutton Hoo.

And it was at this time that Eadulf and his young brother witnessed the baptism of Swithhelm, King of the East Saxons, Essex. At this time Essex was going through a bloody internal conflict between Christian and pagan. The actual baptism was carried out by Cedd, a convert of the Irish missionary Aidan. Cedd, of course, supported the Celtic Rite. He is noted for his role as interpreter between the Irish and Angles at Whitby. Bede claims that after Whitby, Cedd accepted Roman Rite. The evidence, however, is contrary and it is interesting that Cedd died only five months after the decision of Whitby. Cedd appears in a background role in *The Devil's Seal*.

So, these were exciting times for young Eadulf. What happened to him in those early years before he encountered Fidelma at Whitby in 664? Well, his Irish teachers had suggested that he go to Ireland to learn more of the new Faith. With Irish missionaries by this time in all the kingdoms of the Angles and the Saxons – it is no wonder that

WHENCE COMETH BROTHER EADULF?

many Anglo-Saxons journeyed to study at the Irish ecclesiastic and secular colleges. Bede in the 8th century makes a special point of how the nobles and commoners of the Angles and Saxons went to Ireland for their education.

The Irish colleges were famous throughout Europe and Irish *peregrinatio pro Christo* had also established churches and abbeys as far east as Kiev, in the Ukraine, south to Taranto in southern Italy, north to the Faroe Islands and even Iceland. The Dark Ages were not really so dark. It is, perhaps, the myths rather than the history of the period we find easier to accept.

The close relationships between the Anglo-Saxon kingdoms and Ireland tend to be overlooked. An example, Oswy of Northumbria was brought up in exile in what is now Ulster. He married Fín, daughter of an Uí Néill High King, Colmán Rímid. Oswy and Fín's son, Aldfrith was educated at the abbey of Lisgoole, in what is now Fermanagh. He was elderly when his brother was killed, and he was asked to become King of Northumbria in AD 685. He ruled wisely and well and died in AD 705. Aldfrith was an acclaimed poet in the Irish language. Three of these poems are still extant including his praise poem on the beauties and attractions of Ireland which is highly regarded by scholars.

If you like controversy let me remind you that Aldfrith is accepted as King and patron when *Beowulf* was composed, the oldest saga in Anglo-Saxon. In 1923 the great Swedish Celtic scholar, Professor C.W. von Sydow (father of the movie star Max von Sydow), wrote a study arguing that the earlier Irish mythological saga *Táin Bó Fraoch* (not the more popularly known *Táin Bó Cuailgne*) was the inspiration for *Beowulf* – he based the argument on nine significantly close points of identity between the two compositions. I don't mean to name drop but I was having dinner with the late Seamus Heaney, the Nobel Literary Laureate, who was then working on his rendition of *Beowulf,* and I wondered if he was going to refer to this. He replied, wisely, that it was politic to let sleeping (Beo)wulf's lie.

The Irish role in teaching the Anglo-Saxons literacy was a truly remarkable one – for those interested I would recommend Professor Charles Wright's study *The Irish Tradition in Old English Literature* (Cambridge University Press, 1993).

So, Eadulf sets off from Saxmundham to Ireland. Because of the cost of higher education these days it was suggested to me that it must have cost a fortune so only the rich would have gone. Let's quote what

Bede said in the 8th century when the Anglo-Saxon students went to Ireland – "The Irish welcomed them all gladly, gave them their daily food and also provided them with books to read and with instruction how to read, without asking for any payment..."

Eadulf went first to the abbey of Darú, Durrow the abbey of the oaks, now in Offaly, and founded by Colmcille or Columba as he is more popularly known. The *Book of Durrow* is considered one of the great illustrated gospel books of 7th century. It is recorded that students from 18 different countries were studying at Durrow in the mid 7th century.

Eadulf was not only interest in theology, he knew something about the law of his own people, he was also interested in medical matters – that was to come in handy during his subsequent adventures with Fidelma. He left Darú and set off to Tuaim Brecain (today Tomregan in Co. Cavan). That was one of the most famous medical schools in Ireland at the time, founded by a notable scholar and surgeon Bricín. Bricín died in 650, so he was dead by the time Eadulf arrived there.

Eadulf, with diverse interests, was a restless soul. After a year or two there, he dropped out without completing the course in medicine and taking his degree. Oh, yes, the Irish secular and ecclesiastical colleges in the 7th century had a specific degree system. For physicians the Irish laws were very strict on who could practice as a physician. Eadulf probably only just made *fuirmithir*, which implied he had qualified to take a third year of study and could be something like a paramedic. Fidelma, by the way, held the degree in law of *anruth,* the second highest under *ollamh.* Ollamh, by the way, is still the modern Irish word for professor.

Eadulf now had a working knowledge of Irish, of Latin and some Greek, Hebrew and a basic knowledge of the physician's art and his own law. He leaves Ireland and goes on a pilgrimage to Rome and becomes converted to the new Roman liturgy. That is why he then appears at Whitby as part of the pro-Roman delegation. This is the first Fidelma novel – *Absolution By Murder.* When Abbess Etain, a leading advocate on the Irish side, is murdered, King Oswy has a problem. He must be seen to investigate the matter without bias to avoid bitter conflict between members of the delegations – so Fidelma is chosen from the Irish side and Eadulf from the Roman side and ordered to resolve the mystery together.

The next story *Shroud for the Archbishop* finds them both in Rome where Wighard, the Saxon archbishop designate of Canterbury is killed, and an Irish religious accused. Wighard's death in Rome is an historical event. At the end this mystery, Fidelma returns to Ireland while Eadulf is appointed advisor to the Greek Theodore of Tarsus, the new archbishop of Canterbury.

Eadulf, in *The Subtle Serpent*, is eventually sent from Theodore of Canterbury as an envoy to Ségéne, the Chief Bishop of the Irish kingdom of Muman – the province of Munster in Ireland – where Fidelma's brother Colgú mac Failbhe Flann, an historical king, had become king in AD 665. It was the largest and most south westerly of the five kingdoms of Ireland with its ancient capital at Cashel, Co. Tipperary. You may recall that three years ago Queen Elizabeth, on her visit to Ireland, chose only two places outside of Dublin to visit. The first one was Cashel, seat of the Eóghanacht Kings of Muman since the 3rd century – the Eóghanacht being Fidelma's own family.

Anyway, with their reunion in Cashel, Fidelma and Eadulf continued their adventurous life together, uniting both their fascinating cultures in their pursuit of justice for all.

– Peter Tremayne
Originally appeared in *The Brehon*, XIV, 1, January 2015
as "And Not Forgetting Brother Eadulf of Saxmundham"

THE SISTER FIDELMA COMPENDIUM

Brehon Law: The Background to The Sister Fidelma Mysteries

The ancient law system of Ireland, the laws of the Fenechus, which we call the Brehon Laws after the word *breitheamh* – a judge, is the essential background to the Sister Fidelma Mysteries. Fidelma is a qualified advocate of the Brehon system and has to act accordingly.

I grew up knowing about the system. My father, an Irish journalist, had several books on Brehon Law on our bookshelf and I started writing about aspects of Brehon Law in the late 1960s. So, when I started to write the Sister Fidelma Mysteries, in 1993, I was surprised that the Brehon system dumbfounded many readers. The reaction was curious, and it ranged from some readers wondering if I had made up the laws to others who frankly denied they could ever have existed.

Even today, the occasional reader writes in to sharply rebuked me by claiming that such a law would not have been tolerated by Rome. That type of remark simply shows their own ignorance of 7th century Ireland.

I slowly came to the conclusion that, outside the Celtic Studies departments of certain universities, very few people had even heard about the ancient Irish legal system. It had, of course, finally been suppressed in the years following the English Tudor and 17th century Conquests of Ireland. After that, it was the law of the colonial power that was imposed in Ireland. From 1613 the Brehon system, the social system it incorporated, indeed, and Irish language itself was to be abolished by English Statute and Common Law.

Unfortunately, the conquerors always write the history books and today the world tends to perceive Ireland, prior to the 17th century, through the eyes of the English conquest. Sir John Davies (1569-1626) was appointed England's Attorney General of Ireland in the new colonial administration. He naturally claimed that Irish were "uncivilised," "uncouth," "savage" and so on and dismissed the Irish law system as no system at all Propaganda was rolled out in the attempts to destroy the ancient and sophisticated system, which was the nucleus of the Irish social system.

Moreover, the conquerors used physical attempts to destroy the law books and texts and even the lawyers themselves. Even as late as the latter 18th century, anyone caught with an Irish law book could face stringent punishments, transportation or even worse. Some Irish did their best to hide the texts, even placing the vellum in bogs or in ponds.

When one considers this, I admit, it should not have been a surprise that a modern audience was amazed that a Sister Fidelma could appear in such stories and that many readers refused to believe the social background of the stories.

For scholars, during the more liberal days of the mid-19th century, when the Penal Laws in Ireland were relaxed and abolished, it was thanks to Charles Graves (1812-1899), the grandfather of the literary Nobel Laureate, Robert Graves, that knowledge of the Brehon system began to become "respectable." Graves was President of the Royal Irish Academy, and he persuaded the United Kingdom Government to establish a commission to rescue the manuscript and texts of the laws then known to have existed. Using the best Irish scholars of the day, the commission set out to translate and publish them. They were published as *The Ancient Laws of Ireland* in six large volumes between 1865 and 1901.

How old are these laws? We could make the claim that they represent the earliest Indo-European legal system because of the amazing comparisons with the Hindu legal system (Laws of Manu). Many scholars have made studies in this area and one of the leading academics in that area was Professor Myles Dillon (1900-1972), a former President of the Royal Irish Academy and Director of the Dublin Institute of Advanced Studies and School of Celtic Studies. His memorial, unfortunately published posthumously by the Indian Institute of Advanced Study, Simla, was *Celts and Aryans: Survivals of Indo-European Speech and Society* (1974).

Can we be more specific about the date of Brehon Law? According to legendary texts it was an Irish High King Fodhla who first gathered the laws of Ireland in the 8th century BC. But the first known codification, that of collecting the laws in textural form, was said to have taken placed in AD 438 when the High King Laoghaire set up a nine-man commission to examine and revised them in the wake of the coming of Christianity. The names of the nine-man commission, three kings, three lawyers and three judges, are known. And St Patrick was only one member of the commission, although often the entire work is often ascribed solely to him.

While fragmentary texts survive from the 7th and 8th century AD, the first major legal textbooks containing the law survive from the 11th century onwards. More and more of these texts have come to light since the publication of *The Ancient Laws of Ireland.*

As a teenager, the first book I read on Brehon Law, taken from my father's bookshelf, was *The Brehon Laws: A Legal Handbook* by Laurence Ginnell, published in 1894. Ginnell (1854-1923) was a lawyer, a barrister called to both Irish and English Bars, and a Member of Parliament for Westmeath from 1906 until his death. Ginnell approached his interpretation of the system as a modern lawyer. He was one of a group who argued that when Ireland succeeded in becoming independent again, they should try to return to the *spirit* of the Brehon system rather than simply inherited the colonial law under which Ireland had been ruled since 1613, His views were shared by many, including James Creed Meredith, who had been appointed as President of the Supreme Court by Dáil Éireann in 1919. Meredith actually gave a judgement in favour of women's rights under the Brehon system in 1920 declaring English law was retrograde. However, after independence, the new Irish state did not go down that road.

Ginnell's book was a succinct introduction to the system. I moved from that to Dr Patrick Weston Joyce's masterpiece, the two volume *A Social History of Ancient Ireland,* 1903. Joyce's work was sadly neglected after 1919 when Professor Eoin MacNeill (1867-1945), an old academic enemy of Joyce who became Minister of Education in the Irish Free State Government, started to snipe at it. Because of MacNeill's involvement in the independence struggle, his work received greater attention and influence that it would otherwise have done.

In his *Early Irish Laws and Institutions*, published 1927, MacNeill was forced to admit, in his introduction:

"One naturally turns for information to the work of Dr P.W. Joyce, *A Social History of Ancient Ireland*, which was published in 1903. Joyce had a full acquaintance with the material upon which his work ought to depend, so far as this material had been published in his time. Much of what he writes is based on original and laborious investigation, and where he brings forward information of an unfamiliar kind, he usually cites his authorities for it."

So, while praising Joyce, MacNeill tried to claim he worked from printed sources only. Joyce did not simply use printed sources. He knew his way around surviving primary manuscript sources and actually worked on the commission editing and translating the texts for

The Ancient Laws of Ireland. Joyce is scrupulous in manuscript and printed sources. It is interesting that MacNeill provides no source notes, manuscript references or even printed references in his work. His view is usually "trust me, I am a scholar"!

After such a magnificent authority as Joyce, I came to the book that really expanded on the rights of women under the Brehon system. Dr Sophie Bryant's *Liberty, Order and Law Under Native Irish Rule: A Study of the Ancient Laws of Ireland* (1923). This has been a major influence in developing my interest.

Dr John Cameron's *Celtic Law* was published in 1937. Cameron was a Scottish lawyer who again approached the texts from a legalistic viewpoint. From there I went on to discover a volume of *Studies in Early Irish Law* (1936) a collection of academic papers by many of the leading scholars of the time which included some specialist analysis of the role of women under Brehon Law, especially the laws on inheritance and other aspects which would have been a treasure trove to the feminist movements of the 1960s had they realise ancient Irish law could have taught them something.

As I began to develop my adult interest in Brehon Law, I found academics were not neglecting it. Dr Patrick C. Power produced a study in 1976 *Sex and Marriage in Ancient Ireland* which provided an excellent general introduction to this area of the laws.

Then came Professor Fergus Kelly's *A Guide to Early Irish Law*, in 1988. While I do not go along entirely with Professor Kelly's interpretations, and some of the points have been raised with him, this still presents the best general guide to the system. His work also contains a nine-page bibliography of books and articles covering studies and texts on the laws. He published this with the Dublin Institute of Advanced Studies who specialised on producing studies on the individual laws and a bibliography of all the studies, papers, books and so forth published on the law until that time.

The fact that the ancient Irish law system had a common Celtic root with the Laws of Hywel Dda, the ancient Welsh legal system committed to writing in the 9th century, can be seen in Professor T. M. Charles-Edwards *Early Irish and Welsh Kinship* (1993).

The point that I am making, rather than blinding you with a list of books on law, is that there is so much in the printed domain that, if I, as a novelist, was making up the laws for the purpose of writing the Sister Fidelma Mysteries, I would have been torn to shreds by the world of Celtic scholarship.

In recent years, as the Cashel Arts Festival have organised the Féile Fidelma, and invited some of the leading scholars on 7th century Ireland and her laws, I confess I did feel nervous and stood ready to quote my sources and argue my corner. It was a great experience to find that his scholars came along and gave fascinating talks in support of my stories.

I can reassure my readers that the laws and the social system in which Fidelma operates are not the figment of my imagination any more than Umberto Eco's character, Brother William of Baskerville, existed in an entirely fantasy background in *The Name of the Rose*.

Historical novels, whether historical crime novels or any other form, must have a background that is firmly based on the reality of the historical period and that means the reality of the society their code of behaviour, or social systems. Every time Fidelma, or another character, mentions a law, a custom and so on, it is there in the law codes that have come down to us.

It is true that I am writing a fiction story, yet many of the incidents related in the stories are based on, or inspired by, historical events that are recorded in the ancient Irish chronicles and annals. However, I am not setting out to "teach" history or law. My primary concern is to provide entertainment. If I do not, then I have failed as a novelist.

– Peter Tremayne
The Brehon, III, 2, May 2004

THE SISTER FIDELMA COMPENDIUM

About Peter Tremayne

PETER TREMAYNE is the fiction writing pseudonym of the Celtic scholar and author Peter Berresford Ellis.

Peter Berresford Ellis (born 10 March 1943) is a historian, literary biographer and novelist who has published over 100 books to date under his own name and that of his pseudonyms Peter Tremayne and Peter MacAlan. He has also published over 100 short stories. His non-fiction books, articles and academic papers have made him acknowledged as one of the foremost authorities on Celtic history and culture. Under his Tremayne pseudonym he is the author of the international bestselling Sister Fidelma Mystery series. His work has appeared in 25 languages.

Life

Peter Berresford Ellis was born in Coventry, Warwickshire, England. His father was a Cork-born journalist who started his career on the *Cork Examiner*.[1] The Ellis family can be traced in the area from 1288.

PETER TREMAYNE

[2] His mother was from an old Sussex family of Saxon origin able to trace their lineage back through fourteen generations in the same area. Her mother was of a Breton family.[3] Educated at Brighton College of Art and London University. He took a first-class honours degree and his MA in Celtic Studies. He was given a D. Litt (honoris causa) by East London University in 2006 in recognition of his work. He is also a Fellow of the Royal Society of Antiquaries of Ireland (1996) and a Fellow of the Royal Historical Society (1998). He has received numerous awards and honours for his work such as a Bard of the Cornish Gorsedd (1987) for his work

on the history of the Cornish language – *The Cornish Language and its Literature* (published in 1974); an Irish Post Award (1989); Hon. Life President of the Scottish 1820 Society (1989); Hon. Life Member of the Irish Literary Society (2002); he was given a civic reception by the Mayor and Council of Cashel, Co. Tipperary (2004) – the highest civic award Cashel can bestow.[4] He was awarded the French Prix Historia for the best historical mystery novel of 2010 for *Le concile des maudits (The Council of the Cursed)*.

He began his career as a junior reporter on an English south coast weekly, becoming deputy editor of an Irish weekly newspaper and was then editor of a weekly publishing trade journal in London. He first went as a feature writer to Northern Ireland in 1964 for a London daily newspaper which had a profound effect on him. His first book was published in 1968 – *Wales – A Nation Again*, on the Welsh struggle for political independence, with a foreword by Gwynfor Evans, Plaid Cymru's first Member of Parliament. In 1975 he became a full-time writer.

He used his academic background to produce many popular titles in the field of Celtic Studies and he has written numerous academic articles and papers in the field for journals ranging from *The Linguist* (London) to *The Irish Sword: Journal of the Irish Military History Society* (UCD). He is highly regarded by academics in his own field and was described in by *The Times* Higher Education Supplement, London, (June, 1999) as one of the leading authorities on the Celts then writing.

He has been International Chairman of the Celtic League 1988-1990; chairman of Scrif-Celt (The Celtic Languages Book Fair in 1985 and in 1986); chairman and vice-president of the London Association for Celtic Education 1989-1995, and now is an Hon. Life Member); He was also chairman of his local ward Labour Party in London, England, and was editorial advisor on *Labour and Ireland* magazine in the early 1990s. He is a member of the Society of Authors.

Apart from his Celtic Studies interests, Ellis has always been fascinated by aspects of popular literature and has written full-length biographies on H. Rider Haggard, W.E. Johns, Talbot Mundy as well as critical essays on many more popular fiction authors. His own output in the fictional field, writing in the genre of horror fantasy and heroic fantasy, began in 1977 when the first "Peter Tremayne" book appeared. Between 1983 and 1993 he also wrote eight adventure thrillers under the name "Peter MacAlan."[5]

A prolific writer, Ellis has published (as of July 2018) a total of

ABOUT PETER TREMAYNE

101 books, 101 short stories, 8 pamphlets and numerous academic papers and an uncountable number of signed journalistic articles. Under his own name he wrote two long running columns "Anonn Is Anall" (Here and There) from 1987-2007 for *The Irish Democrat* and "Anois agus Arás" (Now and again) from 2000-2008 for *The Irish Post*. This breaks down into 35 titles under his own name and 8 under the pseudonym of Peter MacAlan and 59 under the pseudonym of Peter Tremayne.

He has lectured widely at universities in several countries, including the UK, Ireland, American, Canada, France and Italy. He has also broadcast on television and radio since 1968.[6]

Peter started to write the Sister Fidelma mysteries as short stories in 1993 merely to illustrate how the Brehon laws worked and how a woman could be an advocate of the law system in 7th century Ireland. The stories were so well received that Headline offered him an initial three-book contract to write novels featuring Sister Fidelma. These have proved extraordinarily popular, and several critics have hailed Sister Fidelma as the natural successor to Brother Cadfael.

DOROTHY CHEESMUR ELLIS

This is a compliment that Peter disarmingly rejects, pointing out that Fidelma and Cadfael are poles apart. Fidelma lives in a period 800 years before Cadfael and operates in a cultural and law system that is totally alien to the Cadfael settings. However, he does point out that he owes a surprising debt to Cadfael – the origin of the Peter Tremayne pseudonym.

Writing in *Past Poisons: An Ellis Peters Memorial Anthology of Historical Crime* (ed. by Maxim Jakubowski, Headline, 1998) Peter informs us that Ellis Peters, the creator of Brother Cadfael in 1977, was the pseudonym of Edith Pargetter, famous for her Welsh historical novels. Asked to review the first Cadfael novel *A Morbid Taste for Bones* in the "Catholic Herald" (London), in August 1977, he thought that he could not write the review under his own name in case readers might think Ellis Peters was merely a reversal of Peter Berresford Ellis. He then created Peter Tremayne, using the name of a favourite spot in Cornwall, and a name which he developed into his fiction-writing pseudonym.

THE SISTER FIDELMA COMPENDIUM

With the unparalleled popularity of his 7th century set Sister Fidelma Mysteries, in January 2001, an International Sister Fidelma Society was formed in Little Rock, Arkansas, with a website and producing a print magazine three times a year called *The Brehon*.[7] In 2006 the Cashel Arts Fest[8] established the first three-day international gathering of fans of the series which was held bi-annually and received the full support of the Society. [9] In Fall, 2012, the US publishers McFarland published *The Sister Fidelma Mysteries: Essays on the Historical Novels of Peter Tremayne*. The volume was edited by Professor Edward J. Rielly and David Robert Wooten. ISBN 978-0-7864-6667-2 and eBook ISBN 978-1-4766-0034-5. Print book price was $40. As well as analytical essays, there is a biographical essay which has the full approval of the author.

Citations (references)

1) *The Burning of Cork*, Gerry White and Brendan O'Shea, Mercier Press, Cork, 2006.
2) *The Ellis Family of Millstreet*, Millstreet: "A Considerable Town," Aubane Historical Society, Cork, 2003.
3) *Daisy: Growing Up in a Sussex Village*, Eva Daisy (Randell) Ellis, Hurstpierpoint Historical Society, Sussex, 2003.
4) Entries on Ellis's career at various times can be taken from his entries in the following reference works: *International Authors' and Writers' Who's Who* (Cambridge, UK) from 8th ed 1977 onwards; *Contemporary Authors* (Detroit, USA) from Vols 81, 1979, onwards; *Who's Who in the World* (Chicago, USA), 5th ed. 1980 onwards; *European Biographical Directory* (Belgium) 1990); *Who's Who in International Affairs* (London), 1990; *Who's Who of Authors and Writers* (Europa Publications), 2004; *The Cambridge Blue Book*, (Cambridge, UK), 2005; *The Writers' Directory* (Detroit, USA), 2005.
5) *Book and Magazine Collector*, London, March 1993 (contains an overview of life and work and bibliography to that date).
6) Other details of his fiction work and career are contained in the Tremayne entries in *The Encyclopaedia of Fantasy* ed. John Clute and John Grant, St Martins Press, USA, and Little Brown, UK, 1997; *The Mammoth Encyclopaedia of Modern Crime Fiction*, ed. Mike Ashley, Robinson, UK, and Carroll & Graf, USA, 2002; and *Supernatural Literature of the World, An Encyclopaedia*, edit. S.T. Joshi and Stefan Dziemianowicz, Greenwood Press, USA, 3 vols, 2005.
7) *Book and Magazine Collector*, London, October 2004 (contains a detailed looked at The Sister Fidelma Mysteries).
8) Details of the biannual three-day international gatherings at Cashel on the Cashel Arts Fest website at www.cashelartsfest.com.
9) A profile of, and tribute to, Ellis and his work as an historian appeared in *History Ireland*, Vol 17, No 5 September/October 2009.

The Novels – Synopses

ABSOLUTION BY MURDER, *Headline Book Publishing, London, September 1994. Hardcover, ISBN 0 7472 1106 X, £16.99 Headline Paperback ISBN 0-7472-4602-5, 1995, £4.99; reprint in new jacket November 1998. USA St Martin's Press New York, hardcover ISBN 0-312-13918-7, January 5, 1996, with additional material "Sister Fidelma's World" (an historical note), $21.95 USA Signet Books, New York, September 1997, ISBN 0-451-19299-0 $5.99*

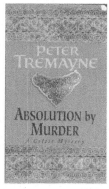

As the leading churchmen and women gather at the Synod of Whitby in AD 664 to debate the rival merits of the Celtic and Roman Churches, tempers begin to fray. Conspirators, greedy for power, plot the assassination of King Oswy of Northumbria. And mysterious, violent death stalks the shadowy cloisters of the Abbey of St Hilda, while outside the abbey walls, the pestilence of the Yellow Plague devastates the countryside. When Abbess Etain, a leading speaker for the Celtic Church, is found murdered at the start of the Synod, suspicion inevitably rests on the Roman faction.

Attending the Synod is Fidelma, of the community of St Brigid of Kildare. Sister Fidelma, an advocate of the Brehon Court, is called upon to investigate the murder. But, because of the acute political tension of the situation, a member of the Roman faction must work with her. Brother Eadulf, a Saxon, is of a family of hereditary magistrates, so he too is eminently qualified for the task. However, the two are so unlike in temperament and cultural concepts that King Oswy describes their partnership as that of a wolf and a fox. But which is which?

More violent deaths follow and the friction among the clerics is beginning to split the kingdom into civil war. Can the solution to the mysteries avert such a disastrous conflict?

ZHE SISZER FIDELMA COMPENDIUM

PRINCIPAL CHARACTERS

The Northumbrian Nobility

Oswy, King of Northumbria

Eanflaed, wife of Oswy

Alhfrith, son of Oswy by his first wife Rhiainfellt, and sub-king of Deira

Cyneburh, wife to Alhfrith, daughter of Penda of Mercia

Wulfric, thane of Frihop, commander of Alhfrith's guard

Alhflaed, daughter of Oswy by Rhiainfellt

Ecgfrith, on of Oswy by Eanflaed

Aelflaed, daughter of Oswy by Eanflaed

At the Abbey of Streoneshalh

Hilda, Abbess of Streoneshalh, cousin to Oswy

Sister Athelswith, *domino* of Streoneshalh

Canna, son of Canna, an Irish astrologer

The church of Columba faction

Colmán, Bishop of Northumbria and Abbot of Lindisfarne

Étain, Abbess of Kildare

Cedd, Bishop of the East Saxons

Cuthbert, Abbot of Melrose, brother of Cedd

Chad, Abbot of Lastingham, brother to Cedd and Cuthbert

Abbe, Abbess of Coldingham and sister to Oswy

Sister Fidelma of Cill Dara (Kildare), a *dálaigh* or advocate of the law courts of 7th century Ireland

Brother Taran, of the land of the Picts

Sister Gwid, of the land of the Picts

The church of Rome faction

Deusdedit, Archbishop of Canterbury

Brother Wighard, secretary to Deusdedit

James, also called Jacobus, an eighty-year-old Roman missionary to Northumbria

Wilfrid, Abbot of Ripon and principal advocate for the Roman faction

Brother Seaxwulf, secretary to Wilfrid

Agilbert, a Frank, Bishop of the West Saxons (Wessex)

Brother Agatho, priest in service to the Abbot of Icanho

ᏔᎻᎬ ᏁᏫᏉᎬᏞᏚ-ᏕᎩᏁᏫᏒᏕᎬᏕ

Brother Athelnoth, a priest
Brother Eadulf, a Saxon monk from the land of the South Folk
Romanus, chaplain to Queen Eanflaed of Northumbria

SHROUD FOR THE ARCHBISHOP, *Head-line Book Publishing, London, January 1995. Hardback, ISBN 0 7472 1140 X. £16.99 Headline Paperback, September 1995 ISBN 0 7427 4848 6 £4.99; reprinted with new jacket November 1998 USA St Martin's Press, New York, Hardcover, September 1996. Price $23.95 ISBN 0-312-14734 1 USA Paperback Signet Books, New York, July 1998, $5.99. ISBN 0 451 19300 8*

Wighard, archbishop of Canterbury, has been discovered garroted in his chambers in the Lateran Palace in Rome in the autumn of AD 664. The solution to this terrible crime appears simple as the palace custodes, its guards, have arrested an Irish religieux, Brother Ronan Ragallah, as he fled from Wighard's chambers. Although the Irish monk denies responsibility, Bishop Gelasius, the nomenclator in charge of running affairs at the Lateran Palace, is convinced the crime is political; Wighard was slain in pique at the triumph of the pro Roman Anglo-Saxon clergy in their debate with the pro-Coloumba Irish clergy at Whitby. There is also a matter of missing treasure; the goodwill gifts Wighard had brought with him to Rome and the priceless chalices sent for the Holy Father Vitalian's blessing have all been stolen.

Bishop Gelasius realises that Wighard's murder could lead to war between the Saxon and Irish kingdoms if Ronan is accused without independent evidence. So, he invites Sister Fidelma of Kildare and Brother Eadulf of Seaxmund's Ham to investigate. They are assisted by a young Roman officer of the Lateran Palace custodes, Furius Licinius. But more deaths must follow before Fidelma is finally able to put together the strange jigsaw in this tale of evil and vengeance.

PRINCIPAL CHARACTERS
Sister Fidelma, of Cill Dara (Kildare), a *dálaigh* or advocate of the law courts of 7th century Ireland

ZHE SISTER FIDELMA COMPENDIUM

Brother Eadulf of Seaxmund's Ham, scriptor or secretary of
Wighard, archbishop-designate of Canterbury

Furius Licinius, *tesserarius* of the *custodes*, officer of Lateran
Palace Guards
Marcus Narses, *decurion*
Marinus, *superesta* or military governor at the Lateran Palace

The Venerable Gelasius, *nomenclator* or chief official to his
Holiness, Bishop of Rome
Brother Donus, his factotum

Brother Cornelius of Alexandria, physician to Vitalian, Bishop
of Rome

Brother Ronán Ragallach, Irish religieux working at the
Munera Peregrinitatist
Osimo Lando, a Greek from Syracuse, sub-prater of the *Munera
Peregrinitatis,* where Ronán works.

Deacon Bieda, in charge of the hostel where Ronán lives near the
Aqua Claudia

Abbot Putoc, of Stanggrund, personal envoy of King Oswy of
Northumbria
Brother Eanred, servant to Putoc and former slave
Brother Sebbi, his adviser
Brother Ine of Kent
Abbess Wulfrun of Sheppey and sister to Queen Seaxburgh of
Kent
Sister Eafa, from Kent

Antonio, son of Nereus, street urchin, candle seller

Deacon Arsenius, in charge of hostel where Fidelma
Sister Epiphania, wife to Arsenius

Nabor, a Roman street tough

SUFFER LITTLE CHILDREN, *Headline Book Publishing, London, October 1995. Hardcover, ISBN 0 7472 1340 2, £16.99 Headline Paperback, June 13, 1996; ISBN 0-7427 4849 4, £5.99; reprinted with new jacket June 1998 USA St Martin's Press, New York, ISBN 0 312 15665 0, August 1997. $23.95. USA Paperback Signet Books, New York, ISBN 0 451 19557 4. February 1999, $5.99*

In the mid 7th century AD the Venerable Dacan, a much respected and beloved scholar of the Celtic Church, has been found murdered while on a visit to the Abbey of Ros Ailithir in the Irish kingdom of Muman.

The Venerable Dacan was a man of Laigin, the brother of its equally beloved Abbot Noe of Fearna, close confident to its newly crowned and impetuous young King. For centuries there has been enmity and tension between the kingdoms of Laigin and Muman and central to their quarrel is the control of the border lands of Osraige. In compensation for the death of Dacan, the young king of Laigin has demanded the land of Osraige – and that will mean bloody war.

Summoned by Muman's dying king to investigate, Sister Fidelma's task is both to solve the mystery of the brutal killing and also somehow to prevent the inevitable war breaking out between the two opposing kingdoms. She sets out for the remote abbey of Ros Ailithir with a warrior named Cass and very little time.

But there are more sinister forces at work behind Dacan's death than just political intrigue. Through a haunting, melancholy atmosphere, Sister Fidelma follows a trail that is as suspenseful as it is tortuous, as complicated as it is surprising.

Pʀɪɴᴄɪᴘᴀʟ Cʜᴀʀᴀᴄᴛᴇʀꜱ
Sister Fidelma of Cashel, a *dálaigh* or advocate of the law courts
    of 7th century Ireland
Cass, a member of the King of Cashel's bodyguard
Cathal, the dying King of Cashel
Colgú, the *tanaíste* or heir-apparent of Cashel, and Fidelma's
    brother

At Rae na Scrine
Intat, a *bó-aire* or local magistrate of the Corco Loígde
Sister Eisten, caring for orphans
Cétach and Cosrach, young brothers
Cera and Ciar, young sisters
Tressach, an orphan boy

At the abbey of Ros Ailithir
Abbot Brocc, a cousin of Fidelma
Brother Conghus, the *aistreóir* or doorkeeper
Brother Rumania, the *fer-tighis* or steward of the abbey
Brother Midach, the chief physician
Brother Tóla, the assistant physician
Brother Martan, the apothecary
Sister Grella, the librarian
Brother Ségán, the *fer-leginn* or chief professor
Sister Necht, a novice and assistant hostel keeper

Men of the Corco Loígde
Salbach, chieftain of the Corco Loígde
Scandlán, his cousin and petty king of Osraige
Ross, captain of a coastal *barc* or sailing vessel

Men of the kingdom of Laigin
The Venerable Dacán, the deceased

Fianamail, the king of Laigin
Forbassach, his Brehon or judge
Abbot Noé, brother of the Venerable Dacan; abbot of Fearna
  and advisor to Fianamail
Mugrón, captain of a Laigin warship
Midnat, a Laigin sailor
Assíd of the Uí Dego, a merchant and sea captain from Laigin

At Sceilig Mhichil
Father Mel, father superior of monastery of Sceilig Mhichil
Brother Febal, a monk

ZHE NOVELS-SYNOPSES

At Molua's House
Brother Molua, who runs an orphanage
Sister Aíbnat, his wife

At the Great Assembly
Sechnassuch, King of Ireland
Barrán, the Chief Brehon of Ireland
Ultan, Archbishop of Armagh, Chief Apostle of the Faith

THE SUBTLE SERPENT, *Headline Book Publishing, London, July 1996. Hardcover, ISBN 0 7472 1651 7. £16.99 Headline Paperback, December 1996, £5.99, ISBN 0 7472 52866; reprinted with new jacket June 1998 USA Hardcover, St Martin's Press, New York, June 1998, $23.95 ISBN 0-312-186703 USA Paperback, Signet Books, New York, October 1999, ISBN 0-451-19558-2 $5.99*

A headless female corpse is found in the drinking well of a remote abbey in south-west Ireland. One hand clasps a crucifix; tied to the other arm is a pagan death symbol...

A merchant ship is encountered under full sail on the high seas off the Irish coast. But the crew and its cargo have vanished – as if by sorcery ...

Whose is the body in the well? Where is the crew of the vessel? Are these bizarre events connected? And if so, who is responsible? The year is AD 666 and Sister Fidelma of Kildare, a religieuse and advocate of the Brehon law courts of the five kingdoms of Ireland, is thrown into another sinister mystery. The intrigue, danger and violence of ancient Ireland are proved palpitatingly real as Fidelma follows a trail of clues to a host of enigmatic suspects; the autocratic Abbess Draigen who has much to hide; the timid Sister Bronach, obviously escaping from something; the sly Brother Febal; and Adna, a petty chieftain with ruthless ambition, amongst many others. As Fidelma slowly begins to unravel the puzzle, the solution appears as complex as it is stunning.

ZHE SISZER FIDELMA COMPENDIUM

Sister Fidelma of Cashel, a *dálaigh* or advocate of the law courts of 7th century Ireland

Brother Eadulf of Seaxmund's Ham, a Saxon monk from the land of the South Folk, her companion

Ross, captain of a coastal *bars* or sailing vessel
Odar, his helmsman

At the Abbey of The Salmon of the Three Wells
    Abbess Draigen
    Sister Siomha, the *rechtaire* or steward of the abbey
    Sister Brónach, the *doirsedror* doorkeeper of the abbey
    Sister Lerben, a member of the community
    Sister Berrach, a handicapped member of the community
    Sister Comnat, the librarian
    Sister Almu, assistant to the librarian

At the fortress of Dan Bet
    Adnár, *bó-aire,* or local chieftain
    Brother Febal, *anam-chara* or soul-friend to Adnár
    Olcán, the son of Gulban the Hawk-Eyed, chieftain of the Beara
    Torcán, son of Eóganán, prince of the Uí Fidgenti and guest of Adnár
    Beccan, chief Brehon, or judge, of the Corco Loigde
    Brother Cillín of Mullach
    Máil, warrior of the Loigde
    Barr, a farmer

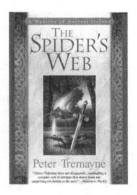

THE SPIDER'S WEB, *Headline Book Publishing, London, April 1997. Hardcover. ISBN 0-7472-1652-5, £16.99 Headline Paperback, September 1997, ISBN 0-7472-5287-4, £5.99: reprinted with new jacket June 1998 USA Hardcover, St Martin's Press, New York, May 1999, $23.95, ISBN 0-312-20589-9. US Paperback Signet Books, October 2000, ISBN 0-451-19559-0, £5.99*

ZHE NOVELS-SYNOPSES

Eber is not a man to make enemies. He is a chieftain with a reputation for kindliness and generosity. Yet, one night, his household is aroused by a scream from his chamber. The servants burst in to find Moen, a young man to whom Eber had extended his protection, crouched over the bloody body of the chieftain. Moen's clothes are drenched in Eber's blood and he is clutching a bloodstained knife in his hand.

There seems no doubt of culpability, but why did Moen kill the gentle an courteous Eber? The problem is made more difficult by the fact that Moen himself cannot tell them – for he is deaf, dumb and blind ...

The case proves to be anything but simple. That is when Sister Fidelma, advocate of the ancient Irish law courts, begins her investigation of the killing in order to present an argument on Moen's behalf before he is condemned. Assisted by the faithful Brother Eadulf, and confronting many enigmatic, intriguing characters, Fidelma finds himself tackling her most difficult case yet. her path to the truth twists and turns with the sinister forces of primitive passions and subtle ambitions – and leads inexorably to a final, stunning denouement.

PRINCIPAL CHARACTERS

Sister Fidelma of Cashel, a *dálaigh* or advocate of the law courts of 7th century Ireland

Brother Eadulf of Seaxmunds Ham, a Saxon monk from the land of the South Folk, her companion

Cathal, abbot of Lios Mhor
Brother Donnán, a *scriptor*
Colgú of Cashel, king of Muman and Fidelma's brother
Beccan, Chief Brehon, or judge, of Corco Loigde
Bressal, a hostel keeper
Morna, Bressal's brother

Eber, chieftain of Araglin
Cranat, Eber's wife
Crón, daughter of Eber and his *tánaiste* or heir apparent
Teafa, Eber's sister
Móen, a blind, deaf, mute

Duban, commander of Eber's bodyguard
Critán, a young warrior
Menma, head stableman at the *rath* of Araglin
Dignait, the stewardess
Grella, a servant

Father Gormán of Cill Uird

Archú, a young farmer of Araglin
Scoth, his fiancée
Muadnat of the Black Marsh, his cousin
Agdae, Muadnat's chief herdsman and nephew
Gadra, a hermit

Clídna, a brothel keeper

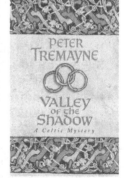

VALLEY OF THE SHADOW, *Headline Book Publishing, London 1998. Hardcover. ISBN 0-7472-2016-6. £16.99 Headline Paperback, August 1998, £5.99 ISBN 0-7472-5780-9. USA Hardcover St Martin's Press, New York, March 2000, $23.95 ISBN 0 32-20939-8. Paperback edition Signet July 2001 $5.99 ISBN 0-451-20330-8*

Sister Fidelma has been sent by her brother, king of Cashel, to Laisre, chieftain of Gleann Geis – the "forbidden valley" – to negotiate permission to build a Christian church and school in his territory, replacing the Druidic sanctuaries. In some remote corners of seventh century Ireland, Christianity has still not displaced the ancient pagan religion, and Laisre's clan is known to be hostile to the new religion, fiercely adhering to the old.

Knowing her mission will be no easy task, Fidelma, accompanied by the Saxon brother Eadulf, enters Gleann Geis. Here they come across the naked, slain bodies of thirty-three young men, curiously placed as if in a sunwise circle. Each body bears the marks of stabbing and garroting; every skull has been smashed in.

THE NOVELS-SYNOPSES

Is this some ritual sacrifice? It bears the hallmark of the ancient threefold death of pagan times. The number thirty-three bears mystical symbolism. What evil lies here? And who is responsible if not the heathens of Gleann Geis?

The solution to the many mysteries Fidelma encounters is not easily arrived at. And as she proceeds through the "forbidden valley" = the valley of the shadow – she embarks on an inquiry fraught with more evil and personal danger than any she has encountered before.

PRINCIPAL CHARACTERS

Sister Fidelma of Cashel, a *dálaigh* or advocate of the law courts of 7th century Ireland

Brother Eadulf of Seaxmund's Ham, a Saxon monk from the land of the South Folk, her companion

At Cashel

Colgú, chieftain of Gleann Geis
Colla, *tánaiste* or heir apparent to Laisre
Murgal, Laisre's Druid and Brehon
Mel, Murgal's scribe
Orla, sister of Laisre and wife to Colla
Esnad, daughter of Orla and Colla
Artgal, a warrior/blacksmith of Gleann Geis
Rudgal, a warrior/wagon-maker of Gleann Geis
Marga, an apothecary
Cruinn, the hostel keeper at Gleann Geis
Bairsech, his wife
Nemon, a prostitute

Brother Solin, a cleric from Armagh
Brother Dianach, his young scribe

Ibor of Muirthemne
Mer, a messenger

Elsewhere

Mael Dúm of the northern Uí Néill, King of Ailech
Ultan, bishop of Armagh, Comarb of Patrick
Sechnassuch of the southern Uí Néill, High King of Ireland

THE MONK WHO VANISHED, *Headline Book Publishing, London, February 1999. Hardcover, ISBN 0-7472-2017-4 £16.99. Headline Paperback, August 1999, £5.99, ISBN 0-7472-5781-7. USA Hardcover, St Martin's Press, New York, $23.95, ISBN 0-312-24219-0*

The Abbey of Imleach, in the southwest Irish kingdom of Muman, now rivals Armagh as the centre of the faith in Ireland. For the founder of the abbey was none other than St Ailbe, the man who brought Christianity to Muman, converted its King Oengus and, together with St Patrick, baptised him at Cashel in AD 448.

But now, calamity has struck the community of the Abbey of Imleach. not only has an elderly brother suddenly disappeared, but, almost worse for the harassed Abbot, the holy relics of St Ailbe have also vanished. St Ailbe's sacred relics are not just the concern of the abbey's community but are a price icon and political symbol of the entire kingdom. So, who would have dared to take them? Both relics and the monk must be found!

Sister Fidelma, together with Saxon brother Eadulf, on a visit to Imleach, are asked to investigate. It seems there is more to the disappearances than meets the eye; much more. Fidelma gradually uncovers one of the most sinister conspiracies she has yet encountered, in which the participators will stop at nothing – even murder – to achieve their aims...

PRINCIPAL CHARACTERS
Sister Fidelma of Cashel, a *dálaigh* or advocate of the law courts
   of 7th century Ireland
Brother Eadulf of Seaxmund's Ham, a Saxon monk from the
   land of the South Folk, her companion

At Cashel
   Colgú of Cashel, King of Muman and Fidelma's brother
   Donndubháin, *tánaiste* or heir apparent to Colgú
   Donennach mac Oengus, Prince of the Uí Fidgente
   Gionga, commander of Donennach's bodyguard

Conchobar, an astrologer and apothecary
Capa, captain of the bodyguard to Colgú
Brehon Rumann of Fearna
Brehon Dathal of Cashel
Brehon Fachtna of Uí Fidgente
Oslóir, a groom
Della, a recluse

At Ara's Well
Aona, the innkeeper
Adag, his grandson

At Imleach
Ségdae, abbot and bishop of lmleach, Comarb of Ailbe
Brother Mochta, Keeper of the Holy Relics
Brother Madagan, the *rechtaire* or steward
Brother Tomar, the stableman
Sister Scothnat, *domina* of the guests' hostel
Finguine mac Cathal, Prince of Cnoc Áine
Brother Daig
Brother Barn, the apothecary
Nion, *bó-aire* (petty-chief) and smith
Suíbne, his assistant
Cred, a tavern keeper
Samradán, a visiting merchant of Cashel
Solam, *dálalgh* of the Uí Fidgente

ACT OF MERCY, *Headline Book Publishing, London, November 1999. Hardcover, ISBN 0-7472-2018-2. £17.99. Headline Paperback, Spring 2000, ISBN 0-7472- 5782-5, £5.99. USA, St Martins Press, New York, hardcover ISBN 0-312-26864-5, $23.95. USA, Signet Books, New York, June 2003, ISBN 0-451-20908-7, $6.50*

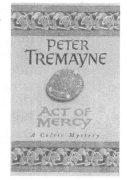

When Sister Fidelma sets out on a pilgrimage to the Holy Shrine of St James in the late autumn of AD 666, her main preoccupation is to reflect on her commitment to the religious life and her relationship with the Saxon monk, Eadulf, whom she has left behind. The arrival, among the small band of pilgrims, of her first love, a man who had deserted her, complicates matters, stirring up memories she would rather forget. But there are more complications to come.

During the first night out, with the ship tossed about by a tempestuous sea, one of the pilgrims disappears, apparently washed overboard. The discovery of a bloodstained robe raises question; was the pilgrim murdered and thrown into the sea?

With the bless of the captain, Fidelma finds herself having to overcome her emotional ties and focus all her abilities on solving the mystery. But death dogs the tiny band of pilgrims in the close confines of the ship. Fidelma finds herself not only battling against the antagonism of her fellow pilgrims but struggling to survive the turbulent elements of the storm-tossed sea, as she attempts to solver a perplexing puzzle. It is not until the Holy Shrine is almost reached – and time is running out – that the amazing truth is uncovered...

Principal Characters

Sister Fidelma of Cashel, a *dálaigh* or advocate of the law courts of 7th century Ireland

At Ardmore (Aird Mór)
> **Colla**, tavernkeeper and trader
> **Menma**, his young assistant

The Pilgrims
> **Sister Canair** of Moville *(Magh Bíle)*, leader of the pilgrims
> **Brother Cian**, a former member of the High King's bodyguard, now of the Abbey of Bangor *(Beannchar)*
> **Sister Muirgel**, of the Abbey of Movilie
> **Sister Crelia** of Moville
> **Sister Ainder** of Moville
> **Sister Gormán** of Moville
> **Brother Guss** of Moville
> **Brother Bairne** of Moville
> **Brother Dathal** of Bangor
> **Brother Adamrae** of Bangor
> **Brother Tola** of Bangor

ȚHE ṄȮVEL5-5ỴṄȮɍ5E5

The Crew of The Barnacle Goose
 Murchad, the captain
 Gurvan, the mate
 Wenbrit, cabin boy
 Drogan, a crewman
 Hoel, a crewman

Others
 Toca Nia, a shipwreck survivor
 Father Pol of Ushant
 Brehon Morann, Fidelma's mentor
 Grian, Fidelma's friend at Tara

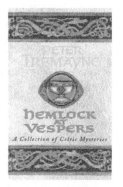

HEMLOCK AT VESPERS – Fifteen Sister Fidelma Mysteries, *Headline Book Publishing, London, March 2000. Hardcover. ISBN 0-7472 7119 4. £17.99. USA Trade Paperback: St Martin's Minotaur, St Martin's Press, New York, March 2000. ISBN 0-312-25288-9 $15.95. Headline paperback, November 2000, ISBN 0-7472-6432-5, £5.99*

    Sister Fidelma originally made her debut as one of the decade's most interesting sleuths in short story form. The red-haired, sharp witted and astonishingly wise religieuse captured the hearts of many readers as she successfully tackled the most baffling of crimes in her other role as *dálaigh* – or advocate – of the law courts of Ireland, using the ancient Brehon Law system. It was the overwhelmingly enthusiastic response to these stories which launched Fidelma as the heroine of a bestselling series of Celtic crime novels set during the mid seventh century AD, *Hemlock At Vespers* is the first collection of these stories ever to be published. With its breathtaking range of settings and crimes, it is guaranteed to entertain and intrigue – and is an anthology that no lover of Celtic culture or historical crime should be without.

OUR LADY OF DARKNESS, *Headline Book Publishing, London, September 2000. ISBN 0-7472-7120-8. £17.99. Headline paperback, May 2001, ISBN 0-7472-6433-3, £5.99. St Martin's Press, September 2002. ISBN 0-312-27295-2 at $23.95. USA Signet Books, New York, publication date June 1, 2004, price $6.50 ISBN 0-451-21221-5*

Arriving home from a pilgrim voyage, Sister Fidelma is told that her faithful Saxon companion, Brother Eadulf, has been found guilty of murdering a young girl. She hastens to the capital of the neighbouring kingdom of Laigin, where he is being held, determined to prove his innocence.

The crime took place at the abbey of Fearna where Fidelma clashes with the equally strong-willed but sinister Abbess Fainder. The evidence against Eadulf seems overwhelming, a terrible sordid story of sex, shame and murder. is it conceivable that Eadulf is actually guilty? Even Fidelma is forced to ask the question.

She has little time to discover the truth, however, for the King of Laigin is determined to make Eadulf an example. He has decided to give in to Abbess Fainder's demand that the ecclesiastical Penitentials from Rome be used and not the native law system, which would have simply meant loss of rights and payment of compensation to the victim's family. Ecclesiastical law demands "an eye for an eye" – Eadulf is due to be hanged.

In the gloomy atmosphere of the menacing abbey, Fidelma, struggling to put aside her emotional involvement, begins the desperate search for the truth; a search that will inspire sheer terror as her toughest investigation yet leads to shocking revelations.

PRINCIPAL CHARACTERS
Sister Fidelma of Cashel, a *dálaigh* or advocate of the law courts of 7th century Ireland

Brother Eadulf of Seaxmund's Ham, a Saxon monk from the land of the South Folk, her companion

Dego, a warrior of Cashel
Enda, a warrior of Cashel

ꙮE NꙮVELꙮ-ꙮYNꙮPꙮEꙮ

Aldan, a warrior of Cashel

Morca, a Laigín innkeeper

Abbess Fainder, abbess of Fearna
Abbot Noé, *anam chara* ("soul friend") of King Fianamail
Brother Cett, a monk of Fearna
Brother lbar, a monk of Fearna
Bishop Forbassach, Brehon of Laigín

Mel, captain of the guard at Fearna
Fianamail, King of Laigín
Lassar, owner of the Inn of the Yellow Mountain, sister of Mel
Sister Étromma, *rechtaire* or stewardess of the abbey of Fearna
Gormgilla, a victim
Fial, her friend
Brother Miach, physician of the abbey of Fearna
Gabrán, captain of a river boat and trader
Coba, a *bó-aire* or magistrate, chieftain of Cam Eolaing
Deog, widow of Daig, who was captain of the watch at Fearna
Dau, a warrior at Cam Eolaing
Dalbach, a blind recluse
Muirecht, a young girl
Conna, a young girl
Brother Martan of the Church of Brigid
Barrán, Chief Brehon of the Five Kingdoms

SMOKE IN THE WIND, *Headline Book Publishing, London, September 2001, ISBN 0-7472-7121-6. £17.99; St. Martin's Press, NYC, July 2003, ISBN 0-312-28780-01, $23.95; Paperback, Headline Book Publishing, March 4, 2002, ISBN 0-7472-6434-1, Price £5.99. Signet, New York, ISBN 0-451-21553-2, June 7, 2005, $6.99*

There seemed no disarray anywhere to account for why the meal appeared to have been deserted halfway through the eating of it. Stools and benches were pushed back as if everyone had risen but he saw nothing that indicated any confusion or panic. At a given moment, before the meal had ended, the brethren had simply stood up, leaving everything in an orderly manner, and vanished!

En route from Ireland to visit the new Archbishop of Canterbury, Sister Fidelma and her faithful Saxon companion, Brother Eadulf, find themselves on the coast of the Welsh kingdom of Dyfed when their ship is blown off course by a storm. The elderly King Gwlyddien is quick to offer hospitality, not last because the famous Irish *dálaigh* may be the only person capable of solving the mystery which has baffled the wisest of men – the entire monastic community of nearby Llanpadern, to which Gwlyddie's eldest son belongs, has vanished into thin air.

Who, or what, is behind the disappearance of the monks? Is it sorcery or some sinister plot – and what does the perpetrator hope to achieve? But before Fidelma and Eadulf can begin to answer these questions, they must contend with the shocking and seemingly unrelated murder of a local girl – a death whose consequences will be more tragic and more far-reaching than anyone can imagine.

Sister Fidelma's tenth full-length mystery takes her to a new Celtic land, where she finds herself embroiled in a case as perplexing as it is spine-chilling.

PRINCIPAL CHARACTERS
Sister Fidelma of Cashel, a *dálaigh* or advocate of the law courts of 7th century Ireland
Brother Eadulf of Seaxmund's Ham, a Saxon monk from the land of the South Folk, her companion

At Porth Clais
Brother Rhodri, of Porth Clais

At the Abbey of Dewi Sant, Menevia
Abbot Tryffin
Gwlyddien, king of Dyfed
Cathen, son of Gwlyddien
Brother Meurig, a *barnwr* or judge of Dyfed
Brother Cyngar, of Menevia
Cadell, a warrior

ZHE NOVELS-SYNOPSES

At Pen Caer and environs
Mair, a victim
Iorwerth the smith, father of Mair
Iestyn, his friend, a farmer
Idwal, a youthful itinerant shepherd
Gwnda, lord of Pen Caer
Elen, Gwnda's daughter
Buddog, a servant in Gwnda's hall
Clydog Cacynen, an outlaw
Corryn, one of his band
Sualda, another of his band
Goff, a smith
Rhonwen, his wife
Dewi, his son
Elisse, the apothecary
Osric, thane of the Hwicce

THE HAUNTED ABBOT, *Headline Book Publishing, London, September 2, 2002, in hardback. ISBN 0-7472-7122-4 at £17.99. February 2003, Headline, London. Paperback. ISBN 0-7472-6435-X £5.99; St Martin Minotaur, New York, ISBN 0-312-28769-0, May 2003, $24.95. Paperback. ISBN 0-451-21716-0. $6.99. December 2005, Signet, New York*

It needed little medical knowledge to realise that Brother Botulf's skull had been smashed in by some heavy, blunt instrument. The realisation came to Eadulf that such wounds could only have bee inflicted by someone whose strength lay in malice. That his friend had been murdered and the event must have occurred scarcely more than a few hours before. At that moment, the wind rose again, shrieking like a chorus of souls in torment shrieking like a presage of evil.

Their business with the Archbishop of Canterbury now complete, Sister Fidelma and Brother Eadulf must make one final journey before returning home to Ireland – to the village of Seaxmund's Ham in the land of the South Folk – where Eadulf grew up. But a mysterious message from his childhood friend, Brother Botulf, finds them making an unexpected detour to the nearby Aldred's Abbey, where Botulf has requested their presence at a very particular time on a very particular day – midnight on the old pagan feast of Yule.

Puzzled and intrigued by their summons, Fidelma and Eadulf battle against the harsh winter storms to make their appointment, only to find they have, nevertheless, arrived too late. Botulf is dead – killed by an unknown hand.

And as they struggle to comprehend this staggering news, it soon becomes clear that the murder of this young monk is not the only trouble facing the abbey. Another less tangible danger threatens – the ghost of a young woman haunts the cloister shadows – a woman some say bears a startling likeness to the Abbot Cild's dead wife. But can Fidelma and Eadulf discover the truth before they themselves fall victim to the danger which pervades the abbey walls?

PRINCIPAL CHARACTERS

Sister Fidelma of Cashel, a *dálaigh* or advocate of the law courts of 7th century Ireland

Brother Eadulf of Seaxmund's Ham, a Saxon monk from the land of the South Folk, her companion

At Cynric's Inn
    Cyrnric, the innkeeper
    'Mad' Mul, a farmer

At Aldred's Abbey
    Abbot Cild
    Brother Botulf, a friend of Eadulf
    Brother Willibrod, the *dominus*
    Brother Osred, the smith
    Brother Higbald, the apothecary
    Brother Redwald, a youthful religieux
    Brother Wigstan
    Brother Beronwulf

In the marshlands
    Aldhere, an outlaw
    Bertha, a Frank, his woman

Wiglaf, one of his band
Lioba, a local peasant girl

On the road
  Dagobert, a Frankish merchant
  Dado, his companion

At Tunstall
  Brother Laisre
  Brother Tola
  Gadra, chieftain of Maigh Eo
  Garb, his son

Sigeric, high steward to Ealdwulf, King of East Anglia
Werferth, commander of his bodyguard

BADGER'S MOON, *Headline Book Publishing, London. Hardback. September 2003. ISBN 0-7553-0223-0. £18.99. Headline, London. Paperback. ISBN 0-7553 0334 9. £6.99. March 2004. St Martin's Minotaur, New York, ISBN 0-312-32341-7, March 2005, $23.95. Signet, New York, July 2006, $6.99*

A series of horrific murders has brought terror to the Kingdom of Muman. Three young girls have been slaughtered with unspeakable violence on the nights of consecutive full moons.

Suspicion falls on three dark strangers from the distant land of Aksum (Ethiopia), who are guests at the Abbey of Finbarr, and a panic-stricken mob attacks the community, leaving the religious in fear for their lives. Sister Fidelma and Brother Eadulf are called in to restore order and it soon becomes clear that while the three mysterious strangers are definitely hiding something, there are other more likely suspects for the murders. What about the ageing Laig, a hermit-like apothecary, who is known to have instructed all three victims about the magic and power of the moon; what sinister truths are hidden in his dark woodland dwelling?

As Fidelma struggles to repair her faltering relationship with Eadulf, can she uncover the truth before the next full moon, when the killer will strike again?

PRINCIPAL CHARACTERS

Sister Fidelma of Cashel, a *dálaigh* or advocate of the law courts of 7th century Ireland

Brother Eadulf of Seaxmund's Ham, a Saxon monk from the land of the South Folk, her companion

At Cashel

    Colgú, King of Muman, Fidelma's brother

    Ségdae, bishop of Imleach, *comarb* of Ailbe

    Sáirait, the nursemaid

At Rath Raithlen

    Becc, chieftain of the Cinél na Áeda

    Adag, the steward to Becc

    Accobrán, *tánaiste*, or heir apparent, to Becc

    Lesren the tanner, father of Beccnat

    Bébháil, mother of Beccnat

    Seachlann the miller, father of Escrach

    Brocc, brother of Seachlann

    Sirin, cook at Rath Raithlen, uncle of Ballgel

    Berrach, aunt of Ballgel, sister to Sirin

    Goll the woodcutter

    Finmed, his wife

    Gabrán, son of Goll

    Liag the apothecary

    Gobnuid, a smith

    Tómma, Lesren's assistant

    Creoda, a tanner's assistant

    Síoda, a boy

    Menma, a hunter

    Suanach, his wife

At the abbey of the Blessed Finnbarr

    Abbot Brogán

    Brother Solam

ᏓᎻᎬ ᏁᎾᏉᎬᏞᏚ-ᏚᎩᏁᎾᏒᏚᎬᏚ

Brother Dangila
Brother Nakfa
Brother Gambela
Brother Túan, steward of the house of Molaga

Conrí, war chief of the Uí Fidgente

THE LEPER'S BELL, *Headline Book Publishing, London, September 6, 2004, in hardback. ISBN 0-7553-0225-7at £18.99. St. Martin's Minotaur, NYC, hardcover, January 2006, ISBN 0-312-32343-3. $23.95. Headline UK paperback, March 5, 2005, £6.99, ISBN 0-7553-0336-5. US paperback, St Martin's Minotaur, October 2006, $13.95, 0-312-36275-7*

Sister Fidelma sets out to solve one of her most dangerous and personal crimes yet.

A servant has been murdered. The baby in her charge has been abducted. Fidelma of Cashel has solved even more horrendous crimes in her career as an advocate of the ancient Brehon Courts of Ireland. But this case is different. For both Sister Fidelma and her companion, Brother Eadulf of Saxmund's Ham, the case is unique because of the personal emotions involved. The baby who has been abducted is their son. What is the motive for their crime? Could someone seeking vengeance on Fidelma and Eadulf have done the deed?

They have made a lot of enemies in their pursuit of justice. Fidelma and Eadulf, ignoring protests that they are too emotionally involved to undertake the investigation, set out on what proves to be one of the most dangerous cases they have ever undertaken...

PRINCIPAL CHARACTERS
Sister Fidelma of Cashel, a *dálaigh* or advocate of the law courts of 7th century Ireland
Brother Eadulf of Seaxmund's Ham, a Saxon monk from the land of the South Folk, her companion

THE SISTER FIDELMA COMPENDIUM

At Cashel
Colgú, king of Muman, Fidelma's brother
Finguine, his *tánaiste* or heir apparent, cousin to Colgú and Fidelma
Ségdae, bishop of Imleach
Brehon Dathal, chief judge of Muman
Cerball, bard to Colgú
Capa, conmander of the king's bodyguard, Gobnat's husband
Gobnat, sister to the murdered nurse Sárait
Caol, a warrior of Cashel
Gormán, a warrior of Cashel
Conchoille, a woodsman
Delia, a former prostiute or *bé táide*
Bishop Petran of Cashel
Brother Conchobar, an apothecary
Cuirgí, hostage chieftain of the Uí Fidgente
Cuan, hostage chieftain of the Uí Fidgente
Crond, hostage chieftain of the Uí Fidgente

At Ara's Well
Aona, the innkeeper
Adag, his grandson
Cathalán, a former warrior

At the Abbey of Imleach
Brother Madagan, the steward
Brother Buite of Magh Ghlas, leader of the pilgrims

At Cnoc Loinge
Fiachrae, the chieftain
Forindain, a dwarf and leader of the *crossan* or travelling players

At Rath na Drinne
Ferloga, the innkeeper

At the Well of the Oak Grove
Conrí, warlord of the Uí Fidgente

ᛏᚻᛁ ᚾᛟᚢᛁᛚᛋ-ᛋᚤᚾᛟᛈᛋᛁᛋ

At Sliabh Mis
   Corb, an itinerant herbalist
   Corbnait, his wife
   Uaman, lord of the passes of Sliabh Mis
   Basil Nestorios, a Persian healer
   Ganicca, an old man
   Nessán, a shepherd of Gabhlán
   Muirgen, his wife

WHISPERS OF THE DEAD – A Collection
of Ancient Irish Mysteries, *Headline Book
Publishing, London. Hardback. ISBN 0-7553-
0229-X. £18.99. US edition – St Martin's Minotaur
(trade paperback), St Martin's Press, New York,
370pp, ISBN 0-312-30382-3. Price $14.95. Pub.
date May 2004. Headline Books, paperback,
London, ISBN 0-7553-0230-5, September 2004.
£6.99*

*"The dead always whisper to us. It is our task
to listen to the whispers of the dead."*
   Whispers of the Dead is a sumptuously rich feast of fifteen short
mystery tales, never before published in book form, featuring the
brilliant and beguiling Sister Fidelma. Although the heroine of a series
of bestselling novels, Sister Fidelma, the seventh-century sleuth of
the Celtic Church, made her debut in short story form. *Hemlock at
Vespers* was the first collection of fifteen early tales. Now *Whispers
of the Dead* brings entirely new adventures.
   This collection contains an astonishing range of crimes and
misdemeanors and seamlessly blends historical detail, character and
story into mysteries that will confound and surprise. *Whispers of the
Dead* is Sister Fidelma at her very best.
   *"In the simultaneously sharp-witted and full womanly figure of
Sister Fidelma, Tremayne has created a heroine whom many readers
will willingly follow"* Kirkus Reviews

MASTER OF SOULS, *Headline Book Publishing, London, ISBN 0-7553-0227-3, price Str£18.99, Pub.date September 5, 2005. US hardback, St Martin's Minotaur, November 14, 2006, $24.94, ISBN 0-312-34832-0. UK paperback, Headline, ISBN 0-7553-0228-1, March 2006, £6.99. US paperback: St Martins Minotaur, New York, ISBN 0-312-37467-4, Price $13.95, September 2007*

A storm-driven night. Wreckers deliberately drive a helpless merchant ship on to a rocky shire on the west coast of Ireland. Abbess Faife, leading a pilgrimage to a holy mountain, is slaughtered, and her six companions, young female religieuse, are abducted. An ageing ecclesiastical scholar is murdered in the oratory of the Abbey of Ard Fhearta. Do these bizarre events have a connection?

Sister Fidelma and her companion, Brother Eadulf, are asked to go to Ard Fhearta to examine the mystery at the request of Abbess Faife's nephew.

But the Abbey of Ard Fhearta stands in the territory of the Uí Fidgente, blood enemies of Fidelma and her brother, Colgú, King of Cashel, for the nephew of Abbess Faife, is none other than Conrí, warlord of the Uí Fidgente.

Many dangers threaten Fidelma and Eadulf from the time of their arrival at the gates of the abbey.

Who is the mysterious "master of souls?" Has the evil Uaman the Leper, Lord of the Passes, returned from what was presumed his watery grave? Is he the shadowy `master" spreading death and corruption across the land? Or is the bombastic chieftain, Slébáne of the Corco Duibhne, playing some malevolent power game of his own? What malicious hazards await Fidelma and her companion on the tiny, storm blown Seanach's Island, where only a small group of hermits are supposed to dwell?

In a brutal and unforgiving seventh-century Irish landscape, Fidelma and Eadulf face one of their most perilous undertakings yet!

PRINCIPAL CHARACTERS
Sister Fidelma of Cashel, a *dálaigh* or advocate of the law courts of 7th century Ireland

THE NOVELS-SYNOPSES

Brother Eadulf of Seaxmund's Ham, a Saxon monk from the land of the South Folk, her companion

On the Sumerli
Esumaro, captain
Coros, his first mate

At Inis
Oleán, leader of the wreckers
Abbess Faire of Ard Fhearta
Sister Eusdan

At Ard Fhearta
Conrí, warlord of the Uí Fidgente
Socht, one of his warriors

Abbot Erc
Brother Cú Mara, the *rechtaire* or steward
The Venerable Cináed, a scholar
The Venerable Mac Faosma, a scholar
Brother Benen, his student
Sister Sinnchéne
Sister Buan, wife to Cináed
Brother Feólaigid, the butcher
Sister Uallann, the physician
Brother Eolas, the *leobhar coimedach,* or librarian
Brother Faolchair, his assistant
Brother Cillín, the *stiúirtheóir conold* or master of music

Mugrón, a merchant
Tadcán, lord of Baile Tade

At Daingean
Slébéne, chief of the Corco Duibhne

At Sliabh Mís
Iobcar, son of Starn the Blacksmith
Ganicca, an old man

At Baile Gabhainn
   Gáeth, the smith
   Gaimredán, his assistant

A PRAYER FOR THE DAMNED, *Headline Book Publishing, London, September 2006. Hardcover, ISBN 0 7553 2836 1, £19.99; Headline paperback, published February 5, 2007, ISBN 978-0-7553-2837-6, Price £6.99. US hardcover: St Martins Minotaur, New York, ISBN 0-312-34833-5, Price $24.95, November 2007. St Martin's Minotaur, 175 Fifth Avenue, New York, NY 10010, paperback ISBN 13-978-0-312-37789-2. Pub. date, September 2008, Price $11.99*

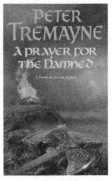

February, AD 668, and Cashel is full of distinguished visitors. The reason Under the old Irish custom, Fidelma of Cashel and Eadulf of Seaxmund's Ham, having been joined together for a year and a day, are to be married. But on the eve of the ceremony, the pious Abbot Ultan, who has travelled from the far north to attend, is found murdered in his chamber. Worst still – one of the most distinguished guests, the King of Connacht, has been seen fleeing from the scene and is charged with the murder. He demands his right to appoint Fidelma in his defence. Quickly Fidelma discovers that Abbot Ultan is not the pious man he was thought to be – indeed, many of the guests have cause to hate him. It is a long weekend of suspicion, fear and more death before Fidelma and Eadulf are able to reveal to their restless and querulous guests the truth behind Ultan's murder.

PRINCIPAL CHARACTERS
Sister Fidelma of Cashel, a *dálaigh* or advocate of the law courts
   of 7th century Ireland
Brother Eadulf of Seaxmund's Ham, a Saxon monk from the
   land of the South Folk, her companion

At the Abbey of Imleach
   Ségdae, abbot and bishop of Imleach
   Brother Madagan, steward of Imleach

ZHE NOVELS-SYNOPSES

Ultán, abbot of Cill Ria and bishop of the Uí Thuirtri
Brother Dróon, scribe and steward of Cill Ria
Sister Sétach, of Cill Ria
Sister Marga, of Cill Ria

At Ardane in the Valley of Eatharlaí
    Miach, chief of the Uí Cuileann
    Brother Berrihert, a Saxon religieux
    Brother Pecanum, his brother
    Brother Naovan, their brother
    Ordwulf, their elderly father and a pagan Saxon warrior

At Cashel
    Colgú, king of Muman, Fidelma's brother
    Finguine, his *tánaiste* or heir apparent, cousin to Colgú and
        Fidelma
    Brehon Baithen, Brehon of Muman
    Caol, commander of the king's bodyguard
    Gormán, a warrior of the guard
    Dego, a warrior of the guard
    Enda, a warrior of the guard
    Brother Conchobhar, an apothecary at Cashel
    Muirgen, nurse to Alchú, son of Fidelma and Eadulf
    Nessán, her husband
    Rónán, a hunter and tracker
    Della, friend of Fidelma and mother of Gormán

Guests at Cashel
    Sechnassach, High King of Ireland
    Brehon Barrán, Chief Brehon of the Five Kingdoms
    Muirchertach Nár of the Uí Fiachracha
    Aidni, king of Connacht
    Aíbnat, his wife
    Dúnchad Muirisci of the Uí Fiachracha
    Muaide, his *tánaiste* or heir apparent
    Augaire, abbot of Conga
    Laisran, abbot of Durrow
    Ninnid, Brehon of Laigin
    Blathmac mac Mael

Coba, king of Ulaidh
Fergus Fanat of Ulaidh, Blathmac's cousin

DANCING WITH DEMONS, *Headline Book Publishing, London, hardcover, 274pp. ISBN 978-0-7553-2838-3, September 2007, £19.99. Headline paperback, ISBN 978-0-7553-2839-0, £7.99, March 2008. St Martin's Minotaur, 175 Fifth Avenue, New York, NY 10010, USA. hardcover. ISBN 0-312-37564-0, Pub. date October 28, 2008. Price $24.95. St Martin's Minotaur, New York, paperback, November 2009, ISBN 978-0-312-58741-3. $13.99*

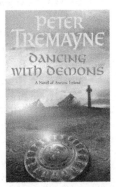

When Sechnussach, High King of Ireland, is found dead in his bedchamber with his throat cut, all clues point to Dubh Duin, the chieftain of the clan Cinál Cairpre. For he was found with the murder weapon in his hand when the High King's guards entered the royal chamber. But rather than surrender, or protest his innocence, Dubh Duin took his own life.

The Chief Brehon of Ireland asks Sister Fidelma to find out what possible motives could have driven Dubh Duin to assassinate the High King. Everyone seems to have an opinion on this shocking murder, but the Chief believes that the real truth is yet to be uncovered. Fidelma, assisted by her trusted partner, Brother Eadulf and accompanied by two Cashel warriors, sets out for the High King's palace at Tara.

Their investigation reveals an intricate web of conspiracy and deception that surrounded Sechnussach while he was alive and one that has only grown more entangled since his death. If those responsible are not discovered in time these intrigues threaten to unbalance the five kingdoms and send them spiralling into a violent and bloody civil war.

PRINCIPAL CHARACTERS
Sister Fidelma of Cashel, a *dálaigh* or advocate of the law courts of 7th century Ireland
Brother Eadulf of Seaxmund's Ham, a Saxon monk from the land of the South Folk, her companion

At Rath na Drinne
Ferloga, the innkeeper
Lassar, his wife

At Cashel
Colgú, king of Muman, Fidelma's brother
Caol, commander of the Nasc Niadh, bodyguards to the Kings of Muman
Gormán, a warrior of the guard

At Tara
Cena Faelad, the new High King
Barrán, Chief Brehon
Sedna, deputy Chief Brehon
Abbot Colmán, spiritual adviser and *rechtaire* or chief steward to the High King
Brother Rogallach, *bollscari* or factotum to the High King
Gormflaith, widow of the High King Sechnussach
Muírgel, eldest daughter of Sechnussach and Gormflaith
Irél, commander of the Fianna, bodyguards to the High King
Erc the Speckled, a warrior of the Fianna
Cuan, a warrior of the Fianna
Lugna, a warrior of the Fianna
Mer the Demented
lceadh the Healer, physician to the High King
Broách, chief female servant
Báine, a maid
Cnucha, a maid
Torpach, a cook
Maoláin, his assistant
Duirnín, a servant
Assíd, a slave
Verbas of Peqini, his master and a merchant
Bishop Luachan of Delbna Mór
Brother Céin, his steward
Brother Diomasach, a scribe
Brotbtr Manchán of Baile Fobhalr
Ardgal, chief of the Cinél Cairpre
Beorhtric, a Saxon warrior

THE COUNCIL OF THE CURSED, *Head-line Book Publishing, London, hardcover, 320pp. ISBN 978-0755328406, July 2008, £19.99. Headline, London, A Format paperback, March 5, 2009, £6.99 ISBN 978-0-7553-49180, Headline, London B Format paperback, March 5, 2009, £7.99, ISBN 978-0-7553-2841-3. St Martins Minotaur, New York, hardcover, ISBN 978-0-312-37565-2. $24.99. Pub. date, November 2009. US paperback edition, St Martins Minotaur, ISBN 978-0-312-60493, November 23, 2010, $14.99*

When Bishop Leodegar of Autun calls upon the church leaders from western Europe to attend a council, it is to be a meeting haunted by sudden death and intrigue. It's AD 670, and the Council of Autun is meeting to discuss serving a final devastating blow to the Celtic Church. But when a conflict between two delegate results in the murder of the chief delegate from Hibernia, the entire Council is in danger. Sister Fidelma and her companion, Brother Eadulf, arrive in Autun to act as advisors to the Irish delegation. Between the autocratic Bishop Leodegar and the malignant abbess, Mother Audofleda, a web of sinister intrigue soon spreads. The theft of a priceless reliquary box, the disappearance of women and children and rumours of a slave trade make this one of the most sinister puzzles that Fidelma and Eadulf have ever faced...

PRINCIPAL CHARACTERS
Sister Fidelma of Cashel, a *dálaigh* or advocate of the law courts of 7th century Ireland
Brother Eadulf of Seaxmund's Ham, a Saxon monk from the land of the South Folk, her companion

At Autun (the religious)
    Leodegar, bishop and abbot of Autun
    Nuntius Peregrinus, the Papal Nuncio or envoy
    Ségdae, abbot and bishop of Imleach
    Dabhóc, abbot of Tulach Óc
    Cadfan, abbot of Gwynedd

Ordgar, bishop of Kent
Brother Chilperic, steward to Leodegar
Brother Gebicca, a physician
Brother Sigeric, a scribe
Brother Benevolentia, steward to Ordgar
Brother Gillucán, steward to Dabhóc
Brother Andica, a stonemason
Abbess Audofleda, the *abbatissa* of the *Donnus Femini*
Sister Radegund, the stewardess of the *Domus Femini*
Sister Inginde
Sister Valretrade

At Autun (the city)
Lady Beretrude
Lord Guntram, her son
Verbas of Peqini
Magnatrude, sister to Valretrade
Ageric, a smith and husband to Magnatrude
Clodomar, a smith
Clotaire III, King of Austrasia
Ebroin, his mentor

At Nebirnum
Arigius, abbot of Neburnum
Brother Budnouen, a Gaul

THE DOVE OF DEATH, *Headline Book Publishing, London, hardcover, 384pp. ISBN978-0755347230, July 2009, £19.99.UK paperback (A Format), 434pp, ISBN 978-0-7553-4724-7, pub. date February 4, 2010, Price Str£6.99 and UK paperback (B Format), 434pp, ISBN 978-7553-5762-8, pub. date February 4, 2010, Price Str£7.99. US hardcover edition St Martins Minotaur, 175 Fifth Avenue, New York, NY 10010. ISBN 978-0-312-55120-9. Pub. October 26, 2010, $25.99. US paperback, Minotaur Books, St. Martins Publishing Group, 175 Fifth Avenue, New*

ZHE SISZER FIDELMA COMPENDIUM

York, NY 10010, USA. September 27, 2011. ISBN 978-0-312-60927-6. Price $14.99

AD 670. An Irish merchant ship is attacked by a pirate vessel off the coast of the Breton peninsular. Murchad, the captain, and a prince from the kingdom of Muman, are killed in cold blood after they have surrendered. Among the other passengers who manage to escape the slaughter are Sister Fidelma of Cashel and her faithful companion, Brother Eadulf. The prince was Fidelma's cousin and she is determined to bring the killers to justice...

PRINCIPAL CHARACTERS

Sister Fidelma of Cashel, a *dálaigh* or advocate of the law courts of 7th century Ireland

Brother Eadulf of Seaxmund's Ham, a Saxon monk from the land of the South Folk, her companion

On the Barnacle Goose
> **Bressal** of Cashel, Fidelma's cousin and envoy of her brother Colgú, King of Muman
> **Murchad**, the captain
> **Gurvan**, the mate
> **Wenbrit**, the cabin boy
> **Hoel**, a crewman

On the island of Hoedig
> **Brother Metellus**, a Roman cleric
> **Lowenen**, the chieftain
> **Onenn**, his wife

On the Rhuis peninsula
> **Abbot Maelcar** of the abbey of the Blessed Gildas
> **Brother Ebolbain**, his scribe
> **Aourken**, a widow
> **Berran**, a drover
> **Biscam**, a merchant
> **Barbatil**, Argantken's father
> **Coric**, his companion

ꙅHE ꓠꙨVELꙅ-ꙅYꓠꙨꝑꙅEꙅ

At the fortress of Brilhag
Macliau, son of the *mac'htiern* (lord) of Brilhag
Argantken, Macliau's mistress
Trifina, Macliau's sister
Iuna, stewardess of the household
Bleidbara, commander of the guard at Brilhag
Boric, his deputy and a tracker
Iarnbud, a *bretat,* or judge to the *mac'htiern* of Brilhag
Riwanon, wife of Alain the Tall, King of the Bretons
Budic, commander of her bodyguard
Ceingar, her female attendant

Alain Hir (the Tall), King of the Bretons
Canao, the *miac'htiern*, Lord of Brilhag
Kaourentin, a *bretat* or judge of Bro-Gernev

At Govihan
Heraclius, an apothecary from Constantinopolis
Koulm ar Maro, "The Dove of Death"

THE CHALICE OF BLOOD, *Headline Book Publishing, London, Pub. July 8, 2010. ISBN 978-0-7553-4725-4. Price £19.99; UK paperback (B format), 433pp, March 2, 2011, ISBN 978-0-7553-5776-5. £7.99; UK paperback, Headline Publishing, 338 Euston Road, London NW1 3BH, UK. ISBN 978-0-7553-5776-5. Price £7.99. February 2011; USA hardcover, Minotaur Books, St Martins Publishing Group, 175 Fifth Avenue, New York, NY 10010, USA, October 25, 2011. ISBN 978-0-312-55152-6. Price $25.99; USA paperback, Minotaur Books, St Martins Press, ISBN 978-1-250-00407-9, August 2012 $14.99*

Ireland AD 670. When an eminent scholar is found murdered in his cell in the abbey of Lios Mór, fear spreads among his brethren: his door was secured from the inside, with no other means of entrance or exit. How did his murderer escape? And what was the content of the manuscripts apparently stolen from the scholar's room?

Abbot Iarnla insists on sending for Sister Fidelma and her companion Brother Eadulf, to investigate the killing. But even before they reach the abbey, there is an attempt on their lives. As the mystery deepens, Fidelma and Eadulf must wrestle with problems of their own, which threatens to separate them forever...

PRINCIPAL CHARACTERS

Sister Fidelma of Cashel, a *dálaigh* or advocate of the law courts of 7th century Ireland

Brother Eadulf of Seaxmund's Ham, a Saxon monk from the land of the South Folk, her companion

At Bingium
Huneric, a hunter and guide
Brother Donnchad of Lios Mór

At Cashel
    Colgú, King of Muman and brother to Fidelma
    Ségdae, Abbot of lmleach, Chief Bishop of Muman
    Brother Madagan, his steward
    Caol, commander of the Nasc Niadh, bodyguards to the King
    Gormán, a warrior of tbc Nasc Niadh
    Brehon Aillín, a judge

At Cill Domnoc
    Brother Corbach

At Lios Mór
    Iarnla, Abbot of Lios Mór
    Brother Lugna, his *rechtaire*, or steward
    Brother Giolla-na-Naomh, the blacksmith
    Brother Máel Eoin, the *bruigad,* or hosteller
    Brother Gáeth, former *anam chara* (soul friend) of Brother Donnchad
    Brother Seachlann, a physician
    Brother Donnán, *scriptor* (librarian)
    Brother Echen, the *echaire*, or stable keeper
    Venerable Bróen, an elderly member of the community

Lady Eithne of An Dún, mother of Brother Donnchad
Glassán, the master builder
Gúasach, his foster-son and apprentice
Saor, a carpenter and assistant master builder

At Fhear Maighe
  Cumscrad, chief of the Fir Maige Féne
  Cunán, his son and assistant librarian
  Muirgíos, a barge master
  Eolann, a bargeman
  Uallachán, chief of the Uí Liathain
  Brother Temnen, librarian of Ard Mór

BEHOLD A PALE HORSE, *Headline Book Publishing, 338 Euston Road, London, ISBN 978-0-7553-7747-3, July 7, 2011, £19.99. Headline Publishing, UK paperback, March 1, 2012, £7.99, ISBN 978-0-7553-7748-0; USA hardcover, Minotaur Books, St Martins Publishing Co., 175 Fifth Avenue, New York, NY 10010, USA. ISBN 978-0-312-65863-2. July 15, 2012, $25.99; US paperback, St Martins Minotaur, June 25, 2013, $15.99, ISBN 978-1-230-02997-3*

It is AD 664 and Sister Fidelma finds herself in the seaport of Genua, en route from Rome back to her native Cashel. Her old teacher, Brother Ruadán, lies dying in the abbey of Bobium – an isolated abbey in a disturbed country where even the Christians are in blood conflict with one another, and the worship of the pagan gods often prevails.

Fidelma is determined to see Brother Ruadán before he dies. But from the moment she enters the beautiful valley of the Trebbia, there is danger on every side. Her dying teacher's last words send her off on her most dangerous adventure where murder follows murder, and a vicious civil war threatens before an extraordinary conspiracy is revealed. And from the start, Fidelma is on her own...

(This story is a chronological sequel to *Shroud for the Archbishop*)

PRINCIPAL CHARACTERS

Sister Fidelma of Cashel, a *dálaigh* or advocate of the law courts of 7th century Ireland

At Genua in the kingdom of the Longobards
Magister Ado of Bobium
Brother Faro
Sister Gisa

In the Trebbia Valley
Radoald, Lord of Trebbia
Wulfoald, commander of Radoald's warriors
Suidur the Wise, physician to Radoald
Aistulf the Hermit

At the Abbey of Bobium
Abbot Servillius
Venerable Ionas, a scholar
Brother Wulfila, steward
Brother Hnikar, apothecary
Brother Ruadán, formerly of Inis Celtra
Brother Lonán, herbalist
Brother Eolann, *scriptor* or librarian
Brother Waldipert, cook
Brother Bladulf, gatekeeper
Romuald of Benevento, Prince of the Longobards
Lady Gunora, his nurse
Bishop Britmund, of Placentia, leader of the Arians
Brother Godomar, his steward

On Mount Penas
Wamba, a goatherd
Hawisa, mother of Wamba
Odo, her nephew, a goatherd
Ratchis, a merchant

At Vars
Grasulf, son of Gisulf, Lord of Vars
Kakko, his steward

THE SEVENTH TRUMPET, *Headline Book Publishing, 338 Euston Road, London, ISBN 978-0-7553-7750-3, July 7, 2012, £19.99. Headline Publishing, UK paperback, March 2013, ISBN 978-0-7553-7751-0. £8.99; US hardcover, St Martins Press, July 7, 2013, $25.99, ISBN 978-0-312-658625. St Martins Minotaur, New York, USA. Paperback – Pub date June 24, 2014, ISBN 978-1-25004-8561*

670 AD. The body of an unknown young noble is found murdered not far from Cashel. The only clue to his identity is the emblem he was wearing – the emblem of the ruling house of the neighbouring kingdom of Laigen. When King Colgú of Cashel sends his sister, Fidelma, and her companion, Eadulf, to investigate, they are propelled into one of their most dangerous and perplexing mysteries. They find themselves struggling with a tangled skein of murder and intrigue, a bewildering conspiracy and, moreover, physical jeopardy.

Is the eruption of violence that has broken out in the west of the kingdom connected? Who is the fanatical figure who leads the violence, claiming to have been summoned by "the seventh angel" to drive the "impure of faith" from the land? What is the mystery that connects the dead noble, a murdered alcoholic priest, and a menacing abbot who has built his abbey into a military fortress rather than a religious community? What evil stirs out of the shadowy Gleann na nGeilt, the Glen of Lunatics? Fidelma herself becomes the victim of abduction and it is up to Eadulf to find and save her from imminent death. Should he beware of the attractive Princess of the Éile or her neighbours, the Osraige, a border people with a reputation for being untrustworthy? Who is the handsome young poet who seems to be a key to bringing together the strands of a complex plot to overthrow the Eóghanacht ruling house of Muman of which Fidelma-s brother is the head? This is one of Fidelma's most baffling investigations yet.

Principal Characters

Sister Fidelma of Cashel, a *dálaigh* or advocate of the law courts of 7th century Ireland

Brother Eadulf of Seaxmund's Ham, a Saxon monk from the land of the South Folk, her companion

At Cluain Mór
  Tóla, a farmer
  Cainnear, his wife
  Breac, his son

At Cashel
  Colgú, King of Muman and brother to Fidelma
  Finguine, son of Cathal Cú-cen-máthair, heir apparent to Colgú
  Segdae, Abbot of Imleach, Chief Bishop of Muman
  Gormán, a warrior of the Nasc Niadh, bodyguards to the King
  Caol, Commander of the Nasc Niadh
  Enda, a warrior of the Nasc Niadh
  Drón, Lord of Gabrán
  Dúnliath, daughter of Drón, Lord of Gabrán
  Ailill, a warrior, foster-son of Drón, cousin of Fidelma and Colgú

At Fraigh Dubh
  Saer, a carpenter
  Brother Ailgesach
  Fedach Glas, the innkeeper
  Grella, his wife
  Brother Biasta

By the River Suir
  Torna, a bard
  Echna, the ferryman

At Durlus Éile
  Gobán, the smith
  Leathlobhair, the half-leper
  Gelgéis, Princess of Éile
  Spealáin, her steward
  Daig, Bishop of the Éile
  Broce, Gelgéis's Brehon
  Áedo, Chief Brehon of Muman
  Étain of An Dún

At Liath Mór
  Abbot Cronán

Brother Anfudán, the steward
Brother Sillán
Ségnat, a hostage

In Osraige
Canacán, a shepherd

At Baile Coll
Coccán, a smith

ATONEMENT OF BLOOD, *Headline Book Publishing, London, July 2013. Hardback £19,99, ISBN 978-077663-7753-4. Headline paperback, February 27, 2014, £7.99, 978-0-7553-7754-1. St Martins Minotaur, New York, USA, Hardcover – Pub date July 22, 2014, ISBN 13: 978-1-25004-6009. $25.99. St Martins Minotaur, New York, US. Paperback – published June 30, 2015, ISBN 13: 978-1-2500 6852-5*

Winter, 670 AD. It is the feastday of the Blessed Colmán, former royal poet of Cashel. King Colgú has invited the leading nobles and chieftains of his kingdom to the festivities. As the feast is about to begin, the gathering is interrupted by the arrival of a religieux from the Abbey of Mungairit claiming that he has an important message for the King.

As he approaches the King, the man draws a knife, and shouting "Remember Liamuin!" strikes. King Colgú is badly wounded and, as the would-be assassin prepares to strike again, the Chief Brehon Áedo is killed trying to protect him. The assassin is slain but Colgú is on the verge of death.

Who is Liamuin? It is a female name. Who is behind the assassination attempt? That is the task faced by Colgú's lawyer sister, Fidelma of Cashel, and her companion, Brother Eadulf. Tracking down the clues, they have to journey into the territory of their archenemies, the Uí Fidgente, Does the evil secret lie in the dark, brooding Abbey of Mungairit, or in the equally threatening mountain fastness ruled by the godless tyrant Fidaig of Sliabh Luachra? Danger and violence are their constant companions until the final surprise revelation.

PRINCIPAL CHARACTERS

Sister Fidelma of Cashel, a *dálaigh* or advocate of the law courts of 7th century Ireland

Brother Eadulf of Seaxmund's Ham, a Saxon monk from the land of the South Folk, her companion

At Cashel

    Colgú, King of Muman and brother to Fidelma

    Finguine, heir apparent to Colgú

    Beccan, steward of the palace

    Áedo, Chief Brehon of Muman

    Aillín, Deputy Chief Brehon

    Caol, Commander of the Nasc Niadh, bodyguards to the King

    Gormán, a warrior of the Nasc Niadh

    Enda, a warrior of the Nasc Niadh

    Dar Luga, *airnbertach* or housekeeper of the palace

    Brother Conchobhar, the apothecary

    Muirgen, Fidelma's nurse

    Nessán, her husband

    Aibell, an escaped bondservant

    Ordan of Rathordan, a merchant

    Spelán, a shepherd

    Rumann, innkeeper

At Ara's Well

    Aona, the tavern-keeper

    Adag, his grandson

At the Abbey of Mungairit

    Abbot Nannid

    Brother Cuineáin, the steward

    Brother Cú-Mara, of Árd Fearta

    Brother Lugna, the abbey's horse-master

    Brother Ledban, an elderly groom

    Maolán, a copyist

ZHE NOVELS-SYNOPSES

By the River An Mháigh
  Temnén, a farmer and former warrior

At the Ford of Oaks
  Conri, warlord of the Uí Fidgente
  Socht, a warrior
  Adamrae (Gláed)
  Brother Cronan
  Sitae the innkeeper

At Dún Eochair Mháigh
  Cúana, steward of the fortress
  Ciarnat, a servant

At the mill of Marban
  Marban, a millwright

Near Rath Menma
  Cadan, a farmer
  Flannait, his wife
  Suanach, an old woman

By the River Ealla
  Fidaig of Sliabh Luachra, chief of the Luachair Deaghaidh
  Artgal, his son

THE DEVIL'S SEAL, *Headline Book Publishing, 338 Euston Road, London, UK. ISBN 978 0 7553 4, Str19.99. Hardback. Pub date July 18, 2014. Headline, UK, paperback, February 20, 2015, ISBN 978 1 47229 8323. St Martins Minotaur, New York, USA, hardcover, July 2015*

"Be warned people of Cashel – the son of chaos will reclaim this place and death and destruction will follow!"
    When a curious deputation of religieux arrives in Cashel, death follows close behind and

Sister Fidelma and her companion, Eadulf, seem unable to stem the bloodshed and discover the sinister reason behind it.

Is one of the deputation responsible? What was the Venerable Verax, the elderly scholar from Rome, hiding? Was there an evil secret behind the austere and arrogant Bishop Arwald of Magonsaete? Indeed, what was the real reason behind Eadulf's own brother, Egric's, unexpected appearance at Cashel to coincide with these events?

Victims and suspects combined to make a tangled skein that results in one of the most complex and bloody mysteries that Fidelma and Eadulf have ever had to face.

PRINCIPAL CHARACTERS

Sister Fidelma of Cashel, a *dálaigh* or advocate of the law courts of 7th century Ireland

Brother Eadulf of Seaxmund's Ham, a Saxon monk from the land of the South Folk, her companion

At Cill Siolán, by the River Siár

Gormán, commander of the Nasc Niadh, bodyguards to the King

Enda, a warrior of the guard

Dego, a warrior of the guard

Brother Siolán

Brother Egric

At Cashel

Colgú, King of Muman and brother to Fidelma

Beccan, *rechtaire* or steward to the King

Dar Luga, *airnbertach* or housekeeper of the palace

Ségdae, Abbot of Irnleach and Chief Bishop of Muman

Brother Madagan, his steward

Aillín, Chief Brehon of Muman Luan, a warrior of the guard

Luan, a warrior of the guard

Aidan, a warrior of the guard

Alchú, son of Fidelma and Eadulf

Muirgen, nurse to Alchú

Brother Conchobhar, an apothecary

Visitors to Cashel
Deogaire of Sliabh Luachra, Brother Conchobhar's nephew
Abbess Líoch of Cill Náile
Sister Dianaimh, her *bann-mhaor* or female steward
Cummasach, Prince of the Déisi
Furudán, his Brehon
Rudgal, an outlaw of the Déisi
The Venerable Verax of Segni
Bishop Arwald of Magonsaete
Brother Bosa, a Saxon scribe
Brother Cerdic, a Saxon emissary
Brehon Fíthel, from the Council of Brehons

In Cashel township
Rumann, tavern-keeper
Della, mother of Gormán
Aibell, friend of Della and Gormán
Muiredach, a warrior of Clan Baiscne

At Eatharlach
Brother Berrihert, a Saxon religieux settled in Ireland
Brother Pecanum, his brother
Brother Naovan, his brother
Maon, of the Déisi

THE SECOND DEATH, *Headline Publishers, 338 Euston Road, London UK. July 16, 2015. Hardcover. Price £19.99. ISBN 978-1-4722-0835-4. St Martins Minotaur, NYC hbk. 978-1250081766, $26.99 July, 26, 2016. Headline paperback, Headline Publishing, 50 Victoria Embankment, London, March 2016, ISBN 978-1-422-0834-7 Price £8.99*

Ireland, AD 671. The Great Fair of Bealtain is almost upon the fortress of Cashel, and a line of painted wagons carries entertainers to mark the occasion. But preparations take a deathly turn when one of the carriages is set alight, and two corpses are found, lying poisoned, within.

As Sister Fidelma and her companion, Eadulf, investigate, they are quickly plunged into the menacing marshlands of Osraige – where the bloody origin of the Abbey of Cainnech is wreaking is still casting a grotesque shadow over the inhabitants and beyond.

What is the symbolism of the Golden Stone, and who are the mysterious members of the Fellowship of the Raven? Fidelma and Eadulf must face a real and mortal danger before they can untangle the evil that strikes at the very heart of the kingdom.

PRINCIPAL CHARACTERS

Sister Fidelma of Cashel, a *dálaigh* or advocate of the law courts of 7th century Ireland

Brother Eadulf of Seaxmund's Ham, a Saxon monk from the land of the South Folk, her companion

At Cashel

    Colgú, King of Muman and brother to Fidelma

    Finguine, *tánaiste* or heir apparent to the kingship

    Alchú, son of Fidelma and Eadulf

    Muirgen, nurse to Alchú

    Dar Luga, *airnbertach* or housekeeper to the palace

    Brother Conchobhar, an apothecary

    Ferloga, visiting tavern-keeper from Rath na Drinne

    Ségdae, Abbot of lmleach and Chief Bishop of Muman

    Fíthel, Chief Brehon of Muman

Warriors of the King's Bodyguard

    Aidan, Acting Commander

    Enda

    Luan

In Cashel township

    Rumann, tavern-keeper

    Cerball, Lord of Cairpre Gabra

Among Cleasamnaig Baodain (Baodain's Performers)

    Baodain, leader of the Performers

    Escrach, his wife

Echdae, a bareback rider
Echna, his partner
Tóla, horse trainer
Ronchú, a conjuror
Comal, his wife

On the marshes in Osraige
Rechtabra, a farmer
Ríonach, his wife
Duach, Rechtabra's friend
Cellaig, Rechtabra's friend

On the Mountains of the High Fields
Brother Finnsnechta, a hermit

At Cill Cainnech
Feradach, *cenn-feadh,* Commander of the township guard
Abbot Saran
Brother Failge, his steward
Ruán, Brehon to Coileach, Lord of the Marshes
Dar Badh, a servant

PENANCE OF THE DAMNED, *Headline hardcover, Headline Publishing, Carmelite House, Victoria Ebankment, London EC4. ISBN 1-4722-0837-9 July 14, 2016. £19.99. Headline UK pbk. March 23, 2017. ISBN 978-1-4722=0838-5. £8.99. St Martins Minotaur, New York, USA, Hardcover – Pub date July 25, 2017, ISBN 13: 978-250-11964-3. $27.99*

Ireland 671 AD. King Colgú of Cashel is shocked to learn that his loyal Chief Bishop and advisor has been murdered in the old enemy fortress of the Uí Fidgente. When word reaches Cashel that the culprit will be executed under new law, a large conflict threatens.

Dispatched to investigate, Sister Fidelma and her companion Eadulf discover that the man facing punishment is Gormán – commander of the King's bodyguard. Fidelma cannot believe Gormán would carry out such and act – and yet he was found locked in a chamber, with the body, weapon in hand. The evidence is stacked against him.

If they are to save Gormán and keep the peace between the kingdoms, Fidelma and Eadulf must find the true culprit. As the threat of war looms, the fate of execution draws ever closer.

PRINCIPAL CHARACTERS

Sister Fidelma of Cashel, a *dálaigh* or advocate of the law courts of 7th century Ireland

Brother Eadulf of Seaxmund's Ham, a Saxon monk from the land of the South Folk, her companion

At Cashel

Colgú, King of Muman and brother to Fidelma

Enda, a warrior of the Nasc Niadh, bodyguard to Colgú

On the road to Uí Fidgente territory

Ciarnat, an attendant in Dún Eochair Mháigh

Conrá, warlord of the Uí Fidgente

Socht, his second-in-command

At Dún Eochair Mháigh

Donennach, Prince of the Uí Fidgente

Brehon Faolchair, his chief judge

Airmid, sister to Donennach and physician to the court

Ceit, *cenn-feadhna* or commander of Donennach's household guard

Lachtna, a guard

Gormán, commander of the bodyguard of the King of Muman

Aibell, wife to Gormán

Étromma, mother of Ciarnat

The religious at the fortress and in the community of Nechta

Abbot Nannid, Abbot of Mungairit

Brother Cuineáin, *rechtaire* or steward to the Abbot of Mungairit

Prior Cuán, the *airsecnap* or Deputy Abbot of Imleach

Brother Tuamán, *rechtaire* or steward to the Abbot of Imleach

THE NOVELS-SYNOPSES

Brother Mac Raith, a scribe of Imleach
Brother Máel Anfaid, a scribe of Imleach
Brother Éladach, *aistreóir,* the doorkeeper of the "Abbey" of
Nechta

Marban, a millwright and uncle to Aibell
Deogaire of Sliabh Luachra, chief of the Luachair Deaghaidh

NIGHT OF THE LIGHTBRINGER, *Headline hardcover, Headline Publishing, Carmelite
House, Victoria Ebankment, London EC4. ISBN
1472238699 June 29, 2017. £19.99. Headline UK
paperback, ISBN 978-1-4722-3870-2, March
2018, Price £9.99; USA edition Severn House,
Tennessee, May 1, 2018, Hardback ISBN 0-7278-
88174 Price $28.99. Severn House Paperback Au-
gust 4, 2020 ISBN 13-978-184751-928-3. $17.95*

Ireland, 671 AD. On the eve of the pagan feast
of Samhain, Brother Eadulf and the warrior, Aidan, discover a man
murdered in an unlit pyre in the heart of Cashel. He has been dressed
in the robes of a religieux and killed by the ritualistic "three deaths."

When a strange woman known as Branche appears in a raven-feather
cloak foretelling of ancient gods returning to exact revenge upon the
mortal world, she is quickly branded a suspect.

But in their search for the killer, Sister Fidelma and Eadulf will
soon discover a darker shadow looming over the fortress. For their
investigation is linked to a book stolen from the Papal Secret Archives
which could destroy the New Faith in the Five Kingdoms... and Fidelma
herself will come up against mortal danger before the case is unraveled.

PRINCIPAL CHARACTERS
Sister Fidelma of Cashel, a *dálaigh* or advocate of the law courts
of 7th century Ireland
Brother Eadulf of Seaxmund's Ham, a Saxon monk from the
land of the South Folk, her companion

THE SISTER FIDELMA COMPENDIUM

At the Lateran Palace, Rome
The Venerable Gelasius, *Nomenclator* of the Lateran Palace
Brother Pothinus Maturis, *Praecipuus* of the Secret Archive
Brother Lucidus, agent of the *Nomenclator*

At Cashel
Colgú, King of Muman and brother to Fidelma
Dar Luga, *ainbertach* or housekeeper of the royal palace
Fíthel, Chief Brehon of Muman
Alchú, son of Fidelma and Eadulf
Muirgen, nurse to Alchú
Nessan, a shepherd, Muirgen's husband
Spélan, a shepherd
Brother Conchobhar, an apothecary
Rumann, the tavern-keeper
Curnan, a woodsman in charge of the Samhain bonfire
Febal, of the Uí Briúin Seóla of Connacht

Warriors of the Nasc Niadh, or Golden Collar, the King's Bodyguard
Gormán, commander
Aidan, second-in-command
Dego
Enda
Luan

Religious council of Cashel
Brother Mac Raith, steward of the Abbey of Imleach
Brother Sionnach of the Abbey of Corcach Mór
Brother Duibhinn of the Abbey of Ard Mór
Brother Giolla Rua of the Abbey of Ros Ailithir

At the Hill of the Bullock
Brancheó, the raven-caller
Torcán, a woodsman
Éimhin, his wife

At Ráth Cuáin Abbey
Abbot Sioda

Brother Tadhg, *aistreóir* or gatekeeper
Brother Gébennach, *leabhar coimedach* or keeper of books
Sister Fioniúr, the herbalist

At Cnocgorm
Erca, the Druid and hermit

Secondary Named Characters
Della, Gormán's mother
Aibell, Gormán's wife
Abbot Cuán of the Abbey of Imleach
Gelgéis, Princess of Éile

BLOODMOON, *Headline Book Publishing, London, July 12, 2018, 352 pages, Hardcover £20.99, Kindle £13.99, ISBN 13 978 147 2238733. Headline UK pbk. March 7, 2019. ISBN 978-1-4722-3872-6. £8.99. US hardback edition Severn House, Tennessee, August 1, 2018, ISBN 978 0 7278 88181, $28.99; US Paperback Severn House, September 2020, ISBN 978 1 8475 1929 0*

Ireland. AD 671. Sister Fidelma has a mission, and she is sworn by oath to reveal her purpose to no other. The secret investigation leads Fidelma and her companions to the abbey of Finnbarr to question the abbot. But before they have a chance to speak to him, the abbot is found murdered – and the young girl suspected of the crime has fled the scene.

Despite their protests, Fidelma's cohorts agree to accompany her in pursuit of the girl for answers. But as vicious rumours spread, accusing Fidelma's family, the Eóghanacht Kings of Cashel, of conspiring to assassinate the High King and abduct his wife, Sister Fidelma's life is placed in mortal danger.

Unable to tell the truth of her quest to anyone, including her husband Eadulf, Fidelma's time is running out – and now she has no choice but to face the challenge, and her enemies, alone.

ZHE SISZER FIDELMA COMPENDIUM

PRINCIPAL CHARACTERS

Sister Fidelma of Cashel, a *dálaigh* or advocate of the law courts of 7th century Ireland

Brother Eadulf of Seaxmund's Ham, a Saxon monk from the land of the South Folk, her companion

Enda, warrior of the Nasc Niadh or Golden Collar, the King of Cashel's bodyguard

At Cluain, in the territory of the Uí Liatháin
    Grella, wife to Cenn Fáelad, High King of the Five Kingdoms
    Cairenn, her companion
    Loingsech, bodyguard to Grella
    Antri of Cluain

At Finnbarr's Abbey, Corcaigh
    Abbot Nessán
    Brother Ruissine, the abbey steward
    Oengarb of Locha Lein, a lawyer
    Brother Lúarán, a physician
    Imchad, a ferryman

In Ciarraige Cuirche territory
    Tassach, a farmer
    Anglas, his wife
    Cogadháin, an innkeeper
    Cogeráin, his son
    Fécho, captain of the *Tonn Cliodhna*, coastal vessel
    lffernán, his chief helmsman

Ard Nemed, the Great Island
    Artgal, Prince of the Cenél nÁeda
    Corbmac, his *rechtaire* or steward
    Murchú, captain of a Cenél nÁeda warship

At Ros Tialláin
    Tialláin, the chieftain
    Gadra, his second in command
    Prince Aescwine, commander of a Gewisse (Saxon) warship

Beorhtric, Aescwine's second in command
Áed Caille, an Uí Liatháin bow-maker and a prisoner
Finsnechta, son of Dúnchad

At Baile an Stratha
    Mother Baine, keeper of a hostel

At the community of Doirin
    Éladach, an Gréicis (the Greek), brother to Glaisne, a prince of
    the southern Uí Liatháin
    Pilib, his *rechtaire* or steward
    Petrán, a warrior

BLOOD IN EDEN, *Headline UK, July 11, 2019, ISBN 978-1472238757, 352 pp hardcover £19.99, Kindle £13,99. Headline UK pbk. March 5, 2020. ISBN 978-1-4722-3676-4. £9.99. US hardback edition, Severn House, Tennessee, July 11, 2019, ISBN 978-0727889362, 320 pp hardcover, $28.99; US Paperback Severn House, August 3, 2021, $17.95, ISBN 978-1780296333*

Ireland AD 671. The hamlet of Cloichán is said to be a veritable Eden, with its prosperous farms and close-knit friendly community.

But when Sister Fidelma and Eadulf arrive a new priest has ordered the villages to lynch a man accused of murdering a local farmer, his wife and two sons. The only evidence they hold against him is the fact that he is a stranger to their land.

Saving the man's life Fidelma is determined that the villagers must give the newcomer a fair trial. But there is to be more blood in Eden and more lives will be lost as long-standing friends become new-found enemies, and no one knows who to trust.

PRINCIPAL CHARACTERS
Sister Fidelma of Cashel, a *dálaigh* or advocate of the law courts of 7th century Ireland
Brother Eadulf of Seaxmund's Ham, a Saxon monk from the

land of the South Folk, her companion

At Cloichín

The victims
Adnán, a farmer
Aoife, his wife
Cainnech, their son
Abel, the second son

The inhabitants
Brother Gadra, a priest
Fethmac, the *bó-aire* or magistrate
Ballgel, his wife
Gobánguss, the blacksmith
Breccnat, his wife
Eórann, mother of Gobánguss
Lúbaigh, a farmworker
Fuinche, his wife
Dulbaire, Lúbaigh's brother
Íonait, a milkmaid
Blinne, her mother, a widow
Tadgán, farmer and cousin to Adnan
Taithlech, a merchant
Flannat, his daughter and widow of Díoma, son of Tadgán

The itinerants
Celgaire
Fial, his wife
Ennec, their baby son

At the Abbey of Ard Fhionáin
Abbot Rumann
Brother Solam, the scholar
Brother Fechtnach, *rechtaire* or steward

At Cnoc na Faille
Conmaol, a claimant to Adnán's inheritance
Slébíne, his son

ZHE NOVELS-SYNOPSES

Tuama, a shepherd

Enda, a warrior of the Nasc Niadh, or Golden Collar, elite
bodyguard to Colgú, King of Muman

THE SHAPESHIFTER'S LAIR, *Headline
UK, July 2020, ISBN 9781472265371, hardcover £20.99. Headline UK paperback
February 2021, ISBN 978-1-4722-6538-
8. Str£9.99; Severn House USA, July
2020, ISBN 978 07278 8964 5, hardcov-
er $28.99. Severn House USA, 26 July 2021, trade
paperback $17.99.*

Ireland. AD 672. The body of a dead man
has been found on a lonely mountain road and
taken to the isolated abbey of Gleann Da Loch for a proper burial.
The abbot quickly identifies him as Brehon Brocc, who had been
travelling to the abbey on a secret mission with Princess Gelgeis
and her steward. When news reaches Colgú, King of Muman, that
his betrothed, Princess Gelgeis, has disappeared, Fidelma with her
trusted companions, Eadulf and Enda, enter the hostile Kingdom of
Laigin in search of the truth.

But one death is quickly followed by another and warnings of
demonic shapeshifters and evil lurking in the mountains must be
taken seriously. Are there really brigands stealing gold and silver from
the ancient mines? And are rumours of a war between the Kingdoms
of Laigin and Muman to be believed? As Fidelma searches for answers,
she must do everything in her power to avoid danger and death in a
land where no one is to be trusted.

PRINCIPAL CHARACTERS

Sister Fidelma of Cashel, a *dálaigh* or advocate of the law courts
of 7th century Ireland

Brother Eadulf of Seaxmund's Ham, a Saxon monk from the
land of the South Folk, her companion

THE SISTER FIDELMA COMPENDIUM

At Cashel
Colgú, King of Muman, Fidelma's brother
Enda, warrior of the Nasc Niadh, warriors of the Golden Collar, the elite bodyguard to King Colgú

Missing in the mountains
Princess Gelgéis of Osraige
Spealáin, her steward

At the Abbey of the Blessed Cáemgen
Cétach, a peddler arriving at the abbey
Abbot Daircell Ciotóg
Brother Aithrigid, his *rechtaire* or steward
Brother Dorchú, the *dorseóracht* or gatekeeper
Brother Lachtna, the physician
Brother Eochaí, the *echaire* or stable master
Brother Gobbán, the smith
Brother Cuilínn, a stable boy

At Láithreach
Iuchra, a soothsayer
Brehon Rónchú, a local judge, who is missing
Beccnat, a *baran* or steward judge, assistant to Brehon Rónchú
Serc, a prostitute
Síabair, the town's physician
Teimel, a hunter and tracker
Muirgel, widow of Murchad, a boatman

At Sliabh Céim an Doire
Corbmac, commander of Dicuil Dóna's warriors

At Ghleann Uí Máil
Dicuil Dóna, lord of The Cuala
Scáth, steward and son of Dicuil Dóna
Aróc, daughter of Dicuil Dóna

At Dún Árd
Garrchú, steward of the mines of The Cuala

Others mentioned
Brehon Brocc, the murdered Brehon
Alchú, son of Fidelma and Eadulf
Tuaim Snámha, petty King of Osraige from AD 660-678
Fianamail of the Uí Mail, King of Laigin from AD 666-680

THE HOUSE OF DEATH, *Headline UK, July 8, 2021, ISBN 978 1 47220540 1, hardcover £20.99; Headline UK paperback March 3, 2022, ISBN 978-1-4722-6541-8. Str£9.99 ; Severn House, USA, September 3, 2021, ISBN 978 0 72788965 2 hardcover $28.99*

Ireland, AD 672, The Feast of Beltaine is approaching and the seven major princes of the kingdom of Muman are gathering at Cashel to discuss King Colgú's policies. Just days before the council meets, Brother Conchobhar, the keeper of the sacred sword, is found murdered.

Sister Fidelma and her brother Colgú fear that the killer had been trying to steal the sword that symbolises the King's authority to rule. And as rumours begin to spread of an attempt to overthrow Colgú, news reaches Cashel that a plague ship has landed at a nearby port, bringing the deadly pestilence to its shores. Amid fear and panic, Fidelma, Eadulf and Enda must work together to catch a killer as the death roll starts to mount...

PRINCIPAL CHARACTERS
Sister Fidelma of Cashel, a *dálaigh* or advocate of the law courts of 7th century Ireland
Brother Eadulf of Seaxmund's Ham, a Saxon monk from the land of the South Folk, her companion

At Cashel
Colgú, King of Muman and brother to Fidelma
Finguine, Prince of Glendamnach, *rodamna* or heir apparent
Dar Luga, *airnbertach* or housekeeper of the royal palace
Fíthel, Chief Brehon of Muman

Abbot Cuán, of the Abbey of Imleach, and Bishop of Cashel
Brother Conchobhar, an apothecary
Brother Laig, a physician
Brother Fidach, a chaplain
Brother Dáire, a librarian
Cainder, a kitchen maid
Sister Ernmas

Warriors of the Nasc Niadh, or Golden Collar
  Gormán, reappointed commander of a *catha*, or battalion, of
    Colgú's warriors
  Enda, commander of the *lucht-tighe*, or household guard
  Luan, a warrior
  Dego, a warrior

In Cashel township
  Rumann, a tavern owner
  Della, Fidelma's friend and mother of Gormán
  Aibell, Gormán's wife
  Gobán, a smith

Princes and guests at Cashel
  Elódach, Prince of the Eóganacht Aine
  Congal, Prince of the Eóganacht Loch Lein
  Furudrán, Prince of the Eóganacht Airthir Chliach
  Moncha, his wife
  Selbach, Prince of the Eóganacht Ráithlinn
  Blinne, his wife
  Esnad, companion to Blinne
  Donennach, Prince of the Uí Fidgente
  Céit, son of Conmael, his bodyguard
  Conrí, warlord of the Uí Fidgente

At Ráth na Drinne
  Ferloga, the tavern-keeper
  Lassar, his wife
  Echdae, a wagoneer from Dairinis

THE NOVELS-SYNOPSES

At Cluain Meala
Arard, *bo-aire* or magistrate

Also mentioned
Prince Cummasach of the Déisi

DEATH OF A HERETIC, *Headline Book Publishing, London, July 21, 2022. hardcover £20.99. ISBN 978 1 47226543 2. Severn House, USA, August 2022, ISBN 978 0 72788966 9 hardcover $28.99*

Ireland, AD 672. The premier abbey of Muman at Imleach Iubhair is being rebuilt when its guests' hostel is razed to the ground by an overnight fire. There is one fatal casualty. Bishop Brodulf of Luxovium, a distinguished visitor and cousin to the King of Franks.

Passing by chance, Fidelma and her companions, Eadulf, with the warrior Enda, are asked by Abbot Cuán to investigate the cause of the fire and death. They find that the bishop had been stabbed to death before the fire had even started.

Thrown into a claustrophobic world of intrigue, treachery and jealousy, where even fundamental religious beliefs are still developing and vehemently disputed, Fidelma and Eadulf are faced with resentment, distrust and a barrier of deceit. The abbey, a leading ecclesiastical teaching institution as well as a conhospitae, housing both sexes, is divided into factions, distrustful of each other.

Can Abbot Cuán trust Prioress Suanach, who is in charge of the sisterhood of the abbey? Can the senior professors trust each other as well as their students, some of whom are Franks from the dead bishop's homeland? What of the dead bishop's own devious companions? Moreover, can suspicion be leveled at the builders working on renovating the abbey under their dominant Master Builder, Sítae?

More deaths are discovered before the complications can begin to unravel in the most intricate mystery ever faced by Fidelma.

THE SISTER FIDELMA COMPENDIUM

PRINCIPAL CHARACTERS

Sister Fidelma of Cashel, a *dálaigh* or advocate of the law courts
of 7ᵗʰ century Ireland

Brother Eadulf of Seaxmund's Ham, a Saxon monk from the
land of the South Folk, her companion

Enda, commander of the warriors of the Golden Collar, the elite
bodyguard to the King of Muman

At Ara's Well

Aona, the innkeeper
Adag, his grandson

At the Abbey of Imleach Iubhair

Abbot Cuán, Abbot and Chief Bishop of Muman
Brother Mac Raith, the rechtaire or steward
Prioress Suanach, head of the sisterhood
The Venerable Breas, the *fer-leginn* or chief professor
The Venerable Lugán, the *leabhar coimedach* or librarian
and master of all students
Brother Anlón the physician
Brother Áedh, in charge of abbey fire fighters
Brother Sígeal, the echaire, master of the stables

The builders

Sítae, *Ollamh-Ailtire*, the master builder
Cú Choille, a missing master carpenter
Patu, a senior carpenter
Mothlach, a stone mason
Tassach, a copper smith

The students

Brother Garb, a senior student
Brother Étaid, his *anam-chara* or soul-friend
Sister Fastrude, a Burgundian student
Sister Ingund, a Burgundian student
Sister Haldetrude, a Burgundian student

THE NOVELS-SYNOPSES

The Frankish visitors
> **Deacon Landric**, the steward to the late Bishop Brodulf of Luxovium in Burgundia
> **Brother Charibert**, servant to Bishop Brodulf

The Chief Brehon's Group
> **Fíthel**, Chief Brehon of Muman
> **Urard**, his secretary and scribe
> **Dego**, warrior of the King, accompanying the Chief Brehon
> **Luan**, a fellow warrior

THE SISTER FIDELMA COMPENDIUM

SISTER FIDELMA SHORT STORIES

COMPLETE LIST OF THE SISTER FIDELMA
SHORT STORIES AND FIRST APPEARANCES
IN THE UK AND USA ONLY

(Unfortunately, unlike the novels, for which "teaser" copy is developed – usually 2 or 3 paragraphs – to include along with a book's listing for sale online, the same is not true for the Fidelma short stories. Thus, we include only such information as will allow the reader to source out these stories from the original publishers, whether in magazines or omnibus mystery books. The two exceptions are "The Lair of the White Fox" and "The Spiteful Shadow," for which we do include this "enticement" text.)

- "Hemlock At Vespers," *Midwinter Mysteries 3*, ed. Hilary Hale, Little Brown, London, October 1993

    o US appearance: *Murder Most Irish*, ed. Ed Gorman, Larry Segriff & Martin H. Greenberg, Barnes Noble 1996

- "The High King's Sword," *Mammoth Book of Historical Whodunnits*, ed. Mike Ashley, Foreword by Ellis Peters, Robinson Books, London 1993

    o US: Carroll & Graf edition, New York

- "Murder in Repose," *Great Irish Detective Stories*, ed. Peter Haining, Souvenir Press, London 1993

- "Murder By Miracle," *Constable New Crime No 2*, ed. Maxim Jakubowski, Constable, London 1993

    o US appearance: *The Year's Best Mystery & Suspense Stories 1994*, ed. Edward D. Hoch, Walker & Co Ltd, New York

- "A Canticle for Wulfstan," *Midwinter Mysteries 4*, ed. Hilary Hale, Little Brown, London 1994

    o US appearance: *Ellery Queen Mystery Magazine*, May 1995

- "Abbey Sinister," *Mammoth Book of Historical Detectives*, ed. Mike Ashley, Robinson Publishing, London 1995
  - US edition by Carroll & Graf New York
- "Tarnished Halo," *Minister Mysteries 5*, ed. Hilary Hale, Little Brown, London 1995
- "The Horse That Died for Shame," *Murder at the Races*, ed, Peter Haining, Orion Books, London 1995
- "The Poison Chalice," *Classical Whodunnits*, ed. Mike Ashley, Robinson Books, London 1996
  - US edition by Carroll & Graf, New York
- "At the Tent of Holofernes," *Ellery Queen Mystery Magazine*, December 1997
- "A Scream from the Sepulchre," *Ellery Queen Mystery Magazine*, May 1998
- "Invitation to a Poisoning," *Past Poisons: An Ellis Peters Memorial of Historical Crime*, ed. Maxim Jakubowski 1998
- "Holy Blood," *Great Irish Stories of Murder and Mystery*, ed. Peter Haining, Souvenir Press 1999
- "Those Who Trespass," *Chronicles of Crime – The Second Ellis Peters Memorial Anthology of Historical Crime*, ed. Maxim Jakubowski, Headline, October 1999
- "Our Lady of Death," *Dark Detectives: Adventures of the Supernatural Sleuths*, ed. Steve Jones, Fedogan & Bremer 2000
- "Like A Dog Returning," *Murder Most Medieval: Noble Tales of Ignoble Demises*, ed. Martin H. Greenberg and John Heifers, Cumberland House, Nashville, Tennessee, USA 2000
- "Who Stole The Fish?," *Murder Through The Ages*, ed. Maxim Jakubowski, Headline Books, London 2000
- "Scattered Thorns," *Murder Most Celtic: Tall Tales of Irish Mayhem*, Martin H. Greenburg, Cumberland House, Nashville, Tennessee, USA 2001
- "Corpse on a Holy Day," *And The Dying Is Easy*, ed. Joseph Pittman and Annette Riffle, Signet, New York, April 2001

SISTER FIDELMA SHORT STORIES

- "Death of an Icon," in a Mike Ashley collection from Robinson, Fall 2001
- "The Astrologer Who Predicted His Own Murder," in *Death By Horoscope*, ed. Anne Perry, Carroll & Graf, New York, Fall 2001.
- "Death of an Icon," *The Mammoth Book of Historical Whodunnits (Brand New Collection)* ed. Mike Ashley, Robinson, London, August 2001 (this is not to be confused with the collection under the same title published in 1993)
- "Whispers of the Dead" has just been published in *Murder Most Catholic: Divine Tales of Profane Crimes*, edited by Ralph McInerny, Cumberland House, Nashville, Tennessee, ISBN 1-58182-260-X, $14.95
- "Gold At Night," *Great Irish Drinking Stories*, ed. Peter Haining, Souvenir Press, London, Fall 2002
- "The Blemish," *The Brehon* (Journal of the International Sister Fidelma Society), Little Rock, Arkansas, September issue (No.3) 2002
- "The Lost Eagle," in *The Mammoth Book of Roman Whodunnits*, ed. Mike Ashley, Robinson, London, August 2003. ISBN 1-84119-685-1. Also Carroll & Graf, New York, simultaneous publication, ISBN 0-7867-1241-4
- "Dark Moon Rising," *The Brehon* (Journal of the International Sister Fidelma Society), Vol.II, No 3. September 2003
- "The Banshee," in *Ellery Queen Mystery Magazine*, New York, February 2004
- "Cry Wolf!" original story for *Whispers of the Dead*, St Martins Press (New York) and Headline (London) March 2004
- "The Fosterer," original story for *Whispers of the Dead*, St Martins Press (New York) and Headline (London) March 2004
- "The Heir Apparent," original story for *Whispers of the Dead*, St Martins Press (New York) and Headline (London) March 2004
- "The Spiteful Shadow" in *The Mammoth Book of Historical Whodunnits* – Third Collection, edited by Mike Ashley, Robinson, London, June 2005 – as *New Historical*

Whodunnits, Carroll & Graf, New York, June 2005; reprinted in An *Ensuing Evil and Others: Fourteen Historical Mystery Stories by Peter Tremayne*, St Martin's Minotaur, New York, January 2006. ISBN 0-312-34228-4

> *When Sister Fidelma arrives at the great Abbey of Durrow on a visit to her old mentor Abbot Laisran, she finds the community reeling from an act of murder. One of their membership, Brother Sioda, has been discovered in his cell with multiple stab wounds to the heart. Everyone is certain that the eccentric Sister Scathach, who foretold the event through whisperings from the Otherworld, is responsible. But Sister Fidelma could never accept such an explanation. For sometimes it is the simplest solutions that hide the most unexpected truths...*

- "Does God Obey his Own Laws?: A Sister Fidelma Mystery," in *Thou Shalt Not Kill: Biblical Mystery Stories*, edited by Anne Perry, Carroll & Graf, New York, December 2005
- "Sanctuary!," *Ellery Queen Mystery Magazine*, New York, May 2006
- "Finnbarr's Bell," *The Holly Bough* (Cork), Christmas 2008
- "The Night of the Snow Wolf," (a novelette) in *The Mammoth Book of Historical Mysteries*, ed. Mike Ashley, Constable Robinson, London, July 2011
- "The Comb Bag," *Ellery Queen Mystery Magazine*, July 2013
- "The Lair of the White Fox" (e-novella) May 5, 2016 Headline Publishing

> *Ireland, AD 659. Sister Fidelma is in her final year of study at Brehon Morann's law school, and en route to visit an old friend, Lúach, in her family home. But things take a sinister turn when Fidelma arrives to discover that Lúach has been missing for five days. Has someone driven her from the enclave of her home, or are there darker forces at work? The deeper Fidelma digs, the more questions she unearths. It's clear that there is far more to Lúach's disappearance than those closest to her are letting on, and only Fidelma has the conviction to pursue the case. Can she untangle the truth in time to save her?*

SISTER FIDELMA SHORT STORIES

THE SISTER FIDELMA COMPENDIUM

PETER TREMAYNE:
MASTER OF THE SHORT STORY

The December issue of the *Ellery Queen Mystery Magazine*, America's oldest continuous crime fiction magazine launched in 1941, contained a new Fidelma mystery. "Catspaw" is unusual in the time scale of most of the stories as it is set during Fidelma's time at Brehon Morann's law school.

Most readers of Peter Tremayne will know that he is a prolific short story writer. *The Irish Post* has commented that "Peter Tremayne is a master of the genre." "Catspaw" is his 100th short story and, of these, 37 stories are Fidelma mysteries.

Of the Fidelma short stories, 30 of them have been gathered and published in two collections. These are *Hemlock at Vespers* (2000) and *Whispers of the Dead* (2004). These were published, more or less, simultaneously, both in the UK and US and became bestsellers. I judge the sales of these by the number if reprints.

Hemlock's US edition reprinted three times in the first year and 10 times by 2008. The UK edition had been reprinted five times by 2004. *Whispers*, in both US and UK, stood at 8 reprints by 2008. Obviously, I am using the number in the 2008 editions that I have.

Different cultures have different tastes and *Hemlock* only went to Spanish (Argentinian), German, Japanese and Breton translations while *Whispers* went to German, French and Spanish (Argentinian) translations.

It is interesting that there are seven more uncollected Fidelma short stories if one counts novella-length stories of which there are two.

What of Peter's other short story output?

His first short story collection was *My Lady of Hy Brasil and other stories* published in 1987 by Donald M. Grant, USA, in 1987. This consisted of six supernatural fantasy stories with original illustrations by Duncan Eagleson, the well-known American artist.

Aisling and other Irish Tales of Terror

was published in 1992 by Brandon Books, Ireland. This contained eleven supernatural short stories that had previous been published in various magazines and anthologies. As well as a paperback edition, this volume as been translated into German in 1999 appearing both in hardback and paperback, and Japanese in 2005. Like most of Peter's books it was highly praised by the Irish critics. Professor Marie Kai called it "Literature" and not merely "genre fiction."

In 2006 St Martin's Press, New York, decided to publish a collection 13 of Peter's non-Fidelma short stories together with an uncollected Fidelma story "The Spiteful Shadow." The title was *An Ensuing Evil*. This volume has never been published in the UK, but in the US it went to four reprints in the first two years.

It was published in Italian and did well in hard cover and paperback. The German translation added two more uncollected Fidelma stories to the collection.

By my reckoning, there are nearly some 40 Tremayne short stories lying hidden in magazines and anthologies.

Thanks to contacts of enthusiasts in various countries, I have been able to put together the following figures:

Of Peter's short stories, apart from appearances in English (this includes US and UK) we have found the short story translations in the following languages: Italian 17, Japanese 15, Breton 12, German 8, Russian 5, Norwegian 4, Czech 5, Irish 4, Cornish 4, French 3, Greek 2, and at least 1 each in Slovak, Manx, Scottish Gaelic, Thai and Chinese.

Now we cannot guarantee that this is complete and that there are no more stories hidden away. Peter himself, when asked, reckons this is probably a fair estimate and he confesses that he has not kept up to date with all the translations of his short stories.

Peter's earlier short stories were actually supernatural thrillers and some fantasy tales. However, what is interesting is that among the later murder mystery short stories we have discovered a detective creation of Peter's that is totally different to Fidelma both in the time period, in culture and in sex.

Master Hardy Drew lives in the last years of the Elizabethan Age and into the start of the Jacobean period. He is a bachelor and the constable of the Bankside Watch in London. Bankside, which still exists in modern London, is on the southern bank of the Thames from Shakespeare's Globe Theatre to London Bridge. Drew has to operate along the squalid waterfront with its notorious Clink Prison. At the same time, he has access to the rakes and nobles who frequent The Globe. The atmosphere is, as one expects of this author, finely written; one can smell the stench of human degradation and poverty, the stale odours of the Thames and we can accompany the young bucks with their perfumed nosegays to attend the latest Shakespearean play. Life at this time was not all glitter and glamour of the upper classes.

There are, unfortunately, only seven short stories featuring the redoubtable Constable, Master Hardy Drew.

One can easily see the author's in-joke in the name. It is a reference to Nancy Drew and the Hardy Boys. These characters were created by American author Edward Stratemeyer. In 1927 he created The Hardy Boys, two boy detectives, and in 1930, he created Nancy Drew, a girl detective. The characters combined in some of the books and in a TV show as "Nancy Drew and the Hardy Boys." Sometimes the books were selling at a million copies a year. Peter once said that while he admired Stratemeyer's output his racism and stereotypes were products of his time and place... Often the books had to be later re-edited to eliminate such abuses.

Peter's Master Hardy Drew, operating in the late 16th century and early 17th century, first appeared to solve a murder on stage at The Globe Theatre in "An Ensuing Evil." The story appeared in an anthology *Shakespeare Whodunnits* in 1997. It was so successful that another anthology was commissioned, (1998), and Peter contributed "Methought You Saw A Serpent." These were edited by Mike Ashley.

Presumably Peter was concentrating on Fidelma for it was not until 2005 that Master Hardy Drew emerged again in "A Walking Shadow" in *The Strand Magazine* (USA). That was followed by "Satan in the Star Chamber" in *Jacobean Whodunnits* and "The Stuart Sapphire" in *Perfect Crimes and Impossible Murders*, 2006. Again the anthologist was Mike Ashley.

There was another pause before "Fear No More the Heat o' the

Sun" appeared in the *Ellery Queen Mystery Magazine* in 2011 and, in the same year, also in *Ellery Queen Mystery Magazine* also published "This thing of Darkness."

There have, sadly, been no more Master Hardy Drew Mysteries.

Of course, the demands on Peter's time is for more Fidelma stories and one can understand how that has precluded him working on to anything else.

However, these were not his only stories that contained a single detective running through them. Some readers will be surprised to know that he has published number of Sherlock Holmes' pastiches. Apparently, so I have read, Peter was intrigued by the fact that the Sherlock and the Holmes families were Anglo-Irish and lived near his own family origin place near Doneraile, Co. Cork. Conan Doyle had stayed there. As we known Arthur Conan Doyle was born in Scotland but of an Irish family. His grandfather, John Doyle (1797-1868), was from Dublin and studied at the school of the Dublin Society gaining a reputation as a caricaturist and in his mid 20s decided to move first to London to try his hand as a portrait painter. In the end he became a popular political cartoonist.

His son, Charles, settled in Scotland and married an Irish woman, Mary Foley. Their son, Arthur Ignatius Conan Doyle, was Jesuit educated and grew up with an acute knowledge of his family's Irish Catholic origins. He visited Ireland often. Small wonder that many of his characters boast Irish names, including his detectives two greatest arch-villains – Professor Moriarty and Colonel Moran. We should not be surprised, therefore, that his detective also bears the names of two well-known Anglo-Irish families. Doyle never speculated on Sherlock Holmes' origins. This gave Peter the freedom to make his Sherlock Holmes a scion of an Anglo-Irish family, educated at Trinity College, Dublin, before winning a scholarship to Oxford – exactly in the manner that Oscar Wilde had done in reality.

The first story "The Affray at the Kildare Street Club" (1997) was set in Dublin's exclusive Anglo-Irish club. This appeared in *New Sherlock Holmes Adventures,* a Mike Ashley anthology. "The Spectre of Tullyfane Abbey" (2001), appearing in *Villains Victorious*, edited by Martin H. Greenberg, Daw Books, took its inspiration from a comment in one of Doyle's stories as did "The Siren of Sennen Cove" (2001) *New Tales of Sherlock Holmes*, edited by Martin H. Greenberg.

Two stories followed in 2003 "A Study in Orange" in *My Sherlock*

PETER TREMAYNE: MASTER OF THE SHORT STORY

Holmes: Untold Stories of the Great Detective edited by Michael Kurland and "The Kidnapping of Mycroft Holmes" which appeared in *The Strand Magazine.*

There was a pause until "The Case of the Panicking Policeman" came out in 2007 in *The Strand Magazine* and finally "The Case of the Reluctant Assassin" in 2010 in *Sherlock Holmes: The American Years* edited by Michael Kurland.

Some of these have been reprinted in other anthologies and, of course, in several translations. This article is concerned with first appearances.

All the stories are first class mysteries. Peter is faithful to Doyle's writings and Holmes and Watson are in keeping with Doyle's attitudes and characterisation. What he adds to this is the Irish background that Doyle would have been acquainted with through his own Irish family. One has to admit that exploring the Irish connection seemed to upset a few critics who believed Sherlock Holmes was the quintessential Englishman and even wanted to claim Conan Doyle was English; hard to accept when one listens to the surviving recordings of his voice with its clear, modulated Edinburgh accents.

Can this be the reason why only one of the seven stories was published in England while the rest were published in the USA or in translation? No matter. Peter is a writer that doesn't mind a little controversy by pointing out the truth as opposed to people's popular misconceptions.

While talking about his short stories, there is one more volume that I should refer to. However, whether it should be included in comments on short stories is a matter of analytical debate. It was a volume published under Peter's original name of Peter Berresford Ellis in 1999. The title was *The Chronicles of the Celts: New Tellings of Their Myths and Legends.* It contained 37 stories from all six Celtic countries (Ireland, Isle of Man, Scotland, Wales, Cornwall and Brittany) complete with a general analytical introduction and a preface to each country's group of myths and legends. It was a 536-page volume published in hardcover in the UK by Robinsons and in the US Carroll and Graf.

The collection was well received; in fact, it was highly praised. But it was not until Constable Robinson issued it in a large paperback format *The Mammoth Book of Celtic Myths and Legends* in 2002 that sales, it seems, took off. My 2015 edition is marked as the 12th reprint. The paperback in the US was issued as *Celtic Myths and Legends* also in 2002 but by 2008 Running Press Book Publishers who had acquired rights and by 2015 had issued the 8th reprint. As far as can be discovered, the book appeared only in Italian translation as *Il Misterioso Mondo dei Celti* in 1999.

We can also reveal that seven of these stories were included in an anthology much earlier than the book, and that was in *The Giant Book of Myths and Legends*, edited by Mike Ashley, published by Paragon Books, of London, in 1995, also published by Barnes & Noble, New York, in 1997.

In conclusion, the short stories are proof, if ever we needed proof, that Peter is one of the most talented and diverse storytellers of his generation. It is hard to think of another writer with such a broad spectrum of subjects; with his prolific output both as a writer of fiction and non-fiction; as both a novelist and a short story writer.

– Christy Gordon
The Brehon, XVI, 1, January 2017

Chronology in The
Sister Fidelma Mysteries

Wuhile each story is complete in itself, and can be read in that fashion, it does add to the reader's interest to know there is a chronology to the novels. Fidelma and Eadulf and the world they live in do age in a logical fashion. We know from Peter that he does have a timeline based on the chronicles and annals, although he admits that he does have to make some arbitrary decisions which he could not do if he was writing non-fiction.

Sometimes the various Irish annals and chronicles do not always agree on the same date for events in the mid-7th century and so Peter has to pick out the date he believes suitable for the story. The variation is not too vast, sometimes only as much as a year out one way or another. All in all, it is argued that the Irish annals and chronicles are highly accurate in their observations.

Dr Dan McCarthy of Trinity College, Dublin, has spoken in praise of Peter's accuracy of dating of certain astronomical observations. Peter had chosen to follow the dates of the Irish annals rather than the Venerable Bede who, now computer checked, showed his timing of an eclipse to be inaccurate.

Peter has pointed out that it is understandable that there might be these slight variations between the annals and chronicles as most copies survive many years after the original. Most copies of the Irish annals and chronicles do not survive intact after the 12th century, through to the 15th century and, of course the famous "Annals of the Four Masters" was composed by four scholars sometime between 1632-1636 but working on early manuscript sources, such as the "Annals of Ulster." Early manuscript fragments the "Annals of Tighernach" survive such as the MS Rawlinson B 488 and B 502.

Peter, while writing "entertainment" as he calls it, always ensures that he is not being anachronistic and that is what makes his books so different. If he says an important event happens either as background or in which Fidelma is involved, you can be assured that he is citing a source in the ancient annals or chronicles.

ZHE SISZER FIDELMA COMPENDIUM

Leaving aside the short story collections in *Hemlock At Vespers* (1999) and *Whispers of the Dead* (2004), there is a strict chronology. The short stories in these volumes seem to be pre-AD 664 as Eadulf does not enter the picture and Fidelma is working alone. The only one exception with "The Lost Eagle" in which Fidelma and Eadulf appear in Canterbury and are on the way to Eadulf's birthplace in Seaxmund's Ham (Saxmundham, Suffolk, in East Anglia), So this has to place the event between *Smoke in the Wind* and *The Haunted Abbot*.

So, the dating in the novels are as follows:

AD 664, historical reference Synod of Whitby. (*Absolution by Murder*, 1994). We meet Fidelma at the age of twenty-seven years old. More details emerged in other books. Peter has hinted at her birth in AD 637. Her brother Colgú is older. They are children of Failbe Flann mc Aedo Dubh, a King of Muman at Cashel. There is another brother Fogartach. Failbe Flann is given a three or four obituary dates in the chronicles around AD 637. In *Chalice of Blood* Fidelma reflects that her mother died in childbirth or soon after and that she had faint memories of her father before he died in battle. For eagle eyes among you, one can trace her education, her decision to study law at Morann's college and then – searching for security – accepting the advice of her elderly cousin Laisran, Abbot of Darú, to enter Cill Dara (Kildare) as a legal advisor. The story "Hemlock At Vespers" tells us why she quite the abbey and took up commissions for kings, bishops and abbots until she settles back in Cashel when her brother succeeds Cathal Cú-cen-máthair as King in AD 665.

AD 664, historical reference Wighard, archbishop designate of Canterbury dies in Rome (*Shroud for the Archbishop*, 1995).

AD 664, Fall. Fidelma visits Bobbio, Northern Italy, on her way back to Ireland where Columbanus founded his famous abbey in AD 613. (*Behold A Pale Horse*, 2011).

AD 665, historical reference, death of Cathal Cú-cen-Máthir of Cashel. Colgú, Fidelma's brother, becomes King. (*Suffer Little Children*, 1995)

CHRONOLOGY IN THE SISTER FIDELMA MYSTERIES

AD 666, January, historical reference Battle of Áine and Fidelma is reunited with Eadulf. (*The Subtle Serpent*, 1996)

AD 666 May, setting Araglin, (*The Spider's* Web, 1997)

AD 666 July, setting Glen Geis. (*Valley of the Shadow*, 1998)

AD 666 September, setting Emly. (*The Monk Who Vanished*, 1999) We now enter some confusion as to the times of the next adventures as they seem to be compressed into a very short space of time. These adventures have to take place between September and December, AD 666. I am not saying that this is impossible but given the nature of the journeys involved, Peter will forgive me for saying that it is squeezing things a little.

AD 666, after September, Fidelma has set off on a pilgrim ship without Eadulf to Santiago di Compostella (*Act of Mercy*, 1999).

AD 666, she has returned to Ireland to save Eadulf who is facing execution in the Kingdom of Laighin (*Our Lady of Darkness*, 2000).

AD 666, shipwrecked in Dyfed (Wales), historical reference Gwlyddien as King of Dyfed. It was known he was king according to the Welsh annals. (*Smoke in the Wind*, 2001)

AD 666, December, Fidelma and Eadulf are in the Land of the South Folk (Suffolk, East Anglia). At the end of this story Fidelma reveals she is pregnant, and they accept a traditional Irish trial marriage of a year and a day. (*The Haunted Abbot*, 2002)

AD 667, October, Fidelma has had her child, a son Alchú, probably born around June. They are back in Muman and seem, from the description that Fidelma is suffering from post-natal depression. (*Badger's Moon*, 2003).

AD 667, November. Fidelma's nurse is killed and Alchú is kidnapped. The setting is Cashel and the Dingle Peninsula. (*The Leper's Bell*, 2004).

THE SISTER FIDELMA COMPENDIUM

AD 668, January. The setting is Árd Fearta (Ardfert) and back to the Dingle Peninsula. (*Master of Souls*, 2005).

AD 668, February. The time has come for Fidelma and Eadulf to have their formal wedding after the year and a day. But there is a murder among the Cashel guests and some scenes are set in the Glen of Aherlow. (*A Prayer for the Damned*, 2006).

AD 669, winter. Historical reference, the murder of High King Sechnassuch by Dubh Duin of the Cineal Cairpre, and accession of Cenn Faelad as High King (*Dancing With Demons*, 2007).

AD 670, Historical reference the Council of Autun in Burgundy, which a set back for the Celtic Church. This was the council where all the religious communities were orders to give up Celtic usages and accept the Rule of Benedict. Fidelma and Eadulf attend. (*The Council of the Cursed*, 2008).

AD 670, early summer. On the return from Autun, Fidelma and Eadulf's ship is attacked off the southern coast of Armorica and they spend time on the Rhuis peninsula where St Gildas established an abbey. Alain II Hir was historical King of Brittany at this time and appears in the story. (*The Dove of Death*, 2009).

AD 670, summer. The setting is the abbey of Lismore (Lios Mhór) where Fidelma and Eadulf investigate an impossible crime. It is important period as it is when Fidelma makes her decision to leave the religious but not the religion. She becomes legal advisor to her brother the King. (*Chalice of Blood*, 2010).

AD 670, early Fall. The story takes Fidelma to Durlus Éile (Thurles) and Osraige (Ossory) important as it involves the girl Fidelma's brother is to marry. (*The Seventh Trumpet*, 2012).

AD 670, November 24, as Peter gives the actual date of the start of this adventure as being of the feastday of St Colmán of Cloyne (*Atonement of Blood*, 2013).

CHRONOLOGY IN THE SISTER FIDELMA MYSTERIES

AD 671, early. Set mostly in Cashel and introduces Eadulf's brother Egric. (*The Devil's Seal*, 2014).

AD 671, April. This is mainly set among the marshlands of Osraige (Ossory) and in Cill Cainnech (Kilkenny). (*The Second Death*, 2015).

AD 671, June. Primarily set in the fortress of a longtime enemy of Cashel, the Uí Fidgente. (*Penance of the Damned*, 2016).

AD 671, October. Set mostly in the heart of Cashel, and we learn of the ritual of the "three deaths." (*Night of the Lightbringer*, 2017).

AD 671, December. A secret investigation leads Fidelma and her companions to the abbey of Finnbarr, where they are caught up in the heart of a rumored conspiracy targeted at Fidelma's family, the Eóghanacht High Kings of Munster. (*Bloodmoon*, 2018).

AD 672, February. Fidelma and Eadulf travel to the ostensibly-idyllic hamlet of Cloichán (Clogheen), said to be a veritable Eden – where a stranger to the village is accused – perhaps falsely – of killing a local man, and is set to hang for the crime. (*Blood in Eden*, 2019).

AD 672, March/April. Fidelma's brother Colgú, King of Muman, sends his sister, Eadulf, and Enda to the hostile mountainous Kingdom of Laigin to the isolated abbey of Gleann Da Loch to investigate the death of a man who was traveling with Princess Gelgeis, Colgú's betrothed. (*The Shapeshifter's Lair*, 2020).

AD 672, April. The Feast of Beltaine approaches, and as the seven major princes of the kingdom of Muman are at Cashel to meet with King Colgú regarding his policies, the keeper of the sacred sword, is found murdered. And am impending plague threatens all involved. (*The House of Death*, 2021).

AD 672, May. The setting is the abbey at Imleach Iubhair (Emly), being rebuilt at the time. A suspicious fire reveals one fatality – Bishop Brodulf of Luxovium (Luxeuil, Haute-Saône, France), a cousin to the King of Franks. Present merely by happen stance, Fidelma and her companions are asked by the Abbot to investigate – and further mysterious deaths ensue. (*Death of a Heretic*, 2022).

So, Peter, in the novels, has taken us through nine exciting years of Fidelma's life since she met Eadulf at the Synod of Whitby. That means she is now 36 years old; her son Alchú is approaching eight years old; but Peter has not made absolutely clear Eadulf's age. It is mentioned somewhere that he was born during the reign of Sigebert, King of the East Angles, who ruled from AD 634-641, when he abdicated and retired to an abbey in favour of his brother Egric. Indeed, Eadulf's brother was named after this King Egric. Both Sigebert and King Egric were killed during a Mercian invasion in AD 641. We should guess, therefore, that Eadulf is a year or two older than Fidelma.

Does chronology matter? We certainly think so when you read the Fidelma saga as a whole.

– David Robert Wooten
Originally an article in *The Brehon*, VIII, 3, September 2014
Updated for this volume

Fidelma: A Life in Dedications

hen authors dedicate their books, there is always a story behind each and every one. Often dedications reflect interesting and fascinating friends and relatives of the author. Some dedications can even give rise to literary mysteries. For example, when Bram Stoker dedicated *Dracula* (1897) to "Hommy Beg" it caused speculation for decades that it was some Turkish potentate. People forgot that Stoker was Irish and a good friend of his was a Manx writer Thomas Hall Caine (1853-1931) who was called by his Manx speaking family and friends "Little Tommy" which in Manx Gaelic vocative was "An Hommy Beg." Speculation was put to rest when Peter Haining and Peter Tremayne published *The Legend of Dracula* (Constable 1997) which was the first biographical study that showed the extent and influence of Stoker's Irish birth and background.

The interesting dedication in Peter Tremayne's Fidelma titles are no exception. Peter has made a point of dedicating each of Fidelma volumes in his series. Each is chosen for special reasons at special moments in his life. Thus, herein is presented a project begun by a late founder member of The International Sister Fidelma Society and active contributor to *The Brehon* – Maurice McCann (1938-2011). In the January 2006 issue of *The Brehon*, Maurice decided to examine the people Peter had dedicated the books up to that date that date. When he died, the list of dedications to that date was published as a tribute to him in the May 2011 issue of *The Brehon*. The listing herebelow brings that project up to date.

1. *Absolution By Murder*, 1994. It was natural that the first Fidelma novel should be dedicated to Dorothea. This was Peter's wife, usually called Dorothy, who tragically passed in 2016.

2. *Shroud for the Archbishop*, 1995. Peter Haining and Mike Ashley. They are well known authors. They are both longtime friends. Peter Haining (now deceased) and Peter went back to the early 1964 and Mike Ashley and Peter to the early 1970s. They individually published two of the first Fidelma stories in anthologies. Peter Haining, in fact, saved Peter from naming his sleuth "Sister Buan" in the very first story he wrote "Murder in Repose." He thought the

name was reminiscent of Bertram Atkey's comical crook "Smiler Bunn." Peter reconsidered the name of his heroine and came up with Sister Fidelma. It was a happy choice.

3. *Suffer Little Children*, 1995. Christopher Lowder is better known as the author and anthologist Jack Adrian, although he has written under a multitude of pseudonyms from Chuck Bainbridge to Jack Hamilton Teed. Chris was editor of the *Six Towns Magazine* in 1966 when he asked Peter to write an article on the author Arnold Bennett (1867-1931). They have been friends ever since. In his role as critic, Jack Adrian was the first to realise the potential of the Sister Fidelma creation.

4. *The Subtle Serpent*, 1996. Penny and David Durrell (David passed in 2016) are friends of Peter and his late wife Dorothy. They lived at the end of the Beara Peninsula in the extreme southwest of Ireland. This is the setting of this novel, an area that Peter knows very well. Penny Durrell is the author of several books on the area and she had paid tribute to Peter's help with her book *Discover Dursey*, 1996. She attended the 2019 Féile Fidelma.

5. *The Spider's Web*, 1997. Terence, The MacCarthy Mór. An unfortunate dedication, and as Peter admits he has tried to get it removed from subsequent editions. At the time, 1997, Terence McCarthy had been recognised for many years by the Chief Herald of Ireland as the descendant of the Eóghanacht kings of Munster and of Desmond and entitled to use this ancient Gaelic title. In 1999, having been recognised by the Irish State and many other heraldic jurisdictions, it was discovered that Terence McCarthy was, in fact, an impostor who had faked his credentials and his recognition was officially removed. Peter (under his nonfiction name of Peter Berresford Ellis) wrote two chapters on the fraud – "The Man Who Would Be Prince" and "The MacCarthy Mór Fraud" – in his book *Erin's Blood Royal*, revised edition from Palgrave, New York, 2002. Peter explains: "At the time of *The Spider's Web*, having accepted the Irish State recognition of the man as being a descendant from the Eóghanacht kings, I felt it natural that I should dedicate one of the Fidelma books to a direct descendant of Fidelma's brother King Colgú. The discovery of the fraud, I admit, was a great embarrassment to me but more so to the Irish State for having recognised him as such for all those years. Even the President of Ireland, Mary Robinson, invited him to a reception at Aras an Uachtaráin, her official residence, as well

as attending a reception for him at Cashel."

6. *Valley of the Shadow*, 1998. Father Joe McVeigh. Father Joe, from Ederney, Co Fermanagh, Ireland, is another longtime friend of Peter and Dorothy and an admirer of Peter's work, although more concerned with his non-fiction historical work. Father Joe, a resolute worker for civil rights in Northern Ireland, is himself an accomplished author and has written several books ranging from *The Wounded Church* (1989), *Renewing the Irish Church* (1993), co-author of *British Injustice in Ireland* (1996), *Crying Out for Justice* (1997), *In Ederney Long Ago* (2000) and many others. Father Joe and Peter have several times appeared as a duo debating the role of St Patrick. Peter played "devil's advocate" arguing that Ireland would have been better off had St Patrick not converted it and Father Joe, of course, took St Patrick's side. The friendly arguments were designed to teach people about St Patrick and his influence. One of their "debates," "Would Ireland Have Been Better Off Without St Patrick?," was published as a pamphlet in 2001.

7. *The Monk Who Vanished*, 1999. Mary Mulvey and the staff of Cashel Heritage Centre. Mary was then manager of the Heritage Centre in Cashel and became a project manager with the Irish Peatland Conservation Council at the Bog of Allen Nature Centre. She was one of the first to welcome Fidelma's links with "Cashel na Rígh" (Cashel of the Kings) and when Peter gave a talk to the Cashel Writers Society in 1997, she presented him with a miniature replica of the sarcophagus panel from Cormac's Chapel on the Rock of Cashel.

8. *Act of Mercy*, 1999. Christos Pittas and Moira (Evans). Christos is a well-known Greek composer who has been a friend of Peter and his late wife Dorothy since 1970, living in the same house. Born in Alexandria and a graduate of the Athens Conservatory, Christos was then a rising musical talent in Greece when he went into exile in London following the 1967 military coup. His fellow composer Mikis Theodorakis (famous for his music for "Z" and "Never On A Sunday") was not so lucky and was imprisoned by the colonels' regime. Christos orchestrated Theodorakis' music smuggled from jail and conducted the London Symphony Orchestra at the Royal Albert Hall in a concert of Theodorakis' music in 1970. This was instrumental in securing the release of the composer. Christos' own career developed into music for theatre and drama and he composed music for over 60 BBC drama productions. Concerts of

his works for orchestra and singers were also performed in, among other famous venues, London's Queen Elizabeth Hall. After 1974, with the fall of the military dictatorship, Christos made his home in both Greece and London. His works have been performed in many countries and he won the Melina Mercouri Prize for his score of Euripedes' "The Phoenician Women" performed at the ancient theatre of Epidaurus in 2002. Moira Evans was also a good friend of Dorothea and Peter and supporter of the Sister Fidelma books, and sadly was to die in 2001, just before her fiftieth birthday (see the dedication to her in *The Haunted Abbot*).

9. *Hemlock At Vespers*, 2000. John Carson. John (1932-2000) was a Canadian who first met Peter in 1978, introduced by a mutual friend. They met again at a literary convention in 1979 when John had become a fan of Peter's work. Over the years, John built up a collection of all Peter's books, short stories and a lot of magazine and newspaper material, asking Peter to sign most of it during his visits to Canada. John rejoiced in the claim to be Peter's "No 1 North American Fan." John worked as an engineer on the dam at Cornwall, crossing the St Lawrence between Ontario and New York, and described himself as "a closet Celt." Peter and Dorothy stayed with John and his family on trips during the 1980s and Peter and John went on several research trips when Peter was writing his novel *The Rising of the Moon* (1987) about the Irish Republican Brotherhood's famous invasion of the provinces of British North America in 1866. John also accompanied Peter when he was lecturing at Sydney University in Cape Breton, Nova Scotia. John was very proud of his large collection of Peter's works and stated that it was his intention to donate it and the correspondence he had with Peter to a local university library. John was diagnosed with cancer in June 1999, just when Peter had decided to dedicate his first short story collection to him. The collection was published in March and John received but, on August 4, 2000, he died at his home in Gravenhurst, Ontario. Peter was saddened when he learnt that John's wish to donate the collection to a university library had not been fulfilled but the books and magazines had been sold to a commercial bookdealer and the collection was broken up. David Wooten managed to secure all Peter's letters to John over the years and these were set back to Peter who now holds them.

10. *Our Lady of Darkness*, 2000. Michael Thomas, literary agent. Peter, at the age of twenty-three, sent his first manuscript, a novel, to the famous London literary agency A.M. Heath & Co Ltd. which had been established in 1919. The agency handled some of the most famous authors including Flann O'Brien, George Orwell, Winston Graham and many others. It was June 1966. Michael Thomas of the agency asked Peter to call in and discuss his work. The upshot was that Michael recognised Peter's talent but told him that he might not be able to sell this first work. However, a year later Michael sold another book written by Peter and remained Peter's agent and literary confidant until his retirement from the company in June 1998. Since then, however, although retired as an active agent, Michael remains chairman of the board of directors. Peter's work was taken over by another director of the company, Sara Fisher.

11. *Smoke in the Wind*, 2001. David R. Wooton [sic], an irritating typo for our director and editor David Wooten. In spite of notes, Peter, like the MacCarthy dedication, has been unable to get the typo corrected. However, we all know of David's great work in creating the International Sister Fidelma Society, and it will not come as a surprise that David is interested and supportive of all Peter's work, non-fiction as well as fiction.

12. *The Haunted Abbot*, 2002. Moira Evans (1951-2001). A sad dedication being an "in memoriam" to a special friend of Peter's and his wife. Moira had been a close friend of Dorothy. She was a schoolteacher, of Irish descendant on her mother's side and therefore fascinated with all things Celtic. She had given Peter an idea used in *Act of Mercy* (see book No. 8) for which she shared a dedication. In the summer of 2001 Moira left for a vacation, with her partner David Ward, in a cottage she owned near Malestroit in Brittany. She had not been there long when she felt ill during the night, was taken into hospital the next morning and was dead in a few days from blood poisoning. Her remains were returned to England. They were taken to where she had bought a cottage in near her only sister's home in preparation for the day she planned to retire from teaching. This was in Weston, near Ilkley, Yorkshire. At the funeral service at the church of All Saints in Weston, the family asked Peter to recite one of Moira's favourite poems – "She Moved Through the Fair" by Pidraic Colum. There was a sad footnote to this. Moira was survived by her younger sister Patricia, born 1954.

Pat, with her husband John Thirlwell, ran a television production company and still found time to raise her young family, two boys and two girls. Patricia was barely fifty when she was diagnosed with a virulent cancer and she died on March 11, 2005, and now lies with her sister at Weston.

13. *Badger's Moon*, 2003. Denis, The O'Long of Garranelongy, and his wife, Lester. The O'Long of Garranelongy has long been recognised by the Chief Herald of Ireland as the descendant of the Eóghanacht Prince Longadh from whom the O'Longs take their name. Peter, and his wife Dorothy, were staying at The O'Long's house in West Cork, and it is in this area (Garran) that Peter set this book, especially at the site of the famous Rath Raithlen whose historic details in the book are accurate.

14. *Whispers of the Dead*, 2004. Sister Fidelma Society members. Peter expressed his gratitude to the "wonderfully supportive" fans who had kept The International Sister Fidelma Society running by their devotion to the books and enthusiasm.

15. *The Leper's Bell*, 2004. Pat and Andrew Broadbent. Dr Andrew Broadbent and his wife Patricia are friends with Peter and Dorothy. Both Andrew and Pat had been married before with children. Both were divorced. They had decided to marry at the famous Iona Abbey, on Colmcille's little island from where Irish missionaries set out to convert the Angles and Saxons to Christianity. Peter and Dorothy journeyed to Iona with other friends to attend the wedding conducted by Father Dennis Touw on June 12, 2003, the date referred to in the dedication. The choir at the service was the famous Napa Valley College Chamber Singers who were visiting Iona all the way from the United States. Some weeks later, at a party and reception in Hampstead, London, which was given for all the friends and relatives unable to get to Iona, Peter had the company in hysterical laughter by a rendition of the wedding adventures on Iona composed as a poem in the style of Robert Service's "The Shooting of Dan McGrew."

16. *Master of Souls*, 2005. Seamus J. King and Treasa Ní Fhatharta (misprint in the Headline edition as Treasa's name unfortunately comes out as Ní Fhartharta). Seamus is a local Cashel journalist as well as author of many books on Irish sport such as *A History of Hurling* (1996) and *The Clash of the Ash in Foreign Fields: Hurling Abroad* (1998). He is also a presenter of local Radio Cashel. Having

become a devotee of Sister Fidelma, and as organiser of the annual Cashel Arts Festival, he instigated an invitation for Peter to officially open the 2004 Arts Festival. The then-American Ambassador to Ireland had opened the 2003 festival. Treasa is an Irish language poetess and actress. She is from the Inis Méain (Inishmaan) in the Aran Islands. It was in her grandparents' cottage that the great Irish playwright J.M. Synge (1871-1909) lived and learnt Irish when staying on the islands. Treasa was the fundraiser and restorer of "Synge's Cottage" run as a museum dedicated to the life and work of Synge. Peter has helped in raising money for the project. Treasa, as the dedication indicates, helped Peter with the old proverb from which the title of this book is taken. "He who despises his own life is soon master of another's – beware, for such a man can become master of souls."

17. *A Prayer for the Damned*, 2006. This is a dedication to Peter's nephew Paul (who came to the first Féile Fidelma) and his wife, Wendy, and sons, Declan, Caleb, and Jamie. Paul Roland Ellis is the son of Peter's brother Paul Alan Ellis (d. 1993).

18. *Dancing With Demons*, 2007. The dedication was to all those people, from ten countries, who attended the very first Féile Fidelma in Cashel during September 2006.

19. *Council of the Cursed*, 2008. The dedication was, sadly, a memorial one to Peter's friend Peter Haining (1940-2007). Peter Haining and Peter arrived in London in early 1964 and worked on rival book trade publications for a while before each moving off to pursue their respective career. Peter Haining became a publisher before expanding his own writing career, becoming a prolific anthologist, novelist, an expert in many areas of popular fiction, and writing non-fiction works on aspects of World War II. It was Peter Haining, in 1993, who persuaded Peter to write the first Sister Fidelma story – a short story, but, when Peter called his sleuth "Sister Buan," he asked him to have second thoughts and approved when Peter came up with the name "Sister Fidelma." Peter therefore attributes him as Sister Fidelma's godfather.

20. *The Dove of Death*, 2009. It is no surprise that a book set in Brittany was dedicated to several Bretons, not the least the man who first suggested to Peter that Fidelma ought to visit this sister Celtic country. That man was Professor Per Denez (1921-2011), a retired professor of Celtic Studies at the University of Rennes, Brittany.

He was one of the leading experts on the Breton language, author of dictionaries, books and papers on linguistics and related Celtic studies as well as writing short stories in Breton himself. Peter first met Per Denez in the 1960s when they were members of The Celtic League. Professor Denez became an admirer of Peter's own work in the field and later an enthusiast of the Fidelma stories. He wrote an article about those stories in the Breton magazine *Al Liamm* in 2007. Another of those to whom the book is dedicated was Bernez An Nail (1946¬2010) who was also a Breton language scholar, a publisher and author, who had been director-general of The Breton Cultural Institute for seventeen years until 2000. Peter first met Bernez in 1985 when Peter was chairman of Scrif-Celt, the Celtic languages book fair. Bernez helped Peter with some of his research on the background for *The Dove of Death*. Tragically, he died before the book appeared in its Breton language translation. Jean-Michel Mahe was the translator, and the book also is dedicated to him. The dedication continues to include enthusiasts such as Yves Borius, mayor from 1989-2001 of Sarshav (Sarzeau) near Brilhag, the setting of the book. An economist working for the Organization for Economic Co-operation and Development, Yves was an accomplished *biniou* player and an enthusiast for the language. Also included, was Hervé Latimier, then a Brehon language editor, who was one of the most enthusiastic reviewers and a translator of Fidelma short stories. Marie Claude and Claud David, who attended the 2008 Féile Fidelma, were hosts to Peter and Dorothy when they stayed in Rennes.

21. *The Chalice of Blood*, 2010. This dedication to David R. Wooten was not only to mark David's ten years as director of the Society as well as editor of *The Brehon*. Where David's last name was previously given as "Wooton" in *Smoke in the Wind* (2001), Peter had tried in vain to get this typo corrected in reprints and subsequent editions. So he decided to make the final corrective with a new dedication, giving the name correctly.

22. *Behold A Pale Horse*, 2011. Peter had given a talk about Fidelma in the cloisters of the famous Bobbio Abbey, in the Trebbia Valley, North Italy, an abbey founded in AD 613 by the Irish missionary teacher St Columbanus. The audience asked if Sister Fidelma could have visited the abbey. This inspired Peter to write the book and therefore dedicate it to those enthusiasts who attended his talk in the ancient abbey.

23 *The Seventh Trumpet*, 2012. Dedicated to Peter's wife Dorothea who had been diagnosed with cancer in 2011. *Is feidir linn* (we can) was a hidden message of hope as Dorothea did not want to share this news with family or friends.

24. *Atonement of Blood*, 2013. Tanya and Marianne were sisters and among Peter's oldest friends. Tanya, then Tanya Lawrence, died on Crete in July 2015. She had invited Peter and Dorothea to join her in the village she where lived there but Dorothea was then too ill to travel. Tanya had just arrived at the house when she had a fatal heart attack. She was the same age as Peter. The dedication also calls on the memory of Tanya and Marianne's father and mother, Cyrille and Odeyne. Cyrille Wolfman (1899-1970), originally a Russian refugee from the Revolution and a decorated (Cross of St. George) officer in the 10th Hussars of the Ukraine during the Civil War, and his wife Odeyne (1907-1966), were friends and neighbours. Cyrille taught Peter most of what he knew about horses because he owned a riding stable when he moved to England. He also taught Peter how to shoot rifles. Peter ghost-wrote Cyrille's story about fighting in the West Russian Volunteer Army of Prince Pavel Bemrondt-Avalov, the Ussuri Cossack leader. The story was published in *Titbits* magazine (March 12, 1967). Odeyne was a Ponsonby and granddaughter of the 4th Earl of Bessborough. Her brother David Ponsonby was a concert pianist, composer, and painter who was living in Paris in 1940, but refused to leave when the Germans entered Paris. He remained in France during the occupation to fight in the French Resistance. He became the only English citizen to be an officer in the French Army and was awarded the Croix de Guerre in the fight against the Nazis. In the dedication Peter fondly recalls the summers with the family sipping lemon tea in the garden, especially the evenings after dinner when David would play for the family. Peter was a subscriber for the posthumous publication of David's memoirs *Fugitive Papers* (2012) and *Scenes from a Life* (2013).

25. *The Devil's Seal*, 2014; and

26. *The Second Death*, 2015; and

27. *Penance of the Damned*, 2016. These three titles were dedicated, in turn, to each of the three children of Dorothea's first cousin, Sandra Peppiatt with whom her relationship was more like a sister. Both Dorothea and Sandra were only children. Their mothers

being sisters of the Italian Volpe family. Dorothea and Peter actually met the month before Sandra married her husband David Peppiatt in 1966. An interesting point is that David Peppiatt, then a headmaster of a school in East Anglia, suggested to Peter that Saxmundham, in Suffolk, was a suitable place for Brother Eadulf to come from. The dedication of No. 25 was to Kate and her husband Dave Clayton and their children. No. 26 to Vick and her husband, Stef Van Leeuwen, and their children, and 27 was to Jonathan Peppiatt, his wife, Helen, and their children; Dorothea and Peter were always considered Aunt and Uncle to the families. Kate has been named as executrix of Peter's estate. She and her mother, Sandra, have been attendees at the Féile Fidelma.

28. *The Night of the Lightbringer*, 2017. This is a sad dedication to Peter's late wife Dorothea Cheesmur Ellis who died March 30, 2016, using the lines that were inscribed on her headstone in Islington Cemetery, North London.

29. *Bloodmoon*, 2018. The dedication reflects on Peter's time dealing with his bereavement and seeking adjustment in the period following Dorothea's death. He classes this as the struggle against "the Laestrygonians, Cyclops and the Wild Poseidon." The references is to a favourite poet of Peter's, C.P. Cavafy (1863-1933), whose lines in *Ithaca* – state *Laistrygonians, Cyclops, wild Poseidon – you won't encounter them unless you bring them along inside your soul, unless your soul sets them up in front of you.*

30. *Blood in Eden*, 2019. Cashel attendees will remember Eleni Triantafillaki and her son Orestes attending the 2019 Féile. Eleni, from Thessaloniki, is a close friend of Peter's as she was of Dorothea, whom she considered her best friend. Peter and Dorothea met Eleni in 1975 when she was working at the BBC in London. Returning to Greece in the early 1980s, having worked in UK local theatre as well as the Young Vic and other London theatres, she was appointed a director of the National Theatre of Greece (of the North) and her productions secured her reputation. Her production of an Angelos Sikelianos (1884-1951) play in Delphi even won her a mention in a Greek encyclopaedia. Eleni helped Peter look after Dorothea in her last months of illness – she flew back and forth from Greece three times during this period. *Blood in Eden* is Peter's tribute. He had also dedicated the first of his fantasy trilogy, *The Fires of Lan-Kern* (1980), to her, and *Celt and Greek* (1997), which was also to her

son Orestes. Eleni and Orestes had driven Peter and Dorothea on an extended trip around Greece during a research tour.

31. *The Shapeshifters Lair*, 2020. Maria Soteriades has been an attendee for many years at the Féile Fidelma. A longtime friend of Peter and Dorothea, she was originally from the Peloponnese, and was working at the BBC in 1969, sharing the same north London house where Peter and Dorothea were living. Maria left the BBC and went to Washington, DC, working in radio before her marriage to a Greek lawyer and hospital administrator, George Matakias, based in Montréal. Settling in the city, she became official media spokesperson (TV and Radio) for the Québec Government on transport, road, and weather conditions. She is now retired, her husband died in 2015, not long before Dorothea. Maria continued to be a frequent visitor to London or hosted when Peter and Dorothea visited Canada. She is also a friend of Eleni. Maria came from Canada to join Eleni in London helping Peter during the last weeks of Dorothea's life and helping Peter with the funeral arrangements. In addition to this book, Peter had dedicated his non-fiction study, *Caesar's Invasion of Britain* (1978), to her. Maria shared Peter's interest in the ancient world and often went on archaeological digs in the Dordogne.

32. *The House of Death*, 2021. "For Susanna Kleeman, welcome to the crazy world of authorship." A neighbour and friend who kept a watchful eye on Peter the during lockdown period as we read in her amusing articles in *The Brehon* (September 2020 and May 2021). Susanna worked in digital tech and published her first fantasy novel *Twice* in 2021, featured in an article in *The Brehon* (May, 2021). Previously, in an eBook, she had published amusing accounts and comments on getting published and other matters in *My Rejections* which she dedicated to Peter. A graduate of Oxford University, she has lived in the US and Canada and taught English in China before returning to work in London.

33. *Death of a Heretic*, 2022. For Caroline Lennon, "the voice of Fidelma;" reader of the English language AudioBooks, making Fidelma come alive on the airways, in appreciation of a talented actress and friend. Caroline is still known for playing the role of Siobhan Hathaway in the BBC Radio's longest running soap "The Archers." She played the role for nine years before her character was "killed off" by the writers, but is still referred to in the series. Born in Co

Wicklow, a graduation of Dublin University, she studied at the Bristol Old Vic. She played Goneril in the 1999 movie *King Lear* starring Brian Blessed. She had also appeared in several television series such as *Casualty*, *London's Burning*, and *The 10½ers*. She has, of course, recorded all the Fidelma novels on Audio and has become known to the Fidelma fandom as "The Voice of Fidelma."

Note: Aficionados, particularly German fans, will comment if we do not acknowledge that there is one Fidelma title, unique to Germany, that has no dedication. This was *Die Wahrheit ist der Lüge Tod* (published by Aufbau, 2018). This was a collection of six short stories which had not been collected in any English or US volumes before. Technically this would have been the 29th Fidelma book in a list of worlds first editions. The volume also contains a German translation of "Sister Fidelma and the Celtic Church" by Frank A. Salamone, published in *The Sister Fidelma Mysteries: Essays on the Historical Novels of Peter Tremayne,* edited Edward J. Rielly and David Robert Wooten, McFarland, North Carolina, 2012.

– Maurice McCann and others
Updated for this volume

SISTER FIDELMA in "ALTERNATE" EDITIONS
(INTERNATIONAL/NON-ENGLISH LANGUAGE, LARGE PRINT, GRAPHIC NOVELS, AUDIOBOOKS)

BOXED SETS
- First four Hobby & Work titles are issued in a boxed set as *Le indagini di sorella Fidelma*. ISBN is 13-978-8878510074 and the box set comes with a gift of a pen.
- UK company Past Times published four boxed sets. Three sets contain three volumes each and one set contains two volumes comprising short stories.
  - *Celtic Whodunnits: The Sister Fidelma Mysteries*, No 0101, 1998
  - *More Celtic Whodunnits: The Sister Fidelma Mysteries* No 9624, 1999
  - *Yet More Celtic Whodunnits: The Sister Fidelma Mysteries*, ISBN 9-9999-9106-8, 2000
  - *Celtic Whodunnits Short Stories* (*Hemlock At Vespers I* and *Hemlock At Vespers II*), ISBN 9-9999-8774-5

WORLD FIRST EDITIONS
(Fidelma novellas and short stories, collected in book form, for the first time)

AUFBAU TASCHENBUCH (Germany)
- *Die Wahrheit ist der Lüge Tod* ("The Lair of the White Fox" and other stories), ISBN 978-3-7466-3372-5, February 16, 2018

LARGE PRINT EDITIONS
- **Magna Large Print Books (UK)**
  - ○ *Absolution By Murder*, 1996
  - ○ *Shroud for the Archbishop*, 1996
  - ○ *The Subtle Serpent*, 1998
  - ○ *The Spider's Web*, 1998
  - ○ *Valley of the Shadow*, 1999
  - ○ *The Monk Who Vanished*, 2000
- **A Vue d'Oeil**
  - ○ *Absolution par le Meurtre*, April, 2007

OMNIBUS EDITIONS
- *The Sister Fidelma 20th Anniversary Collection (Absolution By Murder, Shroud for the Archbishop* and *Suffer Little Children),* available in eBook format (E61630) only, Headline, London, September 2014, ISBN 978-1-472225475
- *Les Deux Premiéres Enquêtes de Soeur Fidelma* (the first two Fidelma titles in French Omnibus), Editions 10-18, Paris, November 2015
- *Le suaire de l'Archevêque suivi de Absolution par le meurtre*, March 2018 (a reprint and new cover of above title)

GRAPHIC NOVEL ADAPTATIONS
The following are adapted by Antonio Muñoz, art by Joseph Ferrer and Carlos Vila.
- *Absolutie door moord* (Dutch, *Absolution by Murder*), ARBORIS, Zelhelm, Netherlands (De Luxe Edition), ISBN 978 903430 5558
- *Absolutie door moord*, ARBORIS, Zelhelm, Netherlands (hardcover edition), ISBN 978 903430 5541

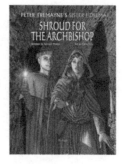

SISTER FIDELMA IN ALTERNATE EDITIONS

- *Absolutie door moord*, ARBORIS, Zelhelm, Netherlands (softcover edition), ISBN 978 903430 5534
- *Absolution By Murder*, (English edition), Zelhelm, Netherlands (softcover edition), 978 908606 0436
- *Lijkwade voor een aartsbisschop (Shroud for the Archbishop)*, ARBORIS, Zelhelm, Netherlands (softcover edition), March 2017
- *Lijkwade voor een aartsbisschop (Shroud for the Archbishop)*, ARBORIS, Zelhelm, Netherlands (hardcover edition), March 2017
- *Shroud for the Archbishop*, (English edition) ARBORIS, Zelhelm, Netherlands (softcover edition), September, 2017

FOREIGN LANGUAGE EDITIONS

VYSEHRAD (Czech Republic)
- *Rozhreseni vrazdou (Absolution By Murder)*, 2004
- *Nechte Malickych (Suffer Little Children)*, 2004
- *Paní tenmot (Our Lady of Darkness)*, August 2005
- *Dym ve vertu (Smoke in the Wind)*, March 2007
- *Opat S Mecem (The Haunted Abbot)*, October 2007
- *Zly Uplnek (Badger's Moon)*, June 2008
- *Zvon Malomocného (The Leper's Bell)*, 2008
- *Pán Dusí (Master of Souls)*, July 2009
- *Modlitba za zatrancence (A Prayer for the Damned)*, December 2009
- *Tenec s Démony (Dancing With Demons)*, July 2010
- *Ztraceny Relikviár (Council of the Cursed)*, November 2010
- *Holubice smrti (The Dove of Death)*, June 2011
- *Kalich Kvre (The Chalice of Blood)*, February 2012
- *Rubás pro arcibiskups (Shroud for the Archbishop)*, October 2012
- *Jezdec vestí smrt (Behold A Pale Horse)*, May 2013
- *Sedmá Polnice (The Seventh Trumpet)*, October 2013

THE SISTER FIDELMA COMPENDIUM

- *Symbol smrti (The Subtle Serpent)*, August 2014
- *Vykouponí krví (Atonement of Blood)*, August 2015
- *Pavoucí Sít (The Spider's Web)*, May 2016
- *Dábloca Pecet (The Devil's Seal)*, 2016
- *Údolí Stínu (Valley of the Shadow)*, September 2017
- *Druhá Smrt (The Second Death)*, April 2018
- *Mnich Který Zmízel (The Monk Who Vanished)*, 2019
- *Pokání Mrtvých (Penance of the Damned)*, October 2019
- *Smrt z Milosti (Act of Mercy)*, November 2, 2020
- *Noc Světlonoše (Night of the Lightbringer)*, June 2021
- *Bloodmoon (2022)*
- *Blood in Eden (2022)*

PANDA BOOKS, EDITORA ORIGINAL (Portugal, Brazil)
- *Morte por Luxúrua (Absolution By Murder)*, the Brazilian (Portuguese) edition of the first of the Sister Fidelma titles from Panda Books of Sao Paolo, Brazil. Published June, 2005, ISBN 85-87537-81-4.

ERA (Bulgaria)
- *Shroud for the Archbishop*, March 2007
- *Suffer Little Children*, August 2007
- *The Spider's Web*, October 2008

EDHASA (Spain)
Hardbacks
- *Absolution Por Asesinato (Absolution by Murder)*, 2001
- *Una Mortaia Para El Arzobispo (Shroud for the Archbishop)*, 2002
- *Sufrid, Pequenos (Suffer Little Children)*, 2002
- *La Serpiente Sutil (The Subtle Serpent)*, 2003
- *La Telaraña (The Spider's Web)*, 2004
- *El Valle de las Sombras (Valley of the Shadow)*, June 2005
- *El Monje Desapapecido (The Monk Who Vanished)*, June 2006
- *Un Acto de Misericordia (Act of Mercy)*, June 2007
- *Nuestra Senora de las Tinieblas (Our Lady of Darkness)*, July 2008

SISTER FIDELMA IN ALTERNATE EDITIONS

Paperbacks
- *La Telaraña (The Spider's Web)*, 2004
- *La Serpiente Sutil (The Subtle Serpent)*, 2005

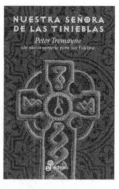

POLAR (Edhasa)
- *Absolución par Asessinato (Absolution By Murder)* February, 2015

QUINTETO (Spanish Paperbacks)
- *Absolution Por Asesinato (Absolution By Murder)*, October 2009
- *Una mortaia para el Arzbispo (Shroud for the Archbishop)* October, 2010

EDICIONES ALTAYA – Colección Historical Crime (Newsstand Editions)
Published in 2007
- o *1 Absolución por Asesinato (Absolution By Murder)*
- o *9 Una mortaia para al Arzobispo (Shroud for the Archbishop)*
- o *15 Sufrid Pequeños (Suffer Little Children)*
- o *23 La Serpiente Sutil (The Subtle Serpent)*
- o *31 La Telaraña (The Spider's Web)*
- o *39 El Valle de las Sombras (Valley of the Shadow)*
- o *45 El Monie Desaparecido (The Monk Who Vanished)*

PEUCO EDITORES (Argentina)
- *Cicuta al Anochecer (Hemlock At Vespers)*, October 2005
- *Susurros de los Muertos (Whispers of the Dead)*, December 2006

- *Sinodo en Witebia (Absolution By Murder)*, 2007
- *Un sudaro para Arzobispo (Shroud for the Archbishop)* May, 2009

HOBBY & WORK (Italy) – Hobby & Work Publishing S.r.l., via Achille Varisco 1, 20052 Monza, MI, Italy
- *L'Abbazia degli Innocenti (Suffer Little Children)*, 2001
- *L'Astuzia del Serpente (The Subtle Serpent)*, 2002
- *I Crimini del Ragno (The Spider's Web)*, 2002
- *Un Sudaio per Il Vescovo (Shroud for the Archbishop)*, 2003
- *Nostra Signora delle Tenebre (Our Lady of Darkness)*, October 2004
- *L'Abate Maledetto (The Haunted Abbot)*, July 2005

- *Delitti di Fuoco (Smoke in the Wind)*, 2006
- *Luna assassina (Badger's Moon)*, December 2006
- *Rintocchi di Morte (The Leper's Bell)*, July 2007
- *Una preghiera per i dannati (A Prayer for the Damned)*, March 2008
- *Danzando con il Diavolo (Dancing With Demons)*, January 2009
- *I neri agenti della notte (An Ensuing Evil)* September, 2009

HOBBY & WORK (Paperbacks) – Hobby & Work Publishing S.r.l., via Achille Varisco 1, 20052 Monza, MI, Italy

- *Nostra Signora delle Tenebre (Our Lady of Darkness)*, March 2009
- *L'Abate Maledetto (The Haunted Abbot)*, March 2009
- *Delitti di Fuoco (Smoke in the Wind)*, July 2009
- *Luna assassina (Badger's Moon)*, July 2009
- *Rintocchi di morte (The Leper's Bell)*, 2010

SISTER FIDELMA IN ALTERNATE EDITIONS

- *Una Preghiera per Dannati (A Prayer for the Damned),* 2010
- *Danzando con il Diavolo (Dancing With Demons),* March 2011
- *I neri agenti della nottee (An Ensuing Evil)* April 2012

TASCABILI EDITORE (TEA) – mass market Italian paperbacks
- *L'Abbazia degli Innocenti,* March 2004
- *L'Astuzia del Serpente,* December 2004
- *I Crimini del Ragno,* May 2005
- *Un Suderio per il Vescovo,* September, 2006

HACHETTE ITALIA (Newsstand paperbacks only) –
SERIES Codici segreti della Storia –
Series No.
- *32. L'Abate Maledetto (The Haunted Abbot),* July 29, 2006
- *36. L'Abbazia degli innocent (Suffer Little Children),* August 28, 2006
- *48. L'astutzia de serpente (The Subtle Serpent),* November 25, 2006
- *49. Un Sudario per il vescovo (Shroud for the Archbishop),* December 2, 2006
- *50. Nostra signora delle tenebre (Our Lady of Darkness)* December 9, 2006

DE LEESKAMER (Netherlands)
- *Absolutie voor moord (Absolution By Murder),* May 2003
- *Lijkwade voor een aartsbischop (Shroud for the Archbishop),* May 2004
- *Moord in de abdij (Suffer Little Children),* June 2005
- *De listige slang (The Subtle Serpent),* May 2006
- *Het web van Araglin (The Spider's Web),* Autumn 2006
- *De vallei van het kwaad (The Valley of the Shadows),* May 2007
- *De verdwenen monnik (The Monk Who Vanished),* October 2007
- *Dood van een pelgrim (Act of Mercy),* May 2008
- *Vrouwe van het duister (Our Lady of Darkness),* October 2008

- *Het klooster van de dode zielen (Smoke in the Wind)*, May 2009
- *De gekwelde abt (The Haunted Abbot)*, October 2009
- *De nacht van de das (Badger's Moon)*, June 2010
- *De leprozenbel (The Leper's Bell)*, October 2011
- *Moord uit de golven (Master of Souls)*, October 2012
- *Een gebed voor de verdoemden (A Prayer for the Damned)*, July 2013
- *Dansen met demonen (Dancing With Demons)*, February 2015
- *Het Valse concilie (Council of the Cursed)*, January 2017
- *De duif des doods (The Dove of Death)*, October 2019
- *De bloedkelk (The Chalice of Blood)*, August 2020
- *Da Zevende Bacuin (The Seventh Trumpet)*, August 2021
- *Forthcoming*
  - *Verlossing door bloed (Atonement of Blood)*
  - *En de hel Volgdw hem (Behold a Pale Horse)*

ROWOHLT (Germany)
- *Nur der Tod bringt Vergebung (Absolution By Murder)* 1998
- *Ein Totenhemd für den Erzbischof (Shroud for the Archbishop)* 1998

AUFBAU TASCHENBUCH (Germany)
- *Nur der Tod bringt Vergebung (new edition)*, 2003
- *Ein Totenhemd für deb Erzbischof (new edition)*, 2003
- *Die Tote im Klosterbrunnen (The Subtle Serpent)*, 2000
- *Tod im Skriptorium (Suffer Little Children)*, 2001
- *Der Tote am Steinkreuz (The Spider's Web)*, 2001
- *Tod in der Königsburg (The Monk Who Vanished)*, 2002
- *Tod auf dem Pilgerschiff (Act of Mercy)*, 2002
- *Vor dem Tod sind alle gleich (Our Lady of Darkness)*, 2003
- *Das Kloster der toten Seelen (Smoke in the Wind)*, July 2004
- *Verneig dich vor dem Tod (The Haunted Abbot)*, January 2005

SISTER FIDELMA IN ALTERNATE EDITIONS

- *Tod bei Vollmond (Badger's Moon)*, June 2005
- *Tod im Tal der Heiden (Valley of the Shadow)*, January 2006
- *Der Tod Soll Auf Euch Kommen (The Leper's Bell)*, June 2006
- *Tod vor den Morgenmesse (Master of Souls)*, February 2007
- *Ein Gebet für Verdammten (A Prayer for the Damned)*, May 2007
- *Tod den alten Gotten (Dancing With Demons)*, July 2008
- *Das Konzil der Verdammten (Council of the Cursed)*, December 2008
- *Der Falsche Apostel (Hemlock at Vespers)*, April 30, 2009
- *Eine Taube bringt den Tod (The Dove of Death)*, January 2010
- *Der Blutkeltch (Chalice of Blood)*, December 2010
- *Die Todesfee (Whispers of the Dead)*, October 2011
- *Und die Hölle folgte ihm nach (Behold A Pale Horse)*, February 2012
- *Die Pforten der Todes (The Seventh Trumpet)*, December 2012
- *Das Sühneopfer (Atonement of Blood)*, December 2013
- *Sendboten des Teufels (The Devil's Seal)*, December 2014
- *Der Lohn der Sünde (The Second Death)*, February 2016
- *Der Tod wird euch verschlingen (Penance of the Damned)*, December 2016
- *Die Wahrheit ist der Lüge Tod ("The Lair of the White Fox" and other stories)*, ISBN 978-3-7466-3372-5, February 16, 2018
- *Ihr Los ist Fersternis (The Night of the Lightbringer)*, October 2018
- *Wer Lügen Sät (Bloodmoon)*, August 16, 2019
- *Die Sünden der Gerechten (Blood in Eden)*, November 2020
- *Tod den finisteren Mächten (The Shapeshifter's Lair)*, translated by Bela Wohl, November 15, 2021, €12.00 ISBN 978-3-7466-3827-0

- *Tod Den Finisten Machten (House of Death)*
- *Forthcoming*
    - *Das Pestschrift (House of Death)* scheduled 2022
    - *Death of a Heretic* scheduled 2023

AUFBAU SPECIAL PROMOTIONAL PAPERBACKS (German)

- *Die Tote im Klosterbrunnen (The Subtle Serpent)*, 9th ed. 2004
- *Nur Der Tod Bringt Vergbung (Absolution By Murder)*, 6th ed. 2005
- *Der Tote am Steinkreuze (The Spider's Web)* October, 2007

CLUB TASCHENBUCH (BERTELSMAN)

- *Tod im Skriptorium*, 2004
- *Tod vor der Morgenmesse – mit Die Freistatt (Master of Souls* with "The Sanctuary," an extra Fidelma short story*)*, October 2007
- *Der Tote am Steinkreuze (The Spider's Web)* October, 2007

RÜTTEN AND LOENING, Berlin

- *Tod im Skriptorium (Suffer Little Children – mit musik CD)*, 2006 (special gift hardcover edition with a CD of Irish music)
- *Tod in der Königsbuirg (The Monk Who Vanished)* October, 2016 (special illustrated collector's item)

VERLAGSGRUPPE WELTBILD

- *Nur der Tod bringt Vergebung*, March 2008
- *Die Tote im Klosterbrunnen*, March 2008
- *Tod in der Kongisburg*, March 2008

WELTBILD-EDITIONEN

A special collector's edition in hardcover which the publishers have announced as "For the first time and the only such publication in the world, there is now a complete Sister Fidelma series in a uniform edition."

SISTER FIDELMA IN ALTERNATE EDITIONS

- *Nur der Tod bringt Vegebung (Absolution By Murder)*, January 2015
- *Ein Totenhemd fur den Erzbischof (Shroud for the Archbishop)*, February 2015
- *Tod im Skriptorium (Suffer Little Children)*, February 2015
- *Die Tote im Klosterbrunnen (The Subtle Serpent)*, March 2015
- *Der Tote am Steinkreuz (The Spider's Web)*, March 2015

- *Tod im Tal der Heiden (Valley of the Shadow)*, November 2015
- *Tod in der Konigsburg (The Monk Who Vanished)*, November 2015
- *Tod aud der Pilgershiff (Act of Mercy)*, December 2015
- *Vor dem Tod sind alle gleich (Our Lady of Darkness)*, 2016
- *Das Kloster der toten Seelend (Smoke in the Wind)*, 2016
- *Verneig dich vor dem Tod (The Haunted Abbot)*, 2016
- *Tod bei Vollmond (Badger's Moon)* 2016

LINGEN VERLAG, Berlin
- *Die Tote im Klosterbrunnen* (popular hardcover edition, June 2006)
- *Nur Der Tod bringt Vergebung* (popular hardcover edition, April 2007)
- *Tod auf dem Pilgershift*, June 2008
- *Tod im Scriptorium*, November 2009
- *Ein Totenhemd für den Erzbishof* (special edition), May 2010
- *Vor dem Tod sind alle gleich*, June 2011
- *Der Tod Soll Auf Euch Kommen (The Leper's Bell)*, July 2013
- *Der Tote am Steinkreuz (The Spider's Web)* September, 2014

DIE ZEIT (special edition from the mass market German newspaper)
- *Das Konzil der Verdammten* (July 2010); Special introduction by Martina Hartmann

THE SISTER FIDELMA COMPENDIUM

EDITIONS 10/18 (France)

- *Absolution par le meutre (Absolution by Murder)*, 2004
- *Le suaire de l'archeveque (Shroud for the Archbishop)*, 2004
- *Les cinq royaumes (Suffer Little Children)*, 2004
- *La ruse du serpent (The Subtle Serpent)*, June 2005
- *Le secret de móen (The Spider's Web)*, 2005
- *La mort aux trois visages (Valley of the Shadows)*, May 2006
- *Le sang du moine (The Monk Who Vanished)*, December 2006
- *La pèlerinage de soeur Fidelma (Act of Mercy)*, May 2007
- *La dame des ténèbres (Our Lady of Darkness)*, November 2007
- *Les disparus de dyfed (Smoke in the Wind)*, April 2008
- *La châtiment de l'au-delà (The Haunted Abbot)*, October 2008
- *Les mystères de la luna (Badger's Moon)*, January 2009
- *De la ciguë pour les veprês (Hemlock At Vespers)*, July 2009
- *La cloche du lépreux (The Lepers Bell)*, November 2009
- *Maitre des âmes (Master of Souls)*, March 2010
- *Une prière pour les damnés (A Prayer for the Damned)*, November 2010
- *Une danse avec les démons, (Dancing with Demons)*, February 2011
- *Le concile des maudits (The Council of the Cursed)*, July 2011
- *La colombe de la mort (The Dove of Death)*, April 5, 2012
- *La parole des morts (Whispers of the Dead)*, July 2012
- *Un calice de sang (The Chalice of Blood)*, February 2013
- *Le cavalier blanc (Behold A Pale Horse)*, October 17, 2013
- *La septième trompette (The Seventh Trumpet)*, 2014
- *Expiation par le sang (Atonement of Blood)*, Autumn 2014
- *Le sceau diable (The Devil's Seal)*, May 2015
- *La confrérie du corbeau (The Second Death)*, June 2016
- *La pénitence des damnés (Penance of the Damned)*, March 2017

SISTER FIDELMA IN ALTERNATE EDITIONS

- *La nuit du porte-lumière (Night of the Lightbringer),* May 2018
- *Une lune de sang (Bloodmoon),* May 2019
- *Du sang au paradis (Blood in Eden),* January 2021
- *Le jeteus de sort (The Shapeshifter's Lair),* August 2021
- *Le conseil de sept (The House of Death)*

FRENCH "BOOK OF THE MONTH CLUB" (GRAND LIVRES DU MOIS)
- *Absolution par le meurtre,* January 2005
- *Le suaire de l'archeveque,* 2005

THEMELIO (Greece)
- *Absolution By Murder* (1996)
- *Shroud for the Archbishop* (1997)
- *Suffer Little Children* (2002)
- *Valley of the Shadow* (2003)
- *Act of Mercy* (2005)
- *Our Lady of Darkness* (2006)

SOGENSHA (Japan)
- *The Spider's Web,* November 2006
- *Suffer Little Children,* September 2007
- *The Poisoned Chalice and other stories,* June 2009
- *The Subtle Serpent,* November 2009
- *Hemlock At Vespers,* July 2010
- *Absolution By Murder,* January 2011
- *Shroud for the Archbishop,* March 2012
- *A Canticle for Wulfstan and other stories,* December 2012
- *The Valley of the Shadow,* December 2013
- *The Monk Who Vanished,* November 2015
- *Whispers of the Dead,* December 2017
- *Act of Mercy,* February 2021
- *Forthcoming*
  - *Cry Wolf (2022)*

FLUID Publishing (Russia)
- *Absolution By Murder*, March 2008

ODAMEES (Estonia)
- *Lunastus mõrva läbi (Absolution By Murder)*, November 2006
- *Peapiiskopi surilina (Shroud for the Archbishop)*, 2007
- *Laske lapsukesed (Suffer Little Children) September*, 2008

VIIKING (Estonia)
- *Kaval madu (The Subtle Serpent) January*, 2018

FEMIS (Poland)
- *Cien Kruczego Skrzydla (Absolution By Murder) September*, 2007

ARGUMENT FORLAG AB (Sweden)
- *Frälsande Mord (Absolution By Murder) September*, 2007

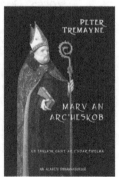

SANDELIN FORLAG (Swedish)
- *Arkebiskopens Hemlighet (Shroud for the Archbishop) April*, 2009

ABER EMBANN (Breizh)
- *Koulm ar Marv (The Dove of Death)*, October 2010
- Kegid d'ar Gousparoù (Hemlock at Vespers) September, 2014

AN ALARC'H (Breizh)
- *Absolvenn dre vuntur (Absolution By Murder)* October 2012
- *Marv an arc'heskob (Shroud for the Archbishop)* October 2016
- *Marc'heger ar Marv (Behold A Pale Horse)* 2019
- *Kuzuligou ar re varv (Whispers of the Dead)* 2022

5I5TER FIDELMA IN ALTERNATE EDITIONS

THE INTERNATIONAL SISTER FIDELMA SOCIETY (Irish Language)
- *Scréach ón Tuama (A Scream from the Sepulchre)* December 2008

AUDIO BOOKS
UK (English Language) Audio Books being released by Headline
- *Absolution by Murder (Sister Fidelma Mysteries Book 1)*, Written by Peter Tremayne; Read by Caroline Lennon; 25-July-2019 Edition EAN\ISBN-13 9781472269812
- *Shroud for the Archbishop (Sister Fidelma Mysteries Book 2)*, Written by Peter Tremayne; Read by Caroline Lennon; 25-July-2019 Edition EAN\ISBN-13 9781472269829
- *Suffer Little Children (Sister Fidelma Mysteries Book 3)*, Written by Peter Tremayne; Read by Caroline Lennon; 25-July-2019 Edition EAN\ISBN-13 9781472269836
- *The Subtle Serpent (Sister Fidelma Mysteries Book 4)*, Written by Peter Tremayne; Read by Caroline Lennon; 25-July-2019 Edition EAN\ISBN-13 9781472269843
- *The Spider's Web (Sister Fidelma Mysteries Book 5)*, Written by Peter Tremayne; Read by Caroline Lennon; 25-July-2019 Edition EAN\ISBN-13 9781472269850

THE SISTER FIDELMA COMPENDIUM

- *Valley of the Shadow (Sister Fidelma Mysteries Book 6),* Written by Peter Tremayne; Read by Caroline Lennon; 25-July-2019 Edition EAN\ISBN-13 9781472269881
- *The Monk who Vanished (Sister Fidelma Mysteries Book 7),* Written by Peter Tremayne; Read by Caroline Lennon; 25-July-2019 Edition EAN\ISBN-13 9781472269898
- *Act of Mercy (Sister Fidelma Mysteries Book 8),* Written by Peter Tremayne; Read by Caroline Lennon; 8-August-2019 Edition EAN\ISBN-13 9781472269904
- *Hemlock at Vespers (Sister Fidelma Mysteries Book 9),* Written by Peter Tremayne; Read by Caroline Lennon; 8-August-2019 Edition EAN\ISBN-13 9781472269911
- *Our Lady of Darkness (Sister Fidelma Mysteries Book 10),* Written by Peter Tremayne; Read by Caroline Lennon; 8-August-2019 Edition EAN\ISBN-13 9781472269928
- *Smoke in the Wind (Sister Fidelma Mysteries Book 11),* Written by Peter Tremayne; Read by Caroline Lennon; 8-August-2019 Edition EAN\ISBN-13 9781472269935
- *The Haunted Abbot (Sister Fidelma Mysteries Book 12),* Written by Peter Tremayne; Read by Caroline Lennon; 8-August-2019 Edition EAN\ISBN-13 9781472269942
- *Badger's Moon (Sister Fidelma Mysteries Book 13),* Written by Peter Tremayne; Read by Caroline Lennon; 8-August-2019 Edition EAN\ISBN-13 9781472269959
- *The Leper's Bell (Sister Fidelma Mysteries Book 14),* Written by Peter Tremayne; Read by Caroline Lennon; 8-August-2019 Edition EAN\ISBN-13 9781472269966
- *Whispers of the Dead (Sister Fidelma Mysteries Book 15),* Written by Peter Tremayne; Read by Caroline Lennon; 22-August-2019 Edition EAN\ISBN-13 9781472269409
- *Master Of Souls (Sister Fidelma Mysteries Book 16),* Written by Peter Tremayne; Read by Caroline Lennon; 22-August-2019 Edition EAN\ISBN-13 9781472269416
- *A Prayer for the Damned (Sister Fidelma Mysteries Book 17),* Written by Peter Tremayne; Read by Caroline Lennon; 22-August-2019 Edition EAN\ISBN-13 9781472269973
- *Dancing with Demons (Sister Fidelma Mysteries Book 18),* Written by Peter Tremayne; Read by Caroline Lennon; 22-August-2019 Edition EAN\ISBN-13 9781472269423

SISTER FIDELMA IN ALTERNATE EDITIONS

- *The Council of the Cursed (Sister Fidelma Mysteries Book 19)*, Written by Peter Tremayne; Read by Caroline Lennon; 22-August-2019 Edition EAN\ISBN-13 9781472269980
- *The Dove of Death (Sister Fidelma Mysteries Book 20)*, Written by Peter Tremayne; Read by Caroline Lennon; 22-August-2019 Edition EAN\ISBN-13 9781472269430
- *The Chalice of Blood (Sister Fidelma Mysteries Book 21)*, Written by Peter Tremayne; Read by Caroline Lennon; 22-August-2019 Edition EAN\ISBN-13 9781472269447
- *Behold A Pale Horse (Sister Fidelma Mysteries Book 22)*, Written by Peter Tremayne; Read by Caroline Lennon; 5-September-2019 Edition EAN\ISBN-13 9781472269454
- *The Seventh Trumpet (Sister Fidelma Mysteries Book 23)*, Written by Peter Tremayne; Read by Caroline Lennon; 5-September-2019 Edition EAN\ISBN-13 9781472269461
- *Atonement of Blood (Sister Fidelma Mysteries Book 24)*, Written by Peter Tremayne; Read by Caroline Lennon; 5-September-2019 Edition EAN\ISBN-13 9781472269478
- *The Devil's Seal (Sister Fidelma Mysteries Book 25)*, Written by Peter Tremayne; Read by Caroline Lennon; 5-September-2019 Edition EAN\ISBN-13 9781472269485
- *The Second Death (Sister Fidelma Mysteries Book 26)*, Written by Peter Tremayne; Read by Caroline Lennon; 5-September-2019 Edition EAN\ISBN-13 9781472269492
- *Penance of the Damned (Sister Fidelma Mysteries Book 27)*, Written by Peter Tremayne; Read by Caroline Lennon; 5-September-2019 Edition EAN\ISBN-13 9781472269508
- *Night of the Lightbringer (Sister Fidelma Mysteries Book 28)*, Written by Peter Tremayne; Read by Caroline Lennon; 5-September-2019 Edition EAN\ISBN-13 9781472269515
- *Bloodmoon (Sister Fidelma Mysteries Book 29)*, Written by Peter Tremayne; Read by Caroline Lennon; 5-September-2019 Edition EAN\ISBN-13 9781472269522
- *Blood in Eden (Sister Fidelma Mysteries Book 30)*, Written by Peter Tremayne; Read by Caroline Lennon; 19-September-2019 Edition EAN\ISBN-13 9781472269393
- *The Shapeshifter's Lair* (Sister Fidelma Mysteries Book 31) Written by Peter Tremayne; Read by Caroline Lennon; 9-July-2020 Edition EAN\ISBN-13 9781472276612

UK (English Language) Audio Books

- *Valley of the Shadow,* read by Marie McCarthy, Magna Story Sound, Long Preston, Yorkshire, UK, ISBN 1-85903-313-X. Time 12 hrs – 9 cassettes
- *A Prayer for the Damned,* read by Annie Farr, Soundings, Isis House, Whitley Bay, UK. ISBN 978-1-84559-646-0. Time 14 hours – 12 Cassettes

- *Dancing With Demons,* read by Caroline Lennon, Soundings, Isis House, Whitley Bay, UK. ISBN 978-1-4079-0431-3. Time 13 hours – 11 CDs
- *Master of Souls,* read by Caroline Lennon, Soundings, Isis House, Whitby Bay, UK. ISBN 978-1-4079-0903-5. Time 13 hours 30 minutes, 12 CDs
- *Council of the Cursed,* read by Caroline Lennon, Oakhill Publishing, 11hrs 8mins. Cassettes ISBN 978 1 84648 600 5 and CDs ISBN 978 1 84648 624 1. May 2009
- *The Dove of Death*, read by Caroline Lennon, Soundings, Isis House, Whitby, UK. December 1, 2009, Cassettes 10-14079141-03 and CDs 13-978-1079141-07
- *Whispers of the Dead,* read by Caroline Lennon, Soundings, Isis House, Whitby, UK, September 2010, CDs ISBN 978-1-4079-2005-4. 12 hrs 30 mins
- *The Chalice of Blood,* read by Caroline Lennon, Soundings, Isis House, Whitby, UK, December 2010, CDs ISBN 978-1-4079-2188-4. 13hrs 30mins
- *Behold A Pale Horse (2012),* read by Caroline Lennon, Soundings, Isis House, Whitley Bay, UK, February 2012, CDs ISBN 978-1-4079-3132-6, running time approx. 12 hours
- *The Seventh Trumpet (2012),* read by Caroline Lennon, Soundings, Isis House, Whitley Bay, UK, February 2012, CDs ISBN 978-1-4079-3350-4, running time approx. 13 hours
- *Atonement of Blood (2014),* read by Caroline Lennon, Soundings, Isis House, Whitley Bay, March 1, 2014, ISBN 978-1-4079-4-5897
- *The Devil's Seal,* read by Caroline Lennon, Soundings, Isis

House, Whitley Bay, UK, October 1, 2014, ISBN 978-1-4079-4767-9
- o *The Second Death,* read by Caroline Lennon, Soundings, Isis House, Whitley Bay, UK, December 1, 2015, ISBN 978-1-4079-5916-0, 9 CDs running time 12 hrs 30 mins
- o *Penance of the Damned,* read by Caroline Lennon, Soundings, Isis House, Whitley Bay, UK, October 2016, 12 hours. ISBN 978-1-4079-6370-9
- o *Night of the Lightbringer (*November 2017*),* read by Caroline Lennon, Soundings, Isis House, Whitley Bay, UK, December 2017, 12 hours, 978-1-4079-69435
- o *Bloodmoon (*November 2018*),* read by Caroline Lennon, Soundings, Isis House, Whitley Bay, UK. 11 hrs30 mins, 978-1-4079-7545
- o *Blood In Eden (*November 2019*),* read by Caroline Lennon, Soundings, Isis House, Whitley Bay, UK. 11 hrs 30 mins, 978-1-4079-84186

GERMAN AUDIO BOOKS

DER AUDIO VERLAG GMBH, BERLIN

- *Tod im Skriptorium (Suffer Little Children),* January 2006, commercial stereo CD from Der Audio Verlag GmbH, Berlin. It comes in two CDs running 106 mins. This is a recording of the play broadcast on German radio WDR5 on July 1 and 2, 2005, and repeated in October. Sissy Höfferer plays Sister Fidelma. The CD comes with a booklet on Peter Tremayne and the Fidelma series with information on leading members of the cast of the production.

DELTA MUSIC (AUDIO BOOKS)
- *Ein Gebet fur
  die Verdammten* (September
  2007), read by
  Susanne Dobrusskin – 5CDs
- *Die Tote
  in Klosterbrunnen* (September
  2007), read by
  Susanne Dobrusskin – 5CDs

**BUCHFUNK AND AUDIBLE
GERMANY**
- *Der Tod wird euch verchlingen (Penance of the
  Damned)*, read by Luise Schubert. Audiobuch CD
  from Buchfunk 12 hrs 22 mins. Also available on Audible
  Germany

**TECHNISAT (Audio Books – all
read by actress Sabine Swobda) –
reissues from Buchfunk**
- *Nur der Tod bringt
  Vergenbung*, 2007
- *Der Kloster den toten
  Seelen*, 2007
- *Tod im der Kongisburg*, 2007
- *Tod im Tal der Heiden*, 2007
- *Der Tod Soll
  Auf Euch Kommen*, 2007

AUDIOBOOKS IN THE USA

*By February 18, 2015, all 27 Fidelma
Mysteries published by that date (up to and
including The Second Death) were produced
by Brilliance Audio on MP3 CDs. After that
title, only downloadable audiobooks were
produced by Audible.com. Audible has the
entire series to date through their service. All
the books were read by Caroline Lennon.*

SISTER FIDELMA IN ALTERNATE EDITIONS

TALKING BOOKS FOR THE BLIND

The following Sister Fidelma titles have been issued by The Library of Congress, Talking Books and Braille Library Blind in the USA:

- *Absolution by Murder*, read by Alita Kiaer, CBA 07675
- *Shroud for the Archbishop*, read by Eileen Grughin, CBA 07676
- *Hemlock At Vespers*, read by Martha Harmon Pardee, RC 061958
- *Whispers of the Dead*, read by Martha Harmon Pardee, RC 061547
- *Suffer Little Children*, read by Phil Regensdorf, 2 cassettes, RC 40925

DUTCH LIBRARY FOR THE BLIND CDs

- *Absolutie voor Moord*
- *Lijkwade voor eern aartsbisshop*
- *Het web van Araglin*

THE SISTER FIDELMA COMPENDIUM

Fidelma Gets Graphic
Sister Fidelma: From Book to Graphic Novel

For more than 20 years now, De Leeskamer has been the publisher of the Fidelma novels in Dutch language. Not so well known is that De Leeskamer has a sister company called Arboris, that started in 1981 and has been publishing comics and graphic novels in Dutch for almost double that period.

Having experience in both fields, it seemed a logical idea to make a combination of the two publishing areas: a graphic novel of a Fidelma story. The idea originated already in the early years of the company, as we asked an artist, who already worked for us making graphic novels, to make the covers for the first Dutch Fidelma novels. This artist, Ken Broeders, also made the drawing of Fidelma that was used for years on banners and flyers for several Féile Fidelmas.

Fidelma by Ken Broeders

Fidelma page by Art Wetherell - The Brehon, I, 1, February 2002

We talked about it with Peter Tremayne, who told me that in 2003 there already had been an attempt to make a comic of the short story *Murder by Miracle*. The English artist Art Wetherell started and drew some pages but died suddenly before he could finish the artwork . It seemed worthwhile to give it another try.

It sounds like a simple idea, but there are a lot of steps to be taken. In fact it took us two years to arrive at a printed result.

As we aimed for a graphic novel of between 48 and 64 pages, we had just about enough room to retell an entire Fidelma novel. A lot of words needed in a novel can be replaced by one simple drawing that tells it all. However, the way a story is told in a graphic novel has its own rules; you can't just start drawing the existing book. Just like in TV-productions, you need a script based on the original book, but taking into account the visual possibilities of the medium. Writing such a script

Fidelma script by Antonio Muñoz

is the work of a specialist. And the next step is of course to find an artist who can bring the characters Peter imagined to life.

Thanks to our experience in the comics-business, we knew that, in Spain, there are many artists who are very good at drawing in a realistic style, the style needed for Fidelma. We contacted a Spanish artist representative and asked him to make some suggestions. We showed him a number of graphic novels with the kind of style we had in mind,

Early sketches for the Fidelma graphic novel

and he came up with a scriptwriter, Antonio Muñoz Lorente, who not only was a very good "scenarist," as we call it in comics, but also was very much interested in history, having written several books on periods in history. As artists a team of two persons was suggested, Josep Lluis Ferrer and Carlos Vila. Josep would do the drawings, and Carlos would then add the backgrounds and colours.

First, of course, they made sketches of Fidelma , in pencil and in full colour. How should she look? Was this the intelligent, somewhat stubborn woman Peter had in mind? Was the clothing like he wanted it to be? And what about the red colour of the hair? The green of the eyes? And Eadulf: What about his clothes, his tonsure?

More sketches were made. Are the monks correct? Is the abbey like it should be? What about the weapons, helmets, tools? The script-writer and the two artists started digging in their collections of books to find documentation, an important task!

What the sketches promised was exactly what we were hoping for!

Then the real work started, the making of the graphic novel. From every description the scenarist made, based on Peter Tremayne's novel, an image had to be made. First as a sketch, later elaborated into a black and white drawing in pencil and ink, and finally in full colour. Sometimes changes were made. For example: look at the first picture on the first page: at first, in the concept sketch, the riders come from the right, in the final picture they come from the left. There is a reason

Left: First concept sketch for a page; Right: Modified version of same page (note difference in positions, perspectives)

behind this: readers (in English and Dutch, at least) read from left to right, so they "ride" with the riders into the story.

There is more to be said about this first page: the first image in the *Absolution by Murder* graphic novel says it all. It shows at once the atmosphere Peter described in the first pages of his novel. Also crucial is the third picture: just the eyes of Fidelma.

The scenarist had understood the significance of these eyes. The entire novel is converted like this into a script, with notes for the artists for every picture. Seven, eight pictures each page, 50 pages or more!

During production, artwork went back and forth to Peter and oc-

Eadulf's dream (original concept)

casionally changes were made, for instance in the tonsure of Eadulf. A more notable change is to be seen when Fidelma is dreaming. In the concept drawing she was naked, but after consultation with Peter Tremayne, it was decided that a naked Fidelma was not quite the atmosphere of the novel. So a negligee was added.

Just drawings aren't enough, obviously. Dialogue is essential. Where do you put the balloons? They mustn't disturb the picture. They ought to be big enough for the spoken words. Most of the dialogue is literally like the dialogue in the novel itself in that same situation, but sometimes the text had to be adapted. The text is too long for that page, too complicated, or not needed, as the drawing already tells us a lot. When Fidelma presents her case in the end, she needs lots of words, but for a comic it has to be limited to the bare essentials.

Eadulf's dream (Fidelma's negligee added)

Principal characters from the graphic novel adaptation of Absolution By Murder

When the story is finished, say after 240 pictures, about 40 weeks later, the book isn't ready yet. A strong cover had to be made. It has to draw the attention of the potential reader. Trial covers are made, changed, adapted, until everybody is happy . And because this is a sophisticated graphic novel, nice looking fly leaves are added, introductions of the writer, scenarist and artists. And then, about five weeks after sending everything to the printer, and – as we already said - two years after starting the production, the book is finally ready. And it is a great feeling to be able to hold it in your hand after such a long time...!

One of the trial covers

– *Hans van den Boom*
Written for this volume

All images, except where noted, courtesy De Leeskamer

THE SISTER FIDELMA COMPENDIUM

Why Cashel?

Back in 1993 I wrote a few short stories with a background of Brehon Law, the ancient law of Ireland, to see if they might work as murder mysteries. They were greeted with enthusiasm, and a publisher offered me a three-book contract if I could write novel-length stories with the same character and background. Nervously, I agreed, little dreaming that twenty years after the first book, and twenty-five titles later, Sister Fidelma would be the subject of the fifth three-day international gathering here in Cashel.

I am often asked to explain why I chose 7th century Cashel as the basic setting for my historical crime series. History apart, I can understand such curiosity, especially when my writing name is "Peter Tremayne" (albeit a good Celtic Cornish name chosen because I lived in Cornwall) and they realise that I was born in Coventry, Warwickshire, and raised mainly in Sussex in England, and that I eventually chose London as my main home.

It is not a complicated story. My father was born and raised in Cork City and started his writing career there on the *Examiner* newspaper. He wound up in London and met my mother, who was from an old South Saxon (Sussex) family. Maybe some future literary commentator will claim that I must see myself as little Alchú, with my parents being a sort of reversal of Fidelma and Eadulf. Not so, but I wish them joy of such speculations. It's all good literary fun.

But let me explain something about my family background(s), as it might make it easier to understand the affinity I have with the ancient kingdom of Muman, the modern province of Munster. The first of my family to arrive in Munster were Breton merchants. The name was then spelt Elys. In 1297 it is recorded that Ricardus Elys held land called Elystoun in the Awbeg Valley, in North County Cork. The name in Irish is Baile Ellis (anglicised as Ballyellis), and townlands were marked as such on the maps. (see "The Ellis Family of Millstreet" in *Millstreet: A 'Considerable Town*; Aubane Historical Society, 2003).

Ballyellis House still stands between Buttevant and Doneraile. The house was built in 1800 by James Barry, whose brother John had married Margaret Ellis in 1772 and she seemed to have had some influence over the house.

The Ellis family did their part in fighting against the Tudor Conquest. There is a reference to "Roger" (Ruaridh) Ellis being pardoned in 1586 as one of 79 men commanded by Donal MacCarthy. He had to leave the Awbeg Valley and live in Castlemaine, and the lands were given to the English adventurer and poet Edmund Spenser (of *The Faerie Queen* fame). But Ruaridh was soon back and helping the O'Sheas attack and burn Edmund Spenser's Kilcolman Castle in 1598. He subsequently fought under Donal MacCarthy and Eóghan MacRory O'More at the Earl of Essex's defeat at Bearna na Cleitidhe (Pass of Plumes), near Portlaoise, in the following year.

Even after the eventual defeat of the Irish forces, we find Ruaridh's son fighting as a "privateer" (a "pirate" in English records) under letters cachet from the Duke of Medici of Florence. He is referred to in records from 1607 to 1627 as captain of the *Tonn Cliodhna* (Cleena's Wave, one of the great mythological waves of Ireland associated with Munster), a ship he harboured in Leamconn (a sheltered harbour on the Mizen Head peninsula, Cork). His ship certainly did not fly the "skull and crossbones," but the flag of Munster, which was the banner of the former Eóghanacht kings and princes. (see "Tonn Cliodhna – The Cork Privateer," *The Holly Bough*, Cork, December 2009).

My branch of the family moved into Cork City in the early 19th century, when William Ellis (1807-1852) established the family there in 1832. A stonecutter, he was very much political, a chip off the old Ellis rebellious block, being a member of the Cork Citizens' Club, supporting Young Ireland's 1848 uprising. His son, Nicholas, joined the IRB, went to the USA and fought in the Civil War in the 20th Kentucky Volunteer Infantry, took part in the Fenian incursion into British North America in 1866, returned home to take part in the 1867 uprising, and was at the action at Ballyknockane. His brother, David, was the ancestor of my direct branch. Politics ran in the family, as Nicholas' son was another William (1873-1951) who was elected to Cork City Corporation in 1916 and became Deputy and Acting Lord Mayor in 1922/24 when Lord Mayor Donal Óg O'Callaghan had to go into hiding. Even my father was an unwilling guest of HM King George V for writing "subversive literature."

My father, a journalist and short story writer, who started his career on the *Cork Examiner* and was an eyewitness to the burning of Cork City in 1920 (see *The Burning of Cork* by Gerry White and Brendan O'Shea, Mercier Press), eventually wound up in Fleet Street, London, when it

WHY CASHEL?

was then a centre of newspaper and magazine publishing.

My mother was working in the West End theatre as a wardrobe mistress with the Matheson Lang Repertory Company. She was from an old family, well known in mid-Sussex, who traced an unbroken line for eleven generations. She wrote a memoir of the early years of her life with some details of the family in *Daisy: Growing Up in a Sussex Village 1897-1919* (published by the Hurst History Study Group). The interesting thing was that her mother, my maternal grandmother, was from a family of Breton exiles, du Lac (then anglicised as DuLake); a Celtic connection again among the Saxons.

I was the only one of my siblings not to have been born in London by the simple the fact that my father, then being a freelance journalist, also volunteered to do some war work. That meant we were in Coventry for most of 1943, and I just happened to arrive in the world at that time.

It was my father who introduced me to Cashel as being the ancient capital of the Munster Kings. As a child, I heard him tell the tales of those Eóghanacht kings, and also the ancient myths of the gods and goddesses, the heroes and heroines, which surround this ancient place. For reasons I can't recall, we usually stayed during vacations in Clonmel, south of Cashel, rather than in Cashel itself.

But ancient legends and history are all around you. South from Cashel to Clonmel you are on the ancient Plain of Femen, where the deities of the Gaels roamed, fought, and loved in the time before time. Look south to Sliabh na mBan (Slievenamon), which you will see when you go on the outing to Coolmore Stud. This is where the Bodh Derg lived, the son of the Good God, "The Dagda." When the gods and goddesses were defeated and driven underground, Bodh Derg became their leader.

They were driven into dwellings under the hills; the *sidh*, the word originally meant hill, and from deities they were denigrated by Christianity to the role of fairies. Even the great god of arts and crafts, Lugh Lamhfada, became known as *Lugh-chromain* (little stooping Lugh), which eventually became Anglicised as leprechaun, a fairy craftsman. No wonder people claim to hear the wail of the banshee – *bean* (woman) *sidh* (now the word for fairies).

It was to the Sidh ar Femen that Midir the Proud fled for sanctuary with the beautiful Étain Echraidhe, with whom he had fallen in love. Midir the Proud was the god who had a mystical cauldron of life, one of the great treasures of the gods, which provided abundance and restored people to life. This Celtic myth is probably the origin of the

Holy Grail motif.

It was here that Fionn Mac Cumhail (Finn MacCool), the great warrior and leader of Fianna Éireann, bodyguards to the High King, became enchanted. Near here Oengus Óg, the god of youth, beauty, and love, found his love, the beautiful Cáer, and they were transformed into swans.

Perhaps it was because of these mythological stories that Eógan Mór founded his royal dynasty at Cnoc Rafann (Knockgraffon), on the Plain of Femen, before his descendant, Conall Corc mac Luigthig, transferred the Eóghanacht capital to Cashel, overlooking the plain.

Seeing the actual places associated with the stories was so much more exciting than just hearing or reading the stories. I fell in love with the countryside. It was doubtless the spur which made me take my first class honours and a master's degree in Celtic Studies.

I often visited Cashel gathering material. One of the good "sources" of interesting information was Pádraig Ó Mathúna, a great silversmith and artist. Dorothy and I used to visit his studio and shop, chatting with him and his wife Siobhán. They had both been pharmacists by training, and, after qualification in Dublin, returned here to Cashel to open a pharmacy. But a deep an abiding fascination with ancient Irish metalwork lured Pádraig into the world of art. His talent soon became obvious. His work is now highly prized.

In 1990 crime hit Cashel. The Mayor's chain of office was stolen. Unfortunately, Fidelma wasn't around to solve the mystery at that time. The outcome was that Pádraig was commissioned to create a new silver chain, and the Mayor was presented with it in 1992. Pádraig also created the Seán Ó Riada (1931-1971) gold medal, created in memory of the great Irish composer who was the single most influential figure in the revival of Irish traditional music. Pádraig made some silver jewellery for my wife.

Pádraig and Siobhán were both walking encyclopaedias of the area, and we were surprised when they decided to move to Kerry and open a studio in Dingle (Daingean, meaning a fortress). As they preferred to express themselves in the Irish language (and, of course, Dingle is a Gaeltacht area where the first language remains Irish), we presumed that they wanted to retire to an Irish language environment.

The Féile Fidema 2012 had a sad ending. Dorothy and I attended the lying in for Pádraig's wife, Siobhán. She had died and was brought back to Cashel for internment. However, the last I heard, Pádraig, at

WHY CASHEL?

the age of 94, remains hale and hearty in Dingle, where his studio still thrives, and the work is carried on by his daughter.

Another great source of local information was Eileen Noonan. In 1995 we took some French friends to stay at her guesthouse on Palmershill. This is Hill House, a house which dates back to 1710, and where, over the years, many Féile attendees stay. Eileen died in November 1999, and Hill House is now owned and run by Carmel Purcell. Carmel has made it one of Cashel's highly recommended B&Bs.

Eileen Noonan was a fount of knowledge, even though she was originally from Princes Street, Cork City, not far away from where my father was born and raised. She was the widow of Dr T. (Tim) J. Noonan (1921-1975), who was a well-known surgeon at the Cashel Hospital. He had graduated in medicine from University College, Cork, and left Ireland to work in Nigeria in 1946. He spent some years there helping the poor and impoverished. He was well respected in his profession and published several papers in *The Lancet* between 1950 and 1964. When he died, a "Surgeon Noonan Society" was formed in 1977 to help fund medical professionals and medicines going to Africa.

When he returned to Ireland, he married Eileen Cronin in 1951. They had seven children and moved into Hill House when Dr Noonan began to work at the Cashel Hospital.

When the Cashel Lions Club was founded in February 1961, it was Dr Noonan who was elected as the first president, serving 1961-62 and again in 1962-63. While I mention this, I feel I must also mention that our dashing master of ceremonies, Séamus J. King, was also president of the Cashel Lions Club several times – 1975-76, 1987-88, and 2010 through to 2012. Interestingly, the inaugural dinner of the club in 1961 was held at the Cahir House Hotel and not in Cashel. I often wondered why? True, Dorothy and I have often enjoyed a dinner in the Cahir House Hotel, which stands on the square in Cahir, a location overlooked by Cahir Castle. For the film and TV buffs among you, it's worth a visit as one of the locations of "Excalibur" and "The Tudors."

More importantly, an Eóghanacht fort stood in the 3rd century where the castle now stands (hence the place name *Cathair* means "stone fort"). This was replaced by a castle built by Conor O'Brien, Prince of Thomond in 1142 just before the Norman invasion. The irony of having Cahir as a location for "The Tudors" is that in 1599 the Earl of Essex besieged it and used artillery to smash its walls and caused its surrender after two months of siege. It was, of course, one of the few victories

Essex could claim for his Tudor monarchs, and when he returned to England a not very grateful Tudor, Elizabeth I, had him executed. Fifty years later the castle surrendered to the Cromwellian forces without a shot being fired. Indeed, the articles of surrender to the Cromwellian army were signed there in 1652.

Nearby is Knockgraffon (Cnoc Rafann – Rafainn's Hill), the site of an early earthwork, standing 60 feet high, which was the place that the Eóghanacht Kings, Fidelma's own family, were said to have been inaugurated before they moved their capital to Cashel in the 4th century. And it was in the nearby ruins of a medieval church that the great Irish historian Seathrún Céitinn, DD (Geoffrey Keating, c.1570-1650) is said to have preached a sermon against the Earl of Inchiquin (Murrough O'Brien of the Burnings), who decided to join the Cromwellian forces. In 1647 Inchiquin and his force approached Cashel and demanded its surrender. The town refused, and 3,000 of its inhabitants were slaughtered. Those survivors who sought sanctuary in the cathedral on The Rock fared no better. Inchiquin ordered his men to fire through the windows before breaking in and finishing the butchery with pile and sword. Céitinn's denouncing of the O'Brien, whose ancestor was the first to surrender his title to Henry VIII and accept an English earldom, caused him to flee into hiding in the caves of the Glen of Aherlow. Céitinn's famous *Foras Feasa ar Éirinn* is one of the Irish language classic histories and said to have been completed some time before 1634.

The great Glen of Aherlow, as many of you know, has featured in the Fidelma stories, particularly in *A Prayer for the Damned*, as well as *The Devil's Seal*. The characters in my books are based on historical reference. Three Saxon brothers – Berrihert, Pecanum, and Naovan – and their father, left England after the Synod of Whitby preferring to stay with Celtic Church usage rather than the Roman Church. They settled in Aherlow. And if you go exploring you will actually find St. Berrihert's Kyle and nearby St Berrihert's Well in the community of Ardane. There is a pilgrimage to these places. The parish priest at Banshea will be able to advise you on locations and pilgrimages.

It was during one of my youthful trips that I was taken to Emly (Imleach Iubhair – the borderland of yew-trees), eight miles west from the town of Tipperary, or Tiobraid Arann (or Ara's Well), both of which feature prominently in the Fidelma series, starting with *The Monk Who Vanished*. Abbot Ségdae of Imleach is, of course, also chief bishop and adviser to Fidelma's brother King Colgú and often appears in the

WHY CASHEL?

stories. Imleach was founded by a pre-Patrician saint Ailbe and, as a matter of fact, the very day the 5th Féile Fidelma opens is his feastday, so let us hope he looks kindly on the gathering. A "Life of Ailbe" has survived and has been edited in *Vitae Sanctorum Hiberniae*, edited by C. Plummer (1910).

The Abbey of Imleach (Emly) was replaced by a cathedral in the 13th century. It remained a "Cathedral City" until 1587, the principal ecclesiastical See of Munster before being combined with the See of Cashel. In the early centuries Imleach was considered just as influential as Armagh, and it was not until the 11th century that the High King Brian Ború acknowledged Armagh as the primacy of Ireland. The cathedral and its buildings at Emly were destroyed in 1607 at the end of the Tudor Wars of Conquest. The modern Catholic Church was built in 1882, but there is little to see of its early glory apart from an ancient weather stone cross in the graveyard said to mark St Ailbe's grave, and there is a holy well called St Ailbe's Well. However, the new church does have some fine stained glass windows, one of which commemorates the famous Eóghanacht King-Bishop of Cashel, Cormac Mac Cuileanáin (AD 836-908), poet, writer, and lexicographer – author of the first surviving Irish dictionary.

The outing organised during the very first Féile Fidelma was a coach trip to Emly, and we returned through the spectacular Glen of Aherlow.

I suppose in dwelling on visits to Cashel I should not neglect to mention the most amazing character one found there in the 1990s. For many, however, the memories are bitter ones. The man was called Terence McCarthy, who claimed to be 51st generation in unbroken male line from King Eóghan Mór of Cashel. He styled himself The MacCarthy Mór, Prince of Desmond.

Now, of course, meeting such a person, albeit one who was very personable and persuasive, in The Cashel Palace, one was immediately suspicious. But after checking, and there was a powerful entry in *Debrett's* – the guide to the titled – I found that the Irish Genealogical Office had confirmed his arms in 1979, accepted his genealogy in 1980, and the Chief Herald of Ireland had given "courtesy recognition" to his titles. Even further, in 1995, the Deputy Prime Minister and Minister of Foreign Affairs had approved these titles to be inserted on his Irish passport. That being so, many foreign heraldic jurisdictions had almost rushed to accord him recognition. He was fêted at receptions given by the then-President of Ireland, Mary Robinson, at Áras an Uachtaráin, the Presidential residence at Phoenix Park, and was guest when she visited The Rock. Faced by that evidence and accepting that the Chief Herald of Ireland and the Irish Genealogical Office knew their business, I accepted the man was genuine. He wasn't.

Two things would come back to bite me because of this. In 1997 I dedicated the fifth Sister Fidelma novel to him – *The Spider's Web*. Whatever else, the man had an excellent library of books on the history of the Eóghanacht. Unfortunately, in spite of my pleas to remove that embarrassing dedication, the books often still appear with my acceptance of his claim.

What was worse, for my academic reputation, I had been working on a non-fiction study of the survivors of the old, titled Gaelic families of Ireland who were recognised by the Irish State. Naturally, a recognised descendant of the Eóghanacht Kings of Munster would feature prominently in such a study. So, *Erin's Blood Royal: The Gaelic Noble Dynasties of Ireland* was published by Constable of London in 1999. The book was in print and about to be distributed when the new Chief Herald of Ireland made the shocking announcement that Terence McCarthy's pedigree was "without genealogical integrity." The man was a fraud.

I was invited to the Chief Herald's office in Dublin and shown the evidence. Giving a quick glance at the files, I could see that any competent historian would have spotted the errors. I could not believe the files that I had been shown would have induced any competent genealogist to have made such recognitions as the Genealogical Office had done. He was from West Belfast, who had taken his degrees in Irish history and heraldry and decided to put his knowledge to use in this amazing scam. I immediately asked my publishers to withdraw my book and I published a statement. Several copies of the book, however, had already been distributed.

Palgrave, a New York publisher, was about to issue the book, but I managed to stop the publication. As they were keen to issue it, I agree to revise the work, spending a couple of years' research and writing a chapter on the McCarthy imposture, and added an introduction to explain why the book had to be rewritten which I entitled "The Man Who Would Be Prince." It was published in March 2002.

The imposture of this man, the details of which are now in the Palgrave, 2002, edition of my book, had a far-reaching effect on many people in many parts of the world, and not just Ireland. At Irish Government level it caused the Irish State to change its practices of "courtesy recognition." Other people sought legal advice to bring actions, but McCarthy had sold his Georgian house and fled his "Munster kingdom" for Tangiers. A large number of people lost considerable amounts of money through the deception (the Director of the Fidelma Society among them). Terence McCarthy is not one of Cashel's most favoured personalities, but certainly he is one that finds a unique place in the modern histories of the town. He has provided a subject of conversation for many in Cashel for over a decade.

During my research in Cashel, I have fond memories of the Bolton Library. This started life as a unique collection of antiquarian manuscripts and books made by Theophilus Bolton, Archbishop of Cashel from 1730 to 1744, whose home is now The Cashel Palace Hotel. The library was originally housed in "The Long Room," which is the room where the talks are given at the Féile Fidelma. Unfortunately, English troops were quartered in this room while putting down the Irish insurrection of 1798 and much damage was done to the collection.

Eventually it was moved to the Chapel House of the Cashel Cathedral in John Street. The library had works from the 12th century, the Nuremburg Chronicle among other things. More importantly, it contained the earliest surviving Irish musical notation and treatise on music written in 1168 before the arrival of the Normans. There were other 16th and 17th century musical manuscripts which were noticed in on an essay "The Musical Books of the Cashel Diocesan Library" by a former Dean R. Wyse Jackson.

The Bolton Library has now been purchased by the University of Limerick, who, sadly, has deemed the Chapter House is no longer a suitable place, and it is removing it to the university library. Of course, one understands the concerns, but the loss to

The Bolton Library, GPA, originally created as the Chapel House situated in the grounds of the Cashel Cathedral Church in John Street, Cashel. Photograph: Patrick Comerford

Cashel and the attraction it holds for scholars will be immense. It is apposite that this Féile will be address by Dr Ann Buckley on ancient music in a place where held the oldest Irish musical manuscript book and one written in Cashel.

The library also has the early editions of Dante, Erasmus, Machiavelli, Calvin, Swift, and others.

In 2010 some Féile attendees remained in Cashel on the Monday following the weekend events and were keen to see some of the treasures of the Bolton Library. But the library was closed on that particular day. I was honoured when Dean Philip Knowles, who was also the curator, allowed me to show the group around, with his assistant, Laura, opening library for us.

My "formal association" with Cashel, if that is the correct phrase, actually started in June 1997. I had been asked by Mary Mulvey, who ran the Cashel Heritage Centre, to give a talk about the Sister Fidelma Mysteries in the Cashel Palace Hotel. The fifth title in the series, *The Spider's Web*, had just appeared. *The Monk Who Vanished* (1999) carried a dedication to Mary and her staff. Mary is now CEO of Greenbox (Responsible Tourism Ltd), which is developing Ireland's first integrated eco-tourism.

I was reminded of this event while I was looking for a reference the other day and found a report of the event in *Red Herrings*, the Bulletin of the Crime Writers Association, September 1997, issue No 49. "This was the first *official* introduction of the Fidelma stories to Cashel, and the event was very successful, organised by the Cashel Heritage and Development Trust Ltd." I am now wondering who sent the report to the journal.

In 2003 a Cashel Arts Fest was established, and the first festival had been opened by Seán Donlon, a former Irish Ambassador to Washington, and Chancellor of the University of Limerick. So, in 2004, I was amazed and flattered when I received a letter from Séamus J, King, representing the Cashel Arts Fest committee, asking me if I would open the second Cashel Festival. Séamus had become an enthusiast of the Sister Fidelma Mysteries. I opened the festival on Thursday, November 11, in the Cashel Palace.

On the Friday there came a big surprise – I was invited to the Town Council Chamber and found that the Mayor and Town Council had unanimously voted me a civic reception and presentation. The Mayor, Councillor Tom Wood, did the honours while Councillor Maureen O'Donoghue presented a bouquet to my wife, Dorothy.

From the Town Hall it was a dash up to Vicars Choral on The Rock

WHY CASHEL?

where I gave a talk about the Fidelma books and their inspiration. It was at the end of that talk, after judging the enthusiastic response, that Séamus then proposed the Cashel Arts committee should examine the idea of organising an event for enthusiasts of the series who wanted to come to Cashel and see the Fidelma's "hometown."

The next morning I had to take a creative writing workshop, and there were also interviews to be done. I was also privileged to meet Professor Marie Kai of Tokyo, who became the translator of the Fidelma titles in Japanese, as well as Dr John Scaggs (then of Limerick University but now Professor of English at Southwestern College, Chula Vista, California), who has written several articles on the Fidelma series.

Within a short time following that visit, the Cashel Arts Fest committee contacted David Robert Wooten of The International Sister Fidelma Society. The result? The first Féile Fidelma was held here at the Cashel Palace hotel from September 8 -10, 2006. It was opened by the Mayor Councillor Paddy Downey, assisted by Councillor John Fahey of the South Tipperary County Council, John Murray, the chair of the Cashel Arts Fest, and, of course, Séamus J, King. There was a pretty powerful array of speakers – Dr Scaggs on "The Impact of Sister Fidelma in Irish Crime Fiction." Talks on aspects of the books were given by Dr Andrew Breeze of Navarra in Pamplona, Spain; Dr Dan McCarthy of Trinity College, Dublin; Professor Máirín Ní Dhonnchadha of National University of Ireland, Galway; Hans van den Boom of de Leeskamer, Fidelma's Dutch publisher, who has since been such a great supporter of the Féile, and, of course, without whom... David Robert Wooten of the International Sister Fidelma Society. Liam ó Duibhir conducted the coach tour to Emly.

That first event was amazing.

And, as an addition, I seemed to have put down another footprint in Cashel, for Olivia Quinlan of the Cashel Heritage Centre had refurbished a guest house on John Street, opposite Cashel Palace, and with my permission called it **The Bruden Fidelma: The Sister Fidelma Guesthouse**, with its rooms named and decorated in keeping with the characters and books. I was invited to cut the ribbon to officially open the guesthouse.

It was such an exciting occasion that I thought 2006 was a year which could not be repeated.

The Cashel Arts Fest committee have proved me wrong. Here we are, 2014, and this is the 5th biannual gathering of enthusiasts in Cashel. A decade has gone by since the Cashel Arts Fest first proposed the idea

WHY CASHEL?

of this three-day gathering in Fidelma's "hometown."

This chronicler of Fidelma's adventures might not be a native of this place, but I hope, in my recording some of my memories of my association with the ancient Eóghanacht capital, I might indicate why it is a special place for me, and a town whose fortunes – past and present – are firmly connected with my life. So, welcome to Cashel of the Kings, to Fidelma's "hometown," and may you all take away with you some of the atmospheric magic of the place. *Dia ar gach bother a rachaidh sibh.*

– Peter Tremayne
From a talk at the 2014 Féile Fidelma

THE SISTER FIDELMA COMPENDIUM

historic Cashel

Ancient capital of the kingdom of Munster, *Caiseal na Rí*, Cashel of the Kings has provided some of the High Kings of Ireland and, on the Rock of Cashel, St Patrick came in the 5th century to baptise the first Eóghanacht king to become a Christian – Óenghus mac Nad Froích.

I take pride in the fact that the Sister Fidelma books are now playing some small part in attracting visitors from many corners of the world and honoured that the books have become a footnote in the long literary history of this ancient town.

Cashel has a literary tradition stretching back to the 5th century. In fact, if we were inclined to boast, we could claim a tradition of well over two thousand, perhaps three thousand years. It has been postulated that the great *forsundud*, the praise poems composed for the Eóghanacht Kings of Cashel, acknowledged as the earliest known Irish poetry because they were first set down in written form in the 5th century AD, were clearly the product of many previous centuries of an oral tradition stretching back to the start of the first millennium Before Christ.

The tale of *Senchas Fagbála Caisil*, "The Story of the Finding of Cashel," is one of the earliest stories that has its provenance here. The Myles Dillon (1900-1972), a scholar I greatly admired, translated and edited one of the best translations and studies of the earliest versions of this story, published in *Ériu*, No XVI (1952). He agreed with a tradition that this saga was first written down by Torna Eigeas the Learned, a scribe who flourished here in the early 5th century. Several of Torna's poems also survive in the *Leabhar na hUidre,* the Book of the Dun Cow. Torna was of the Ciarraigh Lucachra (modern Kerry) and is said to have educated both the Eóghanacht King Conall Corc as well as the famous High King, Niall of the Nine Hostages, progenitor of the Uí Néill dynasty, who died in the early 5th century. Torna acted as an envoy between the High King and King Conall.

"The Story of 'the Finding of Cashel' is about two wandering swineherds who bring their herd of pigs to graze on the Rock of Cashel. As the pigs are grazing, they lay down and, we are told, sleep came upon them, there on the Rock. They slept for three days and three nights. One presumes that they were either very tired or very lazy fellows. One of them, Duirdren, had a vision of a great Yew Tree growing on top of the Rock and of the angel Victor declaring that the Munster noble, Conall Corc, a claimant to the kingship of Munster, should settle there when he would become successful in achieving the kingship and that Cashel would then become blessed as the great capital of the kingdom.

Conall established his fortress on the Rock, making it the centre of his Eóghanacht dynasty that then ruled Munster, with a few violent interruptions from the O'Briens (the Dál gCais), until the Treaty of Glanmire in 1118. It was then that Munster was partitioned into the kingdoms of Thomond (*Tuathmhumhain* – north Munster) and Desmond *(Deasmhumhain* – south Munster). Even afterwards that date, the MacCarthy branch of the Eóghanacht dynasty continued to rule Desmond until the Elizabethan conquests while the O'Briens ruled in Thomond.

The Kings of Muman (Munster) at Cashel
from Conall Corc to Colgú

- **Conall Corca mac Lugaidh** (founded Cashel c. AD 370), *son of Lugaidh mac Ailill Flann Bec*

- **Nad Froích ma Cuirc**, *son of Corc mac Lugaidh*

- **Óenghus mac Nad Froích**, d. AD 492, *son of Nad Froích mac Cuirc*

- **Dauí Iarlaithe mac Maithini**

- **Eochaidh mac Óenghus** (Óengusso) d. AD 523, *son of Óenghus mac Nad Froích*

- **Feidlimid mac Óenghus**, *son of Óenghus mac Nad Froích*

- **Dubh-Gilcach mac Óenghus**, *son of Óenghus mac Nad Froích*

- **Crimthann Srem mac Echdach** d. AD 551, *son of Eochaidh mac Óenghus*

- **Cairpre Cromm mac Crimthann** d. AD 579, *son of Crimthann Srem mac Echdach*

- **Fergus Scannal mac Crimthann Airthir Chliach** d. AD 583, *son of Crimthann Srem mac Echdach*

- **Feidlimid mac Cairpre**, *(possible) son of Cairpre Cromm mac Crimthann*

- **Feidlimid mac Tighernaig** d. AD 592, *son of Tighernaig mac Áedh*
- **Amalgaid mac Éndai**, *son of Éndai*
- **Garbán mac Éndai**, *son of Éndai*
- **Fingen mac Áedo Duibh** d. AD 619, *son of Áedo Duibh*
- **Áed Bennán mac Crimthainn** d. AD 621, *son of Crimthainn mac Cobhtach*
- **Cathal mac Áedo Flaind Chathrach** d. AD 628, *son of Áed Fland Cath*
- **Failbe Flann mac Áedo Dibh** s. AD 637, *son of Áedo Dibh*
- **Cuán mac Amalgaid** d. AD 641, *son of Amalgaid mac Éndai*
- **Máenach mac Fingen** d. AD 662, *son of Fíngen mac Áedo Duib and Mór Muman*
- **Cathal Cú-cen-máthair mac Cathail** d. AD 665/6, *son of Cathal mac Áedo*
- **Colgú mac Failbe Flann** d. AD 678, **brother of Fidelma**, *son of Faílbe Flann mac Áedo Dibh*

By the way, it fell to the descendants of the swineherd Duirdren to pronounce the blessing every year upon each king who succeeded to the throne of Cashel, for which service they received seven *cumals*, the equivalent value of 21 cows, each year. Not a bad income for just having a nap and a weird dream.

Some 531 years before John Bunyan penned his allegory *Pilgrim's Progress* (1678), Cashel had produced it own allegory of a journey to the Christian Otherworld. We can argue that it was the very first European best seller! The author was a monk named Marcus. Marcus left Cashel to join Gilchrist MacCarrthaig, the abbot of Regensburg in Bavaria. Gilchrist was cousin of the King Cormac Mac Carrthaig (AD 1124-1138), who had Cormac's Chapel built on The Rock. Monks from Cashel founded the abbey at Regensburg, and it became one of the most famous Irish monastic foundations in Europe. Its great library is still housed in the Vienna Schottenkloster Archives. There is a whole archive of manuscript books from the medieval period there that has still not been catalogue let alone identified or translated. They are simply classed as `Mumonia' (Munster) archives.

Brother Marcus of Cashel went to Regensberg and while he was there, in 1149, he wrote a saga in Latin called *The Vision of Tnugdal*. It is now regarded as one of the great medieval vision tales of the Christian Otherworld. Tnugdal is a warrior from Cashel who, after dining rather well with some friends in Cork, falls into a deep sleep. In this sleep he journeys on a quest to the Otherworld. There are 154 Latin manuscript copies of this book that still survive from the period and a further 100 copies in all the major European languages including, of course, Irish. This shows you how popular that story was.

Almost at the same time, somewhere between 1127 and 1138, another scribe, working here in Cashel, was writing a fascinating bloodthirsty saga entitled *Caithreim Cheallachain Chaisil* – `The battle career of Ceallachain of Cashel." King Ceallachain, who died in 954, was the Eóghanacht Cashel king who drove the Vikings out of Munster in the 10th century before the High King Brían Ború broke their power in all-Ireland at Clontarf in 1014. This is a full-blooded saga – war, romance, betrayal – it has it all. The only English translation that I have seen available was a translation published in 1905 by the University of Christiana in Denmark.

These tales could well be claimed as the forerunners of modern popular literature.

Even so, we've hardly scratched the surface of Cashel's literary output. Cormac mac Cuileannain, was born here in 836 and became both King and Bishop of Cashel. He was responsible for the compilation known as The *Psalter of Cashel*, which is regarded as a lost work but surviving because so many other writers have quoted extensively from it. It was a work containing the early genealogies of the noble Gaelic families. Cormac was also responsible for *Lebor na gCeart* or the Book of Rights of the Kings, and, of course, the famous *Sanas Chormaic*, Cormac's Glossary, the first known major dictionary of the Irish Language. And if that wasn't enough Cormac's lyric verses also survive in The *Lebor na Nuachonghbhála* or Book of Leinster. Cormac was killed in battle in Kildare in AD 908. He was a man who captured the imagination of many other writers and many poems were composed about him for centuries after his death.

Of course, speaking of Cormac, one should mention his poetess wife Gormflaith (AD 870-919), daughter of Flann Sionna, a High King of Ireland. Her poetry has also survived. The scholar Osbourne Bergin

(1872-1950), a Cork man, made the first edition of her poems generally known in a collection published in 1912.

Even the earliest surviving treatise on music in the Irish language, written in 1168, was penned here in Cashel. This is housed in the Bolton Library, which is well worth a visit. Theophilus Bolton, who was Archbishop of Cashel in 1730, a friend of Jonathan Swift, the Dubliner who wrote *Gulliver's Travels* among other works, set up the library, donating 6,000 volumes from his own library. The volume in which the music text is contained also has other texts suggesting an encyclopaedia of mediaeval knowledge. Bolton Library houses a unique collection of antiquarian works, including the *Nuremburg Chronicle*, and works by Swift, Dante, Calvin, Erasmus and Machiavelli.

Literature, history, music, visual arts, and even architecture – Cashel was a centre for them. The medieval Romanesque style of architecture reached its greatest elaboration in the 12th century Cormac's Chapel on the Rock of Cashel, providing another major point for visitors. Cashel abounds in the richness of the arts. This was once a great intellectual centre for Ireland.

– Peter Tremayne
From a talk at a Féile Fidelma, updated for this volume

THE SISTER FIDELMA COMPENDIUM

Fidelma's Rock? Wait an *Ostint*, not Quite...
BY DAVID ROBERT WOOTEN

e've all seen – those of us who favor Fidelma – several (or dozens? or hundreds?) of various images of The Rock of Cashel, either online or in print. Indeed, The Rock ranks as one of Ireland's top landmarks, and thus appears in every coffee table book of "Beautiful Ireland" (the title may change, but the concept remains the same) that one might find in many a bookstore's shelves.

Further still, those lucky enough to have visited Cashel themselves instantly have that selfsame image of The Rock burned into their memories; when they first rounded a curve, from no matter what direction they might have come, the iconic silhouette of the buildings on that rugged outcropping rising from the plain, both beautiful and awe-inspiring. "There it is! There it is!"

And, to a woman or a man, those who voraciously consume the prose of Peter Tremayne's iconic 7th century sleuth, Sister Fidelma, have engrained in their minds that oddly-mixed cluster of structures as the setting for those murder mysteries *(see collage of The Rock, end of "Why Cashel?" chapter).* Why wouldn't they? That's all that's there is to see.

Mid-19th century drawing of the Rock of Cashel, County Tipperary, Ireland (showing geology of the limestone outcrop) by George Victor Du Noyer [Wikimedia Commons]

Unfortunately, that's all wrong; well, most of it.

"The Rock of Cashel," as it is called, in its current state (not of disrepair, but of buildings, towers, tombstones, and high crosses), looks almost nothing like the geographic/geological landscape anomaly which Fidelma "inhabited."

We can concede the "perimeter wall" which surrounds the property atop The Rock, as it most likely was present during Fidelma's time – but even those walls have most certainly been altered over the centuries, such that they are not the protective barrier in which Fidelma would have been ensconced during her stays/visits to see her brother Colgú, King of Muman, resident at The Rock (in fact, Peter tells us that Fidelma was actually born on The Rock). The very "chronology" of Cashel contradicts what one now sees atop that hillock, and what most presume has been there since "pre-Fidelma."

And the tour guides who would greet and walk you about the property – describing "St Patrick's Cross" (a story for another day), "Cormac's Chapel," The Hall of Vicars Choral, the Round Tower, the Tower House, and the great Gothic cathedral which now holds the place of prominence amongst all the rest, along with the numerous tombstones and crosses that mark those individuals buried atop The Rock – have little to no knowledge of what came before the Round Tower now standing (considered the first "modern" structure still standing, ca. 1100).

However, serious readers of the Sister Fidelma Mysteries, must first break out their "historical bulldozers" and raze everything in that iconic space, present in the 21st century, to the ground. From there, one can begin building a **LIKELY** picture of what ACTUALLY existed thereon prior to, during, and even after Fidelma's tenure.

Why emphasize LIKELY? As one of the primary historical landmarks in all of Ireland, surely there has been extensive archaeological work done at The Rock to discover everything that has ever been erected there – ever since two swineherds ostensibly "discovered" The Rock in the 4th century?

We have ground-penetrating radar for geophysical (geo-phys) surveys (some of which have actually been conducted around The Rock as of this writing). These were conducted by a two-time guest speaker at Féile Fidelmas, Dr Patrick Gleeson, currently a Lecturer in Archaeology at Newcastle University, who spoke to attendees on this very subject. Unfortunately these surveys have been very limited in scope, as allowed by the government. Geo-phys surveys can "bury" down many feet below ground level to find objects and foundations not visible at the surface.

Further still, one could employ LiDAR (an acronym for Light Detection and Ranging) to pulse the grounds in and around the hilltop

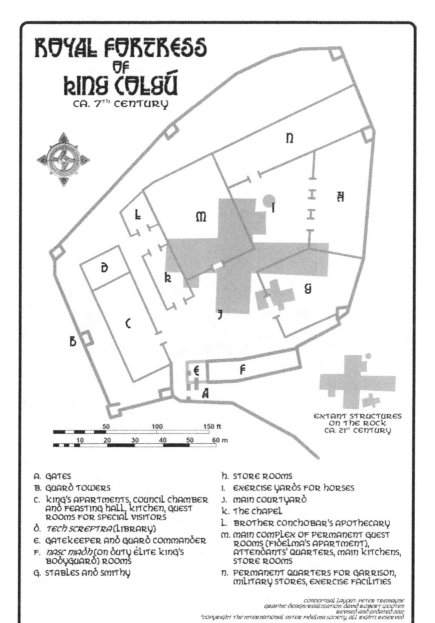

ROYAL FORTRESS
OF
KING COLGÚ
CA. 7th CENTURY

EXTANT STRUCTURES
ON THE ROCK
CA. 21st CENTURY

50	100	150 ft
10 20 30 40 50	60 m

A. GATES

B. GUARD TOWERS

C. KING'S APARTMENTS, COUNCIL CHAMBER
AND FEASTING HALL, KITCHEN, GUEST
ROOMS FOR SPECIAL VISITORS

D. *TECH SCREPTRA* (LIBRARY)

E. GATEKEEPER AND GUARD COMMANDER

F. *NASC NIADH* (ON DUTY ÉLITE KING'S
BODYGUARD) ROOMS

G. STABLES AND SMITHY

H. STORE ROOMS

I. EXERCISE YARDS FOR HORSES

J. MAIN COURTYARD

K. THE CHAPEL

L. BROTHER CONCHOBAR'S APOTHECARY

M. MAIN COMPLEX OF PERMANENT GUEST
ROOMS (FIDELMA'S APARTMENT),
ATTENDANTS' QUARTERS, MAIN KITCHENS,
STORE ROOMS

N. PERMANENT QUARTERS FOR GARRISON,
MILITARY STORES, EXERCISE FACILITIES

with lasers to see what cannot be seen with the naked human eye.

The conundrum with all of this modern technology is that it, as yet, cannot be employed on The Rock of Cashel. Peter Tremayne, in his "condensed" but thorough booklet *Sister Fidelma's Cashel: The Early Kings of Munster and Their Capital* (2008, The International Sister Fidelma Society), succinctly explained the issue at hand:

> *The problem with Cashel is that a proper and detailed archaeological survey of the site, looking beyond the ecclesiastical buildings, is not possible until it ceases to become a sanctified burial ground. So, we may never know if any traces of the ancient stone fortress, referred to as having been built in the time of Conall Corca, or, indeed, any other buildings pre-dating those that still stand, can be found.*

Aerial view of Rock of Cashel, circa 1970, prior to any modern work – Image source: Author David Lippincott for Chassis Plans *[Wikimedia Commons]*

Further still, what stands atop The Rock today is almost completely ecclesiastical in nature; the reader should understand that it was never built that way to begin with. Historical records, too numerable to mention here, confirm that this was the not only the residence of the High Kings of Muman, but their **FORTRESS** as well. As such it would have evoked a vastly different "aura" than the bucolic atmosphere it now belies.

How are we fairly certain of the fortress-nature of The Rock during Fidelma's time, given its intended function(s)? Peter says:

> *The Rock of Cashel is also referred to in texts as* Lios-na-laochru, *The Hill of Heroes, perhaps due to the band of élite warriors who served the Kings as bodyguards...*

These warriors, or Nasc Niadh as they were called:

> *...guarded the High King, [and were] said to have been formed ca. 300 BC by the High King Fiachadh, consisting of twenty-five battalions. Each provincial King had his warrior élite.*

The twenty-five battalions as described here would presuppose a very large force ensconced in and around the fortress that was The Rock of Cashel. According to Peter, "Fidelma's father [Failbe Flann, the 11th King to rule from Cashel] was certainly a warrior king, for he led his army in several battles." And, to further bolster the fortress nature of The Rock, as it was originally constructed, Peter notes "the interesting point, in studying the annals and chronicles, is that during the first two centuries that Cashel was the capital, there appeared no attacks on the powerful centre."

As Peter tells it:

> *It is difficult now to visualise the type of fortress that would have stood in Fidelma's time. We know from the early references that there was one built of stone. I have, in the Fidelma stories, envisaged its basis along the lines of such extant buildings as Staigue Fort, west of Sneem on the Ring of Kerry, whose walls still stand eighteen feet high and thirteen feet thick, enclosing a diameter of 88 feet. This is reckoned to be dated to at least 200 BC.*

The Rock of Cashel, Co Tipperary, Ireland, early 21st century (view from the southwest)

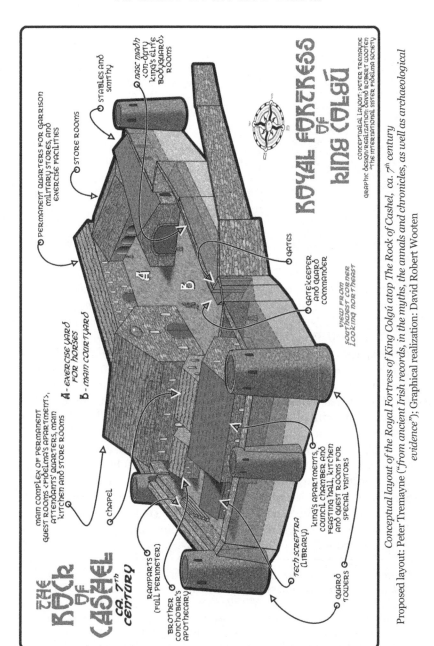

THE
ROCK
OF
CASHEL
CA. 7TH
CENTURY

ROYAL FORTRESS OF KING COLGÚ

main complex of permanent guest rooms <Fidelma's apartments, attendants' quarters, main kitchen and store rooms

RAMPARTS (full perimeter)

chapel

Brother conchobar's apothecary

tech screptra (library)

king's apartments, council chamber and feasting hall, kitchen and guest rooms for special visitors

GUARD TOWERS

A - exercise yard for horses
B - main courtyard

PERMANENT QUARTERS FOR GARRISON military stores, and exercise facilities

STORE ROOMS

STABLES and SMITHY

nasc madh <on-duty king's elite bodyguard> rooms

GATES

GATEKEEPER and GUARD COMMANDER

VIEW FROM SOUTHWEST CORNER LOOKING NORTHEAST

CONCEPTUAL LAYOUT: PETER TREMAYNE
GRAPHIC DESIGN/REALIZATION: DAVID ROBERT WOOTEN
—THE INTERNATIONAL SISTER FIDELMA SOCIETY

Conceptual layout of the Royal Fortress of King Colgú atop *The Rock of Cashel, ca. 7th century*
Proposed layout: Peter Tremayne (*"from ancient Irish records, in the myths, the annals and chronicles, as well as archaeological evidence"*); Graphical realization: David Robert Wooten

Peter Tremayne at the entrance to Staigue Fort (near Caherdaniel, built ca. 400 AD) showing closer detail on the dry stone construction employed

So, defaulting yet again to *Sister Fidelma's Cashel*, Peter notes:

Therefore, in the Fidelma books, I have had to allow a certain amount of imagination in describing the buildings of the royal residence and fortress of the King at Cashel.* However, I have used sources from ancient Irish records, in the myths, the annals and chronicles, as well as archaeological evidence, to reconstruct my idea of Cashel.

To this end, Peter advised, and I generated, a proposed "floorplan" for the space within the perimeter walls (p. 193), walls which, while likely greatly reduced in height since their original construction, still define the "borders" of what was constructed as a fortress. Most of the structures standing on The Rock during Fidelma's would have been of dry-stone construction, with pitched wooden rooftops. Some buildings may have reached as tall as (what we now would measure) two stories, or more.

A pause here to briefly mention a misconception actually promulgated by many "scholars" – that the Irish did not build stone forts until after the 12th century ("Know-Alls' Know Nothing," by the Editor, *The Brehon*, XI, No. 2, May 2012), post-Norman arrival. One such "statement of fact" in correspondence to the International Sister Fidelma Society: "In the 7th century, they would be building huts, stockades and chapels in wood."

---

* Peter will confirm that many is the time he has made such an "I'm just making an educated guess" statement about how he believed The Rock would have appeared during Fidelma's time. My response has always been the same, and one which I gleaned from a movie (and television) series for which both he and I have an affinity: "[I feel] safer about your guesses than most other people's facts."

FIDELMA'S ROCK? NOT QUITE...

While fortresses such as the one under discussion may not have had any true "peer" in 7th century Ireland, there are numerous examples of the dry-stone construction technique in use even prior to the 7th century (e.g. Staigue Fort), not only in defensive structures, but churches and other buildings (examples shown throughout).

In fact, in PW Joyce's *The Story of Ancient Irish Civilisation* (London, 1907), Chapter XIV, "How the Old Irish People Built and Arranged their Houses," he states:

Interior of Staigue Fort for scale, showing remaining stairs to ramparts

...although wood-building was general in Ireland before the twelfth century, it was not universal: for many stone churches... were erected from the time of the introduction of Christianity; beehive-shaped houses, as well as ushers and cashels, were built of stone, without mortar, from pre-historic times: and the remains of these primitive structures—churches, houses, and cahers—are still to be seen in many parts of Ireland. In all these mortarless buildings, the stones, though in their natural state—not hammered or chiselled into shape—are fitted to each other with great skill and accuracy: or, as Petrie expresses it, "with wonderful art."

Thus, no mere palisade of timbers surrounding The Rock, but truly impressive stone construction.

So, from the "conceptual" Royal Fortress of King Colgú, Peter surmises (and historical precedence points to the fact) that the walls surrounding the "mesa" of The Rock would have been much taller (and considerably thicker) than those now extant. A true fortress wall would not have a barrier short enough for a man to be able to overlook standing astride. Therefore, the conceptual fortress walls stand well above the existing stone "fence" now encircling the grounds. But if the walls were that tall, why are they so short now, and where did the material that "heightened" them go?

Once again, there is precedent for the "scavenging" of build-

The well-preserved Grianán of Aileach, which stands on on a high hill in Co. Donegal. Built by the northern Uí Néill about one hundred years before Fidelma's time. Legend has it that the Uí Neill's built their fortress on a more ancient site, claimed in myth as the home of The Dagda, father of the ancient gods of the Tuatha De Danaan. Certainly a centre here was known to Ptolemy in AD 120. A main road approached the fortress in ancient times.

ings no longer in use for building materials to be integrated into new construction (presumably in the growing town of Cashel itself). The same is likely the case with all the materials that would have been torn down after Muirchertach Mac Toirdelbach Mór Ua Briain donated the Royal Fortress on the Rock to the church in 1101.

Peter also notes the rather unusual "sloping" of the west side of the "tableau," believing that the portion of land where he envisions the location of the King's apartments (and Council chamber, feasting hall, etc.) would have actually been level with the higher foundation "slab" upon which the current Gothic cathedral sits; all buildings would have been roughly on the same plane. But if this is the case, why is there now a marked slope down to the west wall?

Again, Peter believes that this missing material may have actually been "quarried" for addition stone materials to build the town below. Thus, the original fortress wall on that side may have also been based on the same level, rather than "dropped down" as it now stands. It is acknowledged that the perimeter wall, as it stands in the 21st century, is a drastically reworked stone "fence" for the cathedral and its outbuildings, which would not have necessitated fortification-like, deep, multi-meter-high walls.

The "towers" shown in the recon-

"Fanciful portrait of Muirchertach" [Mac Toirdelbach Mór Ua Briain], King of Munster and self-proclaimed High King of Ireland – Image source: Wikipedia

struction graphic are problematic at best. They may have been round as shown, or they may have been square (as is usually envisaged when imagining a castle). Unfortunately, there remain no such similar structures in Ireland – of the period – to show precisely how such a fortress would have been laid out. The few forts that remain are the "ring style," as exemplified by Staigue and a handful of similar ruins.

The Gallarus Oratory, on the Dingle Peninsular, Co. Kerry, is a few miles east of Ballyferriter. Again, built using the dry stone method and dated back to Fidelma's time, one of the best examples of the corbel pattern of building applied to a sophisticated rectangular building with a west facing window at the rear.

Again, this is what goes back to the use of what I described as a "likely picture" of Fidelma's "stomping grounds," as we cannot as yet know for certain. Perhaps, one day soon...

And so, while we may still gaze in awe upon the vastly-revised Rock of Cashel as it exists today, Peter neatly closes out his *Sister Fidelma's Cashel* this way:

> *While the remains of the splendid ecclesiastical buildings on The Rock of Cashel visually overpower us, we must remember those who lived there before those buildings were erected.*

– David Robert Wooten
Written for this volume

Exterior of Staigue Fort, showing obvious signs of "scavenging" of stones from the structure over the centuries since its construction, until halted by the government.

THE SISTER FIDELMA COMPENDIUM

TREMAYNE IS NOT A ƉRUIƉ!

I am often puzzled by some of the things that have been said about Peter Tremayne in the guise of "facts." He once asked me to correct some biographical misinformation on the ever-changing Wikipedia. I have tried several times to place an accurate entry on that site, only to quickly have it rewritten by some "know nothing." I finally gave up; guess it was time to be philosophical.

Thankfully, the book I edited with Ed Rielly contains a biographical essay with correct details of Peter's career in it. I had been privileged to have Peter's cooperation in producing it. For those who want the footnote references, we run that on the Society website. Yet I have to say, the inaccuracies that still appear on various websites continue to surprise me, especially when I see them repeated by people who should know better. I refer particularly to some "wannabe" academics. I just wonder how they justify the spurious "facts?"

Needless to say, we all have our opinions, axes to grind and prejudice. That's fine. But opinion is one thing; statements of fact are another.

Some years ago, Anne Louise McKendry, doing post graduate work in Australia delivered a paper to a conference in the USA about Peter's work claiming, among other errors, that the Féile Fidelma, which she thought was organised by the International Sister Fidelma Society and not by Cashel Arts Festival, was a "pseudo academic gathering." You can imagine the affect that had on the many leading academics of Celtic and literary studies who have spoken at the Féile over the years. We wrote to her correcting those errors (and there were several) but we received no acknowledgement although the organiser of the conference was more accommodating.

One of the claims that sometimes appear on the internet is that Peter Tremayne is some sort of New Age Druid creating a fictional world which propagandises New Age Druid philosophies. Peter's opinion in reality is that Druids vanished when the Celtic civilization adopted Christianity. Those who propound this weird claim often believe that Peter makes up everything, including Brehon Law. They do not seem to realise that the Fidelma books are scrupulously based on the ancient Irish law system, reflecting the social system of the time and place. Peter has often given "chapter and verse," his references and where such information can be obtained.

One of the first to propound the idea that Peter was some kind New Age Druid was a Carole Cusack delivering a paper on the Sister Fidelma mysteries to what was supposed to be a Celtic Studies Conference in Sydney, Australia, five years ago. It turned out that Carole Cusack was then a student of religious studies.

It was not the only fact that she managed to get wrong in her very prejudiced account examining the Fidelma Mysteries. She implied Peter had no qualifications in Celtic Studies and wondered how he had very obtained Fellowships of The Royal Historical Society and Royal Society of Antiquaries of Ireland. The answer to that is simple – you have to be proposed, seconded and then elected by your academic peers. She added that he used the Fellowships to promote his fictional work to convince people of his "gravitas." If he had done so, why would he not also throw in his degrees in Celtic Studies? To my personal knowledge, he has never used his Fellowships in this way but, of course, he has no control over what others may claim when speaking about him and his work. Carole Cusack is a case to point.

The late Maurice McCann wrote a corrective to Carole Cusack in 2008 but that went unanswered and so we published it in *The Brehon*. Undeterred Carole Cusack published her ill-considered paper in a volume published by the University of Sydney Press, 2010 where she is now an associate professor in religious studies. As I said at the beginning, she is perfectly free to express opinions, but opinions are one thing; stating as fact things that are untrue to support those opinions is something else.

Peter himself follows the philosophy of Oscar Wilde: it doesn't matter what people say about him so long as they are talking about him.

However, I cannot help reflecting – how can people get away with writing such rubbish?

As "proof" that he is a Druid, some who follow this line refer to a photograph published of Peter clad in the robes of a Bard of the Cornish Gorsedd.

In 1987 he was approached by the council of the Cornish Gorsedd (Gorseth Kernow) asking him if he would accept the honour of bardship in recognition of his work on the Cornish language and culture.

The Cornish Gorsedd was founded in 1928 and exists to maintain the national spirit of Cornwall and to give expression to such spirit;

to encourage the study of Cornish history, the Cornish Language and to foster Cornish Literature, Art and music; to link Cornwall and the other Celtic countries, and to promote a spirit of peace and cooperation among those who work for the honour of Cornwall. It is free from any political or sectarian affinities. There are no "Druids" or "Ovates" in the Cornish Gorsedd; only "Bards."

Its sister organisations are, of course, the Welsh Gorsedd (founded 1792) and the Breton Gorsedd (1901). Invitation to accept a bardship is the equivalent of an honours system. There are no religious or political connotations in any of these organisations.

In 1974 Peter had published a study *The Cornish Language and its Literature* (Routledge Kegan Paul, London) which then became a standard work for Cornish Language Board examinations. In fact, he had first written about the language in *The Linguist* in 1967. This had excited some interest and the editor of *The Cornish Times* asked him to write a regular column on the history of the language which ran from June to December 1968. More academically, he had a paper published in *The Incorporated Linguist* (Journal of the Institute of Linguists) in 1971. That was the year that Tor Mark Press in Cornwall asked him to write a short pamphlet history *The Story of the Cornish Language* which they could sell to tourists. First published in 1971, it has been reprinted regularly ever since.

Peter once told me, in a tone of uncharacteristic commercial regret, that he had sold the copyright to the company. He admitted, however, the company had sent him a "sweetener" now and then because of the continued sales success of the pamphlet.

It was for this body of work that the Cornish Gorsedd asked if he would accept the honour of bardship.

So, on September 5, 1987, he was installed as "Gwas-an-Geltyon" (Servant of the Celts) by the Gorsedd. That did not make him a Druid. Indeed, he is not a Druid anymore than the former Archbishop of Canterbury, Dr Rowan Williams, the former head of the Anglican Church, is one having been made a Bard of the Welsh Gorsedd for his Welsh poetical works. Neither the former UK Prime Minister David Lloyd George, nor the actor Richard Burton ... nor even HM Queen of United Kingdom for that matter were transformed into New Age Druids because they received similar honours. Historians like the late Professor A.L. Rowse, Professor Charles Thomas and so on and many others, who have been given the honour for their contribution to Celtic arts and society, are certainly not New Age Druids.

When Peter later wrote his study of *The Druids*, published in the UK 1994, his UK publishers, thinking most people were more intelligent than they turned out to be, made the mistake of deciding to put a picture of Peter in bardic robes on the back of the hardcover edition. The ignorant who did not know what the Cornish Gorsedd, or indeed the Welsh or Breton Gorsedd were, leapt to the silly conclusion it was some esoteric New Age Druidic organisation.

Thankfully, his US publishers, Eerdmans, did not repeat that mistake. The book did become a bestseller, sold in many languages and in many history book clubs both in the UK and USA.

Peter tells me that the first edition with that photograph created a problem. He told me the following story: "During the many radio interviews I did at the time, I had grown use to some of the bright young media presenters asking me if I was a Druid? Usually, they accepted the explanation so that there was no embarrassment when "on air." However, I went into the LBC studios, the local London radio, to do a piece on "The Frank Bough Show." Unfortunately, Frank Bough, a tried and seasoned presenter was on holiday and so I was faced with a young, inexperienced Chris Mann. Before the "live" programme, I pointed out to his researcher (knowing the average presenter was too "grand" to even bother to look at the book they were discussing) that I was a scholar who had written a serious study on the subject. She assured me that she would particularly brief him on that point.

"I went into the studio. The presenter smiled and nodded absently, a sign from the studio manager and we went live. He brightly announced: "And now we have a real live Druid in the studio.' Aaaragh!!!"

Peter does not have much sympathy with those who have developed an entirely new religion based on the erroneous concepts and inventions of those 17th and 18th century "gentleman antiquaries." "People are free to believe what they like, but it is a pity modern "Druids" have taken the name of the intellectual caste of ancient Celtic society who became absorbed into the new social order brought in by Christianity. Modern day "Druids" bear little relationship to the Druids of the ancient Celts."

Peter is found of using a quote by a friend and colleague, Professor John Carey of University College, Cork, about such matters; "Myth is so much more certain than history. So people prefer the myth but I find the reality much more exciting."

For those who can be bothered to read his views on the reinvention

CREMAYNE IS NOT A DRUID!

of the Druids, they can read his book *The Druids*, chapter 9 entitled "Reviving the Druids." Indeed, even before that study he had made it clear in the epilogue of his *The Celtic Empire: The First Millennium of Celtic History* (Carolina Academic Press, 1990).

– *David Robert Wooten*
The Brehon, XII, 2, May 2013

THE SISTER FIDELMA COMPENDIUM

The Fascination for Sister Fidelma

Peter Tremayne tells Sarah Cuthbertson how his tales of a 7th century Irish lawyer and detective resonate around the world.

Peter Tremayne, pseudonym of Peter Berresford Ellis, was born in Coventry, Warwickshire, on March 10, 1943. His father, from Cork City, was a journalist and writer for the "pulps'. His mother, from an old Sussex family, worked in the London theatre and published a memoir about her childhood. Tremayne admits to a "peripatetic' education. Studying in London, he received a first-class honours degree in Celtic Studies and then a master's degree. However, he decided to follow his father into journalism. He started his career on a weekly newspaper in Brighton, became deputy editor of an Irish weekly newspaper and then editor of a London weekly book trade magazine. His first book, a history of Wales, was published in 1968. He became a full-time writer in 1975. He has guest lectured at universities in the UK, Ireland, Canada and the US etc.

He has received several honours for his work and is a Fellow of the Royal Historical Society, a Fellow of the Royal Society of Antiquaries of Ireland, and was recently made an Hon Life Member of the Irish Literary Society (founded by W B Yeats in 1891, and whose current president is the Nobel Laureate Seamus Heaney). Other honours include an *Irish Post* Award in 1987, inauguration as a Bard of the Gorsedd Kernow for his work on *The Cornish Language and its Literature* (Routledge, Kegan Paul, 1975); an Hon Life Membership of the London Association for Celtic Education (of which he was Chairman in 1989 and Vice-President 1990-1995) and Hon Life President of the Scottish 1820 Society, etc.

He has published 34 titles under his own name (mostly non-fiction but 2 are historical novels); 42 titles as Peter Tremayne and 8 novels as Peter MacAlan. Additionally, he has published 80 short stories, several academic papers and countless signed articles in newspapers and magazines. His work has appeared in nearly twenty different languages.

A new non-fiction work will be published on March 17 entitled *Eyewitness to Irish History* (John Wiley Inc).

The 14th in the Sister Fidelma series, *Whispers of the Dead*

THE SISTER FIDELMA COMPENDIUM

(Headline, hardback, March), is actually the second collection of Sister Fidelma short stories. The Fidelma series are also published in the USA and in nine other languages. Some of the stories have been broadcast on radio in Ireland and Canada.

Did you write fiction before Fidelma?
Yes: I wrote two historical novels under my own name, and I'd written many novels and short stories as "Peter Tremayne'. One of the historical novels under my own name, *The Rising of the Moon* (1987), reached number four on the Irish bestseller fiction lists for several weeks and was optioned for filming almost immediately. It was a story set against the famous Irish Republican Brotherhood's attempted invasion of Canada in 1866 – when 25,000 Irish veterans of the American Civil War tried to occupy part of Canada to force Britain to quit Ireland. It was this "invasion scare' that caused the provinces to unite as the Dominion of Canada in 1867. Alas, the option never reached the filming stage but for a while, in the later years, I was earning more from the option than from sales of the book. Most of the other fiction would be classed as fantasy based on themes from Celtic myths and legends together with a few thrillers.

Presumably, the Sister Fidelma mysteries arose from your studies of Celtic, specifically Irish, history and culture. Which particular aspect(s) gave rise to Fidelma?
I was lecturing at Toronto University on the subject of the role of women in the ancient Celtic world. This was back in the mid-1980s when Umberto Eco's *The Name of the Rose* had just been published in English translation but before the film was made. Also, Ellis Peters' Brother Cadfael books were becoming popular. After I had talked to the students about the role of women in Ireland, the ancient Irish law system, how women could be judges and lawyers and about the conflicts of the Irish, or what we now called the Celtic Church, and Rome, we adjourned across the campus to Dooley's Bar. One of the students, knowing that I wrote some fiction, said the subject of my lecture that day would make good background for a murder mystery in which the sleuth was a female Irish lawyer of the Celtic Church period. The idea was put to the back of my mind. In fact, I did write a non-fiction study, *Celtic Women: Women in Celtic Society and Literature* (Constable, 1995), which explored the matter from the academic viewpoint.

THE FASCINATION FOR SISTER FIDELMA

When did she first appear?
The first four Fidelma short stories were published in October 1993. Many years after that talk in Toronto, an old friend, the anthologist and author Peter Haining, contacted me to say he was looking for an Irish detective tale for an anthology that he was putting together. I wrote the first Fidelma story, Murder in Repose, as a response to his request. In trying to get a name for my sleuth, I decided to use a 7th century Irish name – Sister Buan. Peter came back delighted with the story but pointed out that Sister Buan reminded him of the character of "Smiler Bunn' from the early 20th century crime novels of Bertram Atkey. The name, he pointed out, sounded comical to English ears. I thought for a while and then the name Fidelma came to mind. It, too, was an ancient Irish name but is still used in modern Ireland and is not too "alien' to English ears. So, thanks to Peter ...!

Word of my character spread. So, in October 1993, four different Sister Fidelma short stories came out in four different anthologies. A short time later my agent phoned saying Headline wanted to know if I could write a novel featuring the character and were prepared to offer me a three-book contract. The first book, set against the famous Synod of Whitby in AD 664, appeared from Headline in September 1994. The rest, as they say, is history.

The 14th title is about to be published, the books have sold to the US as well as UK, and in nine other languages to date, and there is a thriving International Sister Fidelma Society based in Arkansas, USA.

In what ways did the Irish Celtic church differ from the Roman church in Fidelma's time?
One could write a book on this; many have, including myself. I wrote *Celtic Inheritance* (1985), which was more a general introduction to the subject. The entity, which we now call the Celtic Church, had developed from the early Christian ideas which had been married into a Celtic cultural ethos. It was not a centralised entity like the Roman Church. Rome was developing new concepts of Christianity – you have only to look at the debates of the early church councils, the new dating of Easter, and also it was becoming feudalised with its bishops exercising authority as temporal princes. But the Celts, including the Irish, adhered to the early philosophies and forms of ritual and dating. There was a marked contrast between Rome and the Celts in terms of asceticism, monastic

extremism, the social order, views on land tenure, which were opposed to Rome's feudal structures and hereditary rights. That brought the Celtic Church into conflict with Rome.

Let's clear up an old myth. The Celtic Church did not disappear after the Synod of Whitby in the 7th century. I'd like a pound, even a euro, for every time I have been assured of this. While King Oswy (of Northumbria) came down in favour of Rome, his cousin Hilda, the abbess of Whitby, actually remained a supporter of Celtic usage until her death. Irish missionaries continued to work in the Anglo-Saxon kingdoms and the church usage in the Celtic countries remained for a long time thereafter. In Ireland, for example, the absorption by Rome didn't really take place until the Synod of Cashel in 1172. But the absorption is long after Fidelma's period, which is the mid-7th century.

The church of Fidelma's age was marked from Rome by a different tonsure for the male religious, by the ritual of service which had more in common with the Eastern Orthodox Church, even the holding up of different fingers (first, second and fourth) to denote the Trinity, with the priest facing the congregation behind the altar instead of before it and so on. Even Greek was in more use as the language of the "sacred texts' than Latin. As for the conflict of philosophies, you only have to examine the teachings of Pelagius (a Celt), who was in conflict with Augustine of Hippo over Fate and Free Will. Pelagius was labelled a heretic and it was claimed he was trying to bring back Druid forms of worship. Over the following centuries, Rome accused the Celtic Church of following Pelagius' heresy. All they were doing was keeping to their own cultural outlook.

Celibacy was not a rule in the Celtic Church but then neither was it in the Roman Church until the time of Pope Leo IX (1049-54). But the Celtic world seemed to have more "mixed houses' (*conhospitae*) than other parts of Christendom. These were religious houses in which men and women lived raising their children in the service of Christ. In Fidelma's day the religious, of whatever rank, could and did marry.

Why did you choose a female protagonist, and a nun in particular?
I chose a female protagonist because this was the most intriguing aspect of the 7th century Irish system which placed women in a co-equal role to men. A fact that seemed forgotten. And it was inevitable that she had to be a religious for, as Fidelma has explained in the stories, in pre-Christian days all the professionals and intellectuals were part of the

THE FASCINATION FOR SISTER FIDELMA

Druid caste whereas, in the early days of Christianity, the vast majority of professionals simply became members of the new religious. It is not something Fidelma particularly likes because her first and main love is law – she is a qualified lawyer and law is her life first and foremost and not religion. She did give up life in the Abbey of Kildare for the reasons explained in the title story of *Hemlock at Vespers*.

What was the position of women in 7th century Irish society generally and the church in particular? Did women have more rights in 7th century Ireland than subsequently?

Under the ancient Irish law system, women occupied a unique place. Simply, the Irish laws gave more rights and protection to women than any other western law code at that time or until recent years. Women could, and did, aspire to all offices and professions as co-equal with men. They could be political leaders, command their people in battle as warriors, be physicians, poets, artisans, local magistrates, lawyers and judges.

Women were protected, under the law, from sexual harassment, against discrimination and against rape. They had the right of divorce on equal terms as their husbands, with equitable separation laws and could demand part of their husband's property as a divorce settlement. They had the right of inheritance of personal property and the right of sickness benefit when ill or hospitalised. They remained the owners of any wealth that they brought into a marriage. Indeed, it was automatic that on divorcing their husband, if he were at fault, they took half of all the joint property accrued during the time of the marriage. The Irish law system was very ancient and sophisticated. While we have fragmentary texts from the early period, the first complete surviving texts do not survive until the 11th century. This law system was finally suppressed following the Tudor Conquest of Ireland at the beginning of the 17th century. During the Penal Years it meant death or transportation to be caught with one of the Irish law books.

It was thanks to Charles Graves, grandfather of the Nobel literary laureate Robert Graves, that many of the Irish legal texts were finally saved. Charles Graves (1812-1899) was President of the Royal Irish Academy, as well as being Anglican Bishop of Limerick. He was an expert on Ogham, the ancient Irish form of writing, and on Brehon Law. He persuaded the British government to set up a commission to rescue the surviving legal books and texts and to edit and translate them. These were published in six volumes from 1865-1901.

It seems from the detail and sense of place that you do intensive research for each novel. How do you go about it?
Accuracy is the first principle. My characters can do nothing that is not consistent with the time, place and social system. I would say that I have probably done the bulk of general background research during the many decades I have been writing of this period of Irish history. When it comes to the setting of each individual novel, I will only write about places I know – places that I've been to. Spirit of place is very important to me. On the technical side, I have to ensure that any law that Fidelma quotes can actually be verified in the ancient law texts. This is something that happens as I go along. An argument on law might arise in the story... then I have to start checking my library to see what the interpretations are. I can neglect writing for days, like Edgar Allan Poe's protagonist, "while I pondered... over any a quaint and curious volume of forgotten lore' – I try to pay particular attention to all aspects of life in 7th century Ireland so that my characters exist comfortably in it and are not modern characters placed against a fictional background and set of events. Once, at Oxford, I was accused of "an anachronism of attitude' – that I had tried to place my modern attitudes in an ancient time when such attitudes could not, according to my accuser, exist. I had to depart from a prepared text to give a lecture on the reality of life in 7th century Ireland.

Do you map out the plot of each novel before starting to write?
Each novel seems to have its own genesis. I try to make a plan and more often the characters take over from me and write the story. I start off thinking that this person is the villain and by the end of the story I find that they have become the hero or heroine. The person that I thought was going to be the victim or the nice person has become the villain. Several times I have given up planning and let the characters, who I now know so well, write the story by their reactions and let the thing work out by itself. That, I know, is not the recommended form, but several times it has worked for me.

It has been my good fortune in life to meet many writers during my career – from James Baldwin to Tom Keneally and from Alex Haley to Hammond Innes. Each will give you a different work method. I used all methods – however the story comes to me.

THE FASCINATION FOR SISTER FIDELMA

Do you have much to do with the International Sister Fidelma Society on the Internet? Where abroad is Fidelma particularly popular?
The International Sister Fidelma Society came into being at the end of 2001 in Arkansas, USA, and has members in over a dozen countries. A local businessman, David Robert Wooten, had asked me back in 2000 if he could put up a Fidelma website. In the first year, so many people contacted him that he asked if I had an objection to forming the Society. I gave it my blessing and am, of course, the patron of the Society. As well as the astonishing website, the Society issues a printed magazine three times a year entitled *The Brehon*. I think the 8th edition of the magazine is shortly to appear. This is a "members only' publication of 16 pages an issue with photographs. The Society even puts out its own sweatshirts, mugs, mousepads and other items. Many of the US members go on trips to Ireland to look at the Fidelma locations, especially Cashel, which is a spectacular place to visit. I am more than happy to answer questions, supply what I can for the Society and its members. They are, after all, the people who pay my wages.

The Fidelma books appear in nine languages and of course the American market is the biggest area where Fidelma is popular. Of the European markets, I find Germany's interest astonishing. Aufbau publishes the series and many of the titles are into their sixth reprint in paperback since they first began in 2000. They have done eight titles to date. I think what particularly warms my sensibilities is that the series appears in Greek from Themelio and has a good Greek following.

What satisfactions does it give you to write fiction about a culture and period you've studied and written about so intensively?
What gives me the most satisfaction is the resonance that Fidelma and her background appear to have had among people in many parts of the world. She and 7th century Ireland have crossed cultural frontiers. I have had fan letters from a lady in Peking, a professor in Japan, and others from Norway to Argentina, from Canada to France, from New Zealand to Spain. But thinking more about your question, I suppose I would consider myself a simple storyteller, an incurable romantic weaving stories mainly, in the first place, for my own entertainment. I would probably be found in ancient times trying to sell literary wares in some marketplace; in ancient Ireland, I might have tried to be the official bard of the High King or even one of the lesser kings. Admittedly,

in that entertainment, there comes the desire to pass on information, to inform, to educate. I am enthused by knowledge and expect other people to be.

Have other writers influenced you?
We were a very literate household. On my mother's side of the family, we boast the poet, playwright and friend of Ben Jonson, Thomas Randolph (1603-1635). On my father's side we have several Irish Ellises who turned out the odd book or two including Henry Ellis (1721-1806), who was an explorer and wrote a bestselling account of one trip in *A Voyage to Hudson's Bay* (1748). My 3-times-great-grandfather was actually publishing books in the 1820s. I think I was reading before I began to walk. Where does the influence start? Of course, writers have influenced me. All writers are influenced by others. But the last person to know of that influence – unless they are consciously borrowing style and so forth – is the writer. The real answer to this question might have to be left to some learned professor or, more probably, an eager graduate student doing a PhD, in analysing my work.

Are there any historical fiction authors whom you particularly admire? If so who – and why?
I used to devour fiction by the metric tonne and still do. It would be impossible for me to start naming names because the list would become endless. I just have to confess to being a voracious reader and, in all genres, – from "popular' literature to "serious' literature, although I do dislike those labels. There are too many pretensions and prejudices that lie behind those categorisations. To start mentioning names would mean that I would have to produce an almost unending list. It would have to start somewhere around Dumas (*père et fils*), J Meade Falkner, R H Dana and then where? From Tolstoy to Walter Macken and from Sholokov to Baroness Orczy to Rafael Sabatini, to Rider Haggard and William Faulkner, Quiller Couch, Elizabeth Gaskell, the Brontës, Norah Lofts... no, the list could go on and on.

Why do you think historical crime fiction is so popular?
This is a difficult one, as I have no idea. To be honest, I have never been a follower of "literary fashions'. In my own writing, I write about what I want to write about. I would hope the Fidelma books sell not because they just happen to be part of a general reading trend measured by

market research – you know, this year yo-yos are the fashion and next year pogo sticks are in! That would be depressing. It would mean that publishers would be publishing only by market research criteria. Mind you, I recall in the late 1960s a Dr Mann doing such market research, mainly employed by Mills and Boon, and trying to forecast trends. No, I would hope people read the Fidelma series because they were first and foremost good entertainment.

What is your opinion on the current state of studies and research into Celtic history and culture?
Celtic Studies certainly lack adequate funding, especially in the area of Irish. An old mentor of mine, Professor Gearóid Mac Eoin of University College, Galway, once pointed out to me that what we know of Irish mythology is based only on translations of 150 manuscript stories. And yet, a further 650 manuscripts are known to exist – and had been identified as early as 1900 by Professor Kuno Meyer. These have simply not been transcribed, let alone edited and translated. In the Vienna repository, into which the vast library of the 11th century Irish foundation of Regensburg was transferred, there is a colossal uncatalogued archive of Irish manuscripts. Vienna is one of many such repositories of Irish manuscripts throughout Europe.

To give you an idea of what is probably lurking in these European archives, where Irish religious went as *peregrinatio pro Christo* during the Dark Ages, let's take Bobbio in northern Italy. Although Umberto Eco (*Name of the Rose*) did not mention Bobbio by name, it was obvious to many of us in the field, that his monastic abbey was modelled on Bobbio, which was closed down in the 19th century. The clues were even carried into the film they made – just look carefully at the library scenes. Its great library and archive was split between the Vatican Secret Archives and some archives in northern Italy such as Padua and Milan. Now Bobbio was founded by St Columban from Ireland at the beginning of the 7th century. Columban is known, among other things, for his famous letter to Pope Boniface IV arguing about the Celtic Church's date for Easter as being more accurate than Rome's new calculations. He was arguing from an Irish calendar, also mentioned in other sources, but which modern scholars had accepted as having been lost for over a thousand years.

In the mid 1980s, in the Biblioteca Antoniana, in Padua, that calendar, the "84 Year Easter Table', was discovered simply by accident.

The very Irish calendar on which Columban based his arguments. An amazing find whose ramifications are still being considered by the academic world. Yet we don't even have the funding to locate and catalogue all the ancient Irish manuscripts in European repositories, let alone work on them. And that is just one aspect of Celtic Studies.

A ridiculous development has recently happened in England, led by a group of academic archaeologists who want to denigrate Celtic Studies. They claim "Celtic' is a 17th century "political invention' and want everyone to refer to the immediate pre-Roman period as "Iron Age'. For Celtic scholars this has become a joke. "Parlez-vous Iron Age?' is the greeting now among Celtic scholars to one another. Celtic is a linguistic term to identify the peoples who spoke a particular branch of the Indo-European languages. Its use as a means of identification is ancient. For those waxing enthusiastic about "Iron Age' people I would simply repeat the comment of Julius Caesar: *"Qui ipsorum lingua Celtae...'* – "In their own language they are called Celts...'

At least, Celtic civilisation, in all its aspects, has been taken as a subject for serious study in many universities throughout the world – even in Japan; Nagoya University has a very respected faculty of Celtic Studies. In fact, the Germans led the way in Celtic Studies from the 19th century. Yet it is in Brittany and these islands that the Celtic languages have survived into modern times and supply the well of knowledge which should not be dismissed so cavalierly.

If I had any wish for a side effect of the international fascination for the Fidelma stories, it would be a hope that the stories encourage an interest in the study of a unique European civilisation and culture.

– *Sarah Cuthbertson*
First published in
Solander: The Magazine of The Historical Novel Society
V.8 No.1 (MAY 2004): 2-66

Frequently Asked Questions

(The answers provided herein were graciously supplied directly by Peter Tremayne/Peter Berresford Ellis himself, with the author's sincere thanks)

As a "prologue" to this highly-educational chapter, I felt the need to include a short article originally published in *The Brehon* (Volume XI, No. 2, May 2012), after the International Sister Fidelma Society received numerous letters and emails from quite well-spoken and well-meaning individuals questioning the amount of actual *research* this "Peter Tremayne" had actually done prior to writing the Sister Fidelma Mysteries.

PETER'S "LACK OF KNOWLEDGE"

We have often pointed out that the problem with the worldwide web is that anyone can say anything and it is not necessarily correct. From time to time, we find that people who know no better have been dismissive of Peter's knowledge of his own field of studies! In spite of Peter's degrees in Celtic Studies, his also being a Fellow of the Royal Historical Society and of the Royal Society of Antiquaries of Ireland, even academics (in both Australia and US, as I recall) have implied our author has no knowledge in the field, and one even referred to the Féile Fidelma as "a pseudo academic gathering." It is highly amusing and rebounds on them rather than on us.

One of our members, responding to such bizarre comments, pointed out that Peter's books on Celtic and Irish mythology, were praised by an Irish newspaper as having done for Irish mythology what Robert Graves had done for Greek mythology. In 1955 Robert Graves published his two-volume guide as The Greek Myths *(an original Penguin Books Publication). The Irish Times pointed out that Peter's book on the Irish myths was "the first attempt to have a full-scale and separate dictionary on the subject."*

Oxford University Press, no less, published two of Peter's books in this field under Peter's own name. A Dictionary of Irish Mythology (first published in 1987) was also issued as an OUP paperback in 1991 and reprinted several times. His Dictionary of Celtic Mythology *(first published in 1992) was also issued as an OUP paperback in 1993.* The Wilson Library Bulletin *found this second book "A fine complement to the many dictionaries of classical mythology."*

Appending this article, it should be noted that on numerous occasions we receive correspondence advising "Peter Tremayne" that he should do some serious non-fiction reading before making such "wild" claims as he does in the Fidelma novels. In fact, to paraphrase quite a few, "Mr. Tremayne should look into the books of Peter Berresford Ellis – someone who <u>REALLY</u> knows his stuff." One needs only scan the checklist of Peter Berresford Ellis's works elsewhere in this book to see that his knowledge is truly encyclopædic in scope.

That bit of housekeeping out of the way, we proceed with the queries that occurred most frequently in our correspondence...

Could members of the religious really get married in Fidelma's time?

Of the numerous and varied questions addressed to the Society, no subject has engendered so many queries than that of clerical marriage. It seems that some readers just cannot accept that there were clerical marriages among the religious in ancient times nor that there were 'mixed communities' in many early religious houses. Peter Tremayne contributed an article in an edition of The Brehon, *and we requested him to expand that article for this publication.*

CLERICAL MARRIAGES: CELIBACY IN FIDELMA'S TIME
In most religions, both ancient and modern, there have always been ascetics who believed that celibacy somehow brought them close to the deity. They have sublimated physical love, a natural life, in a dedication to whatever deity they worshiped. Celibacy within the Western Christian movement was something that took many centuries to become a universally accepted idea, even then it was a means of causing schisms within that movement. Only from the 12th century AD did the Roman Church begin to enforce celibacy among its clerics.

The first disciples of Jesus were, for the majority, married men.

FREQUENTLY ASKED QUESTIONS

Disciples such as Simon Bar-Jonah, nicknamed "The Rock" (Petrus in Latin, Cephas in Greek), the man on whom Jesus is accepted as founding his Church and regarded as the "first Pope." Evidence shows that many of the early Christian religious leaders were married men and women and, moreover, women often took a prominent role in the services. Even many centuries later women in Gaul were officiating over the divine offices and other rituals and that called forth a rebuke from Rome. One has to remember that the Christian movement, like most human movements from the religious to the political, were constantly changing and reforming. Indeed, it was with the 3rd century that the teachings of Gnosticism began to argue that a person could not be married and "religiously perfect."

However, *The Oxford Dictionary of Popes*, edited by J.N.D. Kelly, OUP, 1986, lists no less than 39 Popes as being married. Even the most conservative of Catholic scholars accept than seven Bishops of Rome were married. Moreover, some of the Pope's were succeeded in office by their sons.

Some ascetics, as in other religions, became hermits, shunning society, and removing themselves from "worldly temptation." Such was the idea of St Anthony (born c. AD 250) who took up residence in a deserted fort in Pispir on the Nile. It was from these first Christian "monks" – Anthony and Pachomius – that inspired a former Roman soldier named Martin, born c. AD 315 in Pannonia. He became a hermit in Gaul. By AD 370 he was also a bishop and founder of an entire community. He built his monastery at Marmoutier that still shows its original Celtic name *"mor munntir"* = "place of the great family," for this was in Celtic Gaul. Martin became "Father of Celtic Monasticism" and his ideas spread from Marmoutier to Britain and then to Ireland.

Yet at this stage the majority of priests were married and their children often rose to office in the Church. The Pope St Damascus I (AD 366-384) was the son of the priest St Lorenzo. St Innocent I who was Pope from AD 401-417 was son of Pope Anastasius I (399-401). Popes Boniface (AD 418-422), St Felix (AD 483-492), Anastasius II (AD 496-498) and St Agapitus I (AD 535-536) were all sons of priests while St Silverus (AD 536-537) and John XI were sons of previous Popes and at least three more Popes were also sons of priests.

Ireland was not unique within the wider Christian Church in having married clergy and mixed religious communities were found not confined to Ireland but through Western Christendom.

Yet the ascetic group, advocating celibacy, grew stronger as a political force within the Christian movement. In AD 308 the Council of Elvira in Spain issued a decree that a priest who slept with his wife on the night before Mass could not perform it. In AD 325 the Council at Niceae argued that, after ordination, priests should not marry.

One fascinating point is that the Council of Laodicea in AD 352, ordered that women should not be ordained, showing that at this time women were still being ordained as priests. Early Irish references show that St Brigid of Kildare, (died c. AD 525) herself was ordained as a bishop. She founded her *conhospitae*, or mixed, house with Bishop Conláed. St Hilary in Northumbria is also referred to as being ordained bishop. In AD 494 Pope Gelasius I (492-496) decreed that woman could no longer be ordained as priests. It is fascinating; therefore, we find Bishop Pelagio, in the 12th century, complaining that women were still being ordained in the Western Church and hearing confessions. K.J. Torjesen's book When Women Were Priests, Harper, San Francisco, 1993, discusses the implications of this.

In AD 385, Pope Siricius (AD 384-399), supporting the ascetic lobby, abandoned his wife and children, and ordered that priests should no longer sleep with their wives but he did not go so far as prohibiting marriage.

Clerics marrying remained an unchanging factor of religious life through the 6th century. In AD 567 the 2nd Council at Tours decided to recommend that any cleric found in bed with their wives should be forbidden to perform church rituals and reduced to a lay state. However, in AD 580 Pope Pelagius II (AD 579-590) was not so much bothered with married clergy but with inheritance to their offspring. He ordered that they should not bequeath property acquired in their office as a member of the church to their sons or other heirs. The Roman Church was becoming conscious of the value of property and wanted what had been acquired to remain within the church.

Throughout the 7th century there is much documentary evidence showing that in Frankia and Gaul the majority of clerics, priests, abbots and bishops, were married. In the following century, St Boniface of Crediton (c. AD 675-755), comments that almost no bishop or priest in Germany followed the idea of celibacy. Indeed, well into the 9th century, it was reported at the Council of Aix-la-Chapelle that the inhabitants of monasteries and convents were living together and that where the bishops and abbots were trying to enforce celibacy there were a number of abortions and infanticide taking place to cover up these relationships.

St Ulric of Augsburg (890-973) argued that the Holy Scriptures and logic demanded that the only way to purify the Western Church from the worst excesses of celibacy was to allow the clerics to marry. He points out "When celibacy is imposed, priests will commit sins far worse than fornication." His letter on this matter was later claimed to be a forgery by the pro-celibacy lobby. Ulric's stand is discussed in *Married Priests and the Reforming Papacy: The Eleventh Century Debates*, A.L. Barstow, Edward Mellin Press, Leviston, New York, 1982.

Pope Benedict IX was elected when he was fifteen years old in 1032 because he was connected with the powerful Counts of Tusculum. He resigned the Papacy in order to marry. Gregory VI took over, but Gregory was banished after a few months. Re-elected in 1045, the married Benedict was deposed by Clement II who died shortly after, and Benedict was again re-elected for a third time before finally being deposed in 1048.

Peter Damian (AD 1007-72) a high-ranking ecclesiastic and theologian who became the leading advisor to the Popes and drew them firmly into the celibacy camp. Peter Damian called the wives of clerics "harlots, prostitutes, unclean spirits, demigoddesses, sirens, witches" among other vicious rhetoric. He found an enthusiastic pupil in Hildebrand di Bonizio Aldobrandeschi of Sovana.

When Hildebrand was elected as Pope Gregory VII (AD 1073-1085), he declared, in 1074, that "priests must first escape the clutches of their wives," and then take a pledge of celibacy. But it was Pope Urban II in 1095 who decided to order that the wives of priests be rounded up and sold into slavery. Riots took place in Germany, Italy and France as priests rejected this order. Pope Calixtus II (AD 1119-1124) in 1123 at the Lateran Council decreed that all clerical marries were invalid, a decree later confirmed by Pope Innocent II (1130-1143).

But, by the 15th century, it was reported that 50 per cent of Catholic priests were still married but, of course, this figure actually shows that the long transition from marriage to celibacy had finally begun to take effect.

The Popes themselves were hardly obeying their own rules. We know that Popes such as Innocent VIII (AD 1484-1492), Alexander VI (1492-1503), Julius II (1503-1513), Paul III (1534-1549), Pius IV (1559-1565) and Gregory XIII (1572-1585), each had many illegitimate children. Of these, one of the most notorious was Alexander VI (1492-

1503), a Borgia Pope, who had seven illegitimate children when he was a cardinal and, as Pontiff had an affair with Giulia Farnese, a 19 year old married girl.

Ireland was really no different from the rest of the Western Church in the respect of attitudes to celibacy. Indeed, the decisions in the documentary recounting "The First Synod of Patrick" simply takes married clerics for granted and says that "any cleric from ostiary to priest "whose wife walks about with her head uncovered shall be despised by the laity and separated from the Church." Dr Patrick Power, in *Sex and Marriage in Ancient Ireland*, Mercier Press, 1976, points to the fact that a later Brehon Law actually grades ecclesiastical marriages indicating that married bishops and priests were allotted only two-thirds of the honour price of an unmarried bishop or priest. In spite of attempts to "sanitise" things by those who want to present celibacy as a strict rule of the Faith from early times, the evidence to the contrary is absolutely clear. Attempts to reduce bishops and abbots in Ireland to "semi-religious officials holding hereditary office, sort of like managers for the community" shows no understanding at all of early Irish society.

Some argue that the Irish term for "monk" and "nun" were used strictly in the same way as used in the late medieval Roman Church way, implying that any union between them was forbidden. Of course, the Latin *monachus* is taken from the Greek word for "solitary." It is interesting that, in Latin myth, a name for Hercules (Heracles) was Monoecus – he that dwells alone. When one is talking about an entire community of "monks" it is obvious that word meanings change, so the argument that if someone was a "monk" it must mean they dwelt alone becomes fallacious. However, one argument as been that a "religious monk" meant a celibate person and where reference is made to monks that were married a fall-back defence is that they were not "religious monks." It is true, of course, that *manach* occurs as an Irish legal term as a "tenant of church lands," of which there were two different classes – *sóirmanaigh* and *doirmanaigh*. Indeed, deriving from another etymology, the term *manach* is giving to one who performs feats of skill such as bareback riders who appear at fairs. But anyone dealing with the textual evidence is easily able to different from context who is being spoken of.

The term "nun" derives from the Latin *nonnus* and *nonna* originally applied as terms of respect for elderly people. For example, most Italian speakers will easily recognise the modern terms *nonno* and *nanna* (grandfather and grandmother respectively). The same idea occurs in Old and Middle Irish when the word *caillech* was used for a nun. An abbess was a *cenn caillech*. But the word also applied to an elderly woman or a matron and the same word, in the sagas, applied to a hag, witch or crone. It also became the word for a "veil" obviously from its religious connection.

Those who tend to rely on trying to claim that the words "monk" and "nun" have meant celibate religious since the start of the Christian movement would do better to reflect on the linguistic ideas and changes over the centuries.

One important thing to remember is that Irish society in Fidelma's period was in a state of flux, of tremendous stresses and changes. Nothing was written in stone and there was a great deal of fluidity in ideas relating to church and social matters.

Whereas the *conhospitae*, mixed houses in which religious of both sexes lived and raised their children in the services of the Faith, existed at the same time that the ascetic religious were founding solitary hermitages or single sex communities, to pursue their path to the deity. Abbey communities were changing, some often rejecting the civil (Brehon) laws of Ireland and accepting the harsh, physical punishment orientated, Penententials. But it was all a very slow process. For example, Dr Patrick Power, in *Sex and Marriage in Ancient Ireland*, points out that a Céili Dí "Penetential" does not order excommunication and expulsion for any monk or nun who has a sexual relationship but only prescribes a penance.

The Céili Dí (Servants of God) monastic order, founded in Tallaght by St Mael Ríain (d. 792) certainly approved of celibacy and in the Martyrology of Oengus they believed that a priest could not baptise anyone if they had sexual intercourse. "Baptism comes not from him, after visiting his nun (*nonna*)." Professor Edward C. Sellner (*The Celtic Soul Friend*, Ave Maria Press Inc., Notre Dame, Indiana. 2002) actually picked up on the fact that in later years the Céile Dí, which movement had lasted into the 14th century in parts of Gaelic Scotland, were often married. "This movement consisted of both lay people and ordained, many of whom were married, who wanted to recover the lost traditions of their spiritual ancestors, and thus bring new life into their own churches and monasteries."

In fact, the marriages among the Céili Dí had been remarked back in the late 15th, early 16th century by Canon Alexander Myln (1474-1548) of Dunkeld who wrote his *Dunkeldensis Ecclesiae Episcoporum*, c. 1516. His text has been edited by T. Thomson for the Bannatyne Club 1823-31.

Myln wrote: "In this monastery (Dunkeld) Constantine, king of the Picts, placed religious men, commonly called Kelldedei, otherwise Colidei, that is, God-worshippers, who, however, after the Eastern Church, had wives (from whom they lived apart when taking the sacred offices) as afterwards grew to be the custom in the church of the blessed Regulus, now called St. Andrews."

When Dr William Reeves published his *The Culdees of the British Isles as they appeared in history*, Dublin, 1864, he, too, remarked on the marriage of the Céli Dí quoting from Myln and pointing to such married abbots as Crinan (sometimes Cronan) the Abbot of Dunkeld who married Bethoc, daughter of Maol Callum II (1008-1034) of Scotland, whose son was Duncan I (1034-1040). Duncan, after a disastrous reign, was overthrown by MacBeth, son of Maol Callum II's second daughter Doada. He reigned from 1040-1057 having married Gruoch, grand daughter of Coinneach III (997-1005).

A century before this period, in Ireland, some Kings like Cormac mac Cuileannáin (836-908) were not simply Kings but, in Cormac's case was Bishop of Cashel as well as King of Cashel. He married Gormflaith, daughter of the High King, Flann Sionna mac Maelsechnaill (879-916). Indeed, he was not the first King at Cashel to fulfil a religious role. Fergus Scandal mac Crimthain Airthir Chliach (d. AD 583) was also abbot of Imleach (Emly). Cenn Fáelad gua Mugthigirn (d. 872) not only became King at Cashel but also was another abbot of Imleach, as, indeed, his uncle, Rechtabra (d. 819) had been. Cenn Fíelad's son Eóghan, was not elected to the kingship but succeeded his father as abbot of Imleach. However, Olchobar mac Cináeda (d. 851) succeeded as both King as well as abbot. Certainly, in the annals we find references to the sons of abbots of Imleach, such as Mescell son of Abbot Cumasach. While Emly was important for the Munster ruling house of the Eóghanacht, it is interesting that when the Dál gCais (the Uí Fidgente of the Fidelma stories) had a king on the throne of Cashel in 786 in the person of Olchobar mac Flainn (d. 796/7) he was also abbot of Inis Carthaigh (Scattery Island).

As surnames began to emerge in 11th and 12th century Ireland, we find that Mac an Mhanaigh (MacEvanny) was "son of the monk;" that Mac an tSagairt (MacEntaggart) was "son of the priest" (the same name as McTaggart in Scotland); that Mac Giolla Easpuig (MacGillespie) was "son of the bishop" and Mac Giolla Iosa (MacAleese) was "the son of the devotee of Jesus" – applied to the son of a religious leader. The rights and education of children of clerical marriages, as given in Brehon Law, has been studied in papers printed in *Studies in Early Irish Law*, published by the Royal Irish Academy, Dublin, 1936. These include August Knock's "Die Ehescheidung im Alten Irischen Recht," and Kathleen Mulchrone's "The Rights and Duties of Women with Regard to the Education of their Children."

While King Bishops or King Abbots might be explained as powerful men combining the secular and the religious functions, if anyone really thought that the abbots and bishops in Ireland were only "semi-religious" figures then they should spend a few hours with the Irish Annals, Chronicles, and other texts.

The law text the *Córus Béscnai*, "the regulation of proper behaviour" dealing with the mutual obligations of clergy and laity, can be traced from at least the 8th century. It becomes the third section of the Senchus Mór. It is quoted in both the *Ancient Laws of Ireland* (volume III) and in the *Corpus Iuiris Hibernici*, ed. by D.A. Binchy, Dublin, 1978. It states that the monks (*manaigh*) were of the *fine erluma*, of the kin of the founder of the monastery. Professor Thomas Charles-Edwards, an expert on the laws, has no problem with this and sees this as a single kin-related *tuath* or tribe (clan). One writer has actually argued that this terminology should not be taken literally. That it was symbolic and the kingship was not blood related and that legal writers were employing familiar social and economic ideas of the times to explain things.

Yet it is perfectly clear that in many monasteries in Ireland, those habitants were families that were bound by blood. As Professor Lisa M. Bitel, in spite of her later arguments, confessed in *Isle of the Saints: Monastic Settlement and Christian Community in Early Ireland*, (Cornell University Press, 1990): "Abbots and officers openly supported wives, sons and other kin. They sent their relatives to become officers in nearby monasteries, or they kept sons, brothers, and nephews within their own communities to succeed to offices there. Successive generations of the Maicc Cuinn na mBocht, for example, controlled major monastic offices at Cluan Moccu Nois (Clonmacnoise) for about three centuries. Another family, the Uí Sinaich, battled for and won control of Ard Macha, remaining in power for generations. There is no reason to assume that other monks ignored the example of their abbots and officers."

Indeed, as she points out, echoing Kathleen Hughes in her *Church*

In Early Irish Society, that there was no reason to assume that the brethren in these abbeys remained celibate ignoring the example of their abbots, the officers of the religious houses and, indeed, the bishops and priests. The family within the monastic communities allowed knowledge as well as property to pass on to sons and other family members. T. O'Donoghue, examining a 10th century poem, "Advice to a Prince" (Eriu 9 (1921) pp 43-54), shows that the writer of this poem argues that abbots could most efficiently be succeeded by their sons.

Indeed, this was happening in many religious houses throughout Ireland. The Irish Annals and Chronicles are replete in their references to the children of Abbots (*abbas*). In the *Annals of Ulster* just for the year AD 793 we find recorded not only Dubh Da Leithi, the son of Sinaich, the Abbot of Armagh, but of Cinaed, son of Cumascach, the abbot of Demag, Flaithgel, son of Taichlech, abbot of Druim Rótha and so on. Sons of abbots certainly reached high rank in the Irish Church. For example, Bishop Flann, who died in AD 812, was the son of Cellach, abbot of Finnglas.

And even if one doesn't want to take Irish sources as evidence, let us take an example from the writing of St Bernard of Clairvaux (c.1090-1153) who knew St Malachy (Mael Maedoc ua Morgair – AD1094-1190) of Armagh. Now surely few intelligent people can claim that Armagh and its archbishopric was a "lay" or "semi-religious" house and its archbishop was a "lay manager?" By the time Bernard was writing, the Irish High Kings and, indeed, the Bishop of Rome had accepted Armagh, as the primacy, or chief ecclesiastical centre in Ireland. This was mainly due to the political intervention of the High King, Brían mac Cennátig (d. 1014) perhaps better known as Brían Bórumha. According to the Annals of Ulster, in 1005, Brían acknowledged Armagh as the primatial jurisdiction of Ireland for the first time.

Yet Bernard points out that even "this primatial Holy See" was "held in hereditary succession for they (the Irish) suffered none to be bishops but those who were of their own tribe and family." He mentions that the abbots and bishops of Armagh were married, and fifteen bishops had succeeded by hereditary right at Armagh prior to the election of Archbishop Celsus. In fact, it was not until 1101 at a Council at Cashel, convened by the High King Muirechertach Ua Bríain (d. 1119), who was not only High King but King of Munster (Muman), that the first serious moves were made to enforced clerical celibacy in Ireland. It was at this Council that Muirchertach handed over the historical royal lands of

FREQUENTLY ASKED QUESTIONS

Cashel to the church "without any claim of layman or cleric upon it, but to the religious of Ireland in general." It was, for Ireland, a point where church and state began a separation and, indeed, the pro-celibacy lobby began to have its most significant impact.

Without the Irish more liberal attitude to sexual relations during this period, it would have been a grim society. One of the important studies here remains *The Serpent and the Goddess: Women, Religion and Power in Celtic Ireland* by Dr Mary Condren (1989). Dr Condren has taught at the Harvard Divinity School. Her study was of ground-breaking significance.

What many later scholars who attempt to square the circle, arguing for the tradition of celibacy, try to claim is these married religious were not ordained but were laymen. Such a claim was made for St Celsus, otherwise Cellach Mac Aodh (1079-1129) who inherited the bishopric of Armagh in 1105. Now if St Celsus was a layman, we have a problem. How was he then able to ordain St Malachy (Maelmadoc ua Morgair) as a priest, commission him to reform the church, and then, as he lay dying, appoint him his successor as Archbishop of Armagh?

The short answer to those who attempt to deny that there was clerical marriage in Ireland and deny the existence of many mixed communities, raising their children in the service of the New Faith, is that they can only put forward their argument by distorting or ignoring the evidence.

Perhaps we should reiterate, as most of our readers should know, that Peter, in his other role as the well-known historian Peter Berresford Ellis, took his degrees in Celtic Studies and is a Fellow of the Royal Historical Society and a Fellow of the Royal Society of Antiquaries of Ireland. His non-fiction works are highly regarded.

Why are the measurements in the stories given in the metric form – is this not an anachronism?

OF INCHES, FEET, YARDS, AND MILES – ANACHRONISTIC MEASUREMENTS IN SISTER FIDELMA BOOKS

I might have had an easier life if I had chosen to use Imperial measurements in the Sister Fidelma mysteries. If I had made something measure so many inches, or feet, or distances in so many miles, I might not have had the occasional strident protest that the metric measurements I use are anachronistic to the 7th century.

The amusing point is that those who gleefully point this out think that I ought to be using Imperial measurements. But Imperial measurements are even more anachronistic to 7th century Ireland.

I am well aware that the metric system was first adopted as standard in France in 1799.

Imperial measurements became standard in the United Kingdom in 1838. They arose from an old English system. Let's take some basic measurements. The Old English *ynce* (inch) seems to derive from the Latin *uncia*, a twelfth part of a foot measurement. The Old English *fot* (foot) is the measurement of an average human foot. The yard (Old English *gard*) means a branch or twig used as measuring rod from the mid 15th century, usually indicating a pace. And the Old English *míl* (mile) is from the Roman measure *mille* meaning one thousand paces. Initially the English mile was 1,618 yards but then standardised into 1,760 yards.

Now this Imperial system developed from a base 12 counting system which seems to have entered Europe through the Romans and coming from the Sumerian, Assyrian and Babylonian. Base 12 counting systems were not Indo-European.

The Indo-European systems as made on a base 10 counting system. Pythagorean thinkers believed 10 to be "the first born of the numbers, the mother of all, the one that never wavers, and gives the key to all things." The possible explanation was that the hands were the earliest calculating machine and most Indo-European languages have names for numerals that are derived from the names of the first 10 numbers.

Interestingly, while Irish, as an Indo-European language, follows this decimal system, it bears remains of pre-Indo-European vigesimal reckoning – that is, a base 20 counting system. The following terms occur: 20 = *fiche* (twenty), 30 = *deich ar fiche* (ten and twenty), 40 = *da fiche* (two twenty) and 50 *deich ar da fiche* (ten and two twenty).

Obviously, the English Imperial system was not used in 7th century Ireland and neither, admittedly, was the metric system.

Let us consider what measurements were used. Like most ancient peoples, the Irish fixed the standards of length measurements (called *tomus*) mostly, but not exclusively, on parts of the human body. One of the first tables of these measurements is contained in the Book of Aicill, one of the two great Brehon Law books written in the 5th century AD.

FREQUENTLY ASKED QUESTIONS

The smallest measurement used in ancient Ireland was the length of an average sized grain of wheat – that is *gráinne*.

Three *gráinne* produced the measurement one ordlach. A quicker way to indicate this measurement, than placing three grains together, was usually the length of the top joint of a thumb.

Four *ordlach* produced one bas, usually a palm width measured across the root of the fingers.

There were variations such as the *dorn*, a fist, but even this was broken down into two measurements. The *mail-dorn*, "bare fist" which was a fist with the thumb closed in, and the *airtem*, a fist with the thumb extended.

Going back to the *bas* measurement, three *bas* produced one *troighid*, which is roughly the measurement of an average foot.

Two and a half *troighid* produced a céim and two *céim* produced a *deis-céim* or full pace of a person. Two *déis-céim* produced a *fertach* while twelve *fertach* measured a *forrach*. To make the equivalent of the English mile one would have to estimate some 36.66666 & etc *forrach*.

The greatest distance recorded in early Irish texts was a *toin*. A *toin* was reserved for Irish astronomical observations because it is glossed as being the word for a measurement equivalent to 5000 Greek *stadia*. Now a *stadia* is a distance of 185 to 192 metres (607-630 feet in Imperial measurement). It is from where the word "stadium" derives. So, a *toin* would be the equivalent of between 9250 kilometres and 9600 kilometres. It is mentioned, among other works, in the *Leabhar Mór Mhic Fhir Bhisigh Leccain* (The Great Book of Leccan), now in Trinity College, Dublin.

Great distances in the early period were usually indicated as *asdar* or *aister*, which appears to derive from the Celtic root "to go." Vast distances simply became *cen thomhus* – immeasurable.

So, if I did not wish to be anachronistic, perhaps I should I have started using these ancient measures – with lengthy footnoted explanations.

The obvious answer was that I should render the terms into modern European measurements. And what are modern standard European measurements?

I am well aware that the United States seems to have maintained an affinity to the old Imperial measures.

However, in 1965 the United Kingdom and Ireland officially moved to the metric system and fell in line with the rest of Europe – in fact,

Ireland more rapidly than the UK with road distances in kilometres. Many young people, receiving their education after the 1970s in the UK and Ireland, have difficulty now understanding the old Imperial system. Everyone from 40 years old and under is at home with the metric system.

As an interpreter of 7th century Ireland, I chose to interpret the ancient Irish measurements into the modern standard system. It is as simple as that. Prior to 1965, as I was writing the books in English, I might well be giving Imperial measurements and leaving it to translators of my work into other European languages to translate into their metric system.

I have, incidentally, given the US publishers a choice of translating the European metric system into the Imperial system that is still used there but they seem to believe that most Americans are able to use metric measures as well as Imperial ones. Canada seems to have no problem about the metric system.

The logical conclusion of those trying to claim metric measurements as anachronistic in these books, is the argument that I should also be writing the stories in Old Irish, the Irish for the period, and not English. The other conclusion is that they are indulging in an unconscious cultural imperialism in placing the later English system, now replaced by the modern metric system, back in 7th century Ireland.

I am reading **Whispers of the Dead** *and in two places so far, a reference has been made to "ten minutes" – was this on a sundial or a water clock?*

"WAIT AN OSTINT!" (Ostint = 1 minute, 36 seconds)
While we realise that query is humorous, it raises a point which, although not a frequently asked question, is still valid.
Modern mystery writers can use time very precisely in their stories. Writing such tales set in 7th century Ireland, one has to be more general. However, like metric measurements explained above, one can use internationally accepted standards of time to give general approximations. In modern English, the term "ten minutes" (as in "I'll be ready in ten minutes") is not a precise measurement of time but indicates "in a short while." The term *deich nómíad-shin* (ten minutes ago) is used in Irish but also not as a precise measurement, just as the Irish use forms such as – *gceann tamaill bhig, bomaite ina dhiadh sin* & *nóimíad ina*

FREQUENTLY ASKED QUESTIONS

dhiadh to indicate in a little while. But it is my colloquial English use of time that Patricia has picked up on.

While the question is meant as humorous, it does raise a good point. In the works of several ancient writers, technical chronology is touched on. The ancient Irish also had their time divisions with minute denominations. The following measures are from the Old Irish text *Cath Maige Tuired* (Battle of Moytura) with the equivalents in what is considered modern timing.

- 1 *atam* = a quarter of a second
- 1 *ostent/ostint* (376 *atam*) = 1 mins 36 seconds
- 1 *bratha* (564 *atam*) = 2 mins 24 seconds
- 1 *pars* (940 *atam*) = 4 mins
- 1 *minuit* (1410 *atam*) = 6 mins
- 1 *pongc* (3525 *atam*) = 15 mins
- 1 *uair* (14,100 *atam*) = 60 mins
- 1 *cadar* (quarter of a day) = 6 hours

While the Irish give their lowest time measure as an *atam* (cognate with the Latin *atomus*), in the 8th century the Venerable Bede of Northumbria gave an even smaller measurement for the Anglo-Saxons that was eight times less, being one thirtieth of a second. Such minute measurements are also given in Latin in texts by Isidore of Seville (7th century) and by Rhabanus Maurus, Bishop of Mainz (9th century). Even the ancient Greeks experimented with measurements of time by means of a *clepsydra* (water clock) reckoning that 0.75 litres of water, emptying from a bowl in the *clepsydra*, gave them a measurement of 1 minute. Scholars generally accept that these small measurements were expressions of ideals and not meant as strictly accurate measurements.

The oldest surviving complete version of the text of *Cath Maige Tuired* is an 11th century version. Professor Brian Ó Cuív produced an excellent text and commentary published in Dublin in 1945. A more accessible bilingual text was produced by Dr Elizabeth Gray for the Irish Text Society in 1982. Also, for comparison, a text appeared in the *Irish Archaeological Miscellany*, Vol. I, published by the Irish Archaeological Society, 1848.

For discussions on the "time measurements" see Dr P.W. Joyce's *A Social History of Ancient Ireland* (London, 1903), vol. 2, page 387. There is also a discussion by Whitley Stokes in *The Tripartite Life of*

Patrick, 2 vols, London, 1887. In addition, Dr Stokes and John Stra-chan edited *Thesaurus Paleohibernicus*, 1901, 1903 and Supplement by Stokes, 1910, which also contains useful information.

However, in writing the Sister Fidelma Mysteries, I am aware that one cannot be precise with time, so I try to avoid using these measure-ments. While the ancient Irish had water-clocks and sundials, time, in specific terms, cannot enter into the stories in the way it could it modern stories even though, theoretically, with the *atam* as regarded as a quarter of a second, one might be given an indulgence.

In a couple of the books, the author has Sister Fidelma quote chapter and verse of a Bible passage for Eadulf. It is known that "chapter and verses" were not available until about 1000 years after Fidelma! Does Peter know something that we don't know?

A scholar who writes fiction on historical matters sometimes meets an immovable object in the person of his editor, who insists that his scholarship must taken second place to his readers' understanding. I believe in making things as easy as possible for readers but certainly not writing down to them. But I admit to having some irritating problems during the early years of writing Fidelma stories and these occasionally rear their heads from time to time when readers think they have spotted errors or anachronisms.

Most famously has been my choice of using metric measurements as the closest and most understandable form of interpreting ancient Irish measurements in modern terms. The editor tried to argue for the use of the even more anachronistic English Imperial measurements. Thankfully, I won this argument on the basis that the UK had officially adopted the metric system during the latter half of the 20th century. It is still amazing how many English readers race to inform me that I should be using Imperial measures!

The matter that I did not win in the early days of producing the books is identifying quotations from the Bible. The history of how the Bible was put together should be well known. The Councils and arguments about which books should be included and which left out is fascinating in itself.

I usually work with Jerome's 4th century Vulgate Latin, which version would be known and used in Fidelma's time. It was only in AD 325, just before this, that the New Testament was even divided into paragraphs, let alone chapter and verses.

All well and good for the scholar. But the early editor pointed out that I was not writing an academic book and that modern readers should have quotations identified for them in the modern way. That meant they wanted to use the modern chapter and verse reference, based on the King James version!

I tried to point out that the first English Bible to use chapter and verse division was the 1560 Geneva Bible. They were unmoved.

In vain, I pointed out that it was Cardinal Hugo de Sancto Caro, creating a concordance to the Vulgate, who created the basis of modern divisions about 1244 but Archbishop Langton of Canterbury had also made divisions which Wycliffe accepted for his English version of 1382 and which divisions we now use. As for the sub-divisions in verses, the Italian Dominican Santi Pagnini put the Latin New Testament into verses at the end of the 15th century.

Later William Whittington divided the English into versions – that was 1557.

On this matter the editor would not be moved and I, a humble scribe, succumbed. The editor eventually moved on and I reverted to stopping the anachronistic process, when quoting the Vulgate within the story. There were, of course very few times that this "chapter and verse" quotation system happened. Thankfully, although the Fidelma stories have sold in millions in several languages, only one reader has written in querying this over the entire period.

However, one piece of anachronism which is entirely down to me – *mea maxima culpa!* – is the fact that in *Shroud for the Archbishop* I mention fuschias in Ireland in Fidelma's time. Ooops! What was I thinking? Fuschias, so dominant on the Irish landscape for hundreds of years, did not enter Ireland until the 12th century. Yet no reader has picked that one up.

Can you provide more information on the unarmed combat that Sister Fidelma uses?

TROID SCIATHAGID (Battle Through Defence)
Troid (also *troit*) = fight, battle, quarrel; *sciath* = root word for shield,

defence, protection, guardian (*Royal Irish Academy Dictionary of the Irish Language: based mainly on Old and Middle Irish Materials*)

A Fellow of the Society of Martial Arts in the UK, a professional society which operates the College of Higher Education of Martial Arts, as approved by Privy Council wrote to Peter Tremayne through his publisher, seeking additional information on the martial art he attributes to Sister Fidelma, about which he had never been able to obtain any additional information.

In *Shroud for the Archbishop*, Chapter 13, Sister Fidelma first resorts to an unarmed combat technique which she calls *troid sciathagid* or "battle through defence" and which, she explains to her companion, Brother Eadulf, that Irish missionaries learn as a means of defending themselves without having to resort to weapons.

There is no complete text, so far identified, that has explained in detail how this method of unarmed combat worked. But, from various passing references, I believe we can assume that it was a series of defensive kicks, blows and wrestling holds which are parallels to aikido or a similar method.

Ruairi Ó Flaitheartaigh (1629-1718) in his work *Ogygia seu Rerum Hibernicum Chronologia* stated that Comrac Mac Airt founded three colleges at Tara, one of which was for teaching military science, as well as the use of weapons, strategy and so forth, wrestling and unarmed defence, were taught. Because no ancient reference was given by Ó Flaitheartaigh, Eugene O'Curry (1796-1862) in his three volume study *Lectures on the manners and customs of the Ancient Irish* was inclined to dismiss this reference as he did not think there were "regular professors and a regular system" of military instruction. But O'Curry contradicts himself when he talks about the military training warriors receive as part of a general education. If they received such training it must be that there were people who were qualified to instruct them and on a regular basis.

We can also see from many other references, particularly in the Red Branch Cycle, or Ulster Cycle, of Irish Myth, there is mention of such schools where warriors were so instructed and we find that sons of chiefs and children of the "higher classes" were sent to such schools where they were placed under the instruction of a warrior. Perhaps one of the most famous of these schools was that of Scóthach, a female warrior, who teaches the military arts to Cú Chulainn in the tale *Tochmarc Emire*. It was from Scóthach that the famous Ulster warrior learns the *torann-chless* (thunder feat) by which he could leap over the heads of his enemies when surrounded using no artificial aids. Reference to such tactics is made in *Aided Oenfhir Aife* (or, *The Tragic Death of Aifeás Only Son*) showing that Cú Chulainn relies not only on weapons to defend himself but on physical agility and using his opponent's aggression to bring about their downfall.

In *Cath Fionntrógha* we have a reference to warriors fighting unarmed against one another. Prof. Kuno Meyer interprets this as "wrestling warriors" (1885) and in the version of the Rawlinson B487 manuscript of the 15th century the phrase *tucadar trodchuir trena troid déaroili* is given also implying that they were fighting with their bare hands and had no weapons.

Certainly, wrestling was given high priority on the list of arts taught to Irish children not only as a recreation game and also introduced as a pastime at the fairs but as part of warrior training. And this form of wrestling was particular to the Celts. Indeed, there are countless references to a particular form of Celtic wrestling – even before Agincourt in 1415 it was reported that the Cornish fought under a banner showing two wrestlers in a "hitch" which was looked upon as their national symbol. Geoffrey of Monmouth, Layamon, Spenser and Milton all mention the prowess of Celtic wrestlers. Francois I of France and Henry VIII in 1520 sent Cornish, Welsh and Breton wrestlers to have a match at the Field of the Cloth of Gold. A particular form of wrestling survived in Cornwall, Brittany, Wales and Cumberland so that in the 10th century annual Pan Celtic Wrestling Tournaments were normal and Pan Celtic Gatherings such as those at Lorient & etc. There are references to a similar sort of wrestling surviving in some rural parts of Ireland and some contests taking place at the Donnybrook Fair in the 19th century.

When we find references to peregrinatio pro Christo using *troid sciathagid* to defend themselves from bandits (a mention I think, without checking, in *Essai díun catalogue de la littérature épique de l'Irlande*, Paris, 1883, and talk of it being a defensive art, I think we can only interpret in way I have in the Fidelma books. Especially the references to Irish missionaries being taught to defend themselves "without inflicting violence" – a particular reference in the Mss of the former College of Irish Franciscans, Louvain (*Fourth Report of the Royal Commission on Historical Manuscripts*, 1874).

Of course, I admit that I have taken the few references that I have come upon and made an interpretation for the fiction of the Fidelma novels. It needs more time and more workers in the field to see if more information on this subject can be recovered. Alas, I now do not have time to undertake such a task. But one of the problems in finding dedicated workers in the field is the lack of funding and encouragement of researchers in the field of Celtic Studies.

I was shocked (and still am) when an old mentor of mine Professor Gearóid Mac Eoin, who was at Galway UC, explained to me many years ago that even in the field of Irish mythology we had only scratched the surface of research. Professor Kuno Meyer back in 1900 in his introduction to *Liadain and Curithir* listed 400 sagas and tales in manuscript. But he added a further 100 which had been brought to light since he had completed that list and estimated a further 50 to 100 manuscript tales were probably undiscovered in some repository. Indeed, Dr Eleanor Hull in *The Cuchullin Saga in Irish Literature* (1898) had made a similar estimate.

Professor Mac Eoin pointed out that our knowledge of Irish mythology was based on the translations of only about 150 manuscript tales. That meant in 1900 there were some 400 manuscripts untouched. The punch line is that in spite of this early identification of these manuscripts and the problem, these manuscripts still remain untouched in Old and Middle Irish forms because of lack of funding and academic encouragement. When I, under my own name, published this fact in my *Dictionary of Irish Mythology* (1987), it elicited no response from the Irish Government or Universities. Manuscripts do come to light by pure accident – such as the famous Irish calendar which Columbanus quoted in his argument to Pope Gregory and was thought to have been lost for over 1,000 years. This was found by accident in the Biblioteca Antoniana in Padua in the late 1980s. What a find! But it is all done by hit and miss methods.

I realise that this is not of much help to resolving your specific questions. I believe, from the various shadowy references I have come across by accident, that I have interpreted the term *troid-sciathagid* correctly and, perhaps, somewhere out in the piles of Irish mss that, shamefully, are lying untouched in various repositories, there may well be one which will explain the details of this defensive form.

In the meantime, thank you for your interested and all your support for the Sister Fidelma books which, I hope, will create an awareness among a new generation of the richness of the culture that so desperately needs more qualified workers in the field of all aspects Celtic Studies.

There is mention of a corn mill in **Atonement of Blood,** *but* *everything I've read about corn claims that it didn't get to* *Europe until around 1500 AD.*

This is actually one of the most frequently asked of all the questions we receive from visitors. The answer to this question highlights the fact that, to paraphrase the Irish writer George Bernard Shaw, we are two [or many] nations divided by a common language. Although, so far as we have observed, both Webster's and OED carry the same definitions.

Certainly, in the English Dictionary, "corn" does not only mean maize – and it would certainly not mean maize during the period being written about. You will find that the word "corn" was, and is, used for wheat in England, and oats in Scotland – in fact any local cereal crops, even barley anciently. The word "corn" is found in Old English (Anglo-Saxon), Old Frisian, Old Scandinavia, Old High German, Old Norse, and Gothic – usually as *korn* or *kaurn,* referring to cereal or farinaceous plants; that is, plants yielding flour or starch of a mealy nature. In Old and Middle Irish there are words such as *airmnech* and *arbar,* referring to the growing of such crops, that are translated as "corn" in English – specifically referring to cereal crops – wheat and barley being the main cereal crops farmed in Ireland as early as 4000-2000 BC.

We would like to know more about those people who Peter *Tremayne has mentioned as influencing his interest in the* *ancient Irish law system.*

Peter has written articles for some Irish publications about these individuals and as and when they are available for internet use, Peter is allowing us to post them on the website. In the first of these articles, he talks of the author of the very first book he read on Brehon Law – Lawrence Ginnell (1854-1923).

When the body of Laurence Ginnell, who died in a hotel in Washington, DC, in 1923, was brought back to be buried in his native Delvin,

Co. Westmeath, Ireland, Mrs Margaret Pearse, the mother of Pádraic Pearse (executed leader of the 1916 insurrection), delivered the funeral oration. She reminded those gathered that Ginnell, the radical Member of Parliament for North Westmeath at Westminster, had been popularly known as "The Member for Ireland."

Ginnell was an extraordinary man. He was a lawyer, called to both the Irish and English Bars, and a scholar – writer of some profound legal studies. He was elected to the Westminster House of Commons as a member of the Irish Party in 1906. But after the 1916 Insurrection, he resigned and joined Sinn Féin. He was then re-elected and took his seat in the breakaway Dáil in Dublin and held the seat until his death.

It was boasted that he had been ejected more times from the House of Commons (Westminster) than any other Member for raising controversial issues which made him a thorn in the side of the British Establishment. Even the Irish Parliamentary Party once expelled him for the offence of asking to see the party accounts and later he was bodily ejected from the Free State Dáil.

Yet today his name is unknown, his grave neglected and there is no memorial to the "Member for Ireland."

Ginnell took his degrees in law and was called to both the Irish Bar and the English Bar, having also studied at the Middle Temple. He gave a lecture to the Irish Literary Society in London on ancient Irish law, and this led to his famous book *The Brehon Laws* (1894). He also wrote the controversial study *The Doubtful Grant of Ireland* (1899) on the illegality of the Papal grant of Ireland to the Angevin emperor, Henry II, which supported the Norman invasions.

He was fifty years old when he became involved in politics, and he threw himself enthusiastically into the battle not only for self-government but for the transfer of ownership of the land from the big landlords and their estates to tenant farmers. His campaigns marked a new phase of the Land War and Ginnell was almost a lone voice in the Irish Party whose leadership was disinclined to get involved in more radical policies after the fall of Parnell.

Ginnell was active in the United Irish League and, as a prominent campaigner, he was often arrested by the police and served several short prison sentences.

He was in Dublin in 1916 and there are stories that he was no mere observer of the insurrection. On May 9, as the executions of the leaders were being used to hammer Ireland into submission, it was Ginnell, in the House of Commons, who roared "murderers!" at the Government benches.

Without Ginnell, the hundreds who were being interned in the wake of 1916, would have had no rights or legal representation. He deluged the House of Commons with questions about the internees and the imprisoned insurgents, demanding information, raising questions about the shooting of civilians by the British troops, and he insisted on visiting the internees who had been brought to England and Wales. At one point, the Government banned Ginnell from visiting jails.

At Knutsford Jail, he signed his name as "Labhras Mag Fionngaile" and was immediately fined for "breaking the law" in spite of there being no law against using the Irish version of one's name. He refused to pay, pointing out this fact, but was then jailed for not paying the fine.

In 1917, after consulting with a meeting of his constituents, he resigned from the Irish Party and his House of Commons seat. He joined Sinn Féin and became its joint treasurer. Early in 1918 he was arrested and taken to England to serve a jail sentence for purportedly "agitation" in Co. Westmeath.

In the General Election of 1918, he was again elected to his seat in North Westmeath and this time, with the unilateral declaration of independence, he took his seat in the Dáil. He was appointed Minister for Propaganda. He was arrested in May for belonging to "an illegal assembly" and imprisoned again.

His health was shattered by the years of continued harassment and imprisonment. He was in his late sixties. The English authorities released him in 1920, worried at the deterioration in his health, and the Dáil sent him to Argentina as, effectively, the ambassador of the republic.

He tried to get back to Ireland for the Treaty Debate and even telegraphed from the ship asking that he be allowed to send a proxy vote. He took the Anti-Treaty side during the Civil War, being re-elected as a republican candidate in May that year. In September 1922, at de Valéra's personal request, he was the only republican to enter the Dáil to challenge the legality of the Free State.

He accused deputies who "illegally, at the bidding of a foreign government, did begin civil war" did illegally by decree purport to suppress the Supreme Court of the Republic – and are steadily overthrowing Dáil Éireann and substituting their own personal government."

When his legal questions became too uncomfortable, William Cosgrave moved that Ginnell should be removed from the House. When Ginnell argued they had no right to remove an elected member of Dáil Éireann, Ginnell, aged 70 years, was forcibly dragged out of chamber.

In October 1922, he became a member of the republican "Council of State" formed by de Valéra and was shortly afterwards sent to the USA to help co-ordinate assistance for the republican cause there. He had been very distressed at the developments in the Civil War, not the least by the execution of his friend Erskine Childers, executed on November 27 while an appeal against his sentence was pending before the High Court. Ginnell's last book was The Seventh Year of the Republic: A Defence of Erskine Childers (1923).

He died in a Washington hotel on April 17, 1923, and his body was brought back to his native Delvin, Co. Westmeath, where there were great scenes of national mourning.

Had Ginnell contributed nothing more than his book *The Brehon Law*, a brief introductory study to the ancient Irish law system, a system that was finally suppressed during the 17th century, he would have been deserving of some recognition. But he achieved far more.

It is sad for this writer that Dublin newspapers not so long ago ran an advertisement seeking information about Laurence Ginnell to help the Irish Civil Service with their archives about former members of Dáil Éireann.

Can Peter Tremayne give more details about Dr Sophie Bryant who he says had a great influence on his work and understanding of Brehon Law from a Feminist perspective?

The first woman in the United Kingdom ever to obtain both a Bachelor of Science degree and a Doctor of Science degree was Sophie Willock Bryant (1850-1922) from Sandymount, Dublin. She went on to gain another doctorate, that of Doctor of Literature. She was a brilliant scholar who, in 1898, was the first women ever to be elected by the Convocation of London University to the University Senate.

She was one of the key influences in my own reading and interpretation of ancient Ireland and two of her books still have prominent places on my bookshelves today. Her main influence on me was her classic study Liberty, Order and Law Under Native Irish Rule (1923), published a year after her tragic death when she was overwhelmed in an avalanche while mountaineering on Mont Blanc, in France, at the age of 72!

She was a well-known Alpine climber.

A granite cross still marks her grave in Chamonix-Mont Blanc.

Sophie, she preferred that form than the more formal Sophia, made a groundbreaking analysis of the ancient Irish (Brehon) law system from a feminist viewpoint. She was, of course, a campaigner for women's rights and suffrage. She was president of the Hampstead Suffrage Society and one of the leaders of the 1908 march of the National Union of Suffrage Societies.

She was also an active campaigner for Irish self-government, helping to form a support group in England and lecturing on self-government platforms both in Ireland and England.

Sophie was the daughter of Professor W. A. Willock, a Fellow of Trinity College, Dublin, who had played an important role in the Commission for National Education in Ireland. He privately educated his daughter with the aid of a governess until, aged thirteen, the family moved to London when her father was appointed to the chair of Geometry at London University. Sophie, aged only sixteen, entered Bedford College in 1866, won a science scholarship the same year and took the Cambridge Examination for Girls' matriculation the next year.

Aged nineteen, in 1869, she married Dr W. Hicks Bryant, but found herself a widow one year later when her husband died from cirrhosis. She never married again. She obtained a teaching post in a girls' school in Highgate, north London.

Teaching German and mathematics, Sophie joined the staff of the North London Collegiate School in Camden in 1875. By 1884 she had secured her first doctorate in moral science. By 1895 she was headmistress of the NLCS and one of three women members of the Royal Commission on Secondary Education.

She was a member of the Education Committee of the then London County Council and served on many committees and councils all the way to government level at the then Board of Education.

She became chair of the Teachers' Training College Council, President of the Association of Head Mistresses ad helped with the transfer of Goldsmith's College to London University status.

She was dynamic and active as a "hands on" educationalist. She did not retire as headmistress of the NCLS until 1918, at the age of sixty-eight.

It is amazing that she also found time to study and write. Her degrees in moral science would be the equivalent of degrees in philosophy and psychology today. She wrote many books and countless articles on moral and religious education and also philosophy in general. These included works like *Short Studies in Character* (1894) and *Moral and Religious Education* (1920). She even found time to co-author works on Euclid's *Elements of Geometry*.

Sophie had also studied Old and Middle Irish and had not neglected an interest in the country of her birth and childhood. Indeed, she was a member of the Irish Literary Society, founded in 1891, of which the Nobel Laureate W.B. Yeats became President. She was also a member of the Irish Text Society and the Gaelic League.

She published a volume, *Celtic Ireland* (1889), and then a ground-breaking volume, *The Genius of the Gael: A study in Celtic psychology and its manifestations* (1913). Coming as the Third Reading of the Home Rule for Ireland Bill was passing through the House of Commons, the book was not only an analysis of attitudes in Ireland but also an enthusiastic endorsement of those who sort to re-Gaelicise Ireland.

Sophie's anti-Partition views were clear when she contributed the foreword to W.A. McKnight's book *Ireland and the Ulster Legend: or, the Truth about Ulster* (1921).

However, it was Sophie's study on the Brehon laws of ancient Ireland that had the most lasting impact of her books. It was also her magnum opus.

She wrote it as the new Irish state was coming into being.

"It has also been written throughout in the hope that it might prove to be of interest – perhaps even of service – to my countrymen and countrywomen in the work of social reorganisation which lies before them, and to which so many of them have already put their hand."

It seems that Sophie shared the ideas put forward by many who had studied the ancient Irish laws and thought that, on independence, Ireland should not merely adopt English law, which had been forced on the country during the conquests of the 16th and 17th centuries but turned to the spirit of the native law system and update it for modern usage.

Such a person was the barrister, Laurence Ginnell (1854-1923), a long time Irish National Party Member of Parliament who had changed his attitudes after the 1916 uprising to be elected as one of the earliest

Sinn Féin MPs, being re-elected in 1918 General Election for Westmeath. He served initially as the first Dáil's Director of Publicity before being imprisoned by the British for belonging to "an illegal assembly." Ginnell had written several works among the best known of which was *The Brehon Laws: A Legal Handbook* (1894). [Ginnel's life is dealt with in the above answer to a question. Ed.]

Another legal mind supported the idea was James Creed Meredith, a barrister entrusted by the Irish Government of 1919-21 with drafting a constitution for the new republic and the rules of the law courts. He was appointed by the first Dáil as President of the Supreme Court having charge over what the English called the "Sinn Féin courts." In 1920 Meredith, hearing a case on women's rights, pronounced English law retrograde and applied Brehon law to give judgement in favour of an unmarried mother for medical expenses.

In 1922 Sophie had written: "In the work of regeneration for the future that lies before the Irish people, a more widely diffused and accurate knowledge of the old Irish customs should be of great value, as an inspiring motive force, in recreating gradually, under native rule – by the national organisation of the modern composite Irish race – the old delight in the sanctity of contracts and equitable law which is expressed in the pages of the *Senchus Mor* and the other Irish law tracts."

Sadly, however, with the emergence of the Free State, the idea of updating the progressive principles of the native Irish law system was dropped and English Statute and Common Law were accepted by the newly emerging state.

One tribute I can offer and that is without Sophie Bryant, her work on Brehon Law and women's place within it, my alter ego, Peter Tremayne, might never have created the 7th century Irish sleuth and lawyer, Sister Fidelma, who seems to have found such a remarkable resonance across the world among readers in the ten languages into which she is translated.

It is sad that Sophie's contribution and achievements do not appear to be more widely acknowledged in her native land. However, the archives of the North London Collegiate School, where there is a "Bryant Wing," have kept her papers, among them a Willock family album, relating to her Irish family.

THE SISTER FIDELMA COMPENDIUM

Did Sister Fidelma's world really exist?

ANSWERING CRITICS: FIDELMA'S WORLD DID EXIST

When the Sister Fidelma stories first began to appear, some reviewers expressed their surprise, if not disbelief, that any woman in Fidelma's time could have such rights and exercises such authority. They could not bring themselves to accept that 7th century Irish women could have such roles nor exercise priestly functions and even be ordained bishops in the Celtic Church.

In 1996 Peter Tremayne was invited to talk about his books at St Hilda's College, Oxford, at a "Crime and Mystery Weekend." On the day before he was due to give his talk, a lady in the audience had criticised many modern historical "whodunits" for having an "anachronism of attitude," saying the authors were not dealing with things as they were in the times about which they were writing but placing modern attitudes in their characters. She invoked Tremayne's Sister Fidelma stories as an example saying, Fidelma's world could not have existed.

The next day, Peter tore up his original lecture and began to talk about the role of women in 7th century Ireland.

What the critic in the audience had ignored was that fact that Peter, under his own name, is one of the foremost authorities on Celtic history and culture, who has published many books and studies in this field and lectured widely.

Such criticism, however, caused the publishers to ask Peter Tremayne to add an "Historical Note" to the books to help people realise the background.

In an issue of *The Brehon* we published letters from two Fidelma enthusiasts who were still not sure of the historical background – Father Timothy Cremeens felt that he "[did] not think women were ordained presbyters and bishops in the Celtic Church. I really do not think the historical evidence supports it. If so, I would like to see clear references."

Another reader wondered "did Peter Tremayne make this up or did Brehon law actually see women as being individual, valued members of society?"

We asked Peter to respond.

"I can fully understand why people are amazed when they come across Brehon law and look at the rights accorded to women in 7th century Ireland. We are, after all, the product of many centuries of propaganda against the ancient Irish and their society and this has had an effect on our concepts – and, of course, our concepts not just of the Irish, but the Celts in general. So I don't blame people for asking the questions. I am only irritated with some reviewers attempt to disguise their ignorance in glib and derisory sneers, implying that I am guilty of some fabrication, such as a recent reviewer in *Kirkus Reviews*. Fortunately – over the years – they can be counted on the fingers of one hand and most reviewers are more professional.

"To respond to Val of Sydney: no, I do not make anything up when related to Brehon law. It would be more than my reputation as a scholar is worth, even when writing fiction, to start changing the concepts of Brehon law. There are many academic works, translations and studies on the ancient Irish law system to which people can go to check me out. Don't forget, the Brehon laws survive in writing. We have many fragmentary texts from early Christian times and our earliest most complete text of the laws survive in the Lebar na h Uidri which was compiled at Clonmacnoise c. AD 1100. The chief scribe on this work was Mael Muire Mac Ceileachair who died in AD 1106.

"The grandfather of the literary Nobel laureate, Robert Graves, was Charles Graves (1812-1899) who was President of the Royal Irish Academy and an expert on Ogham and on Brehon law. It was Charles Graves who finally persuaded the British Government to establish a commission to rescue all the manuscript texts then known to exist and edit, translate and publish them. The Ancient Laws of Ireland were published in six large volumes between 1865 and 1901.

"Other manuscript law texts have come to light since then.

"Among the books I especially recommend to students are *A Guide to Early Irish Law* by Professor Fergus Kelly, Dublin Institute of Advanced Studies, 1988; *Liberty Order and Law Under Native Irish Rule*, Dr Sophie Bryant, Harding & Moore, London, 1923; and *Studies in Early Irish Law*, various scholars, Royal Irish Academy, Dublin, 1936 – this volume particularly deals with women's rights. There are many others. I mentioned in a recent talk to the Irish Literary Society, Laurence Ginnell's *The Brehon Laws: A Legal Handbook*. T. Fisher Unwin, London, 1894, which awoke my interested in the subject when I was a boy, it being on my father's bookshelves.

"So, there is no need to wonder whether the society about which I write and in which Fidelma lives is made up or not. Go to source. Check it out for yourselves. Nothing in the Fidelma books is made up, apart from the characters and the stories.

"Turning to Father Cremeens' observation. He is not alone in being dubious that women could exercise priestly functions or even be bishops. One cannot blame him and even some scholars, like Dom Louis Gougard, whose *Christianity in Celtic Lands* (1932) is a seminal study, find themselves uneasy in dealing with the evidence. Dom Louis, who was a Benedictine monk as well as a scholar and admittedly had an axe to grind for Rome, tends to claim that the Celtic women carrying priestly functions were an aberration and seeks to dismiss the idea as not being generally applied. However, the evidence is there as I pointed out in my study *Celtic Women: Women in Celtic Study and Literature* especially in chapter six on "Women in the Celtic Church."

"Once again, I merely present the evidence and it would be more than my reputation is worthy if I could not substantiate my statements without references. The 7th century composition "Hymn to Brigid" tells us that Mel, bishop of Ardagh and Patrick's nephew ordained Brigid as a bishop. Hilda of Whitby and Beverley of York, both abbesses were brought up in the Celtic traditions, were also noted as being bishops. And we have the letter of protest written by Roman clerics to their Celtic brethren demanding that Celts stop allowing women to perform the divine sacrifice of the Mass. There are six pages of bibliography in *Celtic Women*, which will help the serious scholar, so I won't bother to repeat them here.

"Fidelma's world was a reality. It is a pity that it was destroyed. I can only echo a review of a Fidelma book written by the award-winning Irish novelist and scriptwriter Ronan Bennett: "I put down *The Spider's Web* with a sense of satisfaction at a good story well told but also speculating at what modem life might have been like had that civilisation survived."

What was the Yellow Plague that is frequently mentioned in the stories?

THE YELLOW PLAGUE
The Yellow Plague which wiped out one third of the population of Ireland during AD 664-668 is thought to have been a recurrence of the Plague of Justinian which had its origins at Pelusium in Egypt in AD 542. By means of merchant ships it was spread to Constantinople where, in that year, it wiped out 10,000 people in one day. It had reached Gaul by AD 546 where Gregory of Tours (c. AD 538-594) says that its

symptoms compared to *lues inguinaria*, seeming to identify it as a bubonic plague. By AD 547 it had reached the island of Britain where the *Annales Cambriae* (Welsh annals, the earliest copy surviving from the 10th century) record the death from it of Maelgwyn Hir (the Tall), King of Gwynedd. He was one of the most powerful rulers of 6th century Britain who some regarded as the original Arthur being rebuked by Gildas in his *De Excidio et Conquestu Britanniae* (written c. AD 560) and referred to as "dragon of the island" (Pendragon?).

In AD 561-556 the plague is now recorded in Ireland and named in the Irish Annals and Chronicles as the Buidhe Conaill – the Yellow Conaill. We will deal with the meaning of this name in a moment.

In AD 664 the Yellow Plague was devastating Europe once again and estimates of its destruction seem to agree that a third of the population has died from it. The Venerable Bede points out that many prominent people in the Anglo-Saxon kingdoms, such as King Eorcenberht of Kent (AD 640-664) and Bishop Tuda, have succumbed to it and it has swept as far north as Lastingham, in Northumbria.

Bede writes: "This pestilence did no less harm in the island of Ireland. Many of the nobility and of the lower ranks of the English nation were there at that time, who, in the days of the Bishops Finan and Colman, forsaking their native land, retired thither, either for the sake of divine studies, or of a more continent life; and some of them presently devoted themselves to a monastic life; other chose rather to apply themselves to study, going about from one master's cell to another. The Irish willingly received them all, and took care to supply them with food, as also to furnish them with books to read, and their teaching, all gratis."

This passage also underlines the Irish records that many of the Anglo-Saxon kings, princes and nobility went to Ireland to receive their education at this time and were welcomed by the Irish as Eadulf is an illustration in the stories.

The Irish records also name of numerous kings, princes, abbots and bishops from all over the country and recounts the flight of Bishop Colman and his followers from Cork to Inis Bó Finne (Inishboffin) one of the western islands, to escape its ravages. Even the joint High Kings of Ireland, Diarmuid and Blathmac mac Aedha Slaine, were not immune from the *mortalitas magna* and well-known churchmen such as St. Aileran of the Wisdom and St. Féchine of Fore also perished. In one short period four abbots of Bangor – Berach, Cumine, Colm and

Mac Aedha – died one after the other.

The Fáilire Oengus (c. AD 800-850) record that St Ultan, bishop of Ardbraccan in Co Meath, survived the Yellow Plague and established orphanages for the children of those who had perished. To feed the babies he took cows horns, hollowed out with an opening at the smaller end, through which the babies would suckle.

What, then, was the Yellow Plague which caused such a devastation?

The Irish generally record the Yellow Plague as *Buidhe Conaill* and a few times as *chron conaill*. It is often glossed as the *plaga magna* or the *mortalitis magna*. In other countries the Latin name *pestis flava* (yellow plague) also occurs. The Irish word buidhe means yellow and, according to the Royal Irish Academy's *Dictionary of the Irish Language* based mainly on Old and Middle Irish Materials (Compact Edition, Dublin, 1983), the Buidhe Conaill is a relapsing fever with accompanying jaundice. It has been pointed out that while the word Conaill is often given with a capital "C," in the early texts it was given with a small "c" and was thus the genitive of *condall*, meaning "aftermath." There has arisen therefore a confusion among some scholars that the name of the plague was called the "Yellow (Plague) of Conaill" for there is an old Irish name Conall ("strong as a wolf") but, as we now see, it means "yellow aftermath." The other term *chron conaill* means "dark yellow aftermath."

An interesting study on this is Sir W.P. MacArthur's paper "The Identification of Some Pestilences recorded in the Irish Annals' *Irish Historical Studies*, Dublin University Press, vol. vi. (1948-49), pp 169-188.

The Irish for jaundice at this time was *galar buidhe*.

The Oxford English Dictionary has long defined the Yellow Plague as "jaundice," agreed to by most medical historians who believe it to be either a virulent form of jaundice or jaundice as a complication arising after a form of the bubonic plague, which was a condition from inflamed swelling of glandular parts of the body – the lymph nodes or buboes. There would seem no contradiction in either definition.

What exactly is Ogham, which is mentioned in the Fidelma books, and can you explain a little more about it?

Many scholars write this as *ogam*, which is the original form of the word with a dot over the "g" which softens it. Later, the Irish adopted the letter "h" and inserted that after the "g" to indicate the softening process – hence *ogham*.

The bulk of ogham inscriptions survive on stone memorials from the 5th and 6th centuries AD. This form of early writing was named after Ogma, the Irish god of eloquence and literacy.

The letters of the alphabet are represented by varying numbers of strokes and notches. There are 369 known extant inscriptions and of these 121 are in Co. Kerry, where the highest density occurs, with 81 in Co Cork and 47 in Co. Waterford. This leads the scholar Dr Martín Ó Murchá to argue that this form of writing had its origins in the kingdom of Muman (Munster), Sister Fidelma's own country. A few ogham inscriptions are found in other parts of Ireland and then, as the Irish travelled, they occur in South Wales, where the Irish established the kingdom of Dyfed, founded by the Déisi of Munster (there 15 inscribes stones in Pembroke), then in Cornwall, Isle of Man and Scotland.

The old Irish records that ogham was also used on wooden wands (wands of the poets) and carved on bones. However, it is only the stone memorials that appear to have survived to date. The early recorded texts of myths and stories show that ogham was considered a natural form of writing. For example, in the Táin Bó Cuailgne we find Cóchullain carves a warning in ogham and sends it to Ailill and Medb, in the Immran Brain or Voyage of Bran, Bran writes down fifty or sixty quatrains of poetry in ogham. We hear of great libraries of ogham texts in such stories as Baile Mac Buain. In the 3rd/4th century Cosmographia Aethici Istrii – Cosmography of the World by Aethicus of Istria quoted in the later work of Orosius Paulus circa AD 416 – Aethicus says he sailed to Ireland where he remained some time examining their books which he described as ideomochos, implying they were unusual and native to the country.

We owe our knowledge of how to transcribe ogham thanks to a key given in the Book of Ballymote, compiled in Sligo in 1390 by Magnus É Duibhgeínnáin which copies a text that is dated to the 11th century. The book also contains bardic tracts on poetic metre and grammar and an Irish translation of the Aenid. It seems, according to the manuscripts, some letters were added later to the original ogham found on inscriptions, and these introduced symbols for complicated sound values – ea, oi, ui oi, ae and were called *forfeda* (from forfid – additional letters). These represented the *défogur* or double-vowel sounds. More fancifully *forfeda* were given non-Irish values such as K, TH, P, PH and X.

The main letters had the equivalents of A, O, U, E, I; H, D, T, C, Q; B, L, F, S, N; and M, G, NG, Z, R.

There have been several studies of ogham and the surviving inscription. However, the best remains *A Guide to Ogam*, by Damian McManus, An Sagart, Maynooth, 1991. (one of the Maynooth Monographs No 4).

When was the last judgment given under Brehon Law, the ancient native law system of Ireland?

THE LAST JUDGE OF THE BREHON LAWS

You might be surprised to know that it was in 1920. And who gave it? Mr Justice James Creed Meredith, then President of the Irish Supreme Court.

Hearing a case regarding women's rights, Mr Justice Meredith told his court that English Law was retrograde in respect of the rights of women, and he reverted to the Law of the Fénechus which are more popularly known as Brehon Law, deriving its name from the Irish word *breitheamh*, a judge.

It is one of those curiosities that the name of James Creed Meredith has been almost deleted from Irish history. He is given only a few intriguing references in *The Irish Republic 1916-1923* by Dorothy Macardle (1937) and a few passing references in more obscure works such as *Memoirs of Senator James G. Douglas: Concerned Citizen* (1998) and so on.

Yet this was the Quaker lawyer appointed by the First Dáil (1919-21) as its Supreme Court Judge and who was nominated by Eamon de Valéra to chair a committee to draw up the rules of the new courts and provide a constitution for the Irish Republic during the turbulent War of Independence.

Why has he been airbrushed out of history?

James Creed Meredith was born in Dublin in 1875. He came from a family of barristers and lawyers. It was inevitable that he would also study law, graduating from UCD and in 1901 becoming a King's Counsel. This was the equivalent of the modern QC or Queen's Counsel. But Meredith also picked up a master's degree as well as becoming a Doctor of Literature.

He translated Immanuel Kant's *The Critique of Judgement*, published by Clarendon Press, Oxford, which has since become the standard English translation, new editions of which are still published nearly a hundred years later.

Meredith not only believed in Irish independence, but he was fascinated by a new electoral system for Ireland. He was a member of the Proportional Representation Society of Ireland and in 1913 produced one of the many leaflets the Dublin-based organisation published.

Along with Francis Sheehy-Skeffington, the pacifist and writer (1878-1916) and Dermod O'Brien, the painter (1865-1945) he was a member of the United Irish League. The three of them left it to form a more radical and progressive group after disagreeing with John Redmond, the leader of the Irish Party, and his compromising efforts.

Meredith also supported Sir Horace Plunkett (1854-1932) and the writer AE, George Russell (1867-1935) in campaigning to set up an Irish Convention in 1917 to find a path out of the labyrinth of the Nationalist-Unionist stalemate.

Following the Sinn Féin landslide election success in 1918, the unilateral declaration of independence, the Dáil was established as the independent parliament in Dublin in 1919. It was then that Austin Stack, as Minister for Justice, appointed Meredith to draft a constitution and rules of the new Irish Law Courts. He was aided by Arthur Cleary BL, Cahir Davitt BL, Diarmuid Crowley BL, Hector Hughes BL, Conor Maguire and Kevin O'Shiel.

By June 29, 1920, the Dáil approved the establishment of courts of justice and equity to supersede the English colonial courts.

Meredith was appointed President of the Supreme Court, sitting in Dublin, with a minimum two other members of legal qualification and of at least twelve years legal standing. The British administration dismissed the system as "Sinn Féin courts."

Meredith stated that the new republic's courts would administer "the law, as recognised on January 21st, 1919, until amended" except such portion thereof as was clearly motivated by religious or political animosity." Citations could be made to any court ruling from "the early Irish Law Codes, or any commentary upon them in so far as they may be applicable to modern conditions."

And it was customary that when a woman was being tried, a woman judge sat on the Bench. As Dorothy Macardle says:

"In one instance, Judge Meredith, holding that English law was retrograde in the matter before the court – the appeal of an unmarried mother for medical expenses – applied the Brehon Code and gave judgement in favour of the girl. This created an interesting link with old Irish principles of justice and preserved continuity between the old Brehon Law of Ireland and the Republican courts."

The dangerous conditions under which he operated, he was liable to be assassinated by British Intelligence groups or "Black and Tans," did not prevent his work. In 1920 he published an annotated text of The Increase of Rent and Mortgage Interest Restrictions Act, 1920, passed in the London Parliament. The modern law of rent restrictions in the private sector began during World War One when a general shortage of housing led to the passing of a similar 1915 Act. This and other such Acts were consolidated in the 1920 Act, the purpose of which was to provide security of tenure for tenants and to prevent landlords from charging excessive rents.

With the collapse of the republic, the approval of the Anglo-Irish Treaty in January 1922, Meredith ended his tenure as President of the Supreme Court. A new Constitutional Committee was set up with Michael Collins as chair and it is important to note that James Douglas, who took a prominent role on this committee, wrote in his memoirs: "I remember particularly that he (Collins) expressed agreement with the proposal to abolish capital punishment which was in this draft. He said we had had enough executions in Ireland, and that it would be a good thing to see the end of them."

Sadly, in the year that followed Collins' death, those who claimed to follow his vision authorised the execution of 77 political prisoners. Capital punishment was not finally abolished by the Irish State until 1989 although there had been no executions since 1954.

From 1923 Meredith was elected to the senate of the National University of Ireland and remained a member until his death in 1942. He became a judge in the High Court of the Free State from 1924-1936 and then return to the Supreme Court from 1937-1942.

He was one of the presiding judges to oversee the League of Nations' plebiscite on the Saar in 1934/5. After World War I, the Versailles Treaty placed the administration of the Saar Valley in south-west Germany under a League of Nations' mandate, but its rich mines were given to France to exploit. Political pressure in 1934 forced the League to hold a plebiscite, which then restored the territory to Germany.

Meredith was multi-talented, and he also wrote fiction. His novel was published by Brown & Nolan, Dublin, entitled *The Rainbow in the*

Valley (1939) and he also wrote a play – *Nell Nelligan: A romance of the Irish Volunteers*, 1940, the text of which was also published.

James Creed Meredith, one of the most interesting personalities in the founding of the Irish State, who does not even rate a mention in biographical dictionaries of the period, died at his home in Dublin on August 14, 1942.

I am a French fan of the Sister Fidelma books. As someone with a Catholic background, I find Fidelma quite free in her movements, leaving her abbey without restrictions. What were the values of religious vows in those days, the importance of the hierarchy, especially in a religious house like an abbey? Could someone really decide to leave when they wanted? Could they choose to return to the laity without incurring any retaliation from the Church. Or is it that Fidelma is allowed this freedom because she is sister to the King?

As the author has pointed out, those who look for late medieval concepts of the Catholic Church in the rituals and liturgies and practices of the Early Irish Church (or Celtic Church as it is often called) will look in vain.

The author has described in some detail what the church practices in the answers to other questions on this page and there is a recommended reading list of books about the Early Irish Church (above).

You will find that bishops and abbots in Early Irish religious houses acted like chieftains in that they were usually elected and had to obey the commonwealth of the community, rather than imposing their will, otherwise they would be in trouble. In leaving Kildare, Fidelma was only exercising the right shared by everyone, not simply because she was the sister of the King of Muman.

In the 7th century churches in Ireland, there were generally no strict vows such as you mention covering every member of the religious. Ideas varied from area to area, monastery to monastery. "The Rule" of religious houses was not uniform. Some made up their own set of rules, others adopted Roman inspired rules (the Penitential) and many had no rules at all. These were very early days, indeed. We do find, even from Patrick's time, that some of the saints (like Brigid) took vows to serve God but this was a pact strictly between themselves and God, not through the intermediary of a terrestrial authority.

So, some monastic foundations were drawing up rules only in Fidelma's day. The *cuing chróbhadh* or obligations of religious life was often a matter for the individual and not imposed by any single authority. The idea of members of a religious community "retaliating" against an individual because they choose to no longer be part of that community is an alien concept to the cultural attitudes of this time. Certainly, oaths and vows – the *cróbud* or the *moidem*, prescribed in ancient Irish law – were not things to be taken lightly. There were penalties for false oaths or oaths made frivolously. But Irish lawmakers had realised that circumstances could change, and no individual (abbot or bishop) could enforce the conditions of a vow if not freely given. In the case in *Hemlock At Vespers* which you refer to, the abbess had actually been involved in crime and therefore had technically lost her honour-price, releasing Fidelma – and any other member of her community – from any obligation or obedience to her.

From an interview conducted with Peter Tremayne by MysteryTribune.com entitled "A Q&A With The Best Selling Author Peter Tremayne:"

MT: *"Give us a writing tip."*
PT: "The old adage is that writing is one per cent inspiration and ninety-nine per cent perspiration. I agree. The times young hopefuls have come up to me and said 'I would like to be a writer – how should I start.' They seem hurt when I tell them to get a blank paper and pencil and start writing. The fact is that if you really want to write, you don't hang around for the muse, Sit and face that blank paper and start filling it. At the end of the day, even if it is all gobble-de-gook, you might find you have put down an idea that is worth saving."

I am interested in the Early Irish Church and its differences with Rome. Can you recommend some books I can on this?

Peter Tremayne recommends the following reading list. The books are listed by their first publisher and publication date. Some have been reprinted since.

FREQUENTLY ASKED QUESTIONS

- Allcroft, A.H. *The Circle and the Cross*, 2 vols, Macmillan, London, 1927.
- Chadwick, Nora K. *The Age of Saints in the Early Celtic Church*, Oxford University Press, Oxford, 1961.
- De Paor, Móire & Liam. *Early Christian Ireland*, Thames & Hudson, London, 1958.
- De Paor, Liam. *Saint Patrick's World*, Four Courts Press, Dublin, 1993.
- Duke, John A. *The Columban Church*, Oxford University Press, Oxford, 1932.
- Ellis, Peter Berresford. *Celtic Inheritance*, Frederick Muller, London, 1985.
- Gougaud, Louis. *Christianity in Celtic Lands*, Sheed & Ward, London, 1932.
- Graham, Hugh. *The Early Irish Monastic Schools*, Talbot Press, Dublin, 1923.
- Healy, John. *Ireland's Ancient Schools and Scholars*, Sealy, Bryers and Walker, Dublin, 1890.
- Herron, James. *The Celtic Church in Ireland*, Service & Paton, London, 1898,
- Hughes, Kathleen. *The Church in Early Irish Society*, New Universal Library, London, 1906.
- Lehane, Brendan. *Early Celtic Christianity*, Constable, London, 1968.
- MacNaught, John C. *The Celtic Church and the See of St Peter*, Basil Blackwell, Oxford, 1927.
- Ó Cróinín, Dáibhó. *Early Medieval Ireland 400-1200*, Longman, London, 1995.
- Ó hAnluain, Enró. *The First Altars & Early Christian Inscriptions of Ireland*, Dublin, 1935.
- Power, Patrick. *Early Christian Ireland*, M.H. Gill, Dublin, 1925
- Salmon, John. *The Ancient Irish Church*, Gill & Son, Dublin, 1897.
- Stokes, George, T. *Ireland and the Celtic Church*, Hodder & Stoughton, London, 1886.
- Thomas, Charles. *Britain and Ireland in Early Christian Times AD 400-800*, BCA, London.
- Tommasini, Anselmo. *Irish Saints in Italy*, Sands & Company, London, 1937.

- Warren, F.E. *The Liturgy and Ritual of the Celtic Church*, Clarendon Press, Oxford, 1881.
- Zimmer, Heinrich. *The Celtic Church in Britain and Ireland* (trs A. Meyer) David Nutt, London, 1902.

PETER TREMAYNE: MURDERER, DEFENDANT...

PETER TREMAYNE:
MURDERER-DETECTIVE-DEFENDANT-JUDGE-JURY-EXECUTIONER...

At the close of the 2017 Féile Fidelma, when none of us were sure we would ever meet again, I had a discussion with Society member Reidun Drange about compiling all the various methods Peter used to "off" the victims in his books and stories.

I believe both Reidun and I felt this would be a fairly straightforward and quick mission – start with the first chapter in which Peter ends a life without looking back, the title or position of the victim, their full name (where known), the method of murder, the reason for the murder, the location of the murder, ultimately the culprit as well as the culprit's sentence, and their method of punishment. All sounds fairly simple, right? Surely someone who has either written or read all of the books could tick off these details in rapid succession.

Naturally, we turned to the most reliable source – the writer himself. And I must say, approaching him with pen and paper in my hand, champing at the bit... Peter was truly unable to help. Just as with his victims, he dashes them off and never gives them another thought (unless there was a Synod or Council or Eclipse or someone named Peter in the book).

So, the obvious next step was to turn to someone intimately familiar with all of the books, their plots, their locations, their main characters, etc. – Peter Tremayne. Unfortunately, owing to the sheer volume of words Peter has written over the decades, not only Fidelma, but his other fiction, and reams of non-fiction works, such an amout of precise recall was beyond his ken.

Returning to the crux of the matter... **Peter Tremayne: Murderer – Detective – Defendant – Judge – Jury – Executioner**. One can only imagine Peter sitting down to a blank computer monitor, whetting his lips, fingers hovering over his keyboard as he prepares, with bated breath, to slay another named or nameless victim about whom we often know very little, save that one moment he or she was breathing, and the next he was not.

And does Peter limit his gruesome and gory activities to always-deserving characters? Well, some would say that we are all potentially guilty of some major infraction in life, though it may not justify our untimely demise. But no, his are not "simple" deaths. I honestly believe he strolled on over to synonym.com – just as I did – to look up the various like-words for "murder." And I truly believe he is trying to carry out each of the more unique possibilities with each new title.

Now, to get down to the facts and figures, and the aforementioned conversation between myself and Reidun towards the end of the last Féile, the heart of which was: "Wouldn't it be interesting to figure out Peter's most common method of killing people?" And so, we were off...

Ideally, I wanted to arrange the data in such a manner as to ultimately relay the data in a "presentable" format. As a result, the project took almost two full years, extracting every bit of information from the novels (we limited ourselves to the books, and did not include the volume of short stories Peter has written about the good Sister).

For example, a description of strangulations may have ranged from "strangled" to "throttled" to "garroted" (which, technically, is a more "refined" method of strangulation) to "choked to death," etc. For the sake of clarity and brevity, I had to pare these various descriptions down to one term or phrase each.

I confined things to the 30⁺ books only, which include 2 volumes of 30 short stories. Point to be made is that the 7th century was a violent time; skirmishes and battles, the high mortality rate from general illness, and, of course, the famous Yellow Plague that devastated not only the population of Ireland but all of Europe, said to have carried away one-third of the population.

The hundreds of deaths mentioned in the Fidelma books were therefore not always "murders" in the proper sense of the term. People could be killed in a skirmish or out of prejudice by an angry mob, which in this century would be deemed murder, or killed in what we would consider a "war crime" and thus "murder." In our research we have tried to confine ourselves to "secret killings" and thus the true definition of murder; more specifically, those "secret murders" which Fidelma ultimately had to solve in the novels, and not the inevitable "collateral" deaths that occurred as well.

The choice of methods of murder was obviously limited to whatever techniques were available at the time – though Peter has likely not fully plumbed the depths of ALL possible methods of murder.

The conclusion, following the specific criteria of "secret murder" is:

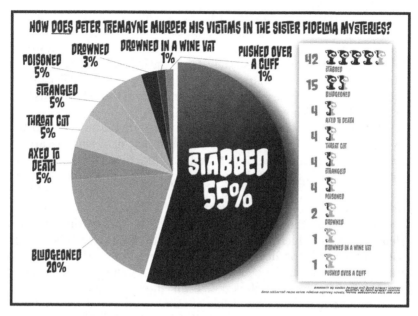

HOW **DOES** PETER TREMAYNE MURDER HIS VICTIMS IN THE SISTER FIDELMA MYSTERIES?

- 42 deaths were stabbings;
- 15 deaths were bludgeoning (hit over the head);
- 4 victims perished by being axed to death;
- 4 victims had their throats cut;
- 4 victims were strangled;
- 4 were poisoned;
- 2 were drowned;
- 1 was drowned in a wine vat; and
- 1 died in a fall (that is, pushed over a cliff)

This would mean that the malevolent Peter Tremayne seems to favor skewering his victims by one method or another, which is, in fact, in keeping with most violent deaths of the period. We have not been specific as to the weapon with which victims were stabbed – knives, daggers, or swords.

The next method seems to be another one in keeping with violent deaths of the time – and perhaps the simplest – being bludgeoned or hit over the head with a blunt instrument.

Surprisingly, at least to me, is that the author only resorts to poison four times, as he does with strangulation.

In researching this subject, I came across another graph taken from the [Irish] Central Statistics Office's website (and I did actually confirm the numbers with a member of that department in Dublin). As it would be virtually impossible to accurately define the Kingdom of Munster – or Muhan – by modern demarcation, at least as far as Garda Divisions, I did turn to Peter to give me his best guesstimate of those Divisions that would fall in the Kingdom of Munster.

However, thanks to Seamus King, who thought the numbers posted by the Statistics Office seemed a bit high, that data was discarded. Seamus actually took the time to make contact with the Garda, and they readily admitted that the system they put in place some years ago is still not working properly, and thus they have no accurate electronic data to show modern homicide statistics.

If you review the "tally" over the 10-plus-year period (in Fidelma's sleuthing) about which Peter has included in the books as of this writing, there have been 350+ deaths.[*] And remember, these particular deaths were "secret murders." I believe we can safely assume Peter has been killing off even more poor folk than even "modern man."

I mentioned Peter's hundreds of other deaths, and not from old age. One figure that arose out of all this research is the number of actual **DEATHS** described in all of these formats. This number is by no means all-inclusive, but I thought it would be interesting to see how many descriptions or enumerations of expiry Peter actually took the time to delineate.

When it comes right down to it, including battles where specific, named characters were described, nameless victims (such as populations of an entire village, or children of an entire orphanage), poor souls who were punished by being worked to death in silver mines, etc., the number jumps much higher than the previous calculations belie.

A **CONSERVATIVE** number of deaths, throughout both books and stories, whether intentional, accidental, virulent, or self-inflicted, totals to **OVER 350** people (to be fair, there was even a listing for the death of a specific dog). Again, this comes from Reidun's extensive research work results.

[*] *Note: The numbers and data reflected in this article and graph reflect information available at the time of the original presentation at the 2019 Féile Fidelma in Cashel. Obviously, readers will discover additional methods of murder by reading the succeeding novels.*

PETER TREMAYNE: MURDERER, DEFENDANT...

I would call those "collateral" fatalities. What did I say Peter's gruesome total was for only 8 years, including all sorts of "incidental" deaths? **350+!** The authorities would certainly be interested in talking to this man.

And also keep in mind that Fidelma can't possibly be solving **EVERY** murder that occurs in Munster. That's like assuming Superman saves every kitten stuck up in a tree or foils all nefarious plans to take over the world. **SOMEONE'S** going to succeed at some point because he's busy saving kittens. Fidelma just works on the "Important" ones.

So doubtless Peter is doing away with dozens and dozens more innocent (or guilty) victims – how else would there be fodder for his future novels? Thus that 375 figure is likely well below his own actual nefarious work.

We must point out, this research can be amended, and we do not claim that the figures are absolutely complete. We present this data here as a general guide. Peter is quite certain that he may have killed more people than we state – though that may simply be his sanguine nature. And, amid the bloody path he leaves in many books, one or two may have been lost along the way.

So, as long as our favorite author's fascination with killing people – at least on the printed page (and all evidence points to this thirst having yet been slaked) – then I believe we can count on even more books and stories by Peter Tremayne – and thus more unique and mysterious (and, more often than not, gruesome) deaths.

Follow-Up...

After the publication of the above article in The International Sister Fidelma Society's journal, *The Brehon*, in January 2020 (following the 2019 Féile Fidelma held September 2019), I quite surprisingly came across an article (reproduced in numerous places after its initial 2015 publication, even unto a January 2020 online article) with a pie-chart (below) entitled "Causes of death in Shakespeare plays."

This infographic looked strikingly familiar to the graphic I produced years later as described above, and which Féile Fidelma attendees first

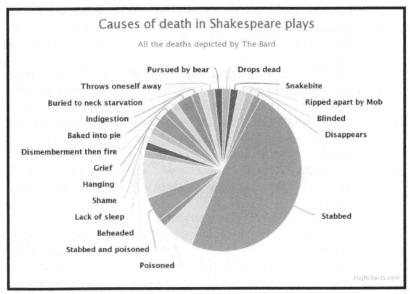

Causes of death in Shakespeare plays

All the deaths depicted by The Bard

Pursued by bear
Drops dead
Throws oneself away
Snakebite
Buried to neck starvation
Ripped apart by Mob
Indigestion
Blinded
Baked into pie
Disappears
Dismemberment then fire
Grief
Hanging
Shame
Lack of sleep
Stabbed
Beheaded
Stabbed and poisoned
Poisoned

Highcharts.com

viewed in September 2019.

One such encapsulated reprint article from 2016 showing the "original" pie-chart, entitled "Totting up the deaths by this and that in Shakespeare's plays," states: "In this tallying, death by being-baked-into-pie is as frequent as death-by-hanging. (The pie death occurs in Titus Andronicus)"

The article continues: "The chart was, reportedly, assembled in connection with a new play in which all those deaths — 74 in total — are re-enacted in a single play written by persons other than Shakespeare. The play, called "The Complete Deaths," produced by the British company Spymonkey, is scheduled to premiere in May 2016." I have not yet searched the internet for reviews of such a play, though I assume it was eventually produced.

"Others have attempted to compile and to some extent analyze some of the death-by-Shakespeare data," according to the article. "One effort is documented in this medical study: "Faints, fits, and fatalities from emotion in Shakespeare's characters: survey of the canon," Kenneth W. Heaton, *British Medical Journal*, 333(7582), December 26, 2015, pp. 1335–1338."

Reidun Drange and I developed the idea for a similar recounting of all the ways Peter Tremayne had killed off his principal (and secondary, and tertiary) murder victims, which sprang forth almost fully-formed during the 2017 Féile. To the best of my knowledge, I had neither seen nor heard of the aforementioned project, pie-chart, or play, unless I randomly scanned past it and it embedded itself in my brain years earlier (highly unlikely).

What is interesting to note is that the 2015 chart and my own were both obviously produced on an Excel spreadsheet, and then that software was allowed to generate the resulting pie-charts. I know this because both charts show the highest "volume" murder method – stabbing – appears in exactly the same position on both charts, and are even colored the same way.

So, while I am certainly not above reproach, I honestly did not knowingly glean such a chart from any resource. Really. I swear upon all of Peter's first editions!

But the coincidence is striking, to be certain.

– David Robert Wooten
Originally presented, somewhat tongue-in-cheek, at the 2019 Féile Fidelma
Published in *The Brehon*, XIX, 1, January 2020
Follow-up article in *The Brehon*, XIX, 3, September 2020

THE SISTER FIDELMA COMPENDIUM

Is There an historical model for Fidelma?

Anyone with a cursory knowledge of Irish myths and legends, or the history of Early Christianity in Ireland with its numerous female saints, and of Irish general history from early times onwards, will know of the prominent role that women have played in Irish culture. It is obvious that they held no servile position and nowhere is this more clearly demonstrated than in the laws on marriage or property in ancient Ireland.

Women could, and did, fulfil any social role as co-equal with men. Indeed, it could even be argued that Ireland produced Europe's first feminist history dating back to at least the early 12th century. This is the *Ban-Shenchus* (The History of Women) a compilation listing the famous Irish women from early times and ending about the 11th century. The work survives in both metrical and prose versions and in several copies. A printed version of the texts, edited by Irish scholar Margaret E. Dobbs., was published in the *Revue Celtique* in 1930-32 (vols XLVII, XLVIII and XLIX.).

Irish mythology is replete with powerful women, whether they are goddesses and Otherworld personages, such as Danú, Éire, Banba, Fótla, Badb, Áine, Brigid and Fand, or female warriors such as Scáthach or Neamhain, or powerful queens such as Scota, Medb and Aoibel, or simply intelligent heroines such as Deirdre, Étain, Fial, Emer and Finnabair. In whatever guise they appear in the myths women are not there for decorative purposes but as the equal to males and often they are more intelligent.

In early history, confusion was often caused when scribes tried to work out whether they were dealing with a mythological figure or an historical figure. At least four different Macha's have been identified from war-goddess to historical queen. Macha Mong-Ruadh is only woman to appear in the lists of pre-Christian High Kings. She is said to have died c. 377 BC and was renowned for building the palace of Emain (Navan). She gave the name to Armagh (Ard Macha) and is claimed to have established Ireland's first hospital Brón Bherg (house of sorrow). In the early Christian period, a St Macha appears as one of the five daughters of a Leinster noble named Léinín who established a community called Cill Iníon Léinín (church of the daughters of Léinín) – modern Killiney, Co. Dublin.

The late Dr Kathleen Hughes and Dr Ann Hamlin, in their book *The Modern Traveller to the Irish Church*, have pointed out that we have the recorded names of no less than 800 prominent Irish female religieuse, now regarded as saints. Women played as great a role as men in the spread of the new religion and in setting up religious communities and colleges. These were powerful women who commanded loyalty and exercised power. Women such as Ita, Brigit, Gobnait of Cork, Albracht of Achonry, Bregha, Moninna, Ercnat and Fanchea of Oriel. And there are even six saints named Fidelma in Early Ireland.

There is more than enough documentary evidence of women's prominent role in ancient Irish society before one recourse to the texts of the ancient Irish law system. For example, from Fidelma's own kingdom of Munster, we find that Uallach, daughter of Muineachain of the Corco Dhuibne (Co. Kerry), was even appointed to be the Chief Ollamh of Ireland in AD 931. She died in AD 934 according to the *Annals of Innisfallen* and was succeeded by Cormacan Eigeas of Ulaidh. To become a Chief Ollamh (the word is still in use in modern Irish as a professor) puts one on the same social as the High King. Professor Máirín Ní Dhonnachadha contributed an excellent piece about Uallach in *The Encyclopedia of Ireland* (2003). Professor Ní Dhonnachadha gave a talk at the first Féile Fidelma in 2006 on another poetess and contemporary of Fidelma, Liadain of the Corcu Duibhne (in Kerry). A contemporary with Uallach was the poetess Gormflaith (c. AD 870-947) who was married to the King of Cashel, Cormac Mac Cuileannáin.

One of the most inspiring women of Cashel was the daughter of King Finghín Mór Mac Carthaigh in the mid 13th century. She was called Étain and commanded a section of her father's army when William de Dene, and his Anglo-Norman army, invaded the kingdom and tried to build castles to use as bases to conquer the country. King Finghín made short work of all six of these castles before his army met the Norman force at Callan near Kenmare on July 24, 1261. The Anglo-Normans had never suffered such a defeat since their arrival in Ireland. Eight Norman barons, 25 knights, and thousands of men-at-arms were slaughtered. However, King Finghín was slain when Milo de Courcy conducted a surprised raid in September, catching the King undefended. Finghín's brother Cormac succeeded him as King.

Still smarting at their defeat at Callan, the Norman Justiciar Richard de la Rochelle together with Walter de Burgo, returned to Munster with a larger army. King Cormac took the field and once again Étain was commanding the right wing of his forces. This battle was fought on the north slopes of An Mhangarta (Anglicised as Mangerton) in Co. Kerry, one of Ireland's tallest mountains. One of the Norman best military commanders, Gerald Roche, said to be `the third best knight in all Ireland" was killed by Cormac, who, in turn, was slain in the closing stage of the battle. But once more, the Anglo-Normans fled from the battlefield and indeed from all Munster. Cormac's son, Donal Rua, became king and was able to reign in peace from 1262-1302. As Professor Edmund Curtis wrote: `For centuries not a single English settler dare now set foot in the country of the Mac Carthys and O'Sullivans ..."

Étain flies all too briefly across these pages of history. But, as a military leader of note, she was not an isolated case as I have pointed out in my study *Celtic Women: Women in Celtic Society and Literature* (1995).

This is by way of a general introduction to underscore the general knowledge that now exists about the prominent role of women in Ireland from early times to modern times. Yet in spite of this, some of my readers wondered whether such a person as Fidelma of Cashel could have existed in reality. Could a woman really be a lawyer in ancient Ireland? This is no reflection on the reader. The only time I get surprised is when someone, without doing the appropriate research, insists that Fidelma is an entire fantasy and could never have existed. I suppose that I grew up with a privileged cultural link. My father had an excellent library of books on Irish history which included many studies on the ancient Irish law system, the Brehon Law.

From such books as Dr Sophie Bryant's *Celtic Ireland* (1889) I learnt `the names of women occur not unseldom in the lists of judges and exponents of law" (p86). In fact, Dr Bryant's major work on the law system *Liberty, Order and Law Under Native Irish Rule* (1923) was one of the first detailed accounts of Brehon Law that I read. Then Dr John Cameron's study *Celtic Law: The Senchus Mór and The Book of Aicill and the Traces of an Early Gaelic System of Law in Scotland* (1937) informed me that `women were regarded as eligible for the office of Brehon" (p.91), gave details of their training and went on to name one lady who held high office in the ancient Irish legal tradition.

The basis for all my reading on ancient Ireland was Dr P. W. Joyce's

A Social History of Ancient Ireland, in two volumes (1903) – a work I feel has never as yet been bettered.

Thus, as I read through the many studies of the Brehon Law system, I not only learnt that women could be lawyers but that they held high office in the Brehon legal system, not only as exponents of law but as writers of legal texts. Eugene O'Curry's *On the Manner and Customs of the Ancient Irish* (1873), refers to the "women of judgement," nine ladies who acted as legal advisers to the High King's family and the actual name of a female judge, who was able to correct a male judge on appeal, was mentioned in *Studies in Early Irish Law,* published by the Royal Irish Academy (1936).

The names of three women lawyers intrigued me. One seems entirely overlooked by many modern writers on the law even though her name was well known enough in the 16th century for the compiler of a dictionary to use it in explaining the full meaning of the word *ech (echta)* as "pure." The dictionary in question was called in modern English *Davoren's Glossary,* published in Halle in 1904, and edited by the scholar Whitley Stokes. *Davoren's Glossary* had been compiled in the 16th century. The manuscript was, in fact, written by Domhnall Ó Duibhdabhoirenn (Anglicised as Davoren), who was born in the early 16th century. He is also credited with the compilation of legal texts as written between 1564-1569 now in the British Library and classed as MS Egerton 88. The Davorens were a well-known family of Brehon lawyers serving the Dal gCais and they ran a law school in the Burren in North Co Clare. In explaining the word *ech (echta)*, Davoren says it meant "pure" as one who describes the purity of the legal judgments of Áine, the daughter of Iugaire. This produces two questions. Was Áine ingine Iugaire one of the Dál gCais lawyers of Munster related to the Davorens? And, secondly, when did she flourish, for, so far, no other references to her have been found, which is surprising if her name was so well known in the 16th century.

It was interesting that thirteen years after Fidelma's appearance, as a Brehon `sleuth" in Munster, another female Brehon detective crime series emerged and also set in Munster. A Cork born children's writer, Cora Harrison, launched her series in 2007 featuring Mara in *My Lady Judge.* I was asked to give a review quote by her publishers. The first thing I notice was the stories were set starting in 1509 and they were called "The Burren Mysteries." It seemed that Cora Harrison was also inspired by Áine, the Dál gCais lawyer mentioned in *Davoren's Glossary.*

AN HISTORICAL MODEL FOR FIDELMA

The other two names mentioned in the ancient texts which intrigued me. The main one was a lady called Dar Í, a female lawyer, who set out the law related to the theft of cows, known as the *Cáin Dar Í*. *Cáin* means `law." Dar Í became of particular interest to me as she initially appeared that she was connected with Muman (Munster). The *Annals of Inisfallen* for the year AD 810 mentions that her law against stealing cows was promulgated in that year. The entry states *"Bo-shlechta la Mumain la Dare ocus la Adhuar macc nEchin."*

I was delighted when I came across a paper on Dar Í by Professor Pádraig Ó Riain of University College Cork, who also gave a brilliant address to the 2010 Féile Fidelma but on an unrelated subject to Dar Í. Professor Ó Riain published his paper "A Misunderstood Annal: A Hitherto Unnoticed *Cáin"* in *Celtica* 21 (1990) pp561-566, *Celtica* is the journal of the Dublin Institute for Advanced Studies.

Dr Ó Riain analysed a translation prepared for the Dublin Institute for Advance Studies and pointed out that the promulgation of the laws of Dar Í and Aduar in AD 810 was not when the laws were written. They were dated to a period two centuries earlier. Also, he pointed out that the translator had translated Dar Í into the masculine form of the name Daire. The entry should have read "the laws concerning cows, of Dar Í and Aduar son of Echen, promulgated in Munster" and taken to mean that two centuries after the laws were written, cow stealing had become so rife in Munster that people had to be reminded of the *existing* law.

Because of the fact that Dar Í's name occurs in other ancient texts the period of her existence is placed between AD 500- 650. If she was alive in the later period, than she is almost a contemporary with Fidelma. Professor Ó Riain points out that her name occurs not only in the annals but the calendar of saints and the genealogies. All the sources give her name as ending with the feminine í. She is referred to in the *Annals of Ulster, Annals of Innisfallen, Chronicon Scotorum, Tripartite Life of Patrick, Martyrology of Tallaght, and of Gorman* and so on.

So, who was Dar Í? The name would appear to mean "daughter of the yew." Like Fidelma, she was not only a lawyer but a religieuse. As St Dar Í she is given two feast days, that of August 8 and of November 2. As Professor Ó Riain states: "(it) does not necessarily imply that we have to do with two or more saints of the same name. The saint is assigned only one pedigree. I take all references to be to the one saint."

Scholars have offered theories as to where she came from, but the most accepted place of origin is in Connacht. P. Grosjean (*Analechta*

Bollandiana, 1963) believes she came from Tirawley, Co. Mayo, because of a record of her meeting with St Cormac of that area. In fact, Professor Ó Riain has pointed out that there was an ancient site called Kildaree (Cill Dar Í = church of Dar Í) in Crossmolina in the area. He also points out there are two other Kildaree place names in Co. Galway. So, all three Dar Í churches are in Connacht.

Three references to her law against stealing cattle being promulgated refer to Munster and Ulster but the fourth records the *re-imposition* of the law in Connacht. This seems to have been done through the efforts of the Connacht King Muirgius mac Tommaltaig (d. AD 815) of the Uí Briuin Aí.

Of Aduar mac Echen whose cattle law was also associated to that of Dar Í in AD 810 little is known apart from that single reference in the annals. He has been identified as being from Osraige, in East Munster, and there is a gloss in the *Lebar na Nuachonghbala,* (Bookf of Leinster) compiled in AD 1150) which speaks of "Aed Cáem as ancestor of Aduar son of Echen, he who made the law" (on cow stealing).

The other prominent lawyer in the ancient texts is a lady called Bríg who corrected the wrong judgement of a male lawyer, Sencha mac Ailella, concerning the female rights of land ownership. The fact that Bríg could overturn a male judgement had also intrigued me as a youth. Not the least was the fact that a lady named Bríg rose to prominent in the church being one of the royal dynasties of the Eóghanacht of Cashel, and yet another Bríg of the Déisi was domicile at the abbey of Lismore. But Bríg was not an uncommon name and because of the lack of a time scale for the judge's existence academics are cautious and describe her as "legendary." One gloss, referred to by Professor Fergus Kelly, "makes her the daughter of the judge she corrected." Professor Kelly's *Guide to Early Irish Law* (Dublin Institute for Advanced Studies, 1898) is the best available guide to the law system. Professor Dáibhí Ó Cróinín maintains Bríg was Sencha's wife and goes further by stating that he believes that Bríg was introduced in the text to help underscore the improved lot of women.

The issue of the law, of the *Din Techtugad*, relating to legal entry of land, and particularly the law on female rights of landownership, is related in Kelly's *Guide* (p187/188) when the judge, Sencha, ruled a female's case could only be conducted in the same manner as a male. But Bríg corrected this by pointing out the law and precedents in support.

This case is not the only one in which Bríg is referred to. She appears

AN HISTORICAL MODEL FOR FIDELMA

also in *Di Chetharslicht Athgabhála* regarding the four divisions of distraint or non-payment of rent or tribute and other matters.

I hope the above will give readers an introduction at least to the subject showing that the status and role of Fidelma is not entirely the figment of the imagination of this poor scribe.

– Peter Tremayne
The Brehon, X, 3, September 2011

THE SISTER FIDELMA COMPENDIUM

Fidelma and Flann Fína

Flann Fína was certainly a fascinating historical character. A romance should have been written so him alone. I will mischievously say Flann Fína was the best Irish King that the Anglo-Saxons ever had.

His mother was the granddaughter of the Irish High King Colmán Rímíd and Flann grew up in Ireland to become a noted poet. He was invited to succeed to the Northumbrian throne in May, 685 and ruled for nineteen years. Flann Fína is better known to the English as Aldfrith.

The historian John Marsden, convincingly argues that Flann Fína, or Aldfrith, was born in 640. So, he is a contemporary of Fidelma who was born in 637.

We will come to Flann's mother and why she took him to Ireland to be raised and educated in a moment. But his father was King Oswy (Oswiu) of Northumbria. Oswy featured in the first Fidelma novel *Absolution By Murder*. That was set during the Synod of Whitby when Fidelma was a twenty-seven-year-old delegate to the debate whether the Northumbrian kingdom would continue to accept the liturgy and philosophies of the Insular Churches, what we loosely call the Celtic Church, or accept the new rules and philosophies from Rome.

Courtyard at Iona Abbey

THE SISTER FIDELMA COMPENDIUM

Oswy of Northumbria was married 3 times. The first wife was Rhianmelt, daughter of the British Celtic king of Rheged, now Cumbria and stretching into Strathclyde, and when she died, Oswy's second wife was Fín, the fair one, as I mentioned, the grand daughter of the Uí Néill High King Colmán Rímíd, whose death is usually given as 604.

Oswy first met Fín in the kingdom of Dál Riada, now southwest Scotland, if you think of Argyll, Scotland – which means the seaboard. It's the area that includes Iona, Mull, Kintyre and so on.

Oswy had been taken into exile there at the age of five in 616 along with his brothers and sisters. They had sought asylum there after their father, King Athelfrith of Northumbria, had been killed by ambitious relatives. Oswy was educated on Iona, the famous holy island of Colmcille, Columba, and lived seventeen years in the Gaelic speaking Dál Riada kingdom. His elder brother, Oswald, became king in Northumbria in 633. Oswy went back with him. And with them they took Irish religious to convert the pagan Anglo-Saxons and scholars to teach them literacy. Oswy succeeded his brother as king in 642.

Oswy and his wife Fín, with their newborn son Flann Fína, lived for a time at a royal centre in Driffield.

But all was not well with Fín and Oswy. Fín knew her husband's family had a nasty habit of bumping off claimants to the kingship and she also knew Oswy had his eyes on another lady called Eanfled from Deria, which is around modern city of York. Flann was still only two or three years old when his mother decided to take her son for safety to her own family, the powerful Uí Néill, in Ireland. So, he grew up, educated in northern Uí Néill territory.

Flann is known to have lived in Lios Gabhail (Lisgoole) in what is now the Co Fermanagh/ Co Cavan border. This was a royal fortress on the west bank of Lough Erne. He is said to have studied under many famous Irish scholars, including Adomnán who devised the *Cáin Adomnán*, a law to protect non-combatants in war... an Irish Geneva Convention if you like. It was passd at the council of Birr, Co Offaly, in 697. Two years after that Adomnán went to Iona and became its 9th abbot ten years later. We'll come back to him in a moment.

Flann Fína was closely related to the scholar and poet Ceann Faolaidh who died in AD 678. Here we have an excellent Fidelma link because Ceann Faolaidh had been a warrior wounded in the head during a conflict at Moira, in Co Down, which took place in the year Fidelma was born in 637. He was taken to be nursed at the medical school set

FIDELMA AND FLANN FINA

The Abbey at Whitby

up by St Brecin called Tuaim Brecain, now Tomregan, on the Ferman-agh-Cavan border.

This was a school not only famous for its medical teaching but for law and for literature. Yes – this is the same medical school where Eadulf, Fidelma's companion, studied the healing arts. Ceann Faolaidh recovered from his wound and eventually became a professor there. For many scholars he is considered as "the father of Irish literature."

So, Flann Fína might have been a fellow student with Eadulf there. Flann Fína achieved a reputation as a poet; at least three of his poems in Irish are extant and surviving in 10th and 12th century manuscripts such as the *Lebor na Nuachongbhala,* an anthology of stories and po-ems compiled in 1150 by Fionn Mac Gormain. We can imagine another possible Fidelma link because Flann Fína actually came to Cashel. He tells us so himself when he writes in one of his poems (translated in English rhyme by Clarence Mangan):

> *I found in Muman, unfettered by any*
> *A king, a princess and nobles with poets a-many*
> *Poets well skilled in music and measure*
> *Prosperous enterprises, mirth and pleasure*
> So, it was happy days in Cashel during Fidelma's time.

Back in Northumbria, in 670 Flann's father, Oswy, died. One of the few Northumbrian kings who actually died of natural causes. Flann's half-brother Ecgfrith became king. He was a son by Oswy's third wife, Eanfled... Oswy had lost no time in marrying her after Fín had gone back to Ireland.

Ecgfrith devoted his fifteen years of kingship to slaughtering his rivals in the family; Flann being in Ireland escaped. Ecgfrith then became busy conquering neighbouring kingdoms. He is recorded as a ruthless tyrant. Even many of the Anglo-Saxon religious and scholars sought refuge in Ireland during his reign, such as Bishop Ecgberht of Ripon. Ecgberht lived in Rath Melsigi, modern day Co Carlow, where he died in 739.

It had already become a centre for Anglo-Saxon religious refugees who went to Ireland after Oswy's ruling at Whitby. Among them was St Wigbert. So, a generation later came Bishop Ecgberht with St Willibrod

Lindisfarne Abbey

who lived in Carlow for thirteen years before going to what is now Germany and founding an abbey. There were mass migrations of Britons as well. When I speak of Britons at this time I mean, of course the original Celtic population of the Britain – the lation of the Britain – the ancestors of the Welsh. Cornish, and Bretons.

Many of you might know that in *A Prayer for the Damned* Fidelma has contact with three Anglo-Saxon religious led by St Berrihert who left Northumbria after Oswy's ruling and actually settled near Cashel in the Glen of Aherlow where they are still remembered. If ever you have time, visit the breathtaking Glen of Aherlow and pause at St Berrihert's Kyle at Ardane, Bansha.

Those of you who have read my historical afterword in *Bloodmoon* will have seen reference to Ecgfrith ordering the first attempted Anglo-Saxon attack on Ireland. It happened in June 684, when the Irish annals say Ecgfrith's warriors, commanded by a warrior called Beorht, devastated the churches and settlements in Brega, south of Tara, taking away many hostages. Among the leading Anglo-Saxons religious and scholars who were outraged by Ecgfrith's attack on Ireland was the Venerable Bede (d. 735) regarded as the first great historian of the English. He condemned the Ecgfrith's attack as on "a harmless race that had always been most friendly to the English."

So, we come to the year 685. Flann's half-brother Ecgfrith was killed while trying to grab more of the Pictish kingdom. He was killed at the battle of Nechtansmere, near modern Forfar. The Pictish king Brude mac Bili drove the Northumbrians back. Northumbria was in turmoil, open to revenge attacks from previous subject kingdoms. Ecgfrith's family were fighting among themselves to grab the kingship.

Flann's half sister Aelflaed, Abbess of Whitby, sought the support of Bishop Cuthbert, Bishop of Lindisfarne – St Cuthbert who had retired to life as a hermit on the Inner Farne Island. He considered the situation was so grave that he left his hermitage and joined her in a plea to Flann Fína to leave Ireland and come to Northumbria to claim the kingship. I think we can safely say that Flann had reservations about the idea before he accepted. In fact, on leaving Ireland he wrote a poem of which 60 lines survive in Irish bardic metre praising and thanking the five kingdoms for their forbearance and hospitality.

Now Flann emerges in Anglo-Saxon history as Aldfrith, uniting the fragmented kingdom and ushering in a golden age of learning. Under his patronage Irish scholars came back into the kingdom. In fact, a year or so after Flann became king, he went to see his old friend Adomnán, the abbot of Iona. Admonán paid many visits to Northumbria and certainly impressed Bede who was a teenager at the time. It is not surprising to find that Flann favoured the rituals and philosophy of the Insular Celtic Church, also encouraging Irish scholars and religious. His arguments with the pro-Roman fanatic, Wilfrid, who had persuaded his father, Oswy, to reject the Irish teachers at the time of Whitby, are documented.

Flann, or Aldfrith, as I say, ushered in a golden age of learning and his patronage produced the famous *Lindisfarne Gospels*, the *Codex Amiatinus* and the first great Anglo-Saxon saga of *Beowulf*. Some experts have claimed that Flann might have had a hand in writing it himself. Some of you may blink at that. Fair enough; there is a controversy about this.

According to the Swedish Celtic scholar C.W. von Sydow (by the way, for movie fans here, he was the father of the movie actor Max von Sydow), in to his study *Beowulfskalden och nordisk tradition* (1923), the author of *Beowulf* was well acquainted with Irish literary tradition. Professor Gerald Murphy in his study on the text points to at least nine similarities between *Beowulf* and the earlier Irish saga *Táin Bó Fraoch*. I emphasise this is not the more popularly known *Táin Bó Cuailgne*. In Fraoch's tale, he sets act to woo Finnbhair and has to fight a water monster.

Professor David Dumville of Cambridge has pointed out that there was a great deal of bilingualism – Irish and Anglo-Saxon – in Northumbria at this period. In 1993 Professor Charles Wright, also of Cambridge, produced the first study of the Irish influence on the beginning of Anglo-Saxon literature *The Irish Tradition in Old English Literature*. His study of the thematic and stylistic links in these first English texts is impressive, especially the cosmology and Celtic myths in texts like "The Devil's Account of the Next World."

Flann was visiting the abbey of St Ercenwald at Barking in Essex when he died and was buried. That was on December 14, 704. Although Ercenwald was dead before this recorded visit – he died in 693 – Ercenwald was from Northumbria. He had been appointed advisor by King Ine of the West Saxons to help develop a law system. West Saxons or Wessex is still used as a title by the English royals today. What's the connection? Flann's wife was Cuthburb, who he had married a few years after becoming king, and she was sister to Ine of the West Saxons. So, here's a thought – could Flann have discussed the Irish law system with Ercenwald and his brother-in-law Ine?

When Flann died of a fever in Barking, his wife went into Ercenwald's abbey becoming abbess there. The abbey was a victim of Henry VIII's dissolution in 1539 but a tower survives, known as the Curfew Tower, in a public open space today called Abbey Green. Sadly, there is no memorial to Flann Fína, or Aldfrith, who we might mischievously call the forgotten Irish king of Northumbria.

– *The Brehon*, XIX, 1, January 2020

A Reflection on Princes, Chiefs, and Chieftains

Alifetime of research has gone into the background of the Sister Fidelma Mysteries. Not only does Peter have his degrees in Celtic Studies and is a Fellow of the Royal Historical Society and Fellow of the Royal Society of Antiquaries of Ireland, but he has written over a score of historical studies. All of this, and more, has cemented his status as one of the leading authorities on the Celts.

As an example, the *Contemporary Review* hailed his book *The Ancient World of the Celts* with the comment – "This book must become the standard introduction for anyone interested in Europe's ancient Celtic civilization."

First published in hardback in 1998 in the UK and US, it had been continuously in paperback edition since 2004. The book received high praise from the academic world. Professor David Rankin, in *The Times Higher Education Supplement* (London), said it was "A vivid and enlightening representation of a fascinating civilization. Anyone interested in the ancient world will find in it an informative and enjoyable adjustment of many assumptions about the Celts."

I make this introduction because here, at the Society, we often get letters from "wannabe critics" who display their ignorance by trying to pick academic faults in the Fidelma books. Peter takes the philosophical line of Oscar Wilde: "there is one thing worse than being talked about, and that is not being talked about."

But, in my opinion, some of these points need correction, especially those written with the arrogance of "one-upmanship," rather than in the tone of inquiry and discussion.

I confess to writing "When Is Corn Not Corn" (*The Brehon*, September 2017), having become fed up with the arrogant notion that corn could only refer to American corn after it was introduced into Europe in the 15th century.

I also confess to writing the 4-page illustrated article (*The Brehon*, May 2012), answering the reader who wrote: "Doesn't Tremayne know that the Irish did not build in stone until after the Normans arrived in the

12th century?" This "authority" went on: "In the 7th century they would be building huts, stockades, and chapels in wood." The photographs of the stone buildings, together with my article, should have made this "authority" bite his tongue.

Other readers assured us that pilgrims from Ireland could not possibly have made a journey from Ireland to Rome in the 7th century. Well, Julius Caesar, and his Roman legionaries, made the trip to Britain in the 1st century BC, not to mention Emperor Claudius coming along with his war elephants a hundred years later! Poor Pelagius, the Christian theologist of the 5th century, must have had trouble booking with his travel agent!

Some of the notions about Ireland in the early medieval period are really startling, as illustrated by a letter from a reading group. It does not reflect well on our general education system.

I was attempting to get some information from Peter about the new Fidelma novel that he is about to deliver to his publishers. He told me that the primary setting is at a time when the seven senior Eóganacht princes meet in Cashel during the Beltaine Feat for council to approve or censure the policies of King Colgú of Muman.

It occurred to me that while everyone (hopefully) has heard of the Ard Rí, or High King of Ireland, we might prepare for letters from the same "know-all" ethos to give us a lecture that princes did not exist in ancient Ireland. Will they inform us that there was no real nobility as we understand it in Ireland? Wasn't Ireland just a collection of isolated tribes ruled by chiefs and chieftains in the same way as we often misperceive the Native American civilizations to be? No. I won't even talk about the Iroquois Confederation that was centuries old when the French followed the English into their territory.

What were the terms for the Irish nobility? We know there was a High King as well as provincial kings. When the English language began to submerge Irish in the 17th and 18th centuries, the old nobles were designated chiefs and chieftains, but these words were used in a sense which makes them less barons, earls, dukes, and kings.

Years before, the Old and Middle English terms "prince" and "duke," both borrowed from Latin, meant "leader" and "chiefs." "Baron" and "earl" in their Middle English forms mean "warrior leaders." The Old English *cyng* was a term for the "scion of nobles" which developed into King and its cognates in all German languages

So, we know Ireland had a basic structure of five kingdoms, which

A Reflection on Princes, Chiefs, and Chieftains

theoretically was ruled by an Ard Ri or High King. These five kingdoms were Muman, Connacht, Ulaidh, and Laigin. Using today's Anglicised names, they are the provinces of Munster. Leinster, Ulster, and Connacht. It was the Vikings who later added the "ster" at the end of Irish names from which the modern Anglicised forms developed.

Now the High King had his own territory, and this was Mide or Meath, and today this includes both Meath and Westmeath. This was the central province, and – no, the Irish word *mid* (center) was not borrowed from English. It is a cognate deriving from the Indo-European common parent and existing in those languages, including in Sanskrit as Má.

The kings of each of the provinces were called the Rí Coigeach – king of a province, Why *coigeach*? Because they were kings of a "fifth" of the country. Even today, when speaking Irish, the word for province is *cúige* – a fifth.

The basic word *aire* is often confused as the nobility and used for various types of a noble. It has its cognate with its Indo-European Sanskrit cousin *ayra*, which a certain German dictator confused as a "race." An *aire* was a landowner, a freeman of society, and there were several additions to the basic word by which to judge their differing status going up to *aire-ard*, high lord. *Bóaire* often appears in Fidelma's time as a minor magistrate – it actually means "cow-lord." An *ócaire* literally means "young lord," but it is interpreted as a lesser lord, not a youth.

The order of nobility in ancient Ireland can be confusing. Brehon Law informs us that a *triath (tríachnaech)* and the female equivalent *triath-ben* is the highest of the 26 titles of dignity. The word is found in various compounds to do with property and high status.

Flaith is another word found in titles – a *banflaith* is a princess – again also used in property status and for a social class of nobility. One could be called a *flaith firian* – righteous prince or *fir flatha* – a true or rightful prince. *Tigerna*e, in its various forms, was a lord but whose status was lower than a *ríaglairí*, a minor ruler who we might call a princeling. Obviously, a *maer* or *mál* was a leading noble or king's steward. The title occurs famously in Gaelic Scotland when Mac Beatha (Mcbeth) was Mormaer of Moray before he succeeded Duncan and not in the way that Shakespeare would have us believe.

However, they were lower in rank to *Rígmál* or *Rógmál* – (used for a great prince). While *rí* is cognate to other Indo-European titles *Raja, Rex*, king. *ró* is Celtic root meaning "great" as seen in the name of the River Rhone – *ró-danus* – great Danu – Danu being the Celtic mother goddess.

Don't forget there were also titles for an heir-apparent such as *Rí Damnae* or *Ró Damna*.

Peter does admit that he has used the term *tánaiste* for an heir-apparent in his books as it also appears as an alternative in ancient texts and is easily recognized today. This word means actually means a "second." And when the modern Irish state came into being, *Tánaiste* was adopted to mean Deputy Prime Minister.

The term *Taoiseach* for Prime Minister was adopted from the Old and Middle Irish *toisech,* which actually means "leader."

In reference to the seven Eóganacht princes, the earliest ancient texts name these as Eóganacht Chaisil (Cashel), Eóganacht Áine, Eóganacht Loch Léin. Eóganacht Glanedamnach, Eóganacht Arann, Eóganacht Raithlinn and Eóganacht Airithir Chliadh. They were all princes.

Peter regards Professor Francis Byrne's book *Irish Kings and High-Kings* (1973), as a seminal study for the ancient kings and their kingdoms.

– David Robert Wooten
The Brehon, IX, 3 September 2020

Reading Fidelma

INCLUDING AN INTERVIEW WITH "THE VOICE OF FIDELMA,"
ACTRESS CAROLINE LENNON

Followers of the Fidelma Mysteries have been able to listen to Fidelma on audio form since the first audio book was issued n 1998. *Valley of the Shadow* was read by Marie McCarthy and a *Prayer for the Damned* was read by Annie Farr for Magna Story Sound (UK). But it was only when the Irish actress Caroline Lennon started to read the books that the series on audio really took off to the extent that fans have hailed her as "The Voice of Fidelma."

She began in 2007 with *Dancing With Demons* and has recorded over a dozen titles for the UK audio publishers Soundings.

However, she has recorded the entire series so far for the USA form Audible, starting in 2015, which specialise in download editions from their website – all titles available to date.

Our membership survey has shown that she is regarded as the most popular reader of the stories so far, and author Peter Tremayne has confirmed that Caroline is his favourite reader to date.

In fact, looking at Caroline, as well as listening to her, we could see that, if that long-awaited television series or film of Sister Fidelma ever emerges, that the producers could do no better than look in her direction.

Caroline was born and brought up in Co. Wicklow, in Ireland, and read Modern English and Modern History at Trinity College, Dublin, Ireland's oldest surviving university, founded in 1592. But Caroline spent most of her time in the Trinity Players, the student drama society. She then progressed to acting with the Dublin Youth Theatre and the Dublin Fringe Theatre. Finally, she went to England and trained at the Bristol Old Vic Theatre School.

Like most actors, she's done a bit of

everything. Her favourite roles so far are Maggie in Brian Friel's *Dancing at Lughnasa* at the Watermill Theatre; Trish in Brian Friel's *Wonderful Tennessee* at the Nottingham Playhouse; Cissie in Arnold Wesker's *Chicken Soup with Barley* at the Nottingham Playhouse and Tricycle Theatre, London; Sandra in Christina Reid's *Joyriders* at Birmingham Rep and its sequel *Clowns* at the Orange Tree, Richmond.

She confesses that she would like to do more film work after appearing in Brian Blessed's film version of *King Lear*, which she found "inspiring." She has appeared on television in the series *London's Burning*, but she would love to do a really good sitcom. She finds each type of acting uses a different part of her, and that's why she never finds it dull. And, she adds, "the great joy of recording audiobooks is that you get to play all the parts!"

She became famous in England for her role in the long running BBC radio series *The Archers*. She played the part of Siobhan for nine years before the writers literally killed off her character in the story. "My character, Siobhan, was originally conceived as a minor one but the audience seemed to take to her and then the writers and producers had a brainwave and thought they could really do something with this. They decided to build this great, slow burning plot with me as the mistress of chief cad, Brian Aldridge, ditching my husband, having a lovechild and generally causing mayhem. It was central to the plot right from the word go that I would produce an heir for Brian (leading to all sorts of inheritance tangles for him and his family) and ultimately pop my clogs. So, no complaints, it was a fantastic storyline."

Listening to her reading of *Master of Souls*, *Dancing With Demons* and *The Council of the Cursed*, among the many other titles, Caroline seems a natural to put over the stories of Sister Fidelma.

Caroline was always interested in history in general, which was why she read it at university. She admits that she only had a sketchy knowledge of the Brehon system from history and her secondary school. "One of the joys of being an audio artist is that you get to learn more about all sorts of things when you research your various books."

Moreover, Caroline feels that it is always very exciting to record a gutsy funny female character with a great mind. She has always been a big fan of detective fiction and the Sister Fidelma stories are right up her alley!

"I think there are lots of reasons why these books have a wide appeal. It's a period in history that hasn't received too much attention. Also, there is a great pleasure in trying to work out how on earth these crimes might be solved without the help of modern science. The settings are so atmospheric, too. It really takes you away from the modern humdrum, and we all need a bit of that.

"And Tremayne's characters are so refreshing, compared to most of those we see in TV detective drama."

Asked if she could explain how she prepares for reading a book like one of the Fidelma novels, Caroline says:

"Well, everybody has his or her way of doing it. I've talked it over with lots of other audiobook readers and we're all different! Myself, I first read the book through just for the story, which sets the creative juices working re: accents/characterisation etc. Any big topics that I might have to do some research on, I make a note of at this point. Then I read it closely again, marking up the text for where I'll emphasise particular words; for change of accent; for pacing and so on. Any words or phrases that are particularly challenging/unusual, I'll practice aloud, too. Like most readers, I do lots of tongue-twisters to keep my "tongue, teeth and lips' ready for action. Audio book reading is the "marathon' of acting. You've got to warm up, it's not for the faint hearted. We'll record for about six solid hours per day."

When we told Caroline that Peter once advised those readers who were concerned about Irish pronunciation to listen to her readings, Caroline said: "That's very kind of him to say. I'm glad that all that preparation and research paid off. Also, it's been great to re-visit speaking Irish; the last time I did that was at school."

Some readers contact The International Sister Fidelma Society from time to time worried that they feel their Irish pronunciation is not quite correct. We carry a guide to pronunciation on our website and in tome of the early editions the publishers tried the experiment of putting the guide in the books. But, as the author himself has often said, reading novels in Russian, French or other languages does not really inhabit the reader, any more than the multitude of "made up" languages that appear in fantasy novels from *Lord of the Rings* to the adventures by Edgar Rice Burroughs.

So, as we noted previously, Caroline has won both the author's and the readers' applause, and IS, quite literally "The Voice of Fidelma."

But this is for the Anglophone speakers. What of the German Fidelma followers?

In 2005 German radio WDR5 broadcast a two-part radio play

adapted from *Suffer Little Children – Tod im Skriptorium* with Sissy Höfferer playing Fidelma. This was so well greeted that it was re-broadcast some months later and then the company issued it as a 106-minute stereo CD in 2006.

In 2007 Germany's Delta Musick issued CDs of Susanne Dobrussskin reading *Die Tote im Klosterbrunnen* (*The Subtle Serpent*) and *Ein Gebet fur die Verdammten* (*A Prayer for the Damned*). These were taken over by in 2016 by LifeTime Audio of Berlin.

At the same time Technisat produce their first six audio books read by Sabine Swobda.

At the start of 2017, Audible of Deutschland, issued a German language download of *Der Tod Wird Euch Verschlingen* (*Penance of the Damned*).

As well as these commercial recordings, an area which is more difficult to find records of, is the audio recording for the blind. We have found five Fidelma books issued on cassette for the USA's Talking Books for the Blind' and three issued in Dutch for the Dutch Library of the Blind.

– The Brehon, VIII, 1, January 2009

A Succinct Review of The Series

"Find out, though the seas rise to engulf us, or the sky falls to crush us; only the truth is sacred."

Series of historical mysteries by British historian Peter Berresford Ellis under the pen name of Peter Tremayne. Sister Fidelma of Cashel is a 7th century Irish religiuse, educated at the abbey of Kildare. Also, sister to King Colgú of Muman (modern Munster), and a trained *dálaigh*, or lawyer, Fidelma travels Dark Age Europe with her friend, later husband the Saxon Brother Eadulf, former *gerefa* (magistrate) of Seaxmund's Ham (modern Saxmundham, Suffolk).

Ellis uses Fidelma and Eadulf to expound to the reader on the society of Ireland during this period, and on the complex web of cultures, places, religions, and rivalries. Irish society was surprisingly Fair for Its Day, compared with its neighbors. The stories often focus on specific points of law, or on comparison between societies and religions. Ellis brings up the following points particularly often:

- Position was not strictly hereditary; kings and chiefs were elected by their families and could be removed from their posts.
- Up until the 9th century or so, many religious houses were co-ed; priests, monks and nuns could marry, and women could be priests and even bishops. At the time of the series, what we now call Catholicism was starting to gain ascendancy over Celtic Christianity, but it was not yet all-powerful.
- Women's rights were relatively progressive. Women could take significant social roles such as warriors, rulers, and lawyers; they could own their own property and have child custody and alimony; they could choose their husbands and divorce them freely.
- There were many laws for the safety of citizens and communities. Trials were a right; innkeepers were required to keep clean establishments and lit lanterns; workers in dangerous professions were required to safeguard their workplaces. There were also many types of legal agreements, for example nine kinds of marriage.

There are [now 33] novels, [two] novell[e], and two anthologies of short stories. The first stories were published in 1993, and the first novel, *Absolution by Murder*, in 1994.

This series provides examples of:

- **Always Murder:** At least three in every novel.
- **Artifact Title:** Sister Fidelma quits the religious life about halfway through the series.
- **Asskicking Equals Authority:** Irish chieftains were required to be of sound body and stepped down when physically unfit. In one book, Colgú is attacked but the assassins don't even try to kill him, just injure and disqualify him for the kingship.
- **As You Know:** Constant, both in-dialogue and out.
- **Busman's Holiday:** Fidelma can't go anywhere without finding a mystery to solve, much to Eadulf's chagrin.
- **Christianity Is Catholic:** Averted every which way; while what will become Catholicism is recognizable, there are undercurrents of conflict both within it (even the Pope, while disapproving, didn't technically outlaw co-ed houses at the time) and between it and Celtic Christianity (different methods of crossing oneself, different tonsures, different official attitudes towards women). Other, more exotic varieties of Christianity also appear, such as Ethiopian.
- **Cliffhanger:** A lot of the books ended with these after the main mystery was resolved, usually with a large hint as to the plot of the next book. Book 2 ended with Fidelma leaving Rome, with her believing she would never see Eadulf again. Another ends with her finding an abandoned, blood-stained ship with Eadulf's satchel (which Fidelma recognises because it contains a distinctive book she gave to him) on it. One ends with Fidelma announcing her pregnancy (to the reader, anyway – opinion differs whether Eadulf knew, and they just didn't mention it aloud). Another ends with Fidelma and Eadulf being handed an urgent letter saying their baby son has been kidnapped.
- **Elective Monarchy:** The Irish system of tanistry comes up frequently.
- **Exotic Detective:** Both to the reader (as a way to introduce a little-known time and culture) and within the story; while Fidelma is well-known and accepted within Ireland, her Saxon friend Eadulf is less welcome, and this reverses itself outside Ireland where women are not expected to be so forthright, or to have such education. Or for a princess of Munster to concern herself with the doings of

commoners who aren't even Irish.

- **Eye Colour Change:** Fidelma's eyes flicker between green and blue when her mood changes.
- **Fiery Redhead:** Fidelma has red hair and acknowledges her quick temper can be a weakness.
- **Footnote Fever:** averted. things other authors might bung in as explanatory footnotes often end up in the main text. See *Shown Their Work* below.
- **Foregone Conclusion:** When a *tánaiste* (heir-apparent) is present, it's possible to look up whether they really did go on to succeed as king. If not, they're likely either to be a victim or exposed as the criminal.
- **Gaslighting:** In a few stories, focusing on the status of mer or the insane.
- **Historical Domain Character:** King Colgú, High King Sechnussach, and several other secular and religious leaders of the period. Novels are set at the Synod of Whitby and Council of Autun.
- **Hooker with a Heart of Gold:** Della, one of Fidelma's closest friends, is a former *be-taide*, or prostitute.
- **Informed Attribute:** Fidelma is regularly described as quirky and with a joy in life, but when she is on a case (pretty much 95% of when we see her), this disappears, and she is irascible and frustrated with her often clueless companions.
- **The Low Middle Ages:** Set in 7th century Ireland.
- **Modest Royalty:** Fidelma, who as a religiuse just wears a habit. Occasionally averted for cause, such as putting arrogant nobles in their place. After she resigns from being a religiuse she dresses in civvies, but still much plainer than you'd expect from royalty, except for special occasions or when she's being official on Colgú's behalf.
- **Politically Active Princess:** Many of the murders have political implications for Colgú and his kingdom of Muman, so Fidelma often has to be diplomatic. It gets to the point where Colgú officially makes her a member of an elite noble fraternity so that she'll have the power to speak for him in certain situations, including legal matters.
- **Pretty Princess Powerhouse:** Unarmed religious were trained in an obscure martial art to protect them during their travels. More than once Fidelma uses this art to subdue armed attackers with her bare hands.
- **Shown Their Work:** Tremayne's lengthy expositions often read

like a university-level dissertation in all aspects of Irish language and culture in the 10th century. He is at pains to explain obscure points of language or law in the text where other authors might employ footnotes.

- **Significant Green-Eyed Redhead:** Fidelma.
- **Succession Crisis:** Many of the stories and novels, though as often focused on the death or selection of an heir, or tánaiste, as on a king or chieftain. Others are about attempts to overthrow kingdoms or ruling families. Kingship could pass between different septs of the same clan.
- **Summation Gathering:** Almost every time. Often justified by Fidelma either presenting the solution before a judge as part of a legal case or having to explain things to someone official or in authority who needs the whole story. Sometimes done so civilians involved in the case don't spend their whole lives wondering what the heck happened or aren't Convicted by Public Opinion.
- **Taking the Veil:** Played with; religious houses even before Christianity were closer to schools than places of worship. Fidelma becomes a religiuse primarily because of the educational opportunities it offers, and gradually withdraws from the religious life.
- **The Watson:** Eadulf. Also, as a foreigner to Ireland, he has constant exposition spouted at him for the readers' benefit.
- **Time Skip:** Despite a normal rate of mystery-solving up to four novels in an in-universe year, there are no volumes between the revelation of Fidelma's pregnancy at the end of one book and sometime after her son's birth over nine months later in the next. Fidelma seems to have solved no mysteries while pregnant, even in the short stories.
- **Will They or Won't They?:** for the first half-dozen or so books, it's all but spelled out that Fidelma and Eadulf are made for each other, but they never seem to do anything about it. But eventually they become a couple, become parents and formally marry.
- **Would Hurt a Child:** In *Suffer Little Children* an orphanage is burned down as part of a complicated plot to murder the heirs to the throne.

– TVTropes.org

PRONUNCIATION GUIDE

Pronunciation Guide
HOW TO PRONOUNCE IRISH NAMES AND WORDS

Irish belongs to the Celtic Branch of the Indo-European family of languages. It is closely related to Manx and Scottish Gaelic and a cousin of Welsh, Cornish and Breton. It is a, very old European literary language. Professor Calvert Watkins of Harvard maintained it contains Europe's oldest vernacular literature, Greek and Latin being a lingua franca. Surviving texts date from the 7th century AD.

The Irish of Fidelma's period is classed as Old Irish, which, after 950 AD, entered a period known as Middle Irish. Therefore, in the Fidelma books, Old Irish forms are generally adhered to, whenever possible, in both names and words. This is like using Chaucer's English compared to modern English. For example, a word such as *aidche* ("night") in Old Irish is now rendered *oiche* in Modern Irish.

There are only 18 letters in the Irish alphabet. From earliest times there has been a literary standard but today four distinct spoken dialects are recognised. For our purposes, we will keep to Fidelma's dialect of Munster.

It is a general rule that stress is placed on the first syllable, but as in all languages, there are exceptions. In Munster the exceptions to the rule of initial stress are a) if the second syllable is long then it bears the stress; b) if the first two syllables are short and the third is long then the third syllable is stressed – such as in the word for fool, *amadán* = amad-awn; or c) where the second syllable contains ach and there is no long syllable, the second syllable bears the stress.

There are five short vowels – a, e, i, o, u and five long vowels – á, é, í, ó, ú. On the long vowels note the accent, like the French acute, which is called a fáda (lit. long), and this is the only accent in Irish. It occurs on capitals as well as lower case.

The accent is important for, depending on where it is placed, it changes the entire word. Seán (Shawn) = John. But *sean* (shan) = old and *séan* (she-an) = an omen. By leaving off the accent on the name of the famous film actor, Sean Connery, he has become "Old" Connery!

For those interested in learning more about the language, it is worth remembering that, after centuries of suppression during the colonial period, Irish became the first official language of the Irish State on independence in

1922. The last published Census of 1991 showed one third of the population returning themselves as Irish-speaking. In Northern Ireland, where the language continued to be openly discouraged after Partition in 1922, only ten-and-a-half per cent of the population were able to speak the language in 1991, the first time an enumeration of speakers was allowed since Partition.

Language courses are now available on video and audiocassette from a range of producers from Linguaphone to RTE and BBC. There are some sixty summer schools and special intensive courses available. Teilifis na Gaeilge is the television station broadcasting entirely in Irish and there are several Irish language radio stations and newspapers. Information can be obtained from **Comhdháil Náisiúnta na Gaeilge, 46 Sráid Chill Dara, Baile Átha Cliath 2, Éire**.

The UK Audio Book versions of the books read by Irish actress Caroline Lennon provide an authentic and excellent way to hear the correct pronunciation.

The Vowels
The short and long vowels are either "broad" or "slender."

The six broad vowels are:
- a pronounced "o" as in cot
- á pronounced "aw" as in law
- o pronounced "u" as in cut
- ó pronounced "o" as in low
- u pronounced "u" as in run
- ú pronounced "u" as in rule

The four slender vowels are:
- i pronounced "i" as in hit
- í pronounced "ee" as in see
- e pronounced "e" as in let
- é pronounced "ay" as in say

There are double vowels, some of which are fairly easy because they compare to English pronunciation " such as "ae" as say, or ui as in quit. However, some double and even triple vowels in Irish need to be learned.
- ai pronounced like "ee" as in see (dálaigh = daw'lee)
- ia pronounced like "ea" as in near
- io pronounced like "o" as in come

PꞀONUNCIATION GUIDE

- ea pronounced like "ea" as in bear
- ei pronounced like "e" as in let
- aoi pronounced like the "ea" as in mean
- uai pronounced like the "ue" as in blue
- eoi pronounced like the "eo" as in yeoman
- iai pronounced like the "ee" as in see

Hidden vowels

Most people will have noticed that many Irish people pronounce the word film as fil'um. This is actually a transference of Irish pronunciation rules. When l, n or r are followed by b, bh, ch, g (not after n), m, or mh, and is preceded by a short stressed vowel, an additional vowel is heard between them. For example, *bolg* (stomach) is pronounced bol'ag; *garbh* (rough) is gar'ev; *dorcha* (dark) is dor'ach'a; *gorm* (blue) is gor'um, and *ainm* (name) is an'im.

The Consonants

- b, d, f, h, l, m, n, p, r, and t are said more or less as in English.
- g is always hard like "g" as in gate
- c is always hard like the "c" as in cat
- s is pronounced like the "s" as in said except before a slender vowel when it is pronounced "sh" as in shin

In Irish the letters j, k, q, w, x, y, or z do not exist, and v is formed by the combination of "bh."

Consonants can change their sound by aspiration or eclipse – aspiration is caused by using the letter "h" after them.
- bh is the "v" as in voice
- ch is a soft breath as in loch (not pronounced as lock!) or as in Bach.
- dh before a broad vowel is like the "g" as in gap
- dh before a slender vowel is like the "y" as in year
- fh is totally silent
- gh before a slender vowel can sound like "y" as in yet
- mh is pronounced like the "w" as in wall
- ph is like the "f" as in fall
- th is like the "h" as in ham
- sh is also like the "h" as in ham

Consonants can also change their sound by being eclipsed, or silenced, by another consonant placed before it. For example, *na mBan* (of women) = nah m'on; or *i bpaipéar* (in the paper) i b'ap'er, or *i gcathair* (in the city) i g'a'har.

- p can be eclipsed by b, t
- t can be eclipsed by d
- c can be eclipsed by g
- f can be eclipsed by bh
- b can be eclipsed by m
- d and g can be eclipsed by n

An Interview With Peter Tremayne

Peter Berresford Ellis is an historian, literary biographer and novelist who has published over 90 books. Under the pseudonym Peter Tremayne, he's the author of the international bestselling Sister Fidelma mystery series. His non-fiction works have made him acknowledged as an authority on Celtic history and culture. He was the first deputy editor of The Irish Post and later a columnist. He was born in Coventry in 1943, the son of a Cork-born journalist. He lives in London.

Who are your heroes?

I have too many heroes (and heroines) covering different fields, but we might make a start in politics, so James Connolly for his philosophies and personal courage.

What song would you like played at your funeral?

Life Gets Teejus, don't it (Walter Brennan)

What record sends a shiver down your spine?

Fortuna Imperatrix Mundi, Carl Orf's setting for Carmina Burana.

What is your favourite place in Ireland?

The Beara Peninsula.

What is your most treasured possession?

At the moment, reasonably good health.

What makes you angry?

Those who make their ignorance into a virtue.

What book influenced you most?

Many books have been influential at various times but the one what really influenced me to start my career was *The Street of Disillusion* by Harry Proctor (1958) an autobiographical account of a Fleet Street reporter when Fleet Street was a centre of journalism.

If you could change one thing in your life, what would it be?
I disobeyed parental advice when I was 18 year old because I thought
I knew better about my career. I didn't. Took me two years to get
back on track. Wish I could change that but then, I suppose I made
it in the end.

What gives your life meaning?
My work and my wife – not necessarily in that order.

Can you tell me a joke?
No good at jokes. More of the slow narrative type, like Dave Allen.
And I use to chuckle away at the *Ripping Yarns* series.

When did you last cry?
Yesterday. Tears come naturally to me at every human tragedy – which
is pretty frequently.

What do you see when you look in the mirror?
A first-class example of the human ageing process.

What is your favourite film and why?
The Uninvited (1944) with Ray Milland and Gail Russell. It's based
on Dorothy Macardle's novel and is the classic ghost story combined
with a whodunnit which, in spite of today's advances in cinematogra-
phy and special effects, has never been bettered for its really chilling
appearance of a ghost on screen.

What is your passion?
Writing.

**What do you have hanging on your walls at home that you
like looking at?**
I like to think that all the pictures on our walls are good to look at.

What was your most formative experience?
As a young reporter in October 1964, newly arrived in Belfast to cover
the General Election, being chased up the Falls Road by a phalanx
of baton-wielding RUC, having witnessed them smashing up the
nationalist campaign office on at Divis.

AN INTERVIEW WITH PETER TREMAYNE

What do you believe in?
Those human beings, left to their own conscience's dictates, can be inherently moral.

What traits do others criticise you for?
For being an optimistic pessimist.

What is the funniest thing you've ever seen or heard?
Collectively, politicians – Shakespeare put it succinctly: `Man, proud man, dressed in a little brief authority, like an angry ape, plays such fantastic tricks before high heaven as makes the angels weep." If not weeping, then you have to start laughing.

What is your favourite word one-liner or retort?
That's an oxymoron – it's usually met with a thunderous silence!

What would your motto be?
The motto of the Ellis family of Cork is `Sperans" (hope) – I am still hoping.

As a child what did you want to be when you grew up?
I was very precocious, so from the age of nine years old, I always wanted to write stories.

Which Irish work would you recommend most highly?
Lebor Gabhala Erenn (Irish Text Society editions, 5 vols.)

– *Martin Doyle*
Irish Post, 9 April 2011

THE SISTER FIDELMA COMPENDIUM

The Sister Fidelma Mysteries: What's The Agenda?

first became interested in the work of the author Peter Tremayne when I started the Research for Writers module with Professor Carl Tighe in October 2004. The module was seen as a rehearsal for this my Independent Studies Project.

On the basis of my research, I wrote an essay on Peter's work entitled *'Exploring the role of a 7th century nun and the ancient Brehon Laws as a formula for success in contemporary creative writing.'* The essay (1) raised many questions I found of interest, why were the readers interested in the life of a 7th century Irish nun and an obscure set of ancient laws, what affect did these laws have on ancient society and did they have any influence on justices today in Ireland? Were a high proportion of the readers Roman Catholic or of Irish descent, did the stories raise political and spiritual issues for the readers. How important to the readers were the sections on women's rights in both church and society. Was there any truth in reports that the books were having a positive affect on the economy of the Irish town of Cashel the setting for many of the Sister Fidelma Mysteries? After reading the essay Carl Tighe suggested I was trying to cover too wide an area and had in fact outlined more than one project.

At this point I was still undecided about my dissertation subject but as suggested, before starting, I visited the Learning Centre and looked at other dissertations by students who had graduated: *Eleanor Craig 1998/99, Case study on Alison Price – Children's writer. Beth Harwood 1998/99, Implications and Benefits of Combining Fact with Fiction. Caroline Armstrong 2003/04, What Roll Does Creative Writing Play in the Evangelical Movement?* I noted that Beth Harwood's dissertation would be more akin to my own project. Even so because they were so wide ranging in subject matter I didn't find them much help, other than to familiarise myself, with what the finished publication should look like.

On further visits to the Learning Centre, I compiled a list of Irish literature to look at but found them all a bit too academic for my purpose. Over the years I'd read a lot of books by contemporary Irish writers such as Roddy Doyle, Frank Delaney, Maeve Binchy and Frank McCourt but

ZHE SISZER FIDELMA COMPENDIUM

I didn't feel I wanted to do my dissertation on any of them. During my studies on the storytelling module with Simon Heywood I'd read a lot of Celtic myth and legend which I'd enjoyed. This perhaps encouraged me to look more into my father's Irish roots and the meaning of my surname, Breheny *(Mac an Breitheamhnaigh)* which translates to son of the Brehon the Irish word for judge.

At some point when I was working on the Research for Writers module, I'd searched the internet for sites about the Irish Brehon Laws. One site that came up was The International Sister Fidelma Society. The site was my introduction to the work of Peter Tremayne the fiction writing pseudonym of Peter Berresford Ellis a Celtic Scholar and expert on the Brehon Laws. Peter Tremayne's bestselling Sister Fidelma Mysteries use a 7th century Celtic nun also *dálaigh* – an advocate of the Brehon Laws to solve crimes. Carl Tighe suggested I could look at how the Brehon Laws influenced Peter Tremayne's writing.

I read the first two books in the series *Absolution by Murder* and *Shroud for an Archbishop*. The stories use events and real people from history as a backdrop for Sister Fidelma and her fellow sleuth, Saxon and lover Brother Eadulf. In the stories Sister Fidelma is present at well known historic events such as the Synod of Whitby in 664 AD where leading churchmen, kings and other notables from history are used as characters in the mysteries. I thought it would be interesting to check the events and characters for accuracy and to look more closely at Peter Tremayne's claims concerning 7th century Irish society.

Reading the first book I found the story line interesting but not as compelling as the Cadfael stories by Ellis Peter's who is generally acknowledged as the doyen of the genre. For me, because of my name the Brehon Laws and the social history were of more interest. Happily when I read the second book set in Rome, I did find it more gripping as a murder mystery and I was intrigued by the comparisons of the Catholic Church of Fidelma's time and the present, typical examples were references to the Pope (2) visiting clergy from other countries (3), the use of gifts as demonstrations of submission (4), celibacy (5), and Rome as a seat of power in the Christian World.

After reading the first two books I spent some time examining the website (www.sisterfidelma.com) in detail, then emailed some questions to David Robert Wooten who is the Director of The International Sister Fidelma Society, an organization set-up to support Peter's work. David's response was immediate and knowledgeable, but he was unable to tell me how many Sister Fidelma books had been sold worldwide. To my surprise he emailed Peter Tremayne on my behalf and within a few hours I had the answer – 1.75 million copies up to December 2004 (6).

I also asked David for a reader profile, he admitted they didn't have one but responded with an email containing the available facts (7).

Without prompting David picked-up on the meaning of my name, Breheny ... son of the Brehon and guessed why I was interested in the books. He correctly told me where my family originated from in Ireland and over the months that followed proved to be a very valuable resource contact. I also placed some questions in the website's Guest Book but received no response.

While studying the website I noticed from Peter Tremayne's biography that he had served a term as the International Chairman of a political pressure group, the Celtic League, from 1988/1990. This prompted me to visit their website which explained their aims and invited visitors to sign-up, free of charge for the League's newsletters. The newsletters are emailed each weekend and cover many political topics applicable to the six Celtic countries, Mannin/Isle of Man, Alba/Scotland, Breizh/Brittany, Cymru/Wales, Eire/Ireland and Kernow/Cornwall. The Articles are wide ranging covering political issues ignored by the British Press, examples of these would be:

- Double standards on terrorism by the French and US governments (8).
- Church reform in Celtic Cornwall (9).
- Radiation pollution in the Irish Sea from Sellafield (10).
- The suspicious deaths of political prisoners in Spanish Jails (11).

Although Peter Tremayne is involved with many Celtic societies and organization's I became interested in his politics after reading comments he made concerning his experiences as a young journalist in Belfast during the 1964 General Election. I wondered if they might have any bearing on his writing.

Once I'd decided to write my dissertation on Peter Tremayne, having found the website so useful and the society director so helpful, I became a full member by paying the sum of £29.95. Membership includes quarterly copies of *The Brehon* the society's journal which I also found to be an excellent resource.

THE SISTER FIDELMA COMPENDIUM

Eventually I read three of Peter's Sister Fidelma Mysteries in chronological order, *Absolution by Murder* 1994, *Shroud for the Archbishop* and *Suffer Little Children*. Like most of his readers with each book I read I became progressively addicted to the stories. For background research I read two of Peter's seventy academic books, *The Celtic Empire* and *The Celtic Woman*. I felt the books confirmed Peter's great knowledge of the subject and for me they established a reality and a trust for me in his fictional work. I was further impressed by a section given over to the Sister Fidelma Mysteries in a new book called *Crime Fiction*, by John Scaggs lecturer in English at Mary Immaculate College, Limerick, Ireland. In it John Scraggs analyses the stories and comments on how Peter uses the past to make sense of the present (12).

I read many academic books on the Celts and for comparison *Boudica, Dreaming the Eagle* by Mander Scott, a creative writer on the Celts, in this book there is an excellent description of a battle between the invading Romans and the Celts. In her notes to the book, she quotes:

'... Concerning her (Boudica) early life there is no written record and thus everything contained in these pages – the people, their life and their dreams – is fiction ...'

Even so, like Peter Tremayne she was for me able to establish a reality based on good historic research of the period. Much of her historical background information can be verified in the writings of the invading Romans, even though they are full of political, cultural and social bias. She also supports her work with a detailed bibliography.

After reading five of Peter's books and a 53 page print out of *The International Sister Fidelma Society* website I had many questions to ask both Peter Tremayne and his readers. I contacted David Wooten at the Sister Fidelma Society who arranged an interview for me with Peter in London for the 15 March.

Before the interview I arranged a tutorial with Moy McCrory my senior course tutor, I asked about content and how many questions would be appropriate. It took me four days to compile a list of possible questions, these totaled ninety-eight, obviously too many. It took me a further day to edit them down to Moy's suggested twelve with a further six questions in reserve. I was concerned that I shouldn't waste Peter's time with inappropriate questions or questions already answered on the website.

WHAT'S THE AGENDA?

I was also keen to ask some personal questions. Questions I felt were relevant to my research, what was he trying to achieve, did he have a political agenda? Had he developed a secret formula? I wanted to know if he was educated as a Catholic, if so, was he still practicing and had his beliefs affected his writing? Was he attempting to use his knowledge of the Roman Catholic Church to influence current issues regarding the ordination of women, married and gay clergy, politics and Northern Ireland? Did he pander to ethnic sentimentality? I wanted to know if he aspired other than to write good historic murder mysteries.

Not knowing what to expect and not wanting to lose his good will before the start of the interview, I emailed my questions to him the day before the interview suggesting that if there were any questions, he objected to them could be cut from the list before we started – there were none. Peter and his wife Dorothy turned out to be friendly and interesting people, going out of their way to be helpful. First, they took me to lunch then back in the relaxed atmosphere of their home Peter answered every question on my list plus many more that grew out of our conversation. The tape-recorded interview lasted one and a half hours and took thirty-three-hours to type. The total word count was 10294.

Later having obtained Peter' approval I sent a transcript of the interview to David Wooten at the International Sister Fidelma Society. After reading it David asked if he could post it, in its entirety on the website and to include some of it in the September edition of *The Brehon Magazine*, his reaction gave me some much-needed confidence.

Because of his political leanings I also asked Bernard Moffatt, Secretary General of the Celtic League for his opinion on Peter Tremayne's work. He replied that he had not read Peter's fictional works but was impressed by both the man and his academic works citing Peter's book *The Celtic Dawn* as the definitive history of the Inter Celtic movement. He also suggested that without the income from his fictional work Peter may not have been able to produce some of his weightier factual tomes (13). I later put this point to Peter who agreed saying that his fiction work had given him financial independence since 1975. However, he stressed that he also enjoyed writing fiction (14).

I discovered that my parish priest Father John Guest, also Vicar General of the Roman Catholic Dioceses of Nottingham and a former head teacher had recently read one of the Sister Fidelma books and had recommended it to the person responsible for adult education in the dioceses. Because of this I felt it would be a golden opportunity to get some feedback from the church, so I also arranged an interview with Father John. The interview was useful in that I was able clarify the churches position on some of current issues raised in the books and to discuss my ideas relating to reader reaction, especially from those with Irish and Catholic backgrounds.

At a second tutorial with Moy McCrory, I discussed my interviews with Peter and Father John Guest and outlined my ideas for the research article. Moy suggested I was overloading myself with research material and it was time to start writing. The same day I spoke to Carl Tighe and discussed what I was trying to achieve, he reminded me that it might not always be possible for me to get the answers I was searching for and warned against getting carried away with my own beliefs when interviewing people. He suggested I try to stay focused on key issues. I think Carl recognized that I was beginning to panic. I had a pile of research material – now I needed to be selective.

Because Peter Tremayne wrote in a highly specialized genre it was difficult to find people who had read his books and whom I could ask to complete a questionnaire. To overcome this problem in November 2005 I emailed over sixty people who'd left comments on the society's website. In a general letter I explained who I was and what I was trying to achieve and asked for their assistance as study partners. I was delighted to receive thirty-six replies from Europe, the USA, Australia and Canada (15).

I then set-up a group email address and on the 10 January 2006 sent out a letter asking the recipients to write and tell me in their own words why they found the Sister Fidelma Mysteries so interesting. Twenty-two readers replied some entering into further personal correspondence and from these contacts a pattern of study began to emerge (16).

One of my study partners, retired sociology professor Bob Piker of Kingston Canada (17) suggested some comparative reading, *The Novice's Tale* by Margaret Frazer an American writer claiming to write in the tradition of Ellis Peter's Brother Cadfael novels. Frazer's main character is also a nun, Sister Frevisse an amateur sleuth in 13th century England. After Sister Fidelma I found the plot weak and in comparison, to Fidelma and Cadfael, Sister Frevisse was a weak character.

For me, it was Margaret Frazer's failure to include enough historic background information and a failure to research her facts correctly that lost my interest. In the story a bottle of wine is used to poison a murder victim (18), research I carried out in conjunction with Professor Bob

WHAT'S THE AGENDA?

Pike established that wine bottles were not used in the way described until 1750 (19). Although glass bottles were used from Roman times wine was stored in barrels or amphora, if bottles were used, they were simply carafes for serving at table. Because of this the writer lost my trust and any further interest in her work.

I kept David Wooten at the International Sister Fidelma Society informed about of my contact with his members and asked about his relationship with Peter Tremayne, I was surprised to learn they had never met.

I prepared a questionnaire of twenty-one-questions based on discussions with all those involved. First, I tested it on friends for feedback, made minor changes, then emailed it to my then thirty-six on-line partners (20), I received fourteen replies. Later my on-line study partner and mentor Bob Piker raised some queries regarding the ethics and sensitivity of some questions – he was the only one to do so but after discussing the matter with him I could see no problems.

As part of my research, I used the interlibrary loan system to borrow volume's I and II of the *Ancient Laws and Institutes of Ireland – Senchus Mor,* these enabled me to cross check some of Peter's claims about the Brehon Laws and saved me several trips to the British Library in London and the Bodleian Library Oxford. When volume II arrived, I was surprised to discover that although printed in 1869 its pages were still uncut – the book had never been read.

And so, armed with my questions some of which I had doubts about ever being able to answer, more research material than I could ever use I started to write my dissertation article.

Reference List

1. Appendix 1. Essay dated 19.04.05
2. Shroud for the Archbishop, by Peter Tremayne. Pub: Headline Book Publishing 1995. ISBN 0-7472-4848-6. Page 11.
3. Shroud for the Archbishop. Page 43.
4. Shroud for the Archbishop. Page 67.
5. Shroud for the Archbishop. Page 175.
6. Appendix 2. David Wooten of the International Sister Fidelma Society. Page 55.
7. Appendix 2. Page 53.
8. Appendix 3. The Celtic League. Page 63.

9. Appendix 3. Page 64.
10. Appendix 3. Page 61.
11. Appendix 3. Page 68.
12. Crime Fiction, by John Scaggs. Pub: Routledge London 2005, ISBN 0-415-31824-6. Pages 133/134.
13. Appendix 3. Page 59.
14. Appendix 4. Peter Tremayne. Page 88.
15. Appendix 5. Study Partner November 2005. Page 91.
16. Appendix 5. Replies from Study Partners January 2006. Page 93 – 110.
17. Appendix 6. Study Partner, Professor Bob Piker. Page 159.
18. The Novice's Tale, by Margaret Frazer. Pub: Berkley Publishing Group, New York 1993. ISBN 0-425-14321-X. Page's 135/136.
19. World Atlas of Wine, by Hugh Johnson. Pub: Mitchell Beazley Limited, London 1971. ISBN 0-85533-002-3. Page 16.
20. Appendix 5. Questionnaire. Page 111.

RESEARCH ARTICLE

For the last year I have been researching the work of Historic Crime Fiction writer Peter Tremayne with the preface that I might discover how and why he uses his knowledge as a Celtic scholar to write and sell books. By analysing his work I had hoped to gain a better understanding of how to succeed as a writer of historic fiction myself. After reading his first three books *Absolution by Murder, Shroud for the Archbishop* and *Suffer Little Children,* I came up with the proposal that Peter might have an agenda that went far beyond the work of most writers. It occurred to me that Peter's books offered the reader more than just a good read and I wanted to know if Peter had developed a new angle on Historic Crime Fiction – perhaps a new formula for success.

Not only do Peter's books offer an insight into a little-known period of Irish history they offer Irish people a pride in their heritage and readers a better understanding of Ireland's historic past achievements and its place in the modern world.

It is my opinion that the trend in recent years has been for Irish writers such as Roddy Doyle and Frank McCourt to project the Ireland of poverty and deprivation in their novels. This may enhance the rags to riches image of Irish people living abroad, but it denies them a pride in their true heritage. For many their understanding of Ireland is the Ireland of their more recent forbearers who left in their millions, during the famines and political upheavals of the 18th 19th and 20th Centuries. It could be said that Doyle and McCourt lay claim to poverty as a uniquely Irish condition of which to be proud of.

Peter Tremayne a respected Celtic scholar has used his great knowledge of Irish history to create a different perspective of Ireland and the Irish. His successful Sister Fidelma Mysteries which have sold almost 2 million copies worldwide feature a seventh century Irish investigator nun, a former member of a religious community founded by St Brigid of Kildare in Ireland. Sister Fidelma the main character belongs to the royal family of Munster and is a *dálaigh*, a judge of the Brehon Laws. In the books we learn that the Brehon Laws are the oldest legal system in Europe and known to have been in existence as early as 700 BC at which time they were held in oral form by the druids. The laws were first written down by St Patrick between 438 and 441 AD (1). Under Brehon Law women had more rights and protection than under any other western law code.

The history of 7th century Ireland is unknown to most people outside of university ancient studies departments but like the world today it was a period of great change and so has many comparisons readers can relate to. While the 7th century represented the "Dark Ages' for the rest of Europe, for Ireland it was a period of "Great Enlightenment.' At this time students from all over Europe and the sons of many Anglo-Saxon Kings studied at the ecclesiastical university of Durrow where it is recorded eighteen different nations were present. At the same time missionaries from Ireland were reconverting pagan Europe and setting up centres of learning from the Faroes in the north to Taranto in southern Italy and as far east as Kiev in the Ukraine.

During the 7th century the Celtic Church was also in conflict with the Church of Rome and in the first book *Absolution by Murder* Peter Tremayne uses the Synod of Whitby in 664 AD as a back drop to the story. The book incorporates real people from history such as Deusdedit Archbishop of Canterbury (2), King Oswy of Northumbria (3) King Loegaire of Ireland (4), real places and real events. The first book set in England not Ireland is seen to illustrate Irish culture as being more refined even more advanced than that of Saxon England.

Readers might get the impression that Sister Fidelma is looking down her nose at her Saxon counterparts especially Saxon Brother Eadulf. Peter Tremayne is continually exposing the reader to little known but controversial historic facts which I feel are the key to holding the reader's interest, especially female readers. For example, we are told that under Brehon Law women had rights (5) not only to property and divorce (for which there were nine reasons they could divorce their husbands) but also within the church where there were women bishops and judges. Equally interesting are the Saxon laws of primogeniture (first born male) which had no standing in Ireland. Peter Tremayne weaves these facts into stories that give the reader a unique insight into a golden age of Irish history.

For me it was the information about the Brehon Laws which held my attention and set me off in search of facts to substantiate his many claims which always stood-up to close scrutiny. For some other readers I'd made contact with it was the power struggle between Rome and the Celtic Church and the fact that women had been bishops in the past and priests married with families. It was interesting to learn that one of the reasons the Church of Rome was against married priests was because they tended to leave their property, which in some cases was extensive, to their children, rather than the church. For me, a practicing Catholic and others I spoke to, Peter was suggesting that the Catholic Church had been misleading us by keeping sensitive secrets, making nonsense of current arguments about married clergy and women priests.

In the same way *The Da Vinci Code,* by Dan Brown has stimulated debate on scripture and dogma, Peter Tremayne's books have stimulated interest in the role of the Catholic in Irish society, marriage, divorce, celibacy, woman priests, women's rights, gay rights, justice, national pride and 7th century history.

Peter peels back years of misinformation to reveal Ireland's untold story, leaving the reader especially those of Irish or Catholic origin, whom I am convinced the books are written for – in a position to better understand their heritage. I believe many Irish people carry a lot of emotional religious and social baggage, the result of centuries of suppression by church and state. When I asked Peter where he himself was coming from spiritually and politically he told me his father had been born a Catholic and studied at a seminary in Ireland before becoming a journalist. But, for most of his life had been an agnostic like Peter, who as a boy had for a while attended a Catholic boarding school (6).

Peter is a lifetime socialist and chairman of his local Labour Party, he sees himself as being left wing. He feels his politics were influenced by his father's family who came from Cork and who had been active Republicans since 1840 (7):

'There's a tradition in the Ellis family of being revolutionaries (8).'

This was interesting background information and brought me to Peter's involvement with the Celtic League a political pressure group run by a man called J B Moffatt living on the Isle of Man. I'd noticed from The Sister Fidelma website that Peter had been chairman of the league for two years', I'd tried to find out more about the league by contacting both BBC Radio Isle of Man and Bernard Moffatt, who continues to email me weekly newssheets (9). Reading between the lines I got the feeling Peter wasn't one hundred percent in tune with the present organisation so I didn't press my questions further:

' ... it's a pan-Celtic movement and ... it was formed in 1961, it ... advocated the   independence ... the setting-up of parliaments in whatever form, each individual countries ... in the six Celtic countries ...because they were Celtic, sharing common links with languages, culture and shared colonial experience. ... there have been some changes ... it wasn't ever seen as just a pressure group ... I wrote a book called the Celtic Dawn which is the history of pan-Celticism, ... still being printed (10) .

I ask about his experiences as a young reporter working in Northern Ireland on the October 64 General Election – hoping he might expand on his republican feelings. On the website he'd said, working in Northern Ireland, had a profound effect on him, so I ask what that effect had been:

'I went across to Northern Ireland, to Belfast to cover the October 64 general election ... from my family traditions I'd heard stories about the North and I'd read histories and books about the North and so I knew that Catholics didn't have civil rights ...

... Forster ... back in 1963, introducing an apartheid cohesion bill in the South African parliament, actually said that he would swap all the apartheid legislation in South Africa for just one clause of the Northern Ireland Special Powers Act ...It's also recorded that Adolf Hitler had admired it.

ZHE SISZER FIDELMA COMPENDIUM

... yet knowing that, it still did not prepare me for what I saw when I arrived at Aldergrove Airport and within twelve hours was being chased down Falls Road by a phalanx of RUC wielding batons and guns and so on and ... seeing a woman at a bus stop with a small child being abused by armed RUC ... simply because s h e w a s Catholic ... And so, it was a very traumatic experience for me as a very young reporter (11).'

I was under no illusions about Peter's political and religious affiliations, but he denied any attempt to influence his readers through his writing.

Next, I wanted to know about the historic source material which he uses as a backdrop for all the Sister Fidelma Mysteries. Apart from a general interest in crime fiction, feedback from his readers indicated to me that it was the historic detail relating to the Brehon Laws, women's rights and the church that most interested them. Like myself, most readers were fascinated by Peter's great knowledge, of this little-known period of history.

I asked Peter if the fact that he had chosen to write about such a short time period (Fidelma's life span) restricted his writing, I had guessed from his comments on the website that not a great deal of historic reference to 7th century Ireland existed.

Peter told me he tries to keep to a chronology which helps him focus on the period and that he checks the Irish Annals and Chronicles for background information, stressing that he never makes-up historic events – whatever he writes about he claims can be authenticated which is confirmed by many of his readers who check-out the facts (12).

He also told me about the Vienna Schottenkloster archive found at the Abbey of Regensburg in Southern Germany which was founded in the 11th or 12th century by Gillcrist MacCarthy the brother of the king of Cashel, the king of Munster. The Schottenkloster archive is a huge collection of Celtic manuscripts taken to Germany from Ireland and recorded by the monks, it still hasn't been indexed and is simply labelled, "The Munster Archive' – no scholar has ever translated them. Peter believes that of all the known Celtic manuscript material in the world only about ten percent has ever been translated (13). It almost makes me want to learn Medieval Latin so I can go and read them.

A recent publicity release issued by the International Sister Fidelma

WHAT'S THE AGENDA?

Society claims that the Sister Fidelma Mysteries are now Ireland's best-selling fiction detective series and Peter, the only living crime writer ever to have been accorded his own literary festival in Ireland. The festival takes place this September at Cashel, Co. Tipperary.

As a Celtic scholar, Peter projects a different view of Celtic culture and history. A view welcomed by people with similar political and cultural sympathies, delighted to discover a more positive perspective of their culture. His books appeal to those who want to learn about a different Ireland, one not written by victor or victim.

Another view of the same history was written by the late English academic John Morris in his book *The Age of Arthur* where the situation is seen from the traditional English viewpoint:

> 'Until the monastic upsurge of the mid sixth century, Ireland was still barbarian, its customs little affected by the impact of Christianity and Roman ideas. The accounts of its last generations, in the years between 480 and 560, describe in detail a still unmodified Iron Age society.
>
> The records of the next century describe the struggle of the Roman religion to transform barbarian Ireland. At first, the monks were in conflict with the powerful Druid, and deeply distrusted those baptised Druids who sought to marry alien worlds. But later the abbot and the bishop replaced the Druid, whose title devolved upon lowly intellectual craftsmen (14).'

It is easy to see where Peter Tremayne is coming from when you read this statement which illustrates the English view of 6th and 7th century Ireland, and which one could say still has implications for the way Ireland is still viewed today by the English. It is perhaps Peter's refusal as a Celtic scholar to see history from an English viewpoint or that of the Church of Rome which appeals to the reader's sense of emotion and justice. His plots are concerned with the relationships between past and present, a blend of old beliefs and new concepts of Christianity and justice. They attempt to make sense of the present "through the past' seeing history as the link to ourselves (15).

I find Morris' attitude derogatory; it conveniently ignores *Ireland's Golden Age of Achievement* referring to Ireland as a barbarian still unmodified Iron Age society. I believe that Peter Tremayne sets out with the Sister Fidelma Mysteries to debunk the historic stereotyping of ancient Ireland by many British writers. I asked Peter about Edward Said's (16) comment that the British used culture to make those they ruled over feel inferior.

'First, you've got to understand what British culture is ... unfortunately the English don't have any sense of their, own history. Now this might sound weird because you get a glazed view all the time. The kings and queens, etc ... kings and queens aren't history ... (17).'

I also asked how he thought the English see the Irish today:

'The English think of the Irish exactly the same as they thought of the Irish a century ago ... they don't understand (18).'

I was interested to see Peter Tremayne also dealing with the tricky question of gay clergy in his second book *Shroud for the Archbishop,* when I asked him if same sex partnerships were taboo or accepted in Brehon Law, he was unsure and said he had debated the point with professor, Fergus O'Kelly who had written what he considered the best guide to the Brehon Law system. Professor O'Kelly said there were only a few references in the laws that referred to the subject and those referred to the law of divorce. From the available information they had decided that same sex partnerships were accepted (19).

There can be no denying the Sister Fidelma website (www.sisterfidelma.com) has become a valuable marketing tool for the Sister Fidelma Mysteries and a platform for the historical, political and social views of Peter Tremayne, but, if we look further, it is more than that. The site containing more than fifty-three-pages is a valuable archive for readers who want to learn more about Sister Fidelma and 7th century Ireland. It contains translations in more than forty languages, information about the author and his academic work and other language editions, interviews, press articles and critical comment, a guide to Irish pronunciation and a direct means of contacting the author for readers wanting clarification of the facts (20) (21).

Without the website interviewing the readers would have been a problem as I'd never met anyone else who had read the books. I wanted to know what it was that held their interest and whether they experienced the same emotional feelings as I had (22)'and more important I wanted to know if they had ancestral links to Ireland. When I'd asked Peter if he had a reader profile, he said he might have started out with one in mind when he wrote the first book, but subsequent fan mail had shown a wider readership (23).

Although I had failed in my attempt to contact non-English speaking fans my own research indicated there was a reader profile. Most of the readers were fans of historic crime fiction most were women, and most were over fifty years of age. A high proportion were practicing Christians and a notable number were descendants of Irish emigrants living in The United States and Australia. Many admitted that when reading the books, they experienced a spiritual link to the people and places mentioned in the stories. Some said reading the books made them proud to be Irish (24). Although the website claims the books are read by people of many faiths all the people, I interviewed were Christians.

High on the list of what readers said they found interesting was the author's academic knowledge of the period, the fact that the main character is a woman, the conflict between the Celtic Church and Rome, the Brehon Laws which many saw as *more just* than many present laws (25), especially when it came to women's rights which some readers felt were more advanced in Fidelma's time. *(In Brehon Law there were a number of advanced concepts but the principle one was that you had compensation for the victim and rehabilitation for the wrong doer)* (26).

When I asked readers if the books posed questions for them in relationship to their beliefs, most felt reading the books had answered many questions, helping them to understand current issues in the Christian community.

Readers without Irish ancestry said the books had increased their interest in the country of Ireland, a man from New Zealand said "he'd thought 7th century Ireland had been a savage place (27),' an American woman with a career in the law said "the stories had helped her be more objective and better appreciate research and investigative concepts (28).' another had developed an interest in ancient trade routes and the bonds developed between nations (29), several people were interested in how the Christian faith had developed as a result of enforced dogma and one woman from Holland took a dim view of Sister Fidelma's activities accusing her of being a power seeking opportunist, even so the lady was an addict and had read fourteen of the books (30).

Of more interest for me, was how the readers related to the stories psychologically. Most agreed it was more than just a good read. When

I asked Peter what he was trying to achieve with his books he told me that he wanted people to be inspired by them and to read more about Irish history and see that Ireland wasn't the backward place presented by the English who had destroyed its culture (31).

With the rediscovery of Celtic tradition in recent years I think many people of Irish origin get quite emotional reading these books especially those living abroad who have a different notion of Ireland. Nostalgia plays a big part in their lives and (32) Tremayne is giving support to these people who are trying to rediscover their heritage and he strengthens his arguments by using facts (33). He's reconnecting them to the old country, but the old country is completely different because he's dealing with nostalgia which means looking back. The Irish in Ireland are asking different questions (34).

What makes' the books interesting for me are the historic facts which Peter as a Celtic scholar presents with authority.

PROCESS ANALYSIS

By the time I started to write I realised I"d spent too much time on research. I had so much material there was no way I could use it all. I'd enjoyed the research but I'd spent too much valuable time on it. At times I'd lost my focus becoming too interested in the subject matter – forgetting about what I was trying to achieve. With deadlines looming I found myself short of time – I just couldn't get started. Worried sick and late in the day I decided to visit the University Learning Centre again to look at more dissertations by previous students. Deborah Sutton who completed her dissertation in 2002/3 summed it all up in her conclusion with words I recognised only to well (1):

'Procrastination, torture, terror, fear.'

She'd even asked herself in those final days of writing if the task was too daunting for her – I gained comfort from the fact that she had finished and been awarded an (A) mark.

The research information I'd collected include downloads from various websites, and numerous interviews with the author and his readers. The most valuable interview was the one carried out with the author Peter Tremayne which ran to 10294 words. It covered eighteen key questions planned in advance plus points of interest which had come up in conversation during the interview. Although Peter had answered every question put to him it was only later when I played back the recording that I realised he'd sidestepped some of the important issues.

Perhaps he didn't have answers, or perhaps it was due to my inexperience as an interviewer, but he left me having to weigh up the evidence on crucial subjects. Later I realised Peter didn't have the answers to all of my questions but what he did have was a successful formula from which I as a writer could learn.

Most successful crime writers have a formula, perhaps the most successful being Agatha Christie with eighty novels and fifty-three plays to her name. A recent documentary on Channel 3 television hosted by Joanna Lumley (2) tried to prove with the use of special computer software that she used simple, but key words over and over again to hypnotise her readers – a great idea but it seemed unlikely.

Like Agatha Christie, Peter's stories have a crime, a detective and a solution and both have more characters than the reader can keep track of and all the characters have a motive for the murder. Both set a fast pace that means the reader doesn't want to put the book down. The pace, because it fast creates an adrenalin rush which can become addictive. Both use complicated plots that keep the reader guessing right until the very end creating an easy but compelling read.

Like Agatha Christie, Peter Tremayne creates a world in which everything is explained in great detail so the reader is picking-up on new information about the people and the history of 7th century Ireland and its position in the world at that time. The world Agatha Christie created for her reader's was the world of the landed gentry and the middle classes. The world Peter Tremayne has created is the world of a 7th century nun, a powerful, single woman playing a key roll in a world most readers had presumed to be a male dominated society. Because of their cultural background many of the readers relate to Sister Fidelma and the world in which she lived and have a desire to learn more about the period. It's an emotional a link to their cultural history which Peter uses.

I started this project on the basis of an emotion. An emotion experienced after reading the first book in a series of eighteen, by Peter Tremayne. The book linked into my Irish heritage in a way no other book ever had – through my surname, Breheny, *Mac an Breitheamhnaigh*, son of the judge, from the start I wanted to know more.

You might ask the question, what's in a name? My answer would be my heritage. Most of the landed gentry in this country claim direct descent from the leaders of the Norman invasion. I remember being amused at the polite one-up-man-ship of one Lord Robert Tamworth eldest son of Earl Ferris when he told me his family title was pre-Norman and one of few Saxon titles to survive the Norman Conquest.

As just another Irish bog trotter I could only be impressed at the length of such a family tree – even though I knew from my grandfather that our family had once held substantial lands in the North before Cromwell had driven them off to live in the bogs of the West. Well, my grandfather used to say "just remember we go back to a time when we were respected by our own people as judges of the Irish Laws – your forefathers were Brehons.' It was proud stuff and as a boy always stirred my emotions, with this information in mind, a year ago I typed the words "Brehon Laws' into a search engine and discovered The Sister Fidelma Mysteries by Peter Tremayne who was writing about things of direct interest to me. I would like to create a web site to further my research, where I can invite comment from people with similar feelings about their heritage this could be a valuable resource for writing.

After reading that first book, *Absolution by Murder* 1994, I had learnt more than ever about my own place in history and it left me with a feeling that Peter Tremayne was on a crusade to educate people who like myself, are the descendants of families that left Ireland long ago. Peter has a skill to transport the reader to another world teaching them things about the Irish they may not have previously known.

Armed with historic facts, Peter is able to give those made to feel inferior by centuries of oppression an interest and a pride in their ancient culture. As I read other books in the series I began to wonder if Peter had a special agenda. Reading the books made me realise I was more interested in the historic facts than the stories. This seemed to be the case with many readers.

If this was the case what was his agenda? Perhaps to influence how the Irish see themselves – by providing a more positive viewpoint, by highlighting feminist rights, or to influence change in the Christian church, even to educate people as a teacher?

I wanted to know if other people experienced the same emotions, I was not sure. I knew from listening to interviews with authors on Radio 4 that people often read meaning into a story never intended by the author. Like me they link historic events to themselves. As we'd learnt last year with Carl Tighe when we studied "Responsibility for Writers,' writers can't always be held responsible for how people interpreted their work. But writers frequently manipulate the reader's emotions which I believe there is evidence of in Peter Tremayne work.

Starting my research was no problem, the problem was staying focused and finishing. I found the subject matter and implications of Peter's stories so interesting I searched too widely. Peter writes about a period of history which is not controversial in the same way writing about the recent Irish troubles might be – so, few none Irish readers could take offence, this widens his readership. The period in history he writes about confronts only the church with hard historical evidence concerning current issues.

I spent hours in the University Learning Centre trying to understand from Irish literature how Irish people think, how confident they are as individuals coming from a culture overshadowed by British rule for hundreds of years. In the case of Catholics, I wanted to know how Catholicism effect's their thought process and whether the spirit of Brehon Law still influences the Irish sense of justice – three-hundred and fifty years after being replaced by English Law, a punishing law and not one of reconciliation like the Brehon Laws.

Moy McCrory suggested I take a look at a book called *The Field Day anthology of Irish Writing*. This went some way to explaining the situation but often through the condescending comments of an English writer. In his *A Description of the Manners and Customs of the Natural Irish*, one such writer Olive Goldsmith in 1759 said, the Irish are:

> ' ... *affable, foolish, hospitable and not to be depended upon ... fawning, insincere, fond of pleasure, prodigality makes them poor, poverty makes them vicious* (3).'

Comparing his own standards, he then spoke of entering an Irish country mansion and its appearance of despair, and the peasant's hovel (blackhouse) with its cow and turf fire with no chimney, saying:

> ' ... *the inhabitants were insensible of their uncomfortable way of living ... excessively cheerful ... a meal of potatoes, butter, and milk ... his host offered to tell him a story – he declined – why – Irish folk law ... he describes a wake where the people, howl, romp and tell stories ... drink muddy ale ...*(3)'

He then describes a Catholic religious meeting in derogatory tone, as a blood-thirsty affair in which priests are as drunk as the people. He attempts to sound polite but he is condescending – today if not then his writing would be viewed as racist. It would be interesting to read an account of Goldsmith's visit from an Irish perspective. We know what the English thought of the Irish and according to Peter Tremayne their opinions haven't changed much (4), but what do the Irish think? This is one of the questions I wanted to answer as an historical writer, could I use my writing to show a different view of Ireland to my readers. Could I use point of view to show a more positive Irish picture? In my letters and questionnaires to his readers I tried to establish if they felt the same way about his books as I did, but this was almost impossible and I was again left to weigh up the evidence and read between the lines.

Many readers did express similar emotions to my own, others said they simply enjoyed reading a different genre of crime novel. In my discussion with Fr John a Catholic priest with much experience of Irish society here and in Ireland, I tried to establish if my own emotions were an Irish trait. Many of the readers I'd been in contact with were of Irish decent living abroad, whose families had left Ireland under hard conditions we discussed if they had less confidence in themselves and their culture.

We decided there was a big difference between the Irish in Ireland, here and abroad (5). For those living in Ireland there's no problem, you're Irish and you're in Ireland, it's your country, your people, your freedom. Those not living in Ireland often find themselves on the defensive because their Catholic or seen as secret IRA supporters. It can be a bit wearing at times, so you keep a low profile, that's how you survive as an outsider.

All this combines into an emotion and an element of nostalgia develops, so your notion of Ireland becomes historical rather than real. I suppose one could claim that Peter Tremayne, through his books is helping them re-connect to the old country, but the old country is not the same. Its nostalgia, because they are looking back, it's also a defence in terms of the society in which they live. But the books are not connecting with the same questions that the Irish in Ireland are asking or talking about. The Irish living abroad are talking about different things and look at things in a different way and it's a high percentage of these people I believe Peter is writing for (6).

Peters use of the Brehon Laws as a backdrop throughout the Sister Fidelma Mysteries appeal to the sense of justice and fair play which has always been a source of pride to the Irish. The laws will be of particular interest to feminists, while women in the Western World have been emancipated for less than a century, women in ancient Ireland were equal to men with regard to education and property and in marriage were the partners and not the property of their husbands (7).

It took English Law and civilization "to put women in their place (8).' The reference books I borrowed from the British Library on the Brehon Laws were amazing to read and supported all Peter's claims. Further information downloaded from websites placed the laws in a modern context noting that they had been used secretly during the Agrarian disputes of the 18th and 19th centuries, by the Sinn Féin arbitration courts during the War of Independence in 1919 and by the IRA in the Peoples Courts of the early 70s (9).

I found it interesting to read in *The Guardian Newspaper* on 15 March (10) this year that the Irish Government under the Pr-Independence Project was reviewing every single law introduced before the country gained independence in 1922. I emailed the project asking if the Brehon Laws were to be placed back on the statute books and if those that banned them were to be removed, I received a pleasant but negative response.

On the 28 March I also attended a lecture given to the Irish Literary Society by Peter Beresford Ellis (the real name of Peter Tremayne) on the life of Dr Sophie Bryant held at the The Quality Hotel, Eccleston Square, London. The lecture was primarily about the Brehon Laws and Dr Bryant's book *Liberty, Order and Law under Native Irish Rule* 1923. I have not quoted from the lecture due to time restraints and the fact that much of the lecture had been covered by other research but attending did allow me to observe the author in his role as an academic and to listen to questions put to him by other academics.

The purpose of my dissertation has been to learn from a successful author, how I might succeed as a writer of Historic Fiction when I leave university. After a painful journey I now have a better understanding of how to undertake research and use it as a Creative Writer. I have a better understanding of reader profiling and I recognise that a winning formula can be simple and repeated many times.

I have gained a great deal of knowledge working on my dissertation much of it due to the author's patience and generosity of spirit. In respect of my working title – **The Sister Fidelma Mysteries – What's the Agenda?** Peter did not admit to having one – so once again I am left to read between the lines. For what its worth, my opinion is that Peter does have an agenda, to pass on his knowledge as a Celtic scholar and Irish Nationalist to those of us interested and in so doing he is able to enjoy what he does best – writing and researching a subject close to his heart.

Reference List
1. *Midland Exposure – The Final Story* by Deborah Sutton 2002/3. Page Conclusion. University of Derby Learning Centre.
2. Documentary – Agatha Christie, Channel 3 Television, hosted by Joanna Lumley 27.12.05.
3. *The Field Day Anthology of Irish Writing* Vol 1, 820-808-916-2-FIE. Pub: Field Day Publications, Northern Ireland. ISBN 0-946755.20.5 Vol 1/2/3. Page 664.
4. Appendix 7. Peter Tremayne Interview 15.03.06. Page 212.
5. Appendix 8. Fr John Guest Interview. Page 229.
6. Appendix 8. Page 230.
7. *Ancient Laws of Ireland, Senchus Mor VII*. Ex-Libris – University of Bristolliensis. Stack DA 25 A2. Pub: Alexander Thom 87 & 88 Abbey Street. Hodges, Foster & Co. 104 Grafton Street. 1869. Laws of Distress, Preface. Page 1vi and 1vii.
8. Appendix 3. The Celtic League. Page 70.
9. Appendix 3 (see ref: 7).
10. Appendix 3. Page 77.

– Peter Breheny
Research Paper For Ba Hons In Creative Writing, April 2006

Successful Time Travel – Peter Berresford Ellis and Writing Historical Detective Stories

Amedieval mystery series in which the sleuth has taken religious vows and mysterious deaths often occur in monasteries...You could be forgiven for thinking that the Sister Fidelma mysteries are yet another imitation of Cadfael.

Sister Fidelma, however, is miles – and centuries – away from Ellis Peters' detective monk. The series is set in 7th century Ireland and Fidelma, though she has taken religious vows, places far more importance on her position as a *dálaigh*, or advocate of the courts, than her commitment to God. She works within Ireland's ancient Brehon laws, a sophisticated legal system which allowed women more rights than under any other Western law code until recent times, including the right to equal men in any profession.

The series' author, Peter Berresford Ellis, (writing as Peter Tremayne), is enthusiastic about this period of Irish history. "The 7th century AD was the start of the "Golden Age' of Irish culture and learning. Students from many parts of Europe attended the great colleges in Ireland for their education. Irish missionaries and teachers travelled through Europe founding colleges, abbeys and churches, spreading learning and literacy in a Europe experiencing what is called the "Dark Ages'. It was anything but a "Dark Age' for Ireland – it was a fascinating and exciting period."

The series of Fidelma novels grew from his desire to introduce this world to a wider audience.

While I was lecturing in the 1980s, I decided to write some short stories to demonstrate how the law and social system of ancient Ireland worked. Demonstrating law naturally led to the mystery story form and what better than a female dálaigh or junior judge as the detective? Such ladies existed, like Darí of Muman (modern Munster). When the short stories were published a publisher asked me if I could use the character in a novel.

THE SISTER FIDELMA COMPENDIUM

There is little difference between writing historical novels and historical detective stories. There should be a plot in both forms, a story that invites the reader in and draws them along, eager to get to a resolution of the mystery or the problem cited. Historical background does not make the story; it is the characters and their backgrounds, their fears, hopes and conflicts that really make the novel in either form.

It is always important for the historical novelist to draw the reader in to the historical time and place, but Peter does not think there is any "easy recipe" for doing this.

You must know your period like the back of your hand. You must know what it is like to really live in that period – even how you would go to the toilet. You must know the plants, the flowers, the animals, the food, the smells – it must be a second home to you. When I am writing I am totally constrained by the laws and social system of the period. I have started off writing a story, checked the law texts and found it would not have arisen in the way I had originally envisioned, or the language would not possess such a cultural concept, so I have had to throw away a good idea. That can be frustrating.

One of the devices Peter uses to help make Fireman's world more accessible for the modern reader is the character of Brother Eadulf, Fidelma's "Watson." Eadulf, a Saxon from England, finds many aspects of Fidelma's world as unusual as the 21st century reader might today. "He appears in the stories as a means through which Fidelma can point out different cultural concepts without lecturing the reader."

Eadulf is more than a "Watson" to Fidelma, however, and as the series progresses the couple fall in love – something not out of the ordinary at the time as clerical marriages had not yet been banned. However, the couple's romantic relationship, along with Fidelma's position as an independent professional woman, have led to a belief among some critics that Peter was inventing the background to the stories – a claim he strenuously denies.

The background is as accurate I can make it. Often even the overlaying murder mystery story is factual as well. The High

SUCCESSFUL TIME TRAVEL

King's murder in Dancing with Demons *(2007) is recorded in the annals. I just supplied the story of how it was resolved.*

My degrees were taken in Celtic Studies, and I have published many books and academic papers in this area. I would not classify myself as a 'real' academic but the leading experts on this period have come out in praise of the Sister Fidelma books. The only people I have found who attempt to throw doubt on the background of the books are those who have never studied the period.

Contrary to the claims of such critics, Peter is quick to stress the importance of historical accuracy when writing an historical novel.

The author should stick to the known facts unless he/she is writing an 'alternative' history, like the recent novel about Hitler in which the writer wrote an account of what might have happened if he had been accepted at the Venice Art Academy. If the story doesn't fit the facts, you should change the story, not vice versa. The historical writer must be disciplined otherwise the sky is the limit – you'd find a Tudor novel in which the Spanish Armada was successful because the writer felt it would make a better story.

Peter does not believe that an historical novel can, or should, speak only about the past, although he is quick to stress that a novelist should never "preach" to the reader.

The ideal historical novel should be able to inform as well as entertain but without ever lecturing to the reader. The reader should be swept along by the tale and then, as they lay aside the book, realise they have learnt something about the period. Without preaching, the author should allow the reader to use the knowledge gained to understand the reality of the present. I was always taught that without a knowledge of the past you cannot understand the present. Without an understanding of the present, you cannot help shape the future.

In the novels Fidelma defends her country's humane punishments (which centred on loss of rights and the payment of fines rather than death or mutilation) against what she sees as the destructive new philosophy of "an eye for an eye" – something which cannot fail to resonate with any reader familiar with subsequent Irish history, particularly events in Northern Ireland.

"A historical novel can never be objective," Peter believes.

History writing is not simply about the enumeration of facts. It is about the moral interpretation of those facts as the historian sees them. The very form in which the historian relates the facts conveys judgement. For example, 'The bottle is half-empty' is a statement of fact. Yet let me put the fact another way. 'The bottle is half full.' It provides us with an entirely different concept of the very same fact. When I see a book claiming to be an 'unbiased study I know it is going to be replete with bias.

Surely, then, the Fidelma books with their emphasis on the rights of women and social justice could not have been written 200 years ago, when such subjects were seen very differently? Perhaps not in England, but Peter suggests that such a series could have been written in Ireland.

Parliament na mBan (The Parliament of Women) was written in the mid seventeenth century. The author argues that men are destroying the world – this is written against the background of the Cromwellian conquest and genocide in Ireland. Women decide to hold their own parliament and enact laws that will change the world and restore it to a natural order. But if the Fidelma series was written against the seventeenth century attempts to eradicate the language, culture and laws of Ireland (it was often a capital offence for an Irish person to possess an Irish law book), Fidelma might have had other problems to occupy her.

Of course, the main purpose of the books is to entertain and, hopefully, the secondary purpose is to show what Ireland was like at this period of the 'Golden Age' of Irish learning. But the first thing is that readers enjoy the books as murder mysteries.

As the novels continued to be published, it seems that Peter achieved at least one of his aims.

– Catherine Green
Writers' Forum, September 2008

FIDELMA: A MODEL LAWYER

Fidelma: A Model Lawyer

idelma, as all readers of Peter Tremayne's many novels and short stories about her know, is a *dálaigh*, a legal term no longer used, and which refers to the profession of advocate before the law courts of Ireland. She is indeed an advocate, but that term does not do justice to her actual legal talents, roles, and accomplishments. My focus in this paper is on Fidelma's multi-faceted performance as a *dálaigh*. At times I will substitute for *dálaigh* a more modern term, "lawyer," knowing that their meanings are not identical, but because I wish to consider the timelessness of Fidelma and how she serves as a model not only for seventh-century advocates but for twenty-first century lawyers, especially American lawyers (since I know them best), but really for lawyers anywhere regardless of the term used or the precise legal system in place.

In truth, no single legal term adequately describes Fidelma. Her achievements grow out of many talents as they grow out of her commitment to law and, even more so, to truth and justice, for the law should be the servant of truth and justice. Nor does she play only one role but rather several interconnected roles. She is a generalist with neither the limited perspective of the specialist nor the superficiality that can sometimes characterize the generalist.

Fidelma, as an advocate, pleads before judges, known in seventh-century Ireland as Brehons. In doing so, she serves the purpose of a modern prosecuting attorney. She offers introductory comments, questions witnesses, and summarizes for the jury, which consists of a Brehon or Brehons, and sometimes others such as a king. Her primary formal objective is to ascertain guilt and bring the guilty party or parties to justice. At times, however, the procedure is more like a grand jury hearing than a trial, with a finding similar to the handing down of an indictment. In *Dancing with Demons*, for example, Fidelma presents her findings before Brehon Sedna. Although summoned to assist with one crime, the murder of the High King, Sechnussach, Fidelma, as often happens, finds that multiple crimes are intertwined. The murder occurs in the middle of a conspiracy to overthrow the existing political and religious order and substitute a perversion of the old religion.

Chief Brehon Barrán is found to be part of the conspiracy, in his case, to satisfy his personal political ambitions. The actual murder, however, was much simpler, involving the servant Cnucha, who resented her humiliating treatment by her lover, the High King. Unaware that the king was already dead, one of the conspirators, Dubh Duin, who had worked his way into the arms of the king's wife in order to gain easy access to the royal quarters, had slit the throat of a man already murdered by the servant.

After listening to Fidelma lay out the conspiracy but before she identifies the actual killer of the High King, Brehon Sedna takes immediate judicial action in suspending Barrán from his nomination as *tánaiste*, or heir apparent, to the new High King, Cenn Faelad, and declaring that Barrán, the murdered High King's daughter Muirgel, and the other surviving conspirators "will be held for the conspiracy in the assassination of Sechnussach" (259). The fate of the murderer also will be decided later. When Eadulf later wonders about Cnucha's future, Fidelma explains that she will be charged with secret killing and undoubtedly have to pay the High King's honor price. Recognizing that the price may well be beyond either Cnucha's or her family's ability to pay, Fidelma notes that she probably will be forced to continue in service as a maid until she pays off her obligation, a punishment not much different from what she has been doing. It is easy to see in this conversation, Fidelma's sympathy for the humiliated mistress, the result of both Fidelma's oft-stated commitment to the rights of women and her view that the king's ill treatment of the servant somewhat diminished the murderer's level of guilt.

Fidelma's sympathy even for a murderer points out another important dimension to her role as a *dálaigh*. The guilty must be brought to justice, but the innocent must be identified as well and freed from unjust punishment. Therefore, Fidelma also serves essentially as a defense attorney as well as the prosecutor. In *Dancing with Demons*, an obvious suspect based on motive is the High King's wife, who has been spurned by her husband and has fallen in love with one of the conspirators. Yet despite some poor judgment on Gormflaith's part, Fidelma recognizes that she is innocent of both the murder and the larger conspiracy.

A Prayer for the Damned, though, presents a different, more focused role, for Fidelma. Here the primary suspect in the murder of a prominent church leader is a king, Muirchertach, king of Connacht, who is accused of murdering Abbot Ultán, the Abbot of Cill Ria. Ultán is a

FIDELMA: A MODEL LAWYER

special emissary from Ségéne, who is seeking recognition as the senior church leader in all of the kingdoms and who, even more importantly, is attempting to impose Roman rule over the church. The accused king asks Fidelma to defend him, setting up the very modern looking legal contest between two individuals specifically designated to defend and prosecute. However, when the suspect is himself murdered and the prosecutor, Brehon Ninnid, after biased and unprofessional conduct, is removed from the case by Barrán, the Chief Brehon of Tara (prior to Barrán's fall, which occurs in the subsequent book), Fidelma reverts to her usual solitary responsibility to unravel the mysteries, discover the guilty, and safeguard the innocent, especially the innocent who appear guilty. So Fidelma, while discovering the murderer of both men, Abbot Augaire of Conga, exonerates the young Sister Marga, who had become a major suspect.

Theoretically, and often in reality, but obviously not always, justice will prevail through the adversarial process involving defense attorney and prosecutor—or in civil cases between lawyers representing their respective clients. Fidelma, however, in combining these roles, must set aside personal preferences in order to seek not only justice but also truth. That she is able to do this is because of her strong commitment to truth, justice, and the law. That commitment is evident repeatedly within the mysteries that she must help unravel.

In *Suffer Little Children*, Fidelma's brother, Colgú, king of Muman, faces possible liability in the death of a respected scholar in an abbey led by a cousin of the king. Colgú asks his sister to be his advocate before the High King's assembly, which will rule on the issue of liability and determine whether Muman will lose a portion of its kingdom. Fidelma's response makes it clear that even truth must override her loyalty to her king and brother: "Tell me this, my brother; suppose my findings are such as support the king of Laigin? . . . Will you accept that judgment under law and meet Laigin's demand?" (24).

Móen, who can neither speak nor hear, is the suspect in a murder committed in *The Spider's Web*. The popular assumption is that he is guilty of killing Aber, his chieftain. However, guilty or not, Fidelma believes that he deserves a fair trial, all the more so because he cannot readily defend himself. Eadulf, Fidelma's longtime partner in solving mysteries and later her husband, wonders, in fact, how he can possibly mount any sort of defense. "If there is a defence, I shall find it," Fidelma states. "But he will not be condemned without a fair trial. On my oath as an advocate of the laws of the five kingdoms, I shall ensure it" (78). Fidelma's commitment to the law and to justice virtually leaps off the page. Much later, after justice has been done, the guilty discovered, and Móen exonerated, the hermit Gadra suggests that the outcome was due to Fidelma's efforts. "It was not the law but the lawyer which provided the key,' interpreted Gadra." Fidelma disagrees and quotes Heraclitus to the effect "that a people should fight for their law as if it were their city wall against an invading army." She adds, sadly, to Eadulf, "I wish I could have convinced him that our law is a sacred thing, the result of centuries of human wisdom and experience to protect us as well as to punish. If I did not believe it I would not be an advocate" (325).

Fidelma recognizes, however, that the law can be distorted by corrupt or incompetent judges or by others involved in safeguarding it; further, the law is not an end but a means. It serves justice as it serves truth. She argues in *A Prayer for the Damned*, "Are we not taught that truth is the highest power, the ultimate cause of all being? So, therefore, we must discover the truth in order that justice might prevail" (188). Fidelma also knows that occasionally even the law must yield for the sake of a higher good. As a young advocate in the short story "Hemlock at Vespers," she struggles to decide whether she "should serve the law or serve justice." In the end, she opts for what she calls "natural justice," choosing to hide the fact of a murder in order to help prevent war and to safeguard her religious community at Kildare (151-55).

This passion for the law, Fidelma recognizes, is more important to her than her status as a religieuse. Near the conclusion of *The Monk Who Vanished*, Fidelma tells Eadulf that she plans to go on a pilgrimage to the tomb of St. James of the Field of the Stars in Iberia (267). She goes for two reasons: to resolve the conflict between her religious vocation and her legal profession, and to sort out her feelings about Eadulf. Unfortunately, on the journey murder and the reappearance of her early lover, Cian, seriously interfere with her plans. Still, she must become involved with the mysteries, not least because mysteries, as we are told in *The Haunted Abbot*, are "like some terrible narcotic to her. She could not let go while there were still questions which needed answers" (187-88). Having once again been called upon to put her legal skills to work, she realizes, reflecting on her future while relaxing in the Iberian port before resuming her pilgrimage, that she had answered one of her two questions. "There was no longer any conflict between her place as a religieuse and her role as a *dálaigh*. Her passion for law left her with no other choice: she would always put law before any contemplative life" (267). As Fidelma states in *The Chalice of Blood*, "My whole being is involved with law and the administration of justice. Not pursuing this will mean the death of my soul. No sacrifice that involves me giving this up is possible" (175).

Professionally, the next logical step up for a lawyer is to become a judge. For Fidelma, that would mean becoming a Brehon. In fact, however, Fidelma does function on occasion as a judge. She hears a land case in *The Spider's Web* because, being "proficient to the degree of *anruth* . . . meant that she could not only plead cases before judges but, when nominated, she could sit to hear and adjudicate in her own court on a range of applications that did not require the presence of a judge of higher rank" (9). In *Smoke in the Wind*, Fidelma and Eadulf find themselves in the kingdom of Dyfed in what today is known as Wales. There she is recruited to solve the mystery of the disappearance of an entire monastic community that has seemingly vanished. Her position as a *dálaigh* is likened to the local position of *barnwr*, or judge (34, 89), and both she and Eadulf are declared "honorary *barnwrs*" (242). Fidelma, in *Badger's Moon*, in consultation with the local chieftain and abbot, formally passes judgment and punishment on a wife who had killed her abusive husband and on the man who had lied in order to protect her (178-79). She refers to herself as a "minor judge" in *The Council of the Cursed* (175). Barrán, Chief Brehon of the Five Kingdoms, tells King Colgú in *A Prayer for the Damned* that his sister should "separate entirely from the religious and become a Brehon instead of just a *dálaigh*. She has the ability to make such sound judgments that she is often wasted in pleading cases before others. . . "(252). Earlier, Colgú, faced with choosing a new Chief Brehon for Muman, had stated in *The Leper's Bell* that "Fidelma is not qualified for the position," explaining that she would need two to four more years of study to rise from the level of *anruth* to that of *ollamh* (249). Later, Fidelma's ambition in that direction does grow and she aspires to become a Brehon. In fact, in *The Chalice of Blood*, she states her desire to leave behind her life as a religieuse and become a candidate for the position of her brother's Chief Brehon despite not holding the degree of *ollamh* (22-27). That desire goes unfulfilled, however, as readers find early in *The Seventh Trumpet* that the Council of Brehons in Muman has chosen someone else to be Chief Brehon (10-11). The loss is disappointing and unsettling, but Fidelma soon throws herself back into her work as a *dálaigh* and legal adviser to her brother. In *The Devil's Seal*, Fidelma has come to recognize that remaining an advocate is her natural role, for it keeps her connected to the people (123).

So what are some of the particular attributes, in addition to her passion for the law and commitment to truth and justice, that help make Fidelma such an extraordinary lawyer (whether prosecuting, defending, or judging), and that induce Barrán, holding the most prestigious legal position in the five kingdoms, to evaluate her so highly?

No lawyer can be outstanding without possessing great knowledge of the law, and great knowledge does not come without considerable study. Fidelma repeatedly demonstrates her familiarity with important legal texts, and her ability to use those texts, showing that the high regard in which her former mentor, Brehon Morann, held her had been realized. Fidelma's meeting her former lover Cian again, in *Act of Mercy*, leads her to recall that unhappy relationship and how severely it had undermined her performance as a student. Fidelma remembers her mentor trying to steer her back onto the right path:

"Let me tell you this, Fidelma of Cashel. Once in a while it transpires that an old teacher, such as myself, encounters a student whose ability, whose mental agility, is so outstanding that it seems that their life, as a teacher, is suddenly justified. The daily chore of trying to impress knowledge into a thousand reluctant minds is more than compensated for by finding one single mind so eager and able to absorb and understand knowledge—and by using that knowledge to make a contribution to the betterment of mankind. All the years of frustration are suddenly rewarded. I do not say this lightly, when I say that I thought that the choice I had made to become a teacher was going to be justified in you." (36)

Indeed, the legal areas in which Fidelma is learned are many. One of her great personal and professional concerns is with the legal protection of women, including their rights within marriage. She knows, for example, precisely the fine provided by the law of the *Fenechus* for a man who kisses or touches a woman against her will (*Shroud for the Archbishop* 135). She refers to the provision in *Bretha Nemed* outlawing harassment or a verbal assault on a woman (*Suffer the Little Children* 233). She recalls that the *Book of Acaill* exempts a woman from liability on some cases if she shows her comb bag and distaff (*The Subtle Serpent* 55), and reflects on the *Uraicecht Bec*, supposedly written by a woman, which discusses women's rights (*Master of Souls* 126). She explains the two types of rape forbidden in law: forcible rape (*forcor*) and other

FIDELMA: A MODEL LAWYER

methods of taking sexual advantage of a woman (*sleth*), such as having sex with a woman too drunk to consent (*The Leper's Bell* 116-17).

Then there is Fidelma's knowledge of marriage law, including the law text *Cáin Lánamna*, which she refers to in answering a question about marriage between social classes (*Valley of the Shadow* 139-41). From the same text, she describes laws on divorce (*Act of Mercy* 79). She discusses dowries (*Smoke in the Wind* 49); is conversant with the specifics of the nine types of union, including *ben charrthach*, the type of relationship that Fidelma first enters into with Eadulf (*The Haunted Abbot* 8-9); explains that an illicit union is one not sanctioned by law (*Master of Souls* 110); delineates the three types of marriages according to the respective social positions of the two spouses (*Dancing with Demons* 119); clarifies the laws of *imscarad*, or divorce (*Dancing with Demons* 121-22); and shares information on a widow's legal standing to inherit her husband's property (*Master of Souls* 244-45).

Fidelma is sympathetic toward women driven by circumstance into prostitution and supportive of them in their attempt to leave that way of life. She befriends Della, for example, and considers her a friend despite the continuing bias toward her by some Cashel residents. In fact, when Fidelma's child, Alchú, is missing and she is questioning her relationship to Eadulf, it is to Della that she pours out her fears and worries, with the former prostitute becoming almost Fidelma's *anam chara*, or soul friend (*The Leper's Bell* 122-23). Nonetheless, Fidelma, as stated earlier, can enforce the law regardless of personal preference. So in *Valley of the Shadow*, she offers the legal opinion, based on the *Berrad Airechta*, that a prostitute may not give evidence against someone (283). In *The Monk Who Vanished*, Fidelma notes that a prostitute also is protected under the law against rape, explaining to Eadulf that she first came to know Della when she represented her when Della was a rape victim. Fidelma further states the legal position "that a prostitute can renounce her previous way of life and, if so, can be reinstated in society" (216-17).

Fidelma's knowledge of law, however, goes well beyond these matters. She has intimate knowledge of the law pertaining to individuals' honor prices, Eric fines, and how the two standards interact. Her references to these matters are numerous throughout the stories; they are so numerous, in fact, that Eadulf also comes to understand the concept of honor price so well that when Fidelma cautions Lesren against making charges that cannot be proved in *Badger's Moon*, Eadulf reflects on the extensive range of honor prices, "from the lowborn to the highest," with the High King at the top. Eadulf himself, as a foreigner, would usually have no honor price, but his marriage to Fidelma, once accepted by her family, settled on him an honor price equal to half of Fidelma's (51-52). The system of honor prices would not have seemed strange to Eadulf, for, as he tells Fidelma in *Shroud for the Archbishop*, his people in his native land had a similar system known as *wergild* (152). The *Eric* fine is based on the honor price of the individual who is harmed or killed, and until satisfactory compensation is rendered, the perpetrator loses a portion or his entire honor price. However, fines may be smaller or greater depending on the nature of the transgression, the degree of harm rendered, and any mitigating circumstances. Homicide committed with the intent to conceal the act resulted, for example, in an additional fine (Bryant 222-23). Regarding the aforementioned case of a woman killing her abusive husband in *Badger's Moon*, which involves the usually heinous act of *fingal*, or kin-slaying, Fidelma imposes no punishment on the woman except for a light fine for delaying to admit what she had done. In coming to this decision, Fidelma explains that she has applied what *Cairde* law says about self-defense (178-79).

At various times in Fidelma's adventures, she expresses legal opinions in many other areas. She realizes that Adnár in *The Subtle Serpent* could be accountable for slander as he accuses Abbess Draigen of murder (79-80); in the same book explains the laws of salvage to Adnár (85); still in the same novel points out to members of the Abbey of the Salmon of the Three Wells that if they kill Berrach, who is a member of their community, they will be guilty of kin-slaying (165-66); questions Ibor in *Valley of the Shadow* as to the legality of selling a horse in light of the law on selling foreign goods stated in *Allmuir Sét* (150-54); and clarifies for Eadulf in *The Spider's Web* that people with physical disabilities, such as Móen, enjoy most of the rights of other members of their community with the exception of not being able to serve as king or chieftain, and that anyone who denigrates someone who is disabled is subject to a fine (92-93);

Fidelma and Eadulf do much traveling, as Fidelma's skills are required not only in Ireland but in England and on the continent as well. Of course, Brehon law does not apply in foreign countries, but in Ireland an area of Brehon law that the much-traveled pair must consider, often from a very practical standpoint, involves taverns and hostels and those who run these establishments. In *The Spider's Web*, Fidelma and Eadulf see a lantern flickering on the top of a post in the distance. Fidelma recognizes the light's meaning, as she knows that "all taverns or public hostels . . . had to announce themselves by displaying a lighted lantern all through the night" (32). Most likely, anyone doing much traveling then would, of course, have known the meaning of the light but might not have known that the law required such a symbol. In *The Monk Who Vanished*, Fidelma explains to Eadulf that some taverns are not licensed. Such places are legal but offer less recourse to legal action for customers if a service, such as the quality of the ale, is substandard. Licensing serves, thus, as a sort of official seal of approval complete with guarantee of quality (97). While traveling through somewhat unfriendly territory in *Our Lady of Darkness*, Fidelma reminds an innkeeper that if he does not provide good service with "good grace," he will have violated the law and be subject to a heavy fine equal to the honor price of the travelers. Further, he could have his inn taken from him and destroyed without compensation. "Do I make the law clear to you, innkeeper?" Fidelma asks (7). Knowing and clearly stating the law, Fidelma fully realizes, can be the difference between a comfortable night in the inn and, at best, rude treatment.

An innkeeper in *Dancing with Demons* worriedly asks Fidelma to examine the body of a man who has died in his inn, for he knows that such a death can put him in jeopardy if he is found to have been neglectful of his duties. Fidelma immediately understands his concern, as the *Bretha Nemed Toisech* offers precise obligations under the law for innkeepers. The innkeeper breathes "a deep sigh of relief" when Fidelma says that he was in no way responsible for the man's death (10-11). As Fidelma, Eadulf, and two members of her brother's bodyguards journey to Tara after the assassination of the High King in *Dancing with Demons*, they stop at a public hostel, a type of establishment, Fidelma knows, differing from private inns in that they are provided by the local chieftain to make available to travelers up to three days of free lodging and food (32-35).

The diversity of mysteries that confront Fidelma requires a wide range of legal knowledge. She is called upon to use her knowledge concerning such disparate issues as boundary fence law (*The Spider's Web* 150-52); legal distinctions among three types of land ("arable land," land of "three roots" [soil able to grow thistle, ragwort, and carrot, and therefore, by extension, many crops], and "axe-land" [covered mainly by trees] (*The Spider's Web* 229-30); legal responsibilities of a miller for injury to people in his mill (*Badger's Moon* 62); methods "of balancing a King's honour with his legal accountability" (*The Monk Who Vanished* 247-48); terms, as stated in the law text *Bretha Crólge*, for arbitrating disputes (*The Monk Who Vanished* 43); sea laws (*Act of Mercy* 66-67, 83-85, 203, 207-08); laws pertaining to mining (*The Monk Who Vanished* 211); one's ability to gain sanctuary (*Act of Mercy* 214; *Our Lady of Darkness* 219-20); appropriate dress according to one's rank in society (*Act of Mercy* 229) and situation, such as functioning as an advocate before the Great Assembly (*Dancing with Demons* 242-43); laws relating to the insane (*The Haunted Abbot* 273, *The Chalice of Blood* 426); fosterage (*The Leper's Bell* 271); care of the elderly (*A Prayer For the Damned* 168); legal limitations of satire (*The Dove of Death* 34-35); the crime of stealing books (*The Chalice of Blood* 263); the law pertaining to builders and craftsmen (*The Chalice of Blood* 100); and on and on. Clearly, her knowledge of the law is deep and extensive; as stated earlier, she combines the qualities of a broadly prepared generalist and a specialist with in-depth knowledge.

However, even Fidelma does not know everything. As accomplished as Fidelma is, she always appears realistic, and part of that realism is that she, like all people, has flaws: personal flaws such as a hot temper that she exercises too often against Eadulf, a failing that she several times acknowledges; and, of course, some imperfection even in her knowledge of the law. As she gazes at the Laigin warship near the Abbey of Ros Ailithier in *Suffer Little Children*, she wishes that she had focused more firmly on the section of the *muir-bretha*, or sea laws, dealing with intimidation. Her immediate impulse, as it should be for any lawyer faced with an issue that he or she is unsure of, is to go to the law books. Consequently, she wonders if the abbey library has copies of relevant texts (106). In *Act of Mercy*, she admits to knowing little about the law of warfare, specifically the fine points of when it is acceptable to kill someone. "A more competent judge is needed to see what must be done," she says. "I know there are circumstances in which the killing of people is justified and entails no penalties" (202). Asked about the rights that a widow religieuse formerly married to another member of the same community has to retain his possessions, Fidelma must consider a legal issue that she "had not considered before and had little knowledge of" (*Master of Souls* 99). Her response is to study the subject in the abbey's library.

These admissions are less indicative of flaws than examples of the inevitable imperfection that characterizes the human condition, and

FIDELMA: A MODEL LAWYER

Fidelma consistently comes across quite definitely as a human being. In fact, no one can be more critical of Fidelma's occasional shortcomings than Fidelma herself. In *Behold a Pale Horse*, she comes late to the realization that a Brother Eolann was part of a plot to help a usurper gain power: "Instead of keeping my own counsel, I thought I could trust the scriptor Brother Eolann because he was from my own kingdom and spoke my language. A silly, arrogant mistake" (349). Later she adds, "I did nothing but allowed myself to be misled by Eolann through my sheer arrogance. ...I regard this as a failure of all my training and faculties. I am ashamed" (367).

So Fidelma possesses passion for the law and admirable knowledge of the law. She also, as stated, willingly engages in continuing research to deepen her knowledge even more. She is, as one might say today, a lifelong learner. But there are yet more skills that she exhibits. She is possessed of a powerfully retentive memory allied with the capacity to judge what is important to remember and what may be discarded. As Eadulf realizes in *Badger's Moon*, "It was her ability to remember all the salient facts that constituted Fidelma's exceptional ability as an investigator and solver of conundrums" (153). Being a good investigator entails more than memory, however; Fidelma points out to Eadulf in *Dancing with Demons*, "One of the secrets of being a good investigator is never to reveal what you know or suspect, and to avoid showing your reactions to what others might tell you. Nor is it wise to suggest ideas to witnesses" (153).

Witnesses play crucial roles in legal cases today, as every lawyer knows. That also was true for Fidelma in seventh-century Ireland. So handling witnesses carefully and effectively is absolutely necessary. She regularly interviews witnesses and does so effectively across the social lines, from commoners to kings. Although she wants witnesses to be forthcoming, she also rejects testimony that is not based on fact. For example, she rebukes Sister Étromma in *Our Lady of Darkness* for identifying a body "before a court if you did not personally know her." Only minutes earlier, Fidelma had reminded the witness that she expected "exactness" in her testimony (75). In *Badger's Moon*, Fidelma reminds Brocc, "You can only give evidence about what you have seen or heard and you must be prepared to swear an oath in support of that evidence" (78). In the same book, she notes that giving "false witness is one of the three great crimes that God avenges most severely" (170). Fidelma also uses her authority to prohibit witnesses from speaking about what they have experienced until such time as Fidelma questions them, a prohibition that she explains in *Master of Souls* (236).

In carrying out the roles that contribute to her overall functioning as a *dálaigh*, including her investigating, partly, of course, through questioning not only witnesses but anyone who may have something to offer toward a solution, Fidelma must know what questions to ask. As she recalls in *The Subtle Serpent*, "[I]t was no use worrying about answers to problems unless she knew the questions that should be asked" (31). Questions, as Fidelma clearly understands, will yield little to the faint-hearted. Assertiveness is required, especially when facing hostility. She often surprises individuals with a forceful assertion of her rights as a *dálaigh* and their responsibility to answer her questions.

Yet Fidelma also knows when to remain silent, even passing up an opportunity to correct someone concerning a principle of law. The young son of Fidelma and Eadulf is kidnapped in *The Leper's Bell*. When an opportunity supposedly arises to gain his safe return by releasing three prisoners, Eadulf cautions against the release without some proof that the author of the ransom note actually has Alchú. Accused of not caring enough about the child, Eadulf angrily retorts, "Do you think that I am not aware that I speak of my own son? I hope everyone present concedes the fact that I am as much concerned in his welfare as anyone else" (102). Fidelma knows that legally Eadulf is wrong, for when the father is a foreigner the mother has sole responsibility for rearing the child. Fidelma starts to correct him but wisely catches herself in time and remains silent. A correction at that point would have been legally correct but extraordinarily cruel to Eadulf.

As Fidelma brings her investigations to a close, she relies on the facts, wherever they may lead, much as a good forensic expert would do today. Faced with no obvious solutions but instead with a variety of seemingly unlikely scenarios, she applies a principle that she learned from her early mentor, Brehon Morann: "If you eliminate the impossible, whatever remains, however improbable, it must be the answer" (*The Monk Who Vanished* 241-42). The principle is so useful that another fictional investigator, many centuries later, Sherlock Holmes, would offer a similar approach. As he states in conversation with Dr. Watson in *The Sign of the Four*, "How often have I said to you that when you have eliminated the impossible, whatever remains, *however improbable*, must be the truth?" (1: 638).

So how is Fidelma a model lawyer? The answer comes in questions:

FIDELMA: A MODEL LAWYER

Do we want an attorney representing us to be highly knowledgeable and passionate about the law, caring deeply for justice? Do we want our lawyer to be skilled in research and willing to admit what she does not know and pursue that knowledge in order to represent us well? Should our legal advocate know how to investigate, and to be assertive, yet, when appropriate, know when to be discreet? We would accept professional ambition, yet we would hope that if our attorney gets passed over for a judgeship, she would still represent us with all of the passion and skill that she exhibited before. However, we might suggest to our attorney that she put her life in jeopardy a little less often than Fidelma does.

There is much more that could be said about Fidelma within this context, but one more topic will have to suffice—a topic that is relevant to the life of a modern lawyer, a seventh-century *dálaigh*, and a great many other people: how to balance personal and professional lives. Fidelma has a traumatic experience with a lover when she is young, an experience that perhaps contributes to her sharp focus on the law rather than on another personal relationship. Finally, however, she meets Eadulf (in *Absolution by Murder*), and, as readers know, eventually marries him, initially through a one-year-long trial marriage, and they have a son, Alchú. The birth of a child, as it does for many couples, introduces a new element into their life together, and it impacts her professional life. So Fidelma is faced with balancing what many people must do: her role as a parent, her role as a spouse, and her professional role. That is no easier for her than for any number of other people, and the struggle to achieve a balance at times places Fidelma in a somewhat unfavorable light but at the same time makes her even more human, even more useful as a model. People learn not only from watching how others succeed but also how others struggle and sometimes fail.

These struggles occur vividly in *Badger's Moon*, with part of Fidelma's difficulty being that motherhood has not lived up to her expectations:

"During the last few days she had not thought once of little Alchú. Did that mean that she was a bad mother? She halted her horse and sat frowning as she considered the matter. She remembered something that her mentor, the Brehon Morann, had once said when judging the case of a neglectful father. "For a woman, giving birth to a child is the path to omniscience." Ever since the birth of Alchú she had been having disturbing thoughts, thoughts which troubled her because she found she did not agree with her teacher. Fidelma had not felt her wisdom increase nor felt any of the joys that she had been told by her female relatives and friends should have been forthcoming. She felt vexed. It was as if she saw Alchú almost as a bond that ensnared her—a curtailment of her freedom rather than something which enriched her. . . . Why didn't she feel those emotions for little Alchú that she had been told to expect? It was not that she did not care about the child, nor feel anything at all, but she had been told that the birth of her child would be an earth-shattering event, one which would change her. It had not. Maybe it was this lack of the fulfillment of the expectation that was the problem and not the relationship with her baby.' (109-10)

In contrast to Fidelma, Eadulf embraces parenthood and longs to be at home with his one-month-old son. When Eadulf makes clear his wish to be back at Cashel with Alchú, Fidelma reacts angrily, to a great extent, as she acknowledges to herself, because of her own feelings of guilt:

"Because my son's name is not always on my lips, it does not mean to say that he is not in my thoughts," she snapped. Her sudden anger was born of guilt that until that very morning Alchú had actually been entirely out of her thoughts.

"We have not discussed our son since we left Cashel." Eadulf spoke softly but with emphasis on the change of personal pronoun. Fidelma flushed guiltily. She knew that Eadulf was justified but, in her guilt, she became more defensive. (*Badger's Moon* 142)

Fidelma admits to Eadulf that since their son's birth she has felt "strangely disturbed. It is as if my mood changes from moment to moment for no apparent reason." She adds, "When I consider my actions with reason, I perceive myself as if some irrational fever has overtaken me. Sometimes I fear for myself. Yet it is only when I think of the baby, Eadulf. My logic remains when I concentrate on other matters. This makes me fear even more." Eadulf replies that he has heard "that sometimes, after a birth, a mother can feel unhappy—" (*Badger's Moon* 143). Fidelma seems to be suffering from what today is known as postpartum depression. She is able to escape that feeling only within her professional life as a *dálaigh*, but even that escape carries with it consequences, such as feelings of guilt.

Eadulf recognizes later in *Badger's Moon* that "he had never seen [Fidelma] attempting to show confidence while being so ill at ease. He was reminded once again that Fidelma seemed to have become a different person from the self-assured, confident *dálaigh* he had fallen in love with. It had all changed with the birth of little Alchú" (173).

FIDELMA: A MODEL LAWYER

So in Fidelma readers see someone who not only must balance a personal life with a professional life that requires many extended periods of time away from her son, but also someone who must contend with feelings of guilt arising from the difficulty of balancing both lives. When Alchú is kidnapped in *The Leper's Bell*, she is completely distraught, even incapable of meaningful action. This is a condition that may seem reasonable, given the abduction of a child, but that is radically different from the Fidelma who has been moving through one extraordinary endeavor after another. At the same time, Fidelma cannot just let herself be the heartsick and worried mother because she knows the expectations that others have for her. "I worry for her," Colgú says. "She is of a disposition that keeps a tight rein on her emotions. She tries to suppress them because she thinks it unseemly to allow others to see her real feelings. It is unnatural to do so." Eadulf responds that Fidelma has been sobbing "her heart out these last few nights until I believe she is unable to conjure up any more tears. Do not mention this to her for, as you say, she would prefer others to think she is in control" (8). In fact, Fidelma has been so overcome by the kidnapping that it fell to Eadulf to describe the clothes that their son had been wearing when abducted (9).

Although most people probably like to think that in a family crisis their family would come together, the reality is often quite different. Many times families have been broken apart by tragedy, and the kidnapping of Alchú, following the tension between Fidelma and Eadulf over parenting priorities, leads Fidelma to pour out "all her fears, her hopes and her worries" to Della (*The Leper's Bell* 123). Fidelma earlier had admitted to herself "that she had not bonded with little Alchú. It had been a painful birth and she had begun to resent the child for keeping her confined in her brother's palace instead of pursuing her passion for law. She knew that Eadulf suspected that she resented the birth of their baby. That made her more angry with him" (98). By the time Alchú has reached three years of age in *The Chalice of Blood*, Fidelma is still conflicted and still feeling guilty (39).

Yet by the end of *Atonement of Blood*, Fidelma appears to be shifting her priorities a bit. Fidelma and Eadulf return to Cashel, finding that her brother, who had survived an assassination attempt, is now out of danger. Before reporting to the King's Council, Eadulf says that Fidelma must first see her brother, and then see their son. "No," Fidelma replies. "We will see our son first—and then I shall see my brother." Fidelma's correction may seem small, but Eadulf recognizes its significance and turns away so that Fidelma will not see him smiling (327).

It would be nice perhaps if all relational problems could be resolved quickly, but it would not be realistic. Finding answers in one's personal life can take much longer than in one's professional life. Fidelma solves many mysteries while still struggling with her own efforts to resolve and balance her personal and professional responsibilities, and find her way forward with husband and son. These personal struggles are one of the great achievements in the Fidelma narrative. They lead readers at times to become angry with her for how she treats Eadulf and to feel that she should focus more on her role as a mother. Fidelma does not appear as a perfect superhero, but she does seem very human. In that way also, she comes off the pages of her novels to serve not just as an engaging fictional character but also as a model. Surely many parents while reading the Fidelma stories have stopped to reflect on their own relationships with their spouse and their children as well as their own struggles balancing personal and professional responsibilities. As Fidelma shows quite clearly, readers can learn much from literature.

WORKS CITED

Bryant, Sophie. *Liberty, Order & Law Under Native Irish Rule: A Study in the Book of the Ancient Laws of Ireland*. London: Harding and More, 1923.

Doyle, Sir Arthur Conan. *The Annotated Sherlock Holmes*. Ed. William S. Baring-Gould. 2 vols. New York: Clarkson N. Potter, 1967.

Tremayne, Peter. *Absolution by Murder*. 1994. New York: Penguin, 1997.

---. *Act of Mercy*. 1999. New York: St. Martin's Minotaur, 2001.

---. *Atonement of Blood*. London: Headline Publishing Group, 2013.

---. *Badger's Moon*. 2003. New York: St. Martin's Minotaur, 2005.

---. *Behold a Pale Horse*. London: Headline Publishing Group, 2011.

---. *The Chalice of Blood*. 2010. London: Headline Publishing Group, 2011.

---. *The Council of the Cursed*. 2008. New York: Minotaur Books, 2009.

---. *Dancing with Demons*. 2007. New York: St. Martin's Minotaur, 2008.

---. *The Devil's Seal*. London: Headline Publishing Group, 2014.

---. *The Dove of Death*. 2009. New York: Minotaur Books, 2010.

---. *The Haunted Abbot*. 2002. New York: St. Martin's Minotaur, 2004.

---. "Hemlock at Vespers." *Hemlock at Vespers: Fifteen Sister Fidelma Mysteries*. New York: St. Martin's Minotaur, 2000. 127-56.

---. *The Leper's Bell*. 2004. New York: St. Martin's Minotaur, 2006.

---. *Master of Souls*. 2005. New York: St. Martin's Minotaur, 2006.

---. *The Monk Who Vanished*. London: Headline Book Publishing, 1999.

---. "Murder in Repose." *Great Irish Detective Stories*. Ed. Peter Haining. New

FIDELMA: A MODEL LAWYER

York: Barnes & Noble, 1993. 337-58.
---. *Our Lady of Darkness*. London: Headline Book Publishing, 2000.
---. *A Prayer for the Damned*. 2006. New York: St. Martin's Minotaur, 2007.
---. *The Seventh Trumpet*. London: Headline Publishing Group, 2012.
---. *Shroud for the Archbishop*. London: Headline Book Publishing, 1995.
---. *Smoke in the Wind*. 2001. New York: St. Martin's Minotaur, 2003.
---. *The Spider's Web*. New York: St. Martin's, 1997.
---. *The Subtle Serpent*. London: Headline Book Publishing, 1996.
---. *Suffer Little Children*. 1995. London: Headline Book Publishing, 1996.
---. *Valley of the Shadow*. London: Headline Book Publishing, 1998.

– Edward J. Rielly
The Brehon, XIV, 3, September 2015
Based on his lecture at the 2014 Féile Fidelma

THE SISTER FIDELMA COMPENDIUM

Smoke in The Wind and The Kingdom of Dyfed

Peter Tremayne's tenth full-length Fidelma mystery *Smoke in the Wind* begins with Fidelma and Eadulf shipwrecked on the shores of the Kingdom of Dyfed. Dyfed was a kingdom in the southwest of what is now Wales, now a Welsh county. The great abbey of Menevia, founded in the 6th century by Dewi Sant (St David), was the main ecclesiastical centre there.

Having left Ireland after the affair of *Our Lady of Death*, Fidelma and Eadulf were en-route to visit the new Archbishop of Canterbury, Theodore of Tarsus, but a storm erupts and their ship founders. They survive and reach shore.

The elderly King Gwlyddien of Dyfed offers them hospitality but there is something on his mind. Knowing of Fidelma's already spreading reputation, he confesses that there is a mystery causing fear and tension in his kingdom. The entire monastic community of nearby Llanpadern has vanished into thin air. The buildings are desolate, their inhabitants gone. Moreover, the King's own son was a member of the community. Who, or what, is behind the disappearance?

This is a fascinating and spine-chilling mystery. Perhaps I should mention there is one "downside" in the book. There is a typographical error in the dedication which renders David R. Wooten as "David R. Wooton." Peter has (apparently) vainly tried to get it corrected in subsequent editions. But at least we know who is meant. The late Maurice McCann (d. 2011) corrected it in his list of Fidelma book dedications in an article in *The Brehon* in January 2006.

Peter also made amends with another dedication to David Robert Wooten in thanks for his then ten years devoted service to the

International Sister Fidelma Society and as editor of *The Brehon*. This was in *The Chalice of Blood*.

One of the fascinating things about Tremayne's descriptions of 7th century Dyfed is that Fidelma finds herself very much at home there. Irish is even widely spoken, the laws are similar and the legal officer of a *barnwr*, is equivalent of Fidelma's office of a *dálaigh*. The social system is similar. This is not entirely due to the fact that the Welsh (perhaps it is better to call them by their native name – *Cymry*, "the comrades," for the word "Welsh" comes from the Anglo-Saxon word *welisc* meaning "foreigners," such name being given them by the English) are Celtic cousins to the Irish.

Originally Dyfed was the tribal homeland of the Celtic Demetae, known as Demetia. The Romans had difficulty exerting their colonial control in this area during their occupation of southern Britain. The Roman fortress at Moridunum Demetarum was abandoned not long after it was constructed about AD 193-217. As Roman colonial rule in Britain waned, Irish settlers started to appear in the area.

Of the approximately 369 Ogham inscriptions (stones bearing memorial inscriptions in an ancient form of Irish), there are 20 in Dyfed alone. According to the Irish annals, in the story of "Expulsion of the Déisi," we are told that the Déisi were a powerful clan in Meath, dwelling on Magh Brega, the Plain of Brega. Their name has come down in the names of the baronies of Upper and Lower Deece. When the daughter of their chieftain, Orba mac Doelte, was raped by Cellach, the son of the High King, Cormac Mac Art, the Déisi demanded compensation under the law. Excuses were made and compensation refused. The brother of the raped girl, Aonghus, lost his temper, cast his spear at Cellach, wounded him but also succeeded in blinding Cormac Mac Art.

For this crime against the High King, the entire Déisi clan were driven into exile. Some settled in southern Muman (around Waterford, Munster) and others journeyed to Cornwall, but a large section of the tribe landed in southern Wales, in the land of the Demetae.

It is fascinating to note that, back in 1988, Peter Tremayne actually wrote a fantasy novel about the exile of the Déisi and their wanderings to Cornwall and Dyfed. *Ravenmoon* was published by Methuen of London in hardback and also issued in paperback in 1989. Baen Books in the USA issued it as *Bloodmist* as a paperback.

The hero is Aonghus mac Orba who, at birth, is given the name Aonghus Gaeladúath – Aonghus of the Terrible Spear – when the druids prophesy he will drive his people out of their lands by a single cast of his spear. The prophecy being fulfilled, Aonghus leads his people in a fearsome story of journeyings, fighting monsters and magic until they reach Dyfed.

In his novel, Peter, in a brief note, admits to being inspired by the Irish manuscript story versions *Inndarba inna nDéisi* and *Tucait indarba na nDéisi* (The Expulsion of the Déisi). He mentions following the text of Professor Kuno Meyer's examination and editing of the manuscripts. Meyers points out that the Laud. MS 610 (Bodleian Library) version, while apparently surviving from the 8th century contains archaic spellings that could even date it as being con temporary with the actual period of the Déisi exile. Professor Kuno Meyer's comments are found in *Anecdota from Irish Manuscripts* vol. I (Halle, 1907).

Historically we are told, after the initial exile, it was Eochaid, son of Artchorp, who flourished c. AD 400, who actually led the Déisi settlement in southwest "Wales." Eochaid became the first Irish King of Dyfed and known as Eochaid Allmuir (Beyond the Sea). By all accounts, the settlement was peaceful. There are no written or archaeological evidence of wars, of slaughter or battles during the period. Perhaps the settlement and transference of kingship was carried out by marriage or alliances.

Eochaid was succeeded by his son Corath, who extended his power east to the borders of Gwent and north to Venedotia so that his son Aedh (c. AD 450s.) had inherited a significant kingdom. Under Aedh's son Tryffin (The Bearded) we see the re-emergence of some Brythonic Celtic names and even Romanised versions of such names such as Aircol Lawhir (Longhand), who is said to have married Clotry, the daughter of Magnus Maximus (D 335-388), the Roman military commander in Britain. He was proclaimed emperor by his troops marched to Italy and was defeated by Emperor Theodosius. Another of his daughters was said to have married Vortigern (Over-Lord) King of southern Britain when the Romans withdrew in AD 410 and who made the mistake of inviting Jutish mercenaries into the country to help him maintain power. These were the first "English" to settle in Britain.

Under his own name, Peter Berresford Ellis, Peter published a fascinating study *Celt and Saxon: The Struggle for Britain AD 410-937* (Constable 1993) which, of course, covers the period. Oddly, *Celt and Saxon* is one of the few titles Peter wrote about the Celts that was never published in the USA. In it, he refers to a recommended study of the period *Ireland and Wales: Their Historical and Literary Rela-*

tionships by Cecile O'Rahilly, Longmans, Green and Co, 1924, which has a section on the Déisi and other Irish settlements in Celtic Britain as well as British Celtic settlements in Ireland – refugees escaping the Roman, Anglo-Saxon, and Norman conquests. There is little new about refugee problems in the world.

The Dyfed king lists record five more kings after Aircol until we come to the king mentioned in *Smoke in the Wind*. This was Gwlyddien ap Nowy, born in AD 609, to became King in AD 640 and died in AD 670. Nowy was son of Arthwyr who died in battle but was said to be devoted to the New Faith and gave much land to the religious communities. Gwlyddien was married to Ceindrych verch Rhiwallon, daughter of the king of neighbouring Brycheiniog. His son, mentioned in *Smoke in the Wind*, was Cathen, and a daughter Sanan became the mother of Elisedd, King of Powys.

Gwlyddien is recorded as defending his kingdom from joint attacks from neighbouring kingdoms in AD 645 or as the Welsh annals describes them as "the hammering of the region of Dyfed." This appears to be an attack by Artglys of Ceredigion in alliance with Morgan ap Arthwyr of Gwent.

Gwlyddien was succeeded by his son Cathen.

Dyfed lasted as an independent kingdom until the reign of Rhodri ap Hyfaidd. He ruled briefly from AD 904-905 when he was beheaded by rivals and the kingdom was eventually incorporated into Deheubarth by the famous Hywel ap Cadell called Hywel Dda (AD 880-950).

Hywel the Good was arguably the greatest of the early Welsh rulers, extending his rule over most of Wales, and famous for ordering the gathering of the Welsh laws and their codification. He set up a commission of six legal scholars under Blegywryd. Known as "The Laws of Hywel Dda" they can be compared for their Celtic commonality with the Brehon Laws and other Celtic law texts.

He could even be regarded as the High King of the Welsh kingdoms and his reign is regarded as a "golden age" in Welsh history.

Considering Fidelma's role and the advance position of women under the ancient Irish laws, an interesting study is *The Welsh Law of Women*, edited by Dafydd Jenkins and Morfydd E, Owen, University of Wales Press, 1980. Dr Andrew Breeze of the University of Navarre, Pamplona, addressed the first Féile Fidelma in 2006 inspired by *Smoke in the Wind*.

He had widely published on the history and literature of medieval

Wales and his volume on *Medieval Welsh Literature* (1997) is regarded as a seminal work.

Dr Breeze subsequently published an article, based on his talk, in *The Brehon* (May 2007) entitled *"Smoke in the Wind*: Historical and Cultural Links of Ireland and Wales in the Seventh Century."

An early admirer of Peter's work, Dr Breeze's most startling revelation was made in his study *The Origins of the Four Branches of the Mabinogi* – the major 12th century work of Welsh mythology. Contrary to the idea of a male scribe as the author, Dr Breeze argued that it was written by a female. He identified her as Gwenllian verch Gruffudd, daughter of Gruffudd ap Cynan, King of Gwynedd. Interestingly, her father, Gruffudd, was actually born in Dublin in 1055 and she was a descendant of Brian Boru.

Gwenllian was born in 1097 and married Gruffudd ap Rhys, King of Deheubarth. When the Normans, having conquered England, began their conquests of Wales, Gwenllian was not the first Celtic woman to take to arms and lead her people in defence of their lands, and her military strategy was regarded with admiration. She became the "Boudicca of Wales" and is often depicted in the mould of Boudicca rallying her troops from a chariot. However, she was eventually defeated, captured, and executed at the battle of Castell Cydweli (Kidwelly) in 1137.

The Origins of the Four Branches of the Mabinogi

Andrew Breeze

Andrew Breeze's controversial book claiming the author of the Mabinogi was a woman

In such a page-turner as *Smoke in the Wind* we find far more than a simple (or, rather, complex) mystery thriller. Tremayne's extensive knowledge of place and time, of culture and attitudes, woven with such consummate ease into his stories, leads one on into an exciting world. The readers are often not aware that they are reading fact within the beautifully told fiction stories. This is what takes the Sister Fidelma

Mystery series out of genre fiction to a higher literary level, and why they continue to have such a following.

– Rhys Williams
The Brehon, XV, 3, September 2016

WHAT THE PRESS HAS TO SAY...

What The Press has say About Peter Tremayne and The Sister Fidelma Mysteries

*T*hrough the years, articles have appeared in the press describing the growing success and popularity of both Sister Fidelma and her author. Presented here is a mere fraction of said articles, representative of what journalists have to say about the series; but not mere criticism of individual books, but indicative of the impact the Sister Fidelma Mysteries have had on detective fiction (and not merely 7th century Irish murder mysteries). Though most are focused on the "beginnings" of the series, it was evident that the team of the good Sister and her creator had already become a "global phenomenon."

SEVENTH CENTURY WHODUNNITS
Books Ireland – September 2004

*A*n Indian publisher recently contacted Peter Tremayne's agent with a view to translating his Sister Fidelma novels into Marathi, a language spoken by some twenty million people in western India. Sister Fidelma is a fictional, seventh-century Irish detective and a trained advocate of Brehon law. As far as we know, the female sleuths of ancient Ireland are not a cult interest in western India, but that may be about to change. The international appeal of

Tremayne's unusual detective series appears to know no bounds. To date, the Sister Fidelma novels have appeared in most European languages, as well as Japanese, and the series is also popular in the US, where one dedicated fan has set up a website (www.sisterfidelma.com), a thrice-yearly magazine called The Brehon and a Sister Fidelma Society with members in twelve countries.

Peter Tremayne is the fiction writing pseudonym of Peter Berresford Ellis, a Celtic scholar born in Coventry in 1943 of Irish and Breton parents. Under his own name, he has written over thirty non-fiction books on subjects as diverse as Welsh nationalism, the Irish working class, Celtic mythology and history, and Captain W. E. Johns, creator of the

Biggles series for children. His fiction spans several genres, including horror, fantasy and contemporary thrillers, as well as the Sister Fidelma series. Ten years after the first Sister Fidelma novel was published – there are now twelve, and two collections of short stories – Tremayne remains pleasantly baffled by the series' phenomenal success.

"It started with a short story, which I wrote just to illustrate how the Brehon laws worked and the position of women in ancient Irish society," he explains. "I had given a lecture on the subject at St Michael's University in Toronto and afterwards some students suggested that it would provide an interesting setting for a novel. Some years later a friend who was compiling an anthology of Irish detective stories asked me to contribute, and that's when Sister Fidelma was born. He liked it and talked to other people about it and as a result, in October 1993, four different Sister Fidelma stories appeared in four different anthologies. Headline got wind of this and offered me a three-book deal to write full-length novels featuring Sister Fidelma. I'm a compulsive writer; when I'm not writing I get broody for my typewriter, and I've been writing the Sister Fidelma books exclusively for the last ten years."

In their depiction of Celtic society, the books are indeed a revelation. Anyone with a passing interest in Irish history will know that ancient Ireland was a great centre of learning, attracting students from around the world and sending teachers and missionaries throughout Europe and beyond.

What is less well known is that the country was also a model of gender equality, more evolved in some respects than contemporary western society. Women could and did aspire to all offices and professions, leading the way in politics and law and taking command on the battlefield as well. They were protected by law against sexual harassment, discrimination, and rape. They had the right to divorce on equal terms from their husbands and had equal inheritance rights.

Tremayne also sheds light on the growing rift between the Celtic Church and Rome, which had begun to reform itself in the fourth century. A great bone of contention was the question of celibacy, which Rome was beginning to embrace. Tremayne says that some of his readers were surprised to find Sister Fidelma, a member of the religious community established by St Brigid in Kildare, marrying her companion, Brother Eadulf, in The Haunted Abbot (Headline 2002), and giving birth to a child. This was her right under both Celtic and Roman law at that time, though Rome had condemned clerical marriages as early as AD 325 and would subsequently ban them altogether.

Though the Sister Fidelma series is rich in history, Tremayne insists that they are, above all, detective stories.

"Generally speaking, somebody, or some bodies, have been found dead, and you want the reader to care about that and to want to find out how it happened. If the reader doesn't engage with that aspect of the novel, then you're doing something wrong. Ancient Ireland and the Brehon system are just an interesting backdrop."

Tremayne's heroine has been favourably compared to Ellis Peters' Brother Cadfael, a medieval monk with a penchant for solving crimes. He rejects the comparison on the grounds that Sister Fidelma was cracking crime 800 years before Ellis Peters' creation, and in a completely different cultural and legal context. But he says he does, indirectly, owe his pseudonym to Cadfael. A former journalist, Tremayne was asked to review the first Cadfael novel in 1977 for *The Catholic Herald*.

"I felt I couldn't write the review under my own name in case readers might think Ellis Peters was merely a reversal of Peter Berresford Ellis. So I decided to use a pseudonym for the first time, taking the name of one of my favourite places in Cornwall, and it proved to be a useful invention."

CELTIC IRELAND YIELDS UP A SUPER SLEUTH
Golden Age Relived through the adventures of Sister Fidelma
Pádraig Ó Cuanacháin
The Holly Bough, December 2001 in *The Irish Examiner*

That period of Irish History between the arrival of Christianity in 432AD and the Norman invasion in the 12th century has rightly been called "The Golden Age." It is not a myth but very much a fact. There were many influences leading to this the Celts brought to Ireland a unique system of organisation and a comprehensive legal system embodied in the Brehon laws. The Celts also excelled in music, dancing and poetry and their culture married very well with Christianity. The greatest flowering of the new order was in the monastic system.

The monasteries and convents in every part of the Island supplied a unique social and economic service. They provided hospitals, food and lodgings for travellers, workshops for the production of illuminated manuscripts and sacred vessels and they were the educators – some of the largest Monasteries such as Clonmacnoise and Durrow were the universities at that time and were attended by students from all over Europe.

The Brehon laws devised and updated every three years, laid the rugs that allow a society to function where everyone was confident of justice and protection. The laws were humane. How many people are aware that the Brehon laws totally prohibited the death penalty no matter what the offence or that compensation and rehabilitation was the objective and not the cruel punishment of offenders? Under this enlightened legal system, women occupied a unique place in society. They had full equality with men and could aspire to be judges, leaders of the clan, doctors and even priests, permitted to celebrate the sacrifice of the Mass. Rome spent much effort in persuading Irish bishops to promote a men-priests-only rule. Women had the right of divorce on equal terms from their husbands and could demand portion of their property as part of a divorce settlement. That sounds very modern indeed. Seen from today's perspective the Brehon laws seemed to maintain an almost ideal environment for women.

In this unique society the divine right of kings was unknown. The eldest son did not automatically become chief after his father's death. Instead, the most suitable family member or a close relative was selected, and the kings and chieftains were, of course, more the servants of the people than their masters. If the ruler failed in his duties to the people, he could be impeached and removed from office.

In this age when entertainment is more in demand than formal lectures, the great challenge was how to make people throughout the world aware of this unique civilisation. Fortunately, Peter Berresford Ellis, the son of a Corkman (a reporter with the Cork Examiner during the War of Independence) has brought the whole period to life by writing a series of books under the pen name "Peter Tremayne" on the adventures of a nun – Sr. Fidelma in the seventh century. It all resulted from the suggestion made by a student at a lecture he gave on Celtic civilisation at a Canadian university. "Why not write stories about Ireland's golden age. Would that not be the best way of telling the world about the wonders of Celtic Ireland?"

That is why we now have a series of 11 books on the life of Sr. Fidelma in the seventh century as she solves a series of mysteries that take her to various parts of Ireland, England, Wiles and even Rome. Born in Cashel and brother of Colgú, king of Munster, she is a *dálaigh*, which means that she is a qualified lawyer In both the criminal code of the senchus mór and the civil code of the *Leabhar Acaill*. She Is also a defender and investigator who has to solve a variety of intriguing mysteries – rather like Sherlock Holmes but she has to tackle even greater problems working always within the framework of the Brehon laws and regulations. She has an assistant, an Irish trained Saxon monk – Brother Eadulf who helps her in treading the right path amidst a myriad of false trails and ever-present dangers.

Incredibly, her adventures have been translated Into Spanish, French, German, Italian, Greek and Dutch. Why is this? Why should foreigners be interested in Celtic Ireland? Well possibly it is not just because they are very good stories but more importantly, they transport the reader back in time to a gentler and more humane era, where everybody had rights that were closely guarded by the Brehon.

Laws. The background detail illustrates life as it was in ancient Ireland – it is wonderfully evocative and stirring. And it leads the reader to wonder what Ireland and maybe the world would be like today if this civilisatlon had flourished instead of being ruthlessly suppressed.

The success of these books all over the world and the certainty of films and a TV series in the future is clear proof once again that Irish culture in all its aspects – music, dance, language, and history is a growth industry throughout the entire world. The challenge for us in the future is to promote this further for the benefit of Ireland's Image and our tourist industry. At the same time we can enrich mankind by showing the world a culture where people and happiness were more important than accumulating wealth and power.

"Mise Éire, sine mé an chailleach Bhearra
Mór mo ghlóir – mé a rug Cú Chulainn cróga"

SISTER FIDELMA AND EARLY CHRISTIAN IRELAND

Ireland's Own – 4 January 2002

All things Irish are a matter of growing interest throughout the world. This is partly explained by the Irish Diaspora. Everywhere people of Irish descent are to be found, very many of them in positions of influence and authority. But there surely is another reason. Maybe Ireland is respected in many lands and in the Third World because of its long struggle for Independence, and its major contribution to the alleviation of human suffering, most especially as a result of its missionary efforts in the establishment of hospitals and schools to assist the poorest of the poor in the Third World.

If there is worldwide interest in Irish music, language, dancing and games it is not just because these embrace a unique culture of great worth, but because Ireland has a special place in the affections of many.

There is also a growing curiosity in a particular area of Irish history. That is the many hundreds of years covering native rule before this was tragically ended by British invasion and oppression. Early Irish history was unique for many reasons, but most especially for the great body of law built up by the Brehons, over a long period of time.

The Irish had their own way of regulating their affairs. The divine authority of kings, the automatic succession of the crown from father to son were unknown – the people themselves elected the new Leader. Chieftains and Kings were more servants of the people than their masters. The Brehon laws compiled by families who traditionally were involved in legal affairs were indeed extraordinary. How many people are aware that Brehon Law totally prohibited the death penalty? Or that compensation and rehabilitation were the objectives rather than the cruel punishment of offenders.

Under these laws, women occupied a unique place. They received more rights and protection than any western code of Law until recent times. They could be Physicians, Judges, Poets and Political Leaders. They had the right of divorce and of property settlement with their husbands.

No wonder that with women regarded as the equals of men, the early Celtic Church had no problem in allowing women priests to celebrate the sacrifice of the Mass, and Rome spent much time in forcing Irish Bishops to comply with the men priests rule.

But, how to explain to ordinary people at the present time how wonderful the system was? Well certainly the world should be most grateful to Peter Tremayne, the pen name of Peter Berresford Ellis, who has already written many books on Irish History such as the "History of the Irish Working Classes' and Celtic Dawn'.

He has written a series of books based on the adventures of an Irish Nun in the seventh century – Sr. Fidelma, whose brother was Colgú, King of Cashel. She was a *dálaigh*, something in the order of an investigator, an advocate, and an upholder of justice for everybody She had studied in a Bardic School, the massive body of law written and codified on the instructions of the High King Laoghaire in AD 438. Possibly he was one and the same Laoghaire who met Naomh Padraig

WHAT THE PRESS HAS TO SAY...

after his arrival in Ireland in 432 AD.

Angela Lansbury of "Murder She Wrote', will come to mind immediately when reading these books, but of course, the good nun, in solving murder mysteries, operated in a completely different environment – where everything had to be done in strict accordance with the Brehon Laws. She had an assistant and friend, Brother Eadulf, an Irish trained Saxon monk, on her many adventures that took her all over Ireland and even as far as England So far there is a series of 10 different books and the remarkable thing is that they have been translated into Spanish, French, German, Italian, Greek, and Dutch. Tens of thousands of copies have been sold in Germany and again, it is a puzzling question as to why Germans and people in Greece could be so absorbed with the adventures of an Irish Nun in Ireland so long ago. Possibly this is because they transport the reader to a gentler, more humane world where people were respected and the rights of all protected.

The cultural splendour of an age of golden enlightenment in Ireland, when Europe existed in the dark ages and when students flocked from all over Europe to be educated in Irish Monasteries is brought to life in the adventures of Sr. Fidelma. It raises the question as to what modern life might have been like if this civilisation had not been ruthlessly suppressed and destroyed.

Cashel, the headquarters of Fidelma, should benefit in its tourist industry, because it is the principle setting for all these books and it must be remembered that this Town was a most important centre of Religious and Celtic civilisation in Ireland.

I do expect that in the future, we will see films, possibly a television series on Sr. Fidelma. Certainly, all this proves that the greatest asset we have in Ireland is all aspects of Irish Culture and long may that culture develop and offer to the people of the entire world hope and consolation and the proof that human beings can indeed be concerned with things other than the accumulation of wealth.

THE CELTIC MYSTERY MAN
Irish Voice (New York) – 21 November 2001

It doesn't sound like a pitch that would work very well with many publishers. Around 666 A.D., a female lawyer (and nun) joins a sea pilgrimage to the Shrine of St. James in modern-day Spain. But the ship is tossed on the turbulent seas, and one pilgrim, Fidelma – sister of a king, and technically an "advocate" of the 7th century Celtic Brehon courts – gets tangled up in a deadly mystery. Sure, blood, gore and, these days, even female heroines are a good sell.

But in the 7th century?

Well, believe it or not, crimefighter Sister Fidelma – the creation of author Peter Tremayne – is a global phenomenon.

"The publishers are knocking down the door for the next one," Tremayne told the *Irish Voice* recently. The author is more surprised than anyone else at his success. This month, Tremayne's tenth Sister Fidelma book, *Act of Mercy: A Celtic Mystery* is released in the U.S. The book has already been a U.K. bestseller, and as with previous Sister Fidelma books such as *The Monk Who Vanished*, expect translations from German to Greek to follow.

All this from a scholar who not long ago was going to dedicate his life to a legal system over 1,000 years old.

"This started... when I was giving a lecture in Toronto trying to explain the finer points of the Brehon law system," Tremayne says from his home in England, referring to the ancient legal system of Celtic lands. "A student later said that instead of giving a long factual spiel about how (the system) operated, why not write some stories. And I did."

The Brehon system, among other things, was open to women at the time. Sister Fidelma informs people about the law, investigates crimes, hears cases and passes judgment.

She is also nun, though the Celtic Church of the 600s was very different from the Rome-centered Church which would later emerge. All of these issues, Tremayne says, apparently fascinate readers – especially when wrapped around a page-turning mystery.

Aside from hot sales around the world, there are several web sites and fan clubs devoted to Sister Fidelma, including sisterfidelma.com. Tremayne also believes his popularity is part of the ongoing boom in Irish culture.

"I've got a following because this is something new, I think it all started with this new Irish renaissance, the Riverdance phenomena. Getting to know your roots and things like that."

Tremayne – his mystery writing pseudonym – has got strong Irish roots of himself.

He was born Peter Berresford Ellis in Coventry, Warwickshire, England, in 1943. His father was a Cork-born journalist who began his career at the Cork Examiner.

WHAT THE PRESS HAS TO SAY...

The Ellis family, Tremayne says, can be traced in that area from 1288. His mother was from a Sussex family of Saxon origin who've spent fourteen generations in the same area.

With Irish, Scottish, Welch and Breton uncles and aunts, Tremayne was seemingly destined to become a world-renowned Celtic expert. He earned degrees in Celtic Studies, but later embarked on a career in journalism.

He began his career as a junior reporter in England, and later became deputy editor of an Irish weekly. He went to Northern Ireland in 1964, which he says had a profound effect on him.

His first book, *Wales: A Nation Again*, was published in 1968, the first of several histories under his born name.

But his worldwide fame will always be with his pen name, the origins of which are not exactly literary.

"Years ago, I went down to live in Cornwall to study the Cornish language ... and Tremayne happened to he a little place (with) three houses, four Methodist chapels, four bars and the best Italian restaurant... It was such a nice place, I said, 'I'll commemorate it,'" Tremayne recalls, with his trademark, jovial laugh.

FIDELMA, THE DASHING
ANCIENT IRISH NUN OF MYSTERY
The Irish Times – 27 October 2001

We've had Celtic mythology; we've had Celtic music; we've had, God help us, Celtic spirituality. You might imagine that certain areas of human endeavour would be beyond the reach of the current craze for all things Celtic – the crime novel, for Instance. But you'd be wrong. Sister Fidelma, a nun who, charges happily around seventh-century Ireland solving murder mysteries, is given her 11th outing in Peter Tremayne's latest book, *Smoke In the Wind*. Miss Marple in a wimple? Not quite. Fidelma is straight out of the *sleuth noir* mould: dark, handsome, a qualified lawyer, an expert horsewoman and – rumour has it – not entirely averse to the idea of sharing a sleeping bag with her sidekick, Brother Eadulf.

However outlandish this may sound; her creator insists that he didn't make it up. "Everything that happens In the Sister Fidelma books is absolutely accurate, historically," says Peter Tremayme, *aka* the Celtic scholar Peter Berresford Ellis. "Under the Brehon laws, women could aspire to be the equals of men in all the professions. They could be doctors, lawyers, teachers, clan leaders, judges." There was even a female bishop, Brigid of Kildare, who died in AD 650.

"Women could also get divorced as easily as men. There were nine reasons for divorce, one of which was if your partner snored. And of course there was no hang-up about celibacy. It was only after the eighth century that all that began to erode, as the Colts moved more into the Roman Idea of legal concepts; but even in the Roman church celibacy wasn't enforced until the time of Leo IX In the 11th century. Then it was enforced very brutally. Loads of the wives of priests committed suicide because the pod Christian pope ordered them to be rounded up and sold into slavery. Great stuff wasn't it?"

Great source material, more like – and Peter Tremayne isn't the only one to have mined it. Inevitably, Sister Fidelma has been compared to Ellis Peters's Brother Cadfael, the mystery-solving monk. "Critics have called her Cadfael's successor, which is nice – but only in the literary sense, because Fidelma is actually eight centuries earlier." Even in the literary sense, however, a race between the two spiritual sleuths is out of the question. "Ellis Peters died a few years ago. She was in her 60s when she got hold of the Cadfael character. It's very sad, really. The success came too late for her to enjoy it."

But Tremayne, who effortlessly brings forth information on the nitty-gritty of life in Celtic Ireland, is noticeably reticent when it comes to giving away any secrets about his own hero's literary future. "She has what we call sexual tension Eadulf," he says, as if that explained everything. "And there have been, um, developments. I do, though, get quite a number of letters from priests and nuns who would – I suspect – rather like to hark back to those days'."

In his "real" incarnation as Celtic Studies scholar, Peter Berresford Ellis is the author of a fistful of non-fiction nooks including *The Celtic Revolution*, *The Celtic Empire*, *A Dictionary of Irish Mythology*, *Wales: A Nation Again*, *Caesar's Invasion of Britain* and *The Problem of Language Revival*.

He is also the author of the definitive story of the Cornish language and literature: "Definitive because it's the *only* history," he says ruefully. His mission has always been to inform the wider public about his chosen fields of interest – so even his Fidelma novels contain explanatory prefaces. But, he says, there's a huge amount of information out there which has – due to the lack of research funding – yet to be processed.

"During the Tudor conquest, a lot of the old Chiefs fled, and they took their bards with them. So all over Europe – in Vienna for example – there are huge numbers of documents that haven't even been catalogued, let alone translated. The same thing happened during the early missionary period, when missionaries were setting up places like Regensburg. What we know of Irish mythology is founded on about one-tenth of known manuscript sources – nobody has ever bothered with the rest. I don't want to launch an attack on academia; it's just that academics tend to bang on about the known stuff, when what's needed is to get into Europe, find those manuscripts, and even just catalogue them, to start with." Still, it may come as something of a surprise to readers accustomed to the Roman view of history (Celts=smelly savages) to discover that the seventh-century Irish were not only assiduous about personal hygiene, but also keen aromatherapists, bathing each evening in tubs that contained sweet-smelling herbs, then toweling off with linen cloths.

Or that the reason why we contemporary Celts often pronounce the world "film' as "fillum' is due to a transference of Irish pronunciation rules into English. Small wonder that Sister Fidelma has her own website, set up by a devotee in Arkansas, which features historical notes, pronunciation guides and such-like (www.sisterfidelma.com).

Celtic chic may have spawned everything from *Riverdance* to born-again Druid separatists, in Derbyshire, but the more we learn about the realities of Celtic Society, says Peter Tremayne, the more we'll learn about ourselves.

THE WISDOM OF SISTER FIDELMA
Tom Chaney, *ColumbiaMagazine.com* – February 2009
Tom reports on a series of mysteries set in seventh century Ireland with detective Sister Fidelma a nun and a brehon, a judge in the courts of the five kingdoms, who is rooted in the old ways but recognizes the coming changes.

For several years now, several of us around and about The Bookstore have eagerly awaited the latest Sister Fidelma novel from the pen of Peter Tremayne. Tremayne is the nom de plume of a renowned scholar of Irish and Celtic matters, Peter Berresford Ellis.

Out of his scholarship Ellis, as Tremayne, has produced a series of mysteries set in 7th century Ireland. His detective is Sister Fidelma – a nun and a brehon, a judge in the courts of the five kingdoms of Ireland. It does not hurt at all that she is also sister to the king of Cashel, one of the five kingdoms.

Fidelma is married to Brother Eadulf, a Saxon priest. They have one son.

Tremayne's latest novel is *Dancing with Demons*. As it opens, the high king of the five kingdoms Sechnussach has been murdered. He is discovered dead in his bedchamber. The obvious suspect is Dubh Duin, a clan chieftain of the old faith, who is found with the murdered king. Dubh Duin is dying of a self-inflicted wound.

He utters a final dying word which muddies the water around the death of Sechnussach.

The Great Assembly of the five kingdoms invites Fidelma to investigate the murder. The solution to the crime involves stolen knives, religious persecution, unreliable help, and secret passageways – enough to keep any aficionado of fictional murder most foul and complicated awake for several nights of good reading.

I'll not give a single clue to who done it. "Twould spoil a good book to know too much too soon. But I do want to talk about a couple of ideas within the book and the series which are of most interest to me.

The stories of Sister Fidelma are set in a time of change in the church in Ireland, indeed a time of change in Irish culture.

A couple of weeks back I talked about Gore Vidal's fine novel, *Julian* set at a time when the Roman empire is adapting itself to the new sect from the eastern end of the Mediterranean – Christianity. The rapid spread of that religion was made possible in part because it was so flexible in accommodating itself to the rituals, holidays and worship places of the existing system of worship.

For instance, the Christian calendar adopted the Roman festival Saturnalia as Christmas. The Lupercalia became, after Augustus, a fertility festival roughly corresponding to our St. Valentine's Day. And there was the Cerealia which in April celebrated the beginning of the fertile crop months.

By the 4th century the new religion was so deeply entrenched in Rome that it was more than a single emperor, namely Julian, could do to root it out.

From the Fidelma novels we learn that three centuries later similar upheavals were happening in Ireland.

Sister Fidelma, a member of a religious order, is married to Brother Eadulf, a Saxon priest – from what was to become England. By the seventh century the rule of Rome was being extended to the far reaches of what was becoming an increasingly Christian world. This brought Rome into conflict with the church in other, differently civilized nations. In Fidelma we have a picture of that conflict. The church in Ireland did not forbid the clergy to marry. The rule of Rome had just instituted the rule of celibacy for all members of religious orders and clergy and was trying to impose this rule in all Christendom. The religious houses of Ireland contained members of both sexes. Rome forbad this. Tremayne pictures a world which in three centuries has moved from the newly adapted Christian world of Rome – establishing itself as the church in the west against the so-called pagan religion – to the seventh century push to establish its rule in the outer reaches of Christianity.

Rome saw danger in the Christianity of Ireland where the church was established on the foundation of a pre-Christian civilization which permitted women to have a significant and equal role in society; which allowed marriage within the ranks of clergy; and which was based on the ancient law of Ireland rather than that of Rome.

It is also interesting that the chief conflict in *Dancing with Demons* is not between the Irish rule and that of Rome, but between Christianity and the ancient, pre-Christian worship in Ireland.

When the golden symbol of the old religion is melted down, Fidelma has reservations.

"Part of my mind agrees," she replied slowly, "yet I cannot help thinking it was made in good faith by our ancestors long before the coming of the word of Christ. It was a sacred and dear object to them. By melting it down, we are in danger of cutting ourselves off from our forefathers. Is that a good thing?...

"Part of me is worried that we are creating a deep abyss between our new world and those of our ancestors in the old world. Once that chasm has been made, we will never be able to re-cross it and know their thoughts, their fears and their hopes... I fear we may soon be stumbling forth in the world, never knowing what knowledge and example our parents would have bequeathed to us."

Yep! History never was so interesting as in the hands of fine historian/novelists such as Gore Vidal and Peter Tremayne.

THE SISTER FIDELMA COMPENDIUM

Fiðelɱa: The Critics Chime In

from newspapers to radio to literary journals to mystery magazines, the critics have been overwhelmingly positive in their effusive praise of Peter Tremayne's storytelling abilities. These are but a few examples of excerpted commentary on Peter and the Sister Fidelma Mysteries.

[T]he clerical detective delights mystery fans with the twining of murder and mysticism, death and divinity. Why does the priest, minister, rabbi, or nun make such a compelling and fascinating detective? Because religious types are natural sleuths in their own right as they sort out the most troublesome realities of society: order and chaos, good and evil, right and wrong. Not unlike the police detective or the gumshoe private eye, the members of the clergy are often faced with the dark side of humanity. But unlike their more mainstream contemporaries, they temper it with an enduring faith in goodness. An ecclesiastical mystery must, above all, represent the faith community with authenticity: the good, the bad and the ugly, from last rites to first communion. [The Sister Fidelma] series had held the interest of mystery readers for over a quarter of a century. Tremayne presents the reader with a winning combination—the convincing character of Sister Fidelma matched by the fascinating depictions of 7th century Ireland. Sister Fidelma, an Irish nun... is possibly the most interesting — and smartest — nun ever to be found on the pages of a clerical mystery. Both heroine and detective, amateur and professional, Sister Fidelma never fails to captivate the reader. — "Divine Mystery: 10 Great Clerical Sleuths - Why Priests, Rabbis, Nuns, and Reverends Solve So Many Crimes," **CrimeReads.com**

Gerry McCarthy in The Sunday Times *(2004) points out that crime fiction "has been undergoing a boom in Ireland," and I think it is important to note that far from being merely a part of this boom, the Fidelma novels were one of the contributing factors that set it in motion –* Dr John Scaggs, **University of Limerick** (Féile Fidelma program booklet, 2006)

Tremayne plays fair with the readers while evoking the period in vivid detail. This long-running series remains as fresh and inventive as ever. — **Publishers Weekly** on *The House of Death*

Fast moving combination of history, mystery and fantasy set in seventh century Ireland... A complex, lovingly written mystery notable for its historical detail and strong heroine. – **Kirkus Reviews** on *The House of Death*

Tremayne returns in top form in his atmospheric 31st whodunit set in seventh-century Ireland ... Tremayne expertly incorporates historical and legal details of the time into the suspenseful plot. This impressive volume bodes well for future series entries. – **Publishers Weekly**, USA on *The Shapeshifter's Lair*

[On Peter Tremayne and Sister Fidelma] Several academics in the field, including Professors Dáibhí Ó Cróinín and Máirín Ní Dhonnchadha and Dr Dan MacCarthy, have attested to the historical authenticity of the Fidelma books. 'Tremayne's' contribution to the popularising of interest in Irish history may now perhaps rival [Peter] Berresford Ellis's!" – **HistoryIreland.com**

One of the best cases for the complex, enchanting Fidelma, whose adventures, rich in historical detail, rarely disappoint. – **Kirkus Reviews**, on *The Shapeshifter's Lair*

Fans of ancient history, myths, and swashbuckling adventure are likely to enjoy this tale set in seventh-century Ireland... This is a challenging and unusual but deeply satisfying and enjoyable historical thriller. – **Booklist**, on *The Shapeshifter's Lair*

Tremayne is one of those very few mystery writers who can complex and bewilder. – **Foyles Bookstore** on *The Shapeshifter's Lair*

Once again, Tremayne (The Chalice of Blood, 2011, etc.) presents a detailed, readable depiction of life in ancient times with a clever mystery neatly woven into the plot. – **Kirkus Reviews**, USA, on *Behold a Pale Horse*

FIDELMA: THE CRITICS CHIME IN

Some interesting facts about Peter Tremayne and the Sister Fidelma series:

1. *The series is set in 7ᵗʰ century Ireland, a place of rival clan territories and five province kingdoms.*

2. *British writer Peter Berresford Ellis, writing under the name Peter Tremayne for this series, is a Celtic scholar and has lectured and written over 30 non-fiction books, most of them about Ancient Ireland. He had also written two historical novels before the Sister Fidelma series.*

3. *A combination of circumstances in the mid-1980s gave him the idea: first, there was the success of Umberto Eco's The Name of the Rose, featuring a series of murders in a 14ᵗʰ century monastery (and the film that followed starred Sean Connery); then there was the popularity of Ellis Peters' Brother Cadfael series. Also, during this time, Tremayne was lecturing at Toronto University on the role of women in the ancient Irish world when a student suggested it would be a great setting for a murder mystery, with a woman lawyer from the period. After the idea percolated a bit, he started writing.*

4. *The series began in the mid-1990s as short stories (of which there are now more than 80), and a year later, the first of the novels was published, Absolution by Murder.*

Sister Fidelma's appeal:

1. *Sister Fidelma, from the religious community of St. Brigid of Kildare, is also a dálaigh (an advocate title in the Irish ancient courts of law). Very few women achieved this status, which required an extensive study of criminal law, and it gives her certain authority and status, which come in handy. She is sort of an ancient Irish Perry Mason.*

2. *This is one nun who hasn't taken a vow of silence and uses her sharp tongue to quell upstart men who think she doesn't know what she's talking about because she's a woman.*

3. *Unlike a cloistered nun, Sister Fidelma travels extensively and consults with kings.*

4. *She is smart, of course, but also doesn't blanch at the sight of blood. And there can be plenty!*

– KB Owens' Masters of Mystery series website

THE SISTER FIDELMA COMPENDIUM

What a magnificent read, this was truly the best historical mystery I have ever read. – Terry Haligan, **Eurocrime** on *The Council of the Cursed*

Fidelma's ability to best opponents, whether in argument, strategy or audacity, makes her a heroine for any age. – **Publishers Weekly**, USA

If you like a good mystery, cleverly plotted and beautifully written, and you have not yet discovered Fidelma, a treasure trove awaits... An example is the first chapter of Dancing with Demons *in which the king's murder on the Hill of Tara combined brilliant imagery and savage detail like that found in a Jacobean tragedy.* – **The Irish Independent**

Tremayne has created a great character in Fidelma and brilliantly conjures the world she inhabits... This is masterly storytelling from an author who breathes fascinating life into the world he is writing about. – **Belfast Telegraph**

We defy anyone picking up a Sister Fidelma Mystery not to be hooked on these superbly written historical thrillers. – **RTÉ** – Raidio Gael-tacha (Book program)

Lovers of historical crime mysteries know they are always in good company with Sister Fidelma. – **Yorkshire Evening Herald**

If there is anyone who has emerged from the crowded field of writers of medieval mysteries to take the place of the late Ellis Peters it is Peter Tremayne – **Denver Post,** USA

Exquisitely crafted... Tremayne continues to provide a superior brand of medieval mystery... – Margaret Flanagan, **Booklist** (New York)

No one can make the seventh century come so alive as the pseudonymous Tremayne, **Library Journal,** USA

Tremayne's books are a delightful respite from the mundane offerings that are available today. – **Anniston Star,** USA

FIDELMA: THE CRITICS CHIME IN

The 7ᵗʰ century husband-and-wife detective team of Sister Fidelma and Eadulf have proved a welcome and original addition to history fiction... finely crafted mysteries... breathing life into the dustiest corners of history and seasoning his plots with a wealth of cleverly observed background detail. Fidelma and Eadulf (are) a splendidly entertaining double act. – **Yorkshire Evening Post** on *The Council of the Cursed*

I had not come across the Sister Fidelma mysteries before I had read this one and I could easily become a fan. What makes these stories is the fast-moving plot alongside the authenticity of the historical background. Those who like detective and historical novels will love this combination. – Bill Spence, **Yorkshire Gazette-Herald** on *The Council of the Cursed*

One of Fidelma's best, and the subject of clerical celibacy is particularly relevant today. – **Kirkus Reviews**, USA, on *The Council of the Cursed*

Readers who love Middle Ages whodunits will want to read A Prayer for the Damned *(as well as previous Sister Fidelma titles) as this series is one of the best being written today. The freshness in Sister Fidelma's latest inquiry is her doubts as to whether she should be released from her vows as a religieuse. The power struggle between Rome's edicts and the Irish Church leaders are meticulously examined even as this serves as a key element to the exciting descriptive plot. Readers gain plenty of insight into 7ᵗʰ century religious and secular politics in Ireland, yet the beauty of Peter Tremayne's skill is he does this while entertaining his fans.* – **Mid-West Book Review**, USA

Perhaps the most successful of the island's (Ireland) current mystery authors is Peter Tremayne, who writes the Sister Fidelma mysteries... The particular pleasure reviewers have praised in these tales is the vivid and accurate re-creation of medieval Irish culture. – **World Literature Today**, USA

Rich in historical detail... Tremayne has produced another winner. – **Publishers Weekly**, USA on *A Prayer for the Damned*

THE SISTER FIDELMA COMPENDIUM

Faithful fans of Fidelma will enjoy another chance to immerse themselves in Tremayne's detailed depiction of medieval Ireland. – **Kirkus Reviews** USA on *A Prayer for the Damned*

The books have it all from action and suspense to a few moments of levity that will have readers searching for more of the author's novels. I am sorry that I did not discover him sooner. – Angel L. Soto, **Eurocrime**

*Detective books have covered many periods in history, none more successfully than (Peter) Tremayne with his much admired series set in 7th century Ireland. –***Oxford Times**, UK

Well written, fast moving and keeps the reader guessing through myriad twists and turns. – **South Wales Argus,** UK, on *A Prayer for the Damned*

Tremayne's formidable mysteries... provides a fascinating and detailed immersion into a highly sophisticated culture as worthy of contemplation today as it was when that culture was the brightest beacon in the European "Dark Ages." – **The Federal Lawyer – Journal of the US Federal Bar Association**

Tremayne writes so authentically about this remote time period that readers will feel they are there in every way. His densely plotted stories are a delight. – (Star review of *Master of Souls*) **Library Journal**, USA

Fidelma's world remains a richly imagined and thoroughly interesting place to spend time. – Yvonne Klein, **Eurocrime**

Tremayne never fails to deliver a fascinating and intriguing read... For all fans of medieval novels, especially mysteries, Tremayne's latest in the Sister Fidelma series is a gratifying read. Though not necessary to enjoy any of the books, it is helpful timeframe-wise, to start the series at the beginning. Even so, any one of Tremayne's (books) is a delightful respite from the mundane offerings that are available today. Tremayne is a "Master" of Mystery. – **Anniston Star,** USA, on *Master of Souls*

FIDELMA: THE CRITICS CHIME IN

Talented author Peter Tremayne guides us back to a time when stepping outside your door was dangerous, when death could strike for no reason. This is a skillfully woven tale made up of several subplots guaranteed to hold your interest. Lifelike characters lay false clues and scatter red herrings across the trails by omission and lies. You'll be hard pressed to decide who to believe. A well-written tale I'm pleased to recommend to anyone who enjoys a really well researched historical story with intrigue and mystery. – **New Mystery Reader**

The reader is left with the smug satisfaction of having digested a fairly erudite volume. There is also the satisfaction of having enjoyed the book... because of Tremayne's story-telling abilities and his talent at evoking scenes and atmosphere... – **Shots** (on *A Prayer for the Damned*)

I have read most of the Fidelma Mysteries and Master of Souls is as fresh as the earlier books. I did not guess the ending so enjoyed right to the last page. Peter Tremayne breathes life into 7ᵗʰ century Ireland. – **Historical Novels Review** (on *Master of Souls*)

The 17th novel of historical detection featuring the marvelous Fidelma and Eadulf (the Dalziel and Pascoe of their day) is rich in atmosphere, clever in the telling and drips with authenticity... this is another terrific novel of ancient Ireland. – review of *A Prayer for the Damned* in **The Huddersfield Daily Examiner**, UK

Tremayne's pitch-perfect 16th mystery to feature Fidelma of Cashel... transports the reader to an unfamiliar time and place with a sure scholarly touch. – **Publishers Weekly**, USA, on *Master of Souls*

Fidelma gathers up all the loose strings of her investigation and brings the case to a stunning conclusion... (*Master of Souls* – star review, a star is assigned to books of unusual merit, determined by the editors) **Kirkus Reviews, USA**

Sister Fidelma is one of the most engaging detectives in modern fiction. – Professor Edward J. Rielly (chair of English Dept., **St Joseph's College**, Maine)

ᚦHE SISTEᚱ FIᚦELᚋA COᚋᚹENᚦIUᚋ

A Prayer For The Damned *is a blessing for the millions of Sister Fidelma's devoted fans around the world. Tremayne's super-sleuth is a vibrant creation, a woman of wit and courage who would be outstanding in any era, but brings a special sparkle to the wild beauty of medieval Ireland. The author sets the scene with meticulous care and develops the plot with intelligence. He always plays fair with his readers, but surprises abound. Half the fun of the Fidelma series is trying to guess what this remarkable woman will do next. Well done!* – **Morgan Llywelyn**, best-selling author of *Lion of Ireland, Finn Mac Cool, The Last Prince of Ireland, Horse Goddess*

What a concept! A seventh century Irish Nancy Drew in the guise of a young female cleric who is a trained dálaigh or legal advocate in ancient Irish law... Fidelma is an original and complex character; brilliant, analytical, emotionally withdrawn, touchy and testy, and conflicted over her relationship with the Irish-trained Saxon, Brother Eadulf. As with the other books in the series, this is a good read, well-paced and suspenseful, sprinkled with Old Irish terms and fascinating detail of early Irish life, food, habits, dress et cetera. I confess to being a fan of the intrepid Sister and this collection of fifteen short stories provides an excellent opportunity for any reader to discover if he or she, too, will succumb to Fidelmania. I'm not surprised there's talk of a television series. An Irish heroine for both the seventh and twenty-first centuries, here is a character more credible and captivating than Xena the Warrior Princess!' – G.V. Whelan (aka the novelist O.R. Melling) writing in **Books Ireland**

An engrossing plot with the right blend of problem-solving and action to keep you hooked. What I also enjoyed was how the period comes alive – Peter Tremayne obviously knows his stuff. – **Belfast News Letter**

Fidelma's popularity is owed entirely to Tremayne's story-telling talents. His characters are vividly drawn, his narrative has pace as well as authority. He may be an expert on the ancient Celts, the Brehon Law system and 7th century Irish history, but he also tells stories that bristle with intrigue and human emotion. Escapist, yes, well-crafted whodunit, most certainly, but this is also fiction with the ring of real history about it. – **Huddersfield Daily Examiner**, UK

FIDELMA: THE CRITICS CHIME IN

There is only one problem with the series – it's too long between each episode. Keep 'em coming, Tremayne. – **The Anniston Star,** USA

The Leper's Bell *is a gripping tale, full of life, interesting diversions, above all a great story that leads us through a maze of possibilities, until, in the end, when we think we have got our man, it turns out to be someone else. Peter Tremayne has served us well yet again.* – **The Tipperary Star**

Sister Fidelma is a hugely well-constructed figment of writer Peter Tremayne's imagination, she is rooted in the reality of 7th century Ireland in which he sets her detective dramas. Since Tremayne launched the Sister Fidelma stories in the early Nineties, she has become a cult figure with even her own website. Much of that is doubtless owed to Tremayne's story-telling talents. His characters are vivid and credible, his narrative gripping and atmospheric. All of it is informed by his credentials as an authority on the ancient Celts, the Brehon law system and 7th century Irish history. This new collection of 15 short stories offers intrigue and entertainment from a world that could so easily have influenced ours. – **Irish Echo**

Every now and again, you come across a book that is so uniquely different as it is accurate to its time period and Peter Tremayne's Sister Fidelma Celtic Mysteries series is just that. The lovely thing about Tremayne's books is his attention to detail. Historically, he keeps it faithfully true without it becoming stale. – **Irish World**

One of the most suspenseful and intelligent series of historical mysteries... Tremayne continues to challenge readers with a compelling combination of church, cultural and legal history, buttressed by intriguingly complex plots and a superlative cast of sympathetic characters. – **Booklist,** New York

This is a cracking whodunnit that offers a generous ration of clues, twists and shocks before the final page. – **Coventry Evening Telegraph,** UK

THE SISTER FIDELMA COMPENDIUM

The Mammoth Encyclopedia of Modern Crime Fiction, compiled by Mike Ashley, Robinson, London, paperback at £9.99, and US edition from Carroll & Graf, New York. Contains a full-page entry on Peter Tremayne and Sister Fidelma. Comments – *this fascinating series is one of a kind...*

Tremayne provides another authentically detailed installment in his exquisitely crafted Sister Fidelma series... decidedly literate and intelligent whodunit... – **Booklist,** USA, on *Act of Mercy*

Tremayne delivers a satisfying cozy with a fascinating historical twist – **The Drood Review of Mystery** – on *Act of Mercy*

The world should be most grateful to Peter Tremayne... The cultural splendor of an age of golden enlightenment in Ireland, when Europe existed in the dark ages and when students flocked from all over Europe to be educated in Irish Monasteries is brought to life in the adventures of Sister Fidelma. – **Ireland's Own**

The detail of the books is fascinating, giving us a vivid picture of everyday life at this time... the most detailed and vivid recreations of ancient Ireland. – **Irish Examiner**

Fidelma is straight out of the sleuth noir mold: dark, handsome, a qualified lawyer, an expert horsewoman... Tremayne effortlessly brings forth information on the nitty-gritty of daily life in Celtic Ireland... (he) has brought our colorful roots to life with (this) crime series... – **Irish Times**, Dublin

Fidelma would put Brother Cadfael to shame as she shows an uncanny talent for treading the right path amid a myriad of false trails, dead ends and pitfalls. – **Irish News**, Belfast

This nun will run and run. Sister Fidelma is no Xena, Warrior Princess – as a lawyer she uses her intelligence and cunning, rather than brute force to solve mysteries. – **Evening Herald**, Dublin

Tense and gripping... compelling, enjoyable adventures. – **Philadelphia Inquirer**, USA

FIDELMA: THE CRITICS CHIME IN

The death of Ellis Peters may have put paid to any more Brother Cadfael mysteries. But fans of ecclesiastical whodunnits can take heart, for the monk detective has a worthy successor in the shape of Sister Fidelma... Our Lady of Darkness... is a riveting tale of murder, duplicity, greed and slavery... Tremayne has created a great character in Fidelma and brilliantly conjures up the world she inhabits. I wonder what the chances are of her reaching the small screen like Cadfael? – **Belfast Telegraph**

Tremayne's – wonderful creation, 7th century Celtic nun Sister Fidelma... he instantly plunges us into Fidelma's arcane but totally accessible world. – **Publishers Weekly,** USA

Our Lady of Death *is one of the best – an excellent mystery with rich helpings of evil and tension. –* **Historical Novel Review**

I like Fidelma. She is intelligent, assertive and full of vitality. As a fan of the Sister Fidelma series of books, I was delighted to learn more about her background from the short stories – Hemlock At Vespers – **Murder Past Tense**

I read Our Lady of Darkness *which gave me great enjoyment and interest. It is excellently done, with an admirable balance between intricacy of plot and persuasive characterization. I wish it every success, and am sure it will be enthusiastically received. Tremayne... has the remarkable capacity to recreate a society of great interest and complexity so that its basic assumptions become clear and are an effective operating context for the characters and the action. It is admirable how he puts the picture together with such a sure and light touch. Readers with no previous knowledge of the period will come away entertained; but also, hardly aware of the process, historically informed. I'm sure it should do a lot here and else where to make people understand what Ireland is, and is about; and will improve general comprehension of the problems faced this century by a new nation-state derived from an ancient and distinctive, repressed but never eliminated, civilization. –* **Professor H. David Rankin** (author of Celts in the Classical World & etc.)

ZHE SISZER FIDELMA COMPENDIUM

It is clear that Peter Tremayne is thoroughly at home with the period about which he writes. Starting with a fascinating historical note, the book is crammed with interesting snippets of information that give the characters credence. His style is racy, his dialogue sharp and with all the aplomb of a 7th century Poirot, Fidelma amasses the facts to reveal the identity of the villain when all are gathered together... I really enjoyed this book, Act of Mercy, *the 8th in a series featuring Sister Fidelma. You can almost taste the salt water, feel the airless crowded conditions aboard ship. The characters are well drawn, each one with a particular weakness – spite, jealousy, cowardice, that sets them apart from the rest – and all the time Fidelma has to fight with her own emotions, resurrected by the presence of the enigmatic Clan.* – Janet Mary Tomson, **Historical Novel Review**

The Sister Fidelma books give the readers a rattling good yarn, but more than that, they bring vividly and viscerally to life the fascinating lost world of the Celtic Irish. I put down The Spider's Web *with a sense of satisfaction at a good story well told but also speculating at what modern life might have been like had that civilization survived.* – **Ronan Bennett**

I can well imagine myself becoming a devotee. The setting is refreshingly different and completely absorbing... a rich array of characters are very well described. Peter Tremayne... evokes perfectly the fascination of this distant age. – Maureen Carlyle, **Shots**

Hemlock at Vespers – *this collection is an essential canonical text for Sister Fidelma acolytes.* – **Publishers Weekly**, USA

In the simultaneously sharp-tongued and full, womanly figure of Sister Fidelma, Tremayne has created a heroine whom many readers will willingly follow – **Kirkus Reviews,** USA

A triumph! Tremayne uses many real characters and events as background, making it all the more convincing and fascinating. He succeeds remarkably in bringing the ancient world to life. – Mike Ashley, **Mystery Scene**

Fast moving – unputdownable! – **Irish Democrat**

FIDELMA: THE CRITICS CHIME IN

The background detail is brilliantly defined... Wonderfully evocative – **The Times**, London

The murders keep us on edge but really the gripping story here is the culture Fidelma represents – **Kliatt**

A brilliant and beguiling heroine. Immensely appealing, difficult to put down. It is reassuring that Sister Fidelma and Brother Eadulf will reappear. The intellectual and physical sparks that are ignited between them light up the pages. – **Publishers Weekly**, USA

A treat for history buffs and historical mystery fans who appreciate strong and intelligent female protagonists – **Booklist**, USA

The Sister Fidelma stories take us into a world that only an author steeped in Celtic history could recreate so vividly – and one which no other crime novelist has explored before. Make way for a unique lady detective going where no one has gone before. – Peter Haining, editor **Great Irish Detective Stories**

I believe I have a tendresse for Sister Fidelma. Ingeniously plotted... subtly paced... written with conviction, a feel for the times, and a chilly air of period authenticity. A series to cultivate. – Jack Adrian, editor **Great Detective Stories from the Strand Magazine**

Definitely an Ellis Peters competitor... the background detail is marvelous – **Evening Standard**, London

One of the most interesting sleuths to come on the scene in recent years – **Ellery Queen Mystery Magazine**, New York

Tremayne's heroine is gutsy. She is funny. As she outwits the dull-witted and silences the foolish with a quick comment, the reader is inclined to murmur "Bravo!" The Spider's Web *is the fifth book in the series. We can only hope there will be a dozen more.* – **Tampa Bay Tribune**, USA

Move over Miss Marple, a new sleuth is on the case – **Hampstead & Highgate Express**, UK

THE SISTER FIDELMA COMPENDIUM

A spunky 7ᵗʰ century heroine... a picture of a world in transition... richly detailed – **Walnut Creek Times**, USA

Sister Fidelma once again works her magic upon readers... Tremayne, as always, makes 7ᵗʰ century Ireland seemed accessible and absolutely fascinating. But it is Fidelma's wit and force of character which really drives this series... and the characters with which Tremayne peoples the abbeys and environs are varied and interesting. A complex plot and good characterization make this a winner especially for historical mystery fans who prefer intellectual style in their mysteries – Clare E. White in **Writers Write**, USA

Fascinating! If you enjoy a good mystery and like reading about history, you'll like Shroud for the Archbishop. *And I know you'll like the Irish detective, Sister Fidelma.* – **Irish American News**

A Brother Cadfael on the distaff side! – **Oxford Times**, UK

An invigorating and stimulating jaunt into the world of soluble murder and apparently insoluble church history. Peter Tremayne creates a seventh century nun who solves murder mysteries in settings of ecclesiastic grandeur, power bunting and intrigue... Entertaining, well paced, interest-sustaining and vivid – Father Des Wilson, **Andersontown News**, Belfast

I can easily see the characters being developed for a television series – **South Wales Evening Post**, UK

Tremayne uses his knowledge well... the books are superbly researched – **The Crimson Circle**, UK

Absorbing... warmly recommended... a good read with evocative atmosphere. – **Cross-ties**

Quite a girl, our Sister Fidelma. The plots are as clever as Fidelma, but the real attraction is Tremayne's feel for the period; a chill, unforgiving time. – **Manchester Evening News**, UK

A 4-Star Recommendation – **Crime Times**, UK

FIDELMA: THE CRITICS CHIME IN

Tremayne spins a rollicking pacey yarn. – **Nuneaton Evening Telegraph**, UK

A credible set of events set against an authentic Celtic background... intriguing and compelling whodunnit which gathers pace to an Agatha Christie-style denouement – **Coventry Evening Telegraph**, UK

On Chalice of Blood – *This exciting murder mystery had me eagerly turning the pages with its intriguing heroine and fascinating setting. The author is an expert in early Irish history so gives an authentic flavour to a well written novel full of suspense... I can understand why she has such a large following. I will look forward to reading more.* – **Yorkshire Gazette-Herald**

Sister Fidelma is fast becoming a world ambassador for ancient Irish culture – **Irish Post**

An outstanding series. – **I Love A Mystery**

The literary successor to Ellis Peters' Brother Cadfael – **Southern Star**, Cork, Ireland

A series which shows no sign of growing tired... two well-delineated leading characters – **Murder: Past Tense** (Historical Mystery Appreciation Society)

Strong historical whodunnits, as sharp as a sword and as colorful as any medieval manuscript – **Northern Echo**, Darlington, UK

[Sister Fidelma] does not disappoint... untangling a complex web of intrigue that moves from one surprising revelation to the next – **Publishers Weekly**, USA

Firmly set in a wild, dangerous time... this historical teaches as it entertains – **Library Journal**, USA, on *Valley of the Shadow*

Tremayne's discriminating sense of history creates a complex mystery for history-mad readers. – **Kirkus Reviews**, USA, on *Valley of the Shadow*

THE SISTER FIDELMA COMPENDIUM

Rich with Irish lore. The Spider's Web *introduces readers to Celtic law, religious and mores in a multi-layered search for a cold-blooded killer.* – **Publishers Weekly**, USA

Fidelma displays her usual knack for uncovering timeless, all too human motives as she solves crimes under the ancient Brehon law system in Ireland. A treasure trove for historical mystery fans. – **Booklist**, USA, on *Hemlock at Vespers*

What do we like best about a Peter Tremayne novel? The historical settings, the complex blend of mystery and adventure... or the characters? How can we not love Sister Fidelma of Cashel as she wends her way through 7th century Europe — seeking truth, narrowly escaping danger? It's impossible to choose; the clever mix of history, mystery and appealingly realistic characters is a perfect concoction. Tremayne, in real life Celtic/Irish scholar Peter Berresford Ellis, has discovered the magic of perfectly balancing rich historic details and clever plot. – **Historical Novel Society** (on *Behold a Pale Horse*)

For those who haven't read Peter Tremayne's previous Sister Fidelma Mysteries, be warned, they are compulsive... Read this and be certain of Tremayne's surefootedness among the intricacies of political and religious life in this ancient Celtic land but also of his certain grasp of atmosphere, of character and place. – **Huddersfield Daily Examiner**, UK

Tremayne has a great world following... once again Fidelma's quest for justice across a treacherous Celtic landscape has a divine authenticity. – **The Oxford Times**, UK

The plot thickens as the story continues, keeping you guessing throughout with the true solution only revealed at the very last. A crime reader's delight. – **Manx Independent**, IoM

A powerful complex whodunit, The Council of the Cursed *is a terrific Dark Age mystery. Fidelma is at her best... The story line is fast paced as Peter Tremayne moves his champion from Ancient Ireland to France in a fabulous entry.* – **The Mystery Gazette**

FIDELMA: THE CRITICS CHIME IN

There is now an ever-growing mass of ardent admirers of Sister Fidelma in this country and worldwide... the series has become hugely popular across the globe and the original hardbacks are becoming increasingly collectible and sought after. – Richard Dalby, **Book & Magazine Collector**, UK

Under his real name, the author is one of the foremost Celtic scholars in the world. His vast knowledge and love of his subject shows in this well-plotted and well-written story. He vividly portrays the day-to-day difficulties of a physically demanding and sometimes harsh life, yet one in which education and knowledge are highly valued. – **Mystery Scene** (No 93)

Tremayne, a master of the medieval mystery – **Booklist**, USA

The characters breathe, the plot twists and turns, and of all the clues scattered amongst the pages, I only managed to spot one. – **Historical Novel Society**, on *The Council of the Cursed*

Drawing on his vast knowledge of ancient Ireland (after The Council of the Cursed) *Tremayne continues his fascinating exploration of medieval religious communities caught between the Rule of Benedict that preached strict sexual abstinence and the Irish tradition of mixed monasteries where marriage was allowed... Essential for series fans and readers who enjoy mysteries with medieval and Irish settings.* – **Library Journal**, USA, on *The Dove of Death*

Like all good mysteries, The Seventh Trumpet *begins with an unidentified corpse... This was the first of Peter Tremayne's novels I've read, but it was his 23rd in the series, so I definitely felt the lack of having read at least some of the earlier books. However, a quick visit to the www.sisterfidelma.com website gave me some missing context and deepened my appreciation for Tremayne's research and the historical accuracy of the novels. Tremayne kept me motivated to read on with a tightly woven story and some fascinating characters. I'd like to read the previous 22 novels.* – **Historical Novel Society**, on *The Seventh Trumpet*

THE SISTER FIDELMA COMPENDIUM

Tremayne creates a compelling character in Sister Fidelma... Whether verbally grilling an archbishop or abbot, a king or queen, an aged physician or pagan lord, Fidelma knows one speed only. Little wonder that there is a Sister Fidelma Society of devoted admirers of Tremayne's protagonist... Tremayne ably paints a compelling and vivid setting. One can practically inhale the scents of an abbey refectory at dinner, the incense used during vespers in the chapel, the manure of a feudal lord's stables, or the salt spray of the ocean. His concise but helpful prologues help sketch the lay of the land in the Irish church of Fidelma's days. Tremayne utilizes careful research and a multitude of details, but the forest is never overly tree-infested, and he gives the reader room to breathe. The plot moves along and never slogs down in a quagmire of facts and figures. [Tremayne tells] a whopping good yarn that lights the path for the reader without giving away the essentials of the mystery. In this, he avoids the oversimplification of many other writers on one hand and the postmodern excess of an Umberto Eco on the other. Some time spent in the company of Sister Fidelma is time well spent. – Luke H. Davis, **Sacred Chao**s, on Tremayne and the Sister Fidelma series

CLERICAL DETECTIVES

SISTER FIDELMA:
A STUDY OF A CLERICAL DETECTIVE

*EDITOR'S NOTE: So extensive are the reviews included herein, it is only proper that we loudly declare a **SPOILERS** alert for any reader who has yet to read one or more of the titles included herebelow.*

SISTER FIDELMA, I am glad to report, has a very prolific author who is still very much alive and busy producing even more stories about her. This is **Peter Tremayne**, the penname of the Irish Post columnist **Peter Berresford Ellis**. The Sister Fidelma stories (only a small part of his total output) are set for the most part in mid-seventh century Ireland at a time when the Roman church was winning power from the Celtic church – and very convincing it all sounds. Tremayne did his degrees in Celtic Studies, is a Fellow of the Royal Historical Society and of the Royal Society of Antiquaries of Ireland and writes with real knowledge and understanding.

Sister Fidelma, when we first meet her, is not only a religieuse, but is a qualified *dálaigh*, or advocate of the ancient laws of Ireland. Don't be put off by the Celtic background – or by the rather difficult Irish names. Everything is clearly explained. Accompanied by her friend, the Anglo Saxon Brother Eadulf (whom, it could well be said, she gets to know better and better from book to book), she experiences all sorts of dramatic and often violent adventures (including one involving an assassination attempt planned at the Synod of Whitby in 664 AD) but what intrigues me most is the picture the books paint of Celtic Ireland at a time when there were still mixed sex monasteries, when monks and nuns were allowed to marry and when women could become lawyers and judges. Fidelma enjoys real respect, power and equality – but no doubt it is a help being sister to the king! At first Sister Fidelma was just featured in short stories, but the later full-length novels are much more satisfying because Tremayne is good at building up suspense and developing attention-grabbing plots: ***Absolution by Murder***, appeared in 1994, and was followed by ***Shroud for the Archbishop*** (1995), ***Suffer Little Children*** (1995), ***The***

Subtle Serpent (1996), *The Spider's Web* (1997), *Valley of the Shadow* (1998), *The Monk Who Vanished* (1999), *Act of Mercy* (1999), *Hemlock at Vespers* (collected short stories, 2000), *Our Lady of Darkness* (2000), *Smoke in the Wind* (2001), *The Haunted Abbot* (2002), *Badger's Moon* (2003), *The Leper's Bell* (2004), *Whispers of the Dead* (more short stories, 2004), and *Master of Souls* (2005). Interestingly, he does not work out his plots in advance, but just lets them develop as he writes. He is perhaps less assured with descriptive passages, as when he writes, "It was a moment of pure chemistry. Some empathy passed from the dark brown eyes of the man into Fidelma's green ones." One way and another, there seems rather a lot about her green eyes and red hair.

Master of Souls *(2005)*

Master of Souls makes a good story. Set in January 668, it starts with wreckers luring a merchant ship onto the rocks, then Fidelma and Eadulf are sent to investigate the murder of an old scholar at the Abbey of Ard Fhearta. As always, the story is full of dramatic action and real surprises, as when it seems that the dreaded Uaman the Leper (last seen by Eadulf being swallowed up by quicksands) has returned to terrorise the neighbourhood.

It is a murderous tale that grips the interest throughout. Fidelma is still very much the leading partner, although "for nearly a year now Fidelma and Eadulf had been joined as *ban charrthach* and *fer comtha*, partners for a year and a day, a legal marriage under the law but a temporary one. After a year and a day, if incompatible, they could go their separate ways without blame and without payment of compensation to one another." Poor Eadulf complains that, instead of settling down together, "We seem to be constantly drifting from one drama to another," and very much misses their baby son Alchú, whom they have had to leave in safe keeping. All this background material is really fascinating, especially as the abbey is "a *conhospitae*, a mixed house in which male and female live together working for the glory of God and where their children are raised to that ideal."

But, in practice, children "are frowned on" and there are those who believe it should become an all-male stronghold. An old monk insists that "a person cannot be married and be perfect. Was it not the Holy Father Gregory the Great who pronounced that all sexual desire is sinful in itself? Fidelma snorted in disgust. "You mean that such a natural desire is therefore evil? Is it then suggested that the God we worship created such an evil?' "We of the religious should live in celibacy,' replied the old man stubbornly. "I adhere to the Council of Laodicea that women should not be ordained and that women presiding at the Eucharistic meals is something that should not be tolerated.' " It all sounds very contemporary.

The 7th century provides a particularly interesting setting because of the mixture of old Celtic Christian and incoming Roman Catholic ideas, mixing with pagan beliefs. As Gaeth, a village blacksmith, says, "We are not Christians ... That is why we dwell apart in order that those would proselytise us do not bother us. Argument is a tedious thing. We each come to the Dagda, the Good God, along our own path." "It seems that you are well-named, Gaeth," Fidelma said, for the name meant clever and wise.

The Irish names aren't always easy to cope with: "There were still members of the Uí Fidgente who refused to accept the rule of Donennach of the Uí Chonaill Gabra. They wanted to see the return of the rule of the old dynasty of the Uí Choirpre Aedba. Yet both families traced their descent to Fiachu Fidgennid." A little of this goes a long way, and it is not really helped very much by the inclusion of several pages of Pronunciation Guide at the end of the book. But skip over the names, and just enjoy the fast-moving story and the convincing background and look out for all the issues that are still relevant today. Recommended.

A Prayer for the Damned (2006)

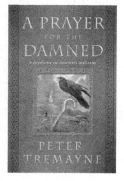

A Prayer for the Damned is set in Cashel in AD 668. The capital is thronged with visitors who have come to celebrate the marriage of Fidelma of Cashel and Eadulf, her long-time Saxon friend. Their trial marriage had lasted for the appointed year and a day, during which little Alchú had been born, but now they had decided to confirm their marriage vows.

But on the eve of the ceremony, the unpopular but supposedly pious Abbot Ultan, who opposed the marriage on the grounds that the religious should not be allowed to get married, is found murdered in his bed chamber. But was he really the virtuous man he claimed to be? Fidelma, appointed to defend Muirchertach Nar, King of Connacht, who has been accused of the brutal murder, discovers that many of the guests have good reason to hate the Abbot. Then another death follows and the wedding has to be further postponed while Fidelma continues her investigations.

This makes a much less gripping story than its predecessors because almost all of it happens in one place, Cashel, and much of it is taken up with Fidelma asking questions about the past rather than having exciting adventures of her own. And the Irish names seem to grow more and more involved, with text like: "I was playing a game of *brandubh* with Dunchad Muirisci of the Uí Fiachracha Muaide until close to midnight." "Dunchad Muirisci, the heir apparent to Muirchertach Nar?" And so it goes on. The game of *brandubh* is not actually explained for another 24 pages.

The arguments about whether or not the religious should be able to marry are of some interest. Fidelma argues that, "Most priests and other religious throughout all the kingdoms of the world still marry. I have heard that this inclination towards celibacy seems to be part of a movement emanating from those who seek to denigrate the role of women in the world." But this is no substitute for exciting action.

Fidelma admits that "to enter a religious house in order to pursue a career in law was but a steppingstone for me. I cannot say that I was really an advocate of the Faith." But, even so, she won't be bullied into disclaiming her vow to serve the Faith and is determined to sort out what has happened. "She felt that old sensation that there was something not quite right." The one person she never seems to spend much time with is her own son Alchú, but then he has a full-time nurse. She is getting rather arrogant too: She compares her pursuit of the murderer to a game of *brandubh*: "The *brandubh* board will now become the great hall where all the players and pieces will be gathered. Before the Chief Brehon Barran, I shall commence my attack. eliminating each suspect before cornering the murderer." And so she does. But it is not one of the more exciting books.

CLERICAL DETECTIVES

Dancing with Demons (2007)

Dancing with Demons includes characters with names such as Mer the Demented, Erc the Speckled and the Lady Gormflaith, so this gets it off to good start! Set in the early winter of AD 669, it is, as the author explains "not so much a *whodunnit* as a *whydunnit* – or is it?"

Sechnussach, High King of Ireland, is found dead in his bedchamber with his throat cut, and Dubh Duin, the chieftain of the clan Cinél Cairpre, the assassin who is caught in the act, stabs himself to death. The Chief Bredon of Ireland asks Sister Fidelma to find out what possible motives could have driven Dubh Duib to murder the High King.

Fidelma, accompanied by her partner (and now husband) Brother Eadulf and two Cashel warriors, sets off for the High King's palace at Tara. This leads on to a series of violent and exciting adventures in which both Fidelma and Eadulf are taken prisoner at the same time, although in different places and by different captors. And, in each case, they are just about to be killed, when their attackers both "fell to the ground," mortally wounded. What a happy coincidence! Usually the author is much more convincing.

Tremayne is usually a good storyteller and he brings his characters to life (he is quite capable of killing them off too, so you can never be sure what is going to happen. But you get involved and this keeps you reading). The Irish background is handled with the author's usual skill, although sometimes he still goes over the top with the Irish names, as when he explains: "Dubh Dahn traced his descent back from Niall's son Cairpre while Sechnussach traced his back to Niall's son Conall and the line of Sil nÁedo Sláine."

The conflict with remaining adherents of the Old (pagan) Faith is well described. But, as Fidelma tells Eadulf, "Part of me is worried that we are creating a deep abyss between our new world and those of our ancestors in the old world. Once that chasm has been made, we will never be able to re-cross it and know their thoughts, their fears and their hopes." Yet this is exactly what this author manages to do.

Fidelma herself is far from a saintly figure. For one thing "she did not believe in miracles of any sort." Years ago, she had been "ill-suited to life as a religieuse at the abbey of Cill Dara" and had soon left it. She is much happier acting as a *dálaigh* ("qualified to the role of *anruth*," as she keeps telling people), who happens also to be sister to a king, and is very conscious of her superior position, so Eadulf usually just does as he's told. When she and Eadulf set off for Tara she says that "it grieves me to desert my son after returning here a short time." Then, when she has solved the mystery, she announces, " "It is time we returned to the peace of Cahil and to our little Alchú. At this rate, our poor child will not know us. We barely spend any time at all with him.' Eadulf grimaced but wisely said nothing." She is hardly the world's most devoted mother.

Ironically, one thing she detested, according to Eadulf, was "arrogance in others," so, imperfect though she may be, she comes across as a real human being. Yet she can be tolerant too: "We do not have a monopoly on all that is good .... The New Faith binds us to have charity towards all and not to fear those who follow different paths."

She makes a shrewd questioner and is at her best when she holds the floor at the Great Assembly, when she produces a whole series of surprises, but all of them credible. Although the pace slackens here and there, her presence holds the interest throughout.

The Council of the Cursed (2008)

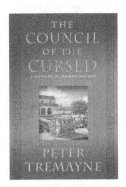

The Council of the Cursed is set in AD 670. Bishop Leodegar of Autun in France has called the church leaders from Western Europe together to deal a final crippling blow to the Celtic Church. But a fierce row soon breaks out and the meeting is brought to an abrupt close. Later that evening the body of one of the delegates is discovered, his skull brutally smashed. The council is under threat – but from whom? Fortunately, Sister Fidelma and Brother Eadulf have been called to Autun to act as advisers to the Irish delegation and they soon find themselves involved in a terrifying murder investigation, having to confront not only the autocratic bishop Leodegar but the malignant abbess, Mother Autofleda. Fidelma discovers that women and children seem to have been disappearing without trace. Could the Abbess have some involvement with the slave trade?

The story gets off to a slow start with all the bickering beween delegates, and it is only when Fidelma starts on a dangerous exploration of the *Domus Femini* (women's quarters), that excitement really builds up. Fidelma herself gets bitten by an adder, almost squashed by a falling statue, and eventually gets knocked out, so, once she is hot on the trail, there is no lack of incident.

As always, the background details are full of interest, as when Fidelma is horrified to discover that "the farm work *(at the abbey)* is done by the slaves and supervised by the brethren." Slavery is an idea that she finds repugnant. Since Bishop Leodegar had taken over a year before, the abbey was no longer a mixed house. As a monk told her, "Many here still have wives and even children in the adjoining *Domus Femini* – wives we had to put from us if we wished to continue as religious here."

Fidelma raised an eyebrow. "*Put* from you?" she queried. "Declare before God and the bishop that we no longer recognized our marriage vows because God had the greater calling on us," confirmed Brother Chilperic.

"And what would have happened had you not done so?"

"We would have had to leave and seek another place."

Usually, the most boring parts of detective stories are the pages and pages of detailed explanations that bring them to an end, but here all is explained by Fidelma in front of the whole abbey, and it makes an exciting conclusion, even if, ultimately few of the characters are to meet a very happy ending.

The Dove of Death (2009)

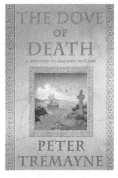

The Dove of Death is set in the summer of AD 670. An Irish merchant ship is attacked by a pirate vessel off the coast of one of the Southern kingdoms on the Breton peninsular. Murchad, the captain, and Bressal, one of his passengers, are killed in cold blood after they have surrendered. Amongst the passengers who manage to escape the slaughter are Sister Fidelma and Eadulf. Safely ashore, a grim task confronts Fidelma. Bressal had been her cousin and Murchad a friend of long standing. Fidelma is determined to bring the killers to justice, spurred on not only by the fact that the killing demands family retribution, but also by her training as an advocate of the law system of her own land. Fidelma's task is not an easy one as her only clue was that the attacking vessel was carrying on its sails the symbol of a dove – the insignia of her Breton host.

There are some really exciting moments as when Fidelma's ship comes under attack, led by a captain who "appeared to be a young man, but he was shrouded from head to foot in white so that his face was not seen." He had a peculiarly shrill voice too, and we are given occasional clues as to who this might be, but it needs Fidelma's particular skills (including her ability to recognise the ship's cat, and to identify arrows) to sort this all out.

The author is, of course, a historian and this sometimes leads him into telling us more than we really want to know, as when he explains, "After Canao died, his one surviving brother, Macliau, became King – and when *he* died, his son, another Canao, became King. Then he died and Judicael of Domnonia claimed the kingdom. In fact, Judicael claimed kingship of all the Bretons and also descent from Waroch. So he named the kingdom as Bro-Waroch, the country of Waroch."

On the other hand, other historical details are fascinating, as when Fidelma is questioned by her rescuer, Brother Metullus, about the way that "even a woman could succeed to be head of the family in your land."

"It is so."

"It would not be allowed in Rome."

"So I learned," agreed Fidelma. "In your republic, a man had complete control over his wife and family, like property .... "

"And your ways are better?" challenged the Brother.

"Our ways are different," conceded Fidelma, "but, on balance, I would argue that life for our people is, in many ways, better. But each society has to develop according to their beliefs and conscience. My argument with Rome is that what is good for Rome is not good for the rest of the world, whether imposed by the military legions that dominate the world or by the Church in Rome that tries to tell people how to behave even in lands far distant, with different customs and ways of looking at the world." This leads to an interesting discussion about Rome's claims for supremacy, which Fidelma, of course is not prepared to accept. She has no objection to services being held in Latin but explains that, "We prefer to conduct our services in the language of the sacred texts – which is Greek." Another revealing detail – nothing to do with the plot, but intriguing, nevertheless.

The highly dramatic use of a secret weapon (liquid fire) eventually determines the outcome of an exciting sea battle, and in a dramatic finale Fidelma exposes the identity of the mysterious and murderous person in white. This final denoument comes as a surprise to everyone, and once again (unlike so many long explanatory endings) holds the interest throughout.

Fidelma's long-suffering husband, Brother Eadulf, manages to get himself almost drowned on two separate occasions, but otherwise just meekly obeys Fidelma's numerous instructions, reminding her on occasions that it was a long time since they had seen their young son back at home. There's no doubt about who wears the trousers in this family!

The story offers the usual combination of gripping action (including murderous attacks, rape and stabbings) and difficult names, leading to sentences like, "I am told that his Cousin Finsnechta Fledach, the son of Dúnchad, who was brother to Cenn Fáeled's father, has raised objections." Unfortunately, though, the Breton setting proves less interesting than previous ones, and you cannot help but feel that the author may be running out of new ideas.

The book ends with Fidelma wondering "whether she should give up the symbols of religious life. That would not be difficult for her, as she had never really been committed to them .... She was no religious at heart. She knew it. She even challenged some of the basic dogmas of the Faith where she felt they needed it." So her final thought is "about leaving the religious altogether and taking her place in the role that she had, unofficially, long since filled. That was the role as a legal adviser to her brother, Colgú, King of Cashel." Perhaps that would also give the author some new ground to explore.

The Chalice of Blood (2010)

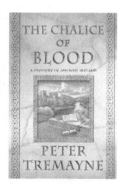

The Chalice of Blood sees Fidelma finally rejecting her life as a religieuse, but, as she explains," I am not rejecting the Faith ... The Church has little need of me to serve the Faith, but the law does have need of me." Her ambition is to become the Chief Brehon of her brother's kingdom of Muman. Meanwhile she is going through a very awkward time in her marriage to Eadulf who wants to continue his life as a religieux and is opposed to her pursuing a career in law. But for Fidelma, "The law comes first, and Faith comes second."

When an eminent scholar is found murdered in his cell in the Abbey of Lios Mór, fear spreads among his brethren; his door was secured from the inside, with no other means of an exit. How did the murderer escape? And what was the content of the manuscripts apparently stolen from the scholar's room? Abbot Iarnla insists on sending for Fidelma to investigate the killing and asks that the reluctant Eadulf should come too. But even before they reach the abbey walls, there is an attempt on their lives. Fidelma realises that "she could not really contemplate an existence without Eadulf's support. Who else would tolerate her sharp temper?" But she cannot make up his mind for him ....

The story gets off to an arresting start and holds the attention throughout. It is no mean feat to achieve this in such a long-running series, which makes it such a happy contrast to so many of the overlong series described in these pages. Occasionally Fidelma verges into the pompous, as when Eadulf tells her, "I realise that it is your brother who is trying to mend fences; it was not your doing to bring me back to Cashel." She then replies "It is not that I regret his interference, Eadulf. I welcome it as a means whereby we might try to rebuild our relationship on a better footing. I am firm in my resolve to pursue the course I have set myself. I would be a hypocrite to do otherwise. How that will square it with whatever else must be taken into consideration .... Well, we must talk more clearly when there are no other problems to distract our thoughts." "Agreed, Eadulf replied with a smile, and you feel that he sees through her pomposity and really understands her.

So the reader becomes involved in their relationship as well as in the intricacies of the plot which make this an exciting and engrossing story. When it comes to uncovering the truth and standing up to her critics, Fidelma proves to be as formidable as ever. And the graphic descriptions of life at the time (and to the critical writings of the second century Greek philosopher Celsus) add to the interest.

Behold a Pale Horse (2011)

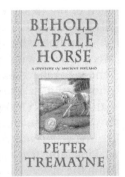

Behold a Pale Horse is set back in AD 664 when Sister Fidelma had found herself in the seaport of Genua en route from Rome back to her native Cashiel. Her old teacher, Brother Ruadan, lies dying in the abbey of Bobium – a disturbed country where even the Christians are in bloody conflict with one another, and the worship of pagan gods often prevails.

Fidelma is determined to see Brother Ruadin before he dies, not realising that her dying teacher's last words would send her off on a dangerous adventure where murder follows murder and a vicious civil war is a constant threat.

As always, it all gets off to a good start and there is plenty of action in the story which is the only one in the series (excluding the short stories) that is out of chronological order, as its real place would be just after *Shroud for the Archbishop*. This, and the absence of Brother Eadulf, make it just a bit less appealing than usual, and it is not always easy to remember who is who, and there are times when not all the chunks of history and elaborate explanations seem to be absolutely necessary.

But there is still plenty to hold the interest as when we read of all the in-fighting between traditionalists and followers of Arius (who had taught that "There could be only one God. While God the Father had existed eternally, God the Son, born as Jesus, did not and was therefore created by, and thus inferior, to God. He even argued that this meant, at one time, Christ *(and the Holy Ghost)* did not exist." It was this dismissal of the doctrine of the Trinity that had led to him being declared a heretic at the First Council of Nicaea and all his works being banned.) Fidelma, we are told, "saw a logic to the argument, which she had never heard before." She felt that "Surely there was no needs to kill one another over that?" But then she also had her doubts about the omnipotence of God – but, of course, she had never been "passionate abour religion." However, she remains a formidable and intriguing character – and it is a considerable achievemnent that the author has managed to sustain her appeal through such a long series of books.

The Seventh Trumpet (2012)

The Seventh Trumpet is set in Ireland in the harvest season of AD 670, and follows on from *The Chalice of Blood*. When the body of a murdered young noble is discovered not far from Cashel, the King calls upon Fidelma (she has given up being Sister Fidelma, more's the pity) and her companion Eadulf (who keeps pointing out he is an Angle not a Saxon so often that it gets rather repetitive) to investigate. The only clue to the noble's identity is an emblem originating from the nearby kingdom of Laign. Could the murder be somehow related to the violence erupting in the west of the kingdom? The turmoil is led by a fanatical figure claiming to have been summoned by "the seventh angel'

to remove the "impure of faith' from the land, and Fidelma and Eadulf soon find themselves struggling with a complicated mix of murder and intrigue, involving the dead noble, a murdered alcoholic priest, and a menacing abbot who has built his abbey into a military fortress. When Sister Fidelma herself becomes the victim of abduction, it is, as you'd expect, up to Eadulf to find and save her from imminent death, so that the mystery can be solved.

The story has its interesting touches such as the way that Fidelma disapproves of her royal brother's intended marriage partner and seems to sulk after not being appointed Chief Brehon, although she admits, without enthusiasm, that the man appointed "does have much more experience than I do." However, as she points out to Eadulf, "I have not left the religion, only the religious." Anyway, for years now, she had "acted independently of any Rule or religious authority. To be honest, and I'm sure that you would admit it, my recent leaving was a formality only." Eadulf still does not really approve of this and keeps on wearing the robes of a religieux.

There are the usual informative explanations of life at the time, as when we are told that "The *daer-fuidir* was the lowest of the social classes in all the five kingdoms. They were usually criminals, and liable to pay a fine or compensation, or sometimes they were even captives taken in battles from other lands. Fidelma knew that a *daer-fuidir*, if he showed remorse and industry, had the ability to progress to the level of *saer-fuidir*. That meant he could be allocated land from the common-wealth of the clan and be allowed to work it in order to pay off the debt to society. Some *daer-fuidir* could accumulate sufficient wealth and status to move forward to become a clansman, a *ceile*, with full rights."

Interesting too is the description of eating habits of the time: "There were even basins of water provided, for the custom was to use a knife in the right hand and eat with the fingers of the left hand, leaning them in the water and drying them with a *lambrat* or hand cloth."

Unfortunately, though, the story gets off to a slow start and offers less dramatic action than previous ones. You begin to wonder if it's really worth working through the welter of confusing Irish names as it only begins to come to life with the kidnapping of Fidelma – but even this lacks the usual excitement (she is found and rescued comparatively easily) and you have to wait until the storming of the enemy fortress before it gets really exciting.

At one point, a warrior suggests, "We should move on. The longer we stay here discussing things, the more dangerous it becomes." In fact, in this story a great deal of time is spent discussing possibilities and theorising about what might or might not have happened, and this is no substitute for a really gripping plot.

Even Fidelma herself doesn't seem to be quite as interesting or attractive a character as she once was. She seems to get more and more pompous, as when she pronounces, with reference to the drunken Brother Ailgesach, "Intoxication to this degree is reprehensible in one who aspires to be a religious." And it is the long-suffering Eadulf, not her, who first points out that Brother Ailgesach had been murdered whereas Fidelma had supposed he had just choked to death on his own vomit. And it is Eadulf who works out the direction in which her kidnappers' boat must have gone. He seems to have more of the best lines too as when, complaining about being on horseback so often, he comments "I have been sea-sick many, many times. Is there such a malady as horse-sickness? If so, I have had it."

Atonement of Blood (2013)

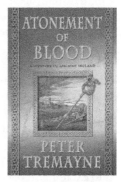

Atonement of Blood is set in the winter of 670 AD. King Colgú has invited the leading nobles and chieftains of his kingdom to a feast day. The gathering is interrupted by a religieux claiming that he has an important message for the King. Suddenly, the man, shouting "Remember Liamuin!' stabs King Colgú. The assassin is slain but Colgú is on the verge of death. Who is behind the assassination attempt? The King's sister, lawyer Fidelma of Cashel, and her husband, Brother Eadulf, are charged with solving the mystery. They must journey into the territory of their archenemies, the Uí Fidgente, where they uncover dark secrets from the past. It all gets very complicated, and even Eadulf admits, "I have never encountered such confusion before."

The story gets off to a really good start with plenty happening to hold the interest, but the plot and lengthy explanations get increasingly tortuous and become bedded down in sentences like "When Nissan had founded the abbey, it was under the patronage of Lomman, son of Erc, Prince of the Uí Fidgente. When Nessan died it was endowed by Prince Manchin, son of Sedna, who claimed descent from Cormac Casa, who maintained that that his people were senior to the Eóghanacht in their claim to the Kingdom of Muman." There is still some exciting action, but Fidelma's lengthy interrogations provide the reader with quite a challenge. Even so, she still has some arresting things to say, such as: "It is said that there are three kinds of men who fail to understand women: young men, old men and middle-aged men."

As usual Fidelma gets herself ambushed and assaulted several times while her son, 3-year-old Alchú, remains left at home under the care of a nurse/foster-mother. Only Eadulf seems to spare him a thought. Fans will still enjoy it, but, except for the opening chapters, the sparkle and brightness of invention of the earlier books are understandingly fading.

The Devil's Seal (2015)

The Devil's Seal is set in the Ireland of AD 671. When a curious deputation of religieux (including the Pope's brother) arrives in Cashel, their motive for coming is far from clear: "It seems," says King Colgú, "that these people have made a very long journey simply to engage in an exercise of pointless speculation and argument." But then one of them is murdered. Is one of them responsible? What was the Venerable Verax, the scholar from Rome, hiding? Was there an evil secret behind  the austere Bishop Arwald? Indeed, what was the real reason behind Eadulf's younger brother Egric's unexpected appearance at Cashel – could he be the culprit? It had been over ten years since Eadulf had last seen him.

Unfortunately, the story lacks some of the suspense, dramatic action and excitement of earlier books, even although there are some eight violent deaths "if you count the boatmen" – and the usual attempt is made on Fidelma's life. Instead, there's a great deal of talk and conjecture which, in the words of King Colgú, begins to get "exceedingly boring."

The lengthy and not always all those relevant explanations of past history, customs and folklore can be quite hard to follow, as here: "Oswy wanted new missionaries to preach the Faith among the Cruthin over whose kingdom he ruled as lord .... Last year, before spring was on us, Oswy died. The Cruthin were then ruled by Drust, son of Donal, who had been a client king under Oswy. The Cruthen had long chafed under what they saw as rule by foreigners, and now they rose up in rebellion .... Things were also changing in Oswy's kingdom. There was a confusion of sub-kings of Deira and Northumbria, each vying for power. Wilfrid, who had led the pro-Roman faction at the great debate at Streonshalh, had obtained almost a king-like power. He began ensuring the removal of many of those who were of the old Columban Church, like Bishop Chad. Presumably he wanted them removed from any position where they might harm his Roman party. Even Oswy's wife, Eanfleda, and her daughter had fled for safety into the abbey of the dead King's relative, Hilda,who also still favours the teaching of Colmcille. Apparently, Wilfrid had full permission of Theodore of Canterbury to pursue these policies, and now Theodore had designated Wilfrid as Bishop of Northumbria."

It was more interesting too when Fidelma still had a religious vocation even if she was "always better suited to law." Even so, she is quite ready to turn down the position of Chief Brehon because she prefers "to be involved in administering the law." It is with people that she (rightly) thinks her strength lies so she is "content to remain an advocate." But she proves a better inquisitor than detective, for in this story her chief suspect manages to get himself murdered.

As you would expect from this author, there are still interesting parts as when Eadulf's unpleasant brother Egric fails to impress Fidelma's four-year-old son Alchú, and there is also a gripping, indeed quite horrifying, description of an amputation carried out by Eadulf. Eadulf, despite his Christian calling, seems quite happy to reassure his dying brother that "If you truly believe in the house of Vali, you will speed yourself to Asgard *(Woden's castle)*, little brother. Woden will be waiting for you ...." "God's speed, little brother," Eadulf wept. "May Woden be ready to greet you in Gladsheim. And may my God forgive me for helping you journey to him rather than to the Heaven of the Christians." So by now even Eadulf does not seem to take his own religion too seriously.

The Second Death *(2015)*

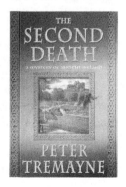

The Second Death follows after the previous book and is also set in Ireland in AD 671. It is almost time for the great fair of Bealtain, and a line of painted wagons is carrying entertainers to Cashel to mark the occasion when one of the carriages is set alight and two corpses are found. Could they have been poisoned? As Sister Fidelma *(she is really no longer a Sister but it is explained that that is how people still think of her, and the publishers*

have good commercial reasons to still refer to her as such on the cover) and her husband, Eadulf, investigate, they are quickly confronted by the mysterious members of the Fellowship of the Raven, and some really exciting situations develop against a background of violent struggles between adherents of the Old Faith and the New Faith of Christianity.

This book marks a real return to form and, once Eadulf gets kidnapped, certainly builds up the suspense. it makes an exciting read. It is interesting too to learn more about Fidelma, who admits that it was a mistake for her to have ever joined the religious just because at the time she "needed some security in life." She can get very sarcastic when talking to her brother, King Colgú: "It was not the first time that Eadulf had witnessed a sibling spat between the two red-haired offspring of King Failbe Flann. They both had short tempers *(and)* did not tolerate fools gladly." She can be impatient too and, when she makes a mistake and gets angry with herself, is liable to get angry with other people too. She seems a very real human being, if not always an entirely attractive one – but it comes as a surprise when she is referred to as still being "a young woman." She must wear her years well, particularly after all the extraordinary adventures she has been through!

Penance of the Damned *(2016)*

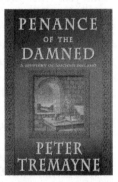

Penance of the Damned follows on from the previous book and is set later in A.D. 671. King Colgú of Cashel is shocked to learn that his loyal Chief Bishop and advisor has been murdered in the old enemy fortress of the Uí Fidgente. When word reaches Cashel that the culprit will be executed under new Penitential law, a larger conflict threatens. Dispatched to investigate, Fidelma and her husband Eadulf discover that the man facing punishment is Gorman – commander of the King's bodyguard. But Fidelma cannot believe Gorman would carry out such an act – and yet he was found locked in a chamber with the body, weapon in hand. The evidence is stacked against him. If they are to save Gorman and keep the peace between the kingdoms, Fidelma and Eadulf must find the true culprit.

As always, the author insists on using as many Irish names and as much Irish vocabulary as he can, although this means he also has to offer numerous translations, a process that can get distinctly clumsy

CLERICAL DETECTIVES

as when Colgú tells Fidelma that he must set off alone into dangerous country and she replies: "Alone? Why not with a *cath*, or battalion, of your *Nasc Niadh*, your bodyguard?." The Irish background is convincingly represented, although pages of sometimes quite unnecessarily detailed explanations of Irish history and customs sometimes slow the action down so that it is only after about a hundred pages that the exciting action really starts.

There are a lot of theological arguments about "Penitentials" that the new self-appointed and hateful Abbot of Imleach is seeking to impose, but there is no really clear explanation of what these are, despite the fact that, as one of the characters put it, they have been "so laboriously" discussed. Fidelma (who explains "I have left the religious – which is not to say I have left the religion") eventually unmasks the abbot for what he is, and the situation is saved by the totally unexpected arrival of Prince Deogaire who suddenly bobs up on page 312. His arrival is a bit too glib – but it's still a good story.

Night of the Lightbringer (2017)

Night of the Lightbringer Is set in Ireland in late 671 A.D. On the eve of a great pagan feast (which "the new faith had not been able to suppress and therefore had tried to absorb"), Brother Eadulf and the warrior Aidan discover a man murdered in an unlit pyre in the heart of Cashel. He had been dressed in the robes of a religieux and killed by the ritualistic "three deaths." When a strange woman, known as Brancheo, appears in a raven-feather cloak, fortelling ancient gods returning to exact revenge upon the mortal world, she is quickly branded a suspect.

Fidelma (who is still wrongly called *Sister* Fidelma on the cover and publisher's blurb, but is now acting as legal adviser to her brother the king), helped by husband Eadulf, discovers a link to a mysterious missing book that has been stolen from the Papal Secret Archives and could lead to the destruction of Christendom. Hardly the world's most original idea!

Fidelma, to whom "law and justice are more important than which ideas one should adopt with regard to religion," and who had been craving for "some real mystery to unravel, some conundrum that needs an explanation," proves once again to be a dogged investigator, and there is plenty for her to look into, including a heavily fortified nearby abbey which has adopted the heretical Psilanthropist belief that Jesus was an ordinary man, and where she spots what may be the missing book.

As always, there are some fascinating glimpses into life at the time, as when it is explained that "there are six classes of tooth injury and the penalties vary according to the social status of the victim," but some of the other historical explanations seem over-lengthy, as do Fidelma's extended interrogations of possible suspects. She turns out to be remarkably agile so, when she decided to break into the heretical abbey, "it took her but little time to scale the wooden walls of the Abbey's garden" before clambering up ivy to reach a conveniently open window and once again "surprisingly, it did not take her too long." Then equally conveniently, she was able to eavesdrop a totally incriminating conversation before being knocked out, "falling into a dark space, twisting and turning in a never-ending abyss." It all seems a little too predictable. After her inevitable if rather unconvincing rescue, the story ends with a lengthy series of explanations by Fidelma which come as something of an anti-climax.

Despite a slow start, the story does have some exciting moments, but not as many as in the best of the earlier books.

Bloodmoon (2018)

Bloodmoon is also set in 671 A.D. and continues from where the previous book left off. It describes how Fidelma (she is, of course, no longer Sister Fidelma despite what it says not only on the cover but even on the list of characters) has a mission, but is sworn by a mysterious *guis*, a secret oath, to reveal her purpose to nobody, not even Eadulf, her husband (who oddly is described just as her *companion* in the list of characters), who accompanies her but feels natural resentment about being kept in the dark.

Fidelma says they, together with the warrior Enda, should travel to the abbey of Finnbarr to question the Abbot. But before they have a chance to speak to him, he is found murdered – and the young girl suspected of the crime has fled the scene. This leads to Fidelma travelling far by land and water while vicious rumours are spreading, accusing her family, the Eóganacht, of conspiring to assassinate the High King and abduct his wife, and Fidelma's own life is repeatedly threatened and she has to rely on her own skill at unarmed combat before being shipped off to be a slave. You can't complain that nothing happens! It is all more interesting than the previous book as there are many more dramatic incidents that make vivid reading, but the pace is slowed down by the inclusion of lengthy explanations couched in language like this: *"Your brother is not the only Eóganacht Prince, lady. Finnbarr's Abbey is in the territory of the Eóganacht Raithland and Nessan was of that branch. But are there not also the Eóganacht Aine, the Airthir Chliach, the Glemdamnach, the Locha Lein? Don't forget even the Uí Fidgenti claim to be Eóganacht, as descendants of Cormac Cas, the brother of Eóghan."* Even with the accents left out, as here, it doesn't exactly flow smoothly from the tongue, and there are other examples too of the author telling us much more than we really need to know. Even Eadulf gets to wondering "why there was never a simple answer" and Fidelma herself admits,"It all seems so confusing." But it still makes an enjoyable read.

Blood in Eden (2019)

Blood in Eden is set in Ireland in AD 672. The hamlet of Cloichin is said to be a veritable Eden, with its prosperous farms and close-knit, friendly community. But when Sister Fidelma and Eadulf arrive, they soon find that the garden is not without its serpents: a new priest has ordered the villagers to lynch a man accused of murdering a local farmer, his wife and two sons. The only evidence they hold against him is the fact that he is a stranger to their land. In the dramatic opening, Fidelma saves the man's life, determined that he should have a fair trial, but finds that one problem leads to another, and we end up with "six murders, one being an illegal hanging, and one abduction plus an attempted murder ... oh, and a second attempt at an illegal hanging." Not to mention a possible attempt on Fidelma's life.

The villagers are led on by murderous Brother Garda, who calls himself Father, (much to Fidelma's disgust) and who champions the New Faith that has come from Rome. He tries to dismiss Fidelma and her legal authority, telling her, "You cite your pagan law when you should be obeying the laws given you by the New Faith ... You will obey the law of God or perish." But Fidelma is never one to give in to threats and is quick to remind Garda and everyone else of her legal qualifications, until even Eadulf wearily complains that he has heard of them "enough times."

Much of the appeal of the story lies in the vivid description of life at the time, as when we learn about the inheritance rights of women, the fosterage system for children, and still-surviving pre-Christian beliefs about the Otherworld, the land of the Ever Young: "When someone died in this world, that were reborn in the next. When someone died in the Otherworld, they were reborn in this." So, death in this world was a time for rejoicing "because it means a soul has been reborn in the Otherworld. We mourn birth in this world because it means a soul has died in the Otherworld."

As always, the Irish names can get very confusing, but there is plenty here to hold the interest. It is the 30th book in the series, and one cannot but congratulate the author on such an achievement, even if the list of principal characters at the front still shows Fidelma as Sister Fidelma and describes Eadulf as her companion not her husband.

The Shapeshifter's Lair (2020)

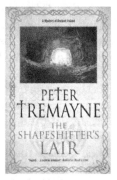

The Shapeshifter's Lair is set in AD 672. When Abbot Daircell identifies a dead body as that of Brehon Brocc, who had been travelling to the remote abbey on a secret mission with Princess Gelgeis (who was betrothed to King Colgú), Colgú sends his sister, Fidelma, to find out what has happened to the missing princess. This gets the story off to an interesting start, especially as there was still widespread belief in the Aos Sí, "supernatural demons who seduce the unwary into their mountain lairs" and become demonic shapeshifters who can transform themselves into the bodies of wild animals.

Further deaths follow and Fidelma learns about possible brigand activity involving the old gold and silver mines and at times this gets rather tedious. However, helped by Eadulf and the warrior Enda, Fidelma successfully finds the missing princess. It seems a pity that Fidelma had left the religious but she tells Eadulf that she had only joined those who had taken advantage of the New Faith "to obtain security." Interesting new characters include the cackling old soothsayer Iuchra and the arrogant

CLERICAL DETECTIVES

young Aroc who proudly identifies herself as the daughter of a nobleman and tries, unsuccessfully of course, to put Fidelma in her place.

The House of Death (2021)

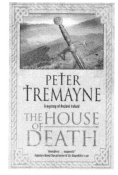

The House of Death starts in April 672 as the once druidic Feast of Lá-Bealtaine is approaching. The seven senior princes of the kingdom of Muman are gathering at Cashel to discuss King Colgú's policies. Just days before the council meets, Brother Conchobhar, the keeper of the sacred sword, is found murdered. Fidelma fears that the killer may have been trying to steal the sword that symbolises her brother's authority to rule. Then news reaches Cashel that a plague ship has landed at a nearby port, bringing the deadly pestilence ashore and causing dismay and panic (all very reminiscent of Covid, in fact). As the death toll mounts, Fidelma, Eadulf, and Enda, the commander of the household guard, face imminent death in their struggle to discover what is going on.

As usual, the story gets off to a really interesting start, and the action scenes (including the discovery of hidden underground chambers, once reputed to be the entrance to the Otherworld) certainly hold the interest, even if this sometimes flags during some of the lengthy conversations in which Fidelma gets engaged. However, there are some new and entertaining characters, such as the arrogant and vain physician, Brother Laig, and the demanding Brother Fidach who insists on being addressed as Father, in keeping with the latest teaching from Rome. Fidelma disagrees with him about this and also much prefers the old idea of confessing sins to a soul friend rather than to a priest like him.

There is also Sister Ernmas, a strange and sinister mystery religieuse with a talent for vanishing at will. Even Fidelma does not know what to make of her, and finds it all very frustrating. And Fidelma is far from happy when the Chief Brehon arrives, as his is a role that she had so much wanted for herself that she had formally left the religious life in order to make herself more available.

There is the usual plethora of difficult, if not impossible, Irish names, and you can't help wondering if the author isn't sometimes having a private joke by seeing how many he can include in a single paragraph. But, although this is the 32nd book in the series, it still makes an engaging read.

THE SISTER FIDELMA COMPENDIUM

Editor's note: The reviewer of these novels also has an extensive website of numerous other clerical detectives. Of interest to Fidelma fans is the good Sister's "ranking" in two separate listings (among several others).

When answering his own question – "Which Are The Very Best Clerical Detectives?" – of the mere handful he lists out of the hundreds on his website which he has read AND reviewed:

- **Sister Fidelma** (by Peter Tremayne). A fascinating portrayal of 7th century Ireland when the Celtic church allowed monks and nuns to marry, there were mixed sex monasteries, and women could rise to high levels in the legal profession.

And in his "A Beginner's Guide to Detective Nuns (of whom there are too many, particularly medieval ones)," at the very top of his list:

- The most intriguing and most well-connected nun?
  - **Sister Fidelma**

– Philip Grosset
www.detecs.org

A Checklist of the Works of Peter Berresford Ellis

SISTER FIDELMA SERIES

Listed in chronological order of UK publication – novels and collections of short stories, as Peter Tremayne:

- *Absolution By Murder* (1994)
- *Shroud for the Archbishop* (1995)
- *Suffer Little Children* (1995)
- *The Subtle Serpent* (1996)
- *The Spider's Web* (1997)
- *Valley of the Shadow* (1998)
- *The Monk Who Vanished* (1999)
- *Act of Mercy* (1999)
- *Our Lady of Darkness* (2000)
- *Hemlock At Vespers* (2000)
- *Smoke in the Wind* (2001)
- *The Haunted Abbot* (2002)
- *Badger's Moon* (2003)
- *Whispers of the Dead* (2004)
- *The Leper's Bell* (2004)
- *Master of Souls* (2005)
- *A Prayer for the Damned* (2006)
- *Dancing With Demons* (2007)
- *The Council of the Cursed* (2008)
- *The Dove of Death* (2009)
- *The Chalice of Blood* (2010)
- *Behold a Pale Horse* (2011)
- *The Seventh Trumpet* (2012)
- *Atonement of Blood* (2013)

- *The Devil's Seal* (2014)
- *The Second Death* (2015)
- *Penance of the Damned* (2016)
- *Night of the Lightbringer* (2017)
- *Die Wahrheit ist der L'ge Tod* (world first of uncollected novellas and short stories) (2018)
- *Bloodmoon*(2018)
- *Blood in Eden* (2019)
- *The Shpeshifter's Lair* (2020)
- *The House of Death* (2021)
- *Death of a Heretic* (2022)

NON-FICTION
Listed in chronological order under first world publication (mainly UK but with first US publication where applicable).

- *Wales – A National Again: The Nationalist Struggle for Freedom*, Foreword by Gwynfor Evans MP. Library 33 Ltd., London, 1968
- *The Scottish Insurrection of 1820*, Co-authored with Seumas Mac a' Ghobhainn. Foreword by Hugh MacDiarmid. Victor Gollancz Ltd, London, 1970
- *The Problem of Language Revival: Examples of Language Survivals*, Co-authored with Seumas Mac a' Ghobhainn, Club Leabhar Ltd., Inverness, Scotland, 1971
- *A History of the Irish Working Class*, Victor Gollancz Ltd, London, 1972
- *James Connolly: Selected Writings*, Edited with an introduction. Pelican Books, Penguin Ltd., London, 1973. (1st US edition, Monthly Review Press, hardcover, New York, 1973)
- *The Cornish Language and its Literature*, Routledge & Kegan Paul ltd, 1974
- *Hell or Connaught: The Cromwellian Colonisation of Ireland 1652-1660*, Hamish Hamilton, London, 1975. (1st US edition, St Martin's Press, hardcover, New York, 1975)

A PETER BERRESFORD ELLIS CHECKLIST

- *The Boyne Water: The Battle of the Boyne, 1690*, Hamish Hamilton, London, 1976 (1st US edition, St Martin's Press, hardcover, New York, 1976)
- *The Great Fire of London: An Illustrated Account*, New English Library, London, 1977
- *Caesar's Invasion of Britain*, Orbis Publishing, London, 1978. (1st US edition, New York University Press, hardcover, 1980)
- *H. Rider Haggard: A Voice from the Infinite*, Routledge & Kegan Paul, London, 1978
- *Macbeth: High King of Scotland 1040-57*, Frederick Muller Ltd, London, 1980. (1st US edition, Barnes & Noble, New York, 1993)
- *By Jove, Biggles! The Life of Captain W.E. Johns*, Co-author Piers Williams, W.H. Allen, London 1981
- *The Liberty Tree – A Novel*, Michael Joseph, London, 1982
- *The Last Adventurer: The Life of Talbot Mundy 1879-1940*, Donald M. Grant Publishers Inc, Rhode Island, USA. 1984
- *Celtic Inheritance*, Frederick Muller Ltd, London, 1985. (1st US edition, Dorset Press, hardcover, New York, 1992)
- *The Celtic Revolution: A Study in Anti-Imperialism*, Y Lolfa Cyf, Ceredigion, Wales, 1985
- *The Rising of the Moon: A Novel of the Fenian Invasion of Canada*, Methuen, London, 1987. (1st US edition, St Martin's Press, hardcover, New York, 1987)
- *A Dictionary of Irish Mythology*, Constable, London, 1987. (1st US edition, ABC Clio, hardcover, Santa Barbara, California, 1989)
- *The Celtic Empire: The First Millennium of Celtic History 1000 BC-AD 51*, Constable, London, 1990. (1st US edition, Carolina Academic Press, hardcover, North Carolina, 1991)
- *A Guide to Early Celtic Remains in Britain*, Constable Guides, London, 1991
- *Dictionary of Celtic Mythology*, Constable, London, 1992. (1st US edition from ABC Clio, Santa Barbara, California, 1992)
- *Celt and Saxon: The Struggle for Britain AD 410-937*, Constable, London, 1993
- *The Celtic Dawn: A History of Pan Celticism*, Constable, London, 1993

THE SISTER FIDELMA COMPENDIUM

- *The Book of Deer (Constable Library of Celtic Illuminated Manuscripts)*, art by Roy Ellsworth and text by Peter Berresford Ellis. Constable, 1994
- *The Druids*, Constable, London, 1994. (1st US edition, Wm. Eerdmans, hardcover, Grand Rapids, Michigan, 1995)
- *Celtic Women: Women in Celtic Society and Literature*, Constable, London, 1995. (1st US edition, Wm. Eerdmans, Grand Rapids, Michigan, 1996)
- *Celt and Greek: Celts in the Hellenic World*, Constable, London, 1997
- *Celt and Roman: The Celts in Italy*, Constable, London, 1998. (1st US edition, St Martin's Press, hardcover, New York, 1998)
- *The Ancient World of the Celts*, Constable, London, 1999. (1st US edition, Barnes & Noble, New York, 1999).
- *The Chronicles of the Celts: New tellings of their myths and legends*, Robinson, London, 1999. (1st US edition, Carroll & Graf, hardcover, New York, 1999)
- *Erin's Blood Royal: The Gaelic Noble Dynasties of Ireland*, Constable, London, 1999. (1st US edition, extensively revised and expanded, Palgrave/St Martin's, hardcover, New York, 2002)
- *Over the Hills and Far Away: A Hurstpierpoint Soldier in Wellington's Army*, Hurst History Study Group, Hurstpierpoint, Sussex. 2002
- *Eyewitness to Irish History*, John Wiley & Sons Inc, New York, 2004
- *The Shadow of Mr Vivian: The Life of E. Charles Vivian 1882-1947* PS Publishing, UK. September 2014, ISBN 978-1-848637-83-2

PAMPHLETS

Some of Ellis's pamphlets have been previous listed on sites as books. But these pamphlets are:

- *The Creed of the Celtic Revolution*, Introduction By F.A. Ridley, Medusa Press, London, 1969
- *The Story of the Cornish Language*, Tor Mark Press, Cornwall, 1971

A PETER BERRESFORD ELLIS CHECKLIST

- *Revisionism in Irish Historical Writing: The New Anti-Nationalist School of Historians*, A Connolly Association Broadhseet, London, 1989. (Text of Peter's 1989 C. Desmond Greaves Memorial Lecture at Conway Hall, London)
- *The Cornish Saints*, Tor Mark Press, Cornwall, 1992
- *Orangeism: Myth and Reality*, Connolly Association Broadsheet, London, 1997. (Text of Peter's lecture at the Irish Labour History Museum, Dublin, 1995)

AS PETER TREMAYNE

As well as the Sister Fidelma series, under the pseudonym "Peter Tremayne," Ellis has written many novels and short stories, the majority inspired by Celtic myth and legend.

- *The Hound of Frankenstein*, Ventura Books, London, 1977. (1st US edition included in *The Mammoth Book of Frankenstein*, Carroll & Graf, New York, 1994)
- *Dracula Unborn*, Corgi/Bailey Bros, London, 1977. (1st US edition, Walker & Co, hardcover, New York, 1979)
- *Masters of Terror 1: William Hope Hodgson*, Edited and introduced. Corgi Books, London, 1977
- *The Vengeance of She*, Sphere Books, London, 1978
- *The Revenge of Dracula*, Bailey Bros, Folkestone, 1978. (1st US edition, Donald M. Grant Inc, Rhode Island (illustrated collectors' edition) 1978; 1st popular edition from Walker & Co (hardcover) New York, 1979
- *The Ants*, Sphere Books, London, 1979. (1st US edition, Signet Books, paperback, New York, 1980)
- *Irish Masters of Fantasy*, Introduced and edited. Wolfhound Press, Dublin, 1979
- *The Curse of Loch Ness*, Sphere Books, London, 1979
- *The Fires of Lan-Kern*, Bailey bros, Folkestone. 1980. (1st US edition, St Martin's, hardcover, New York, 1980)
- *Dracula, My Love*, Bailey Bros, Folkestone, 1980. (1st US edition, Dell/Emerald, paperback, New York, 1983)
- *Zombie*, Sphere Books, London, 1981. (1st US edition, St Martin's Press, paperback, New York, 1987)

ZHE SISZER FIDELMA COMPENDIUM

- *The Return of Raffles.* Magnum/Methuen Books, London 1981
- *The Morgow Rises!* Sphere Books, London, 1982
- *The Destroyers of Lan-Kern*, Methuen, London, 1982
- *The Buccaneers of Lan-Kern*, Methuen, London, 1983
- *Snowbeast!* Sphere Books, London, 1983
- *Raven of Destiny*, Methuen, London, 1984 (1st US edition, Signet Books, paperback, New York, 1986)
- *Kiss of the Cobra*, Sphere Books, London, 1984
- *Swamp!* Sphere Books, London, 1984 (1st US edition, St Martin's Press, paperback, New York, 1989)
- *Angelus!* Panther Books, London, 1985
- *Nicor!* Sphere Books, London, 1987
- *Trollnight*, Sphere Books, London, 1987
- *My Lady of Hy Brasil and other Stories*, Donald M. Grant Inc, Rhode Island, USA, 1987
- *Ravenmoon*, Methuen, London, 1988 (1st US edition, Baen Books, paperback, New York, 1988)
- *Island of Shadows*, Methuen/Mandarin, London, 1991
- *Aisling and other Irish Tales of Terror*, Brandon Books, Ireland, 1992
- *An Ensuing Evil: Fourteen Historical Mystery Stories*, New York, 2006

KINDLE EDITIONS – EBOOKS

Endeavour Press Ltd
- **Peter Tremayne**
  - *The Return of Raffles* 1981 pub date – May 1, 2017

- **Peter MacAan**
  - *The Judas Battalion*, 1983 – January 2, 2017
  - *Airship*, 1984 – February 12, 2017
  - *The Confession*, 1985

A PETER BERRESFORD ELLIS CHECKLIST

- ○ *Kitchener's Gold*, 1986 – April 9, 2017
- ○ *The Valkyrie Directive*, 1987 – April 3, 2017
- ○ *The Doomsday Decree*, 1988 – June 26, 2017
- ○ *Fireball*, 1991 – May 1, 2017
- ○ *The Windsor Protocol*, 1993 – June 26, 2017

Venture Press (Imprint of Endeavour Press Ltd)
All Peter Tremayne titles

- ○ *Raven of Destiny*, 1984 (Irish mythos/fantasy trilogy) – September 26, 2018
- ○ *Ravenmoon*, 1988 – June 13, 2017
- ○ *Island of Shadows*, 1991 – May 11, 2017
- ○ *The Vengeance of She*, 1978 – October 4, 2018
- ○ *The Ants*, 1979 – May 2, 2017
- ○ *The Curse of Lock Ness*, 1979 – August 7, 2017
- ○ *Zombie*, 1981
- ○ *The Morgow Rises*, 1982 – April 28, 2017
- ○ *Kiss of the Cobra*, 1984 – Juune 29, 2017
- ○ *Swamp*, 1985 – July 5, 2017
- ○ *Nicor!*, 1987 – March15, 2017
- ○ *Trollnight*, 1987 – November 22, 2017
- ○ *Snowbeast* – October 25, 3017

SHORT STORIES

For avid collectors of Ellis's work, it should be noted that as of 2018 he has produced over 100 short stories, including 1 short story as Peter MacAlan and 1 story as Peter Berresford Ellis.

- "What's In A Name?" (as Peter Berresford Ellis) *Stornoway Gazette*, Scotland, April 24, 1971
- "The Eye of Shiva" (as Peter MacAlan) The Mammoth Book of Historical Detectives, ed. Mike Ashley, Robinson, London, 1995. Subsequently reprinted as by Peter Tremayne in the collection *An Ensuing Evil*

Non-Fidelma Short Stories as Peter Tremayne

- "Plant Change!," *Camden Journal*, London, December 21, 1979
- "The Ploughing of Pra-a-Ufereth," *Cornish Banner*, August 1 and November 1, 1980
- "Dracula's Chair," *The Count Dracula Fan Club Book of Vampires*, ed. Jeanne Youngson, Adams Press, Chicago, USA, 1980
- "Reflections on a Dark Eye," *Fantasy Tales*, London, Spring, 1981
- "The Lane," *Fantasycon VII Programme Booklet*, Birmingham, July 1981
- "The Hungry Grass," Freak Show Vampire, ed. Jeanne Youngson, Adams Press, Chicago, 1981
- "The Storm Devil of Lan-Kern," *Fantasy Tales*, Winter 1982
- "Snakefright," *Eldritch Tales*, Kansas, USA, February 1983
- "The Imshee," *Weirdbook*, USA, July 1982
- "The Kelpie's Mark," *Fantasy Macabre*, London, July 1983
- "The Last Gift," *Masters of Terror 1: Peter Tremayne*, British Fantasy Society, London, March 1984
- "The Hudolion," *Eldritch Tales*, Kansas, USA, May 1984
- "My Lady of Hy-Brasil," *Kadath*, Genoa, Italy, Fall 1984
- "Feis na Samhna," *Feasta*, (Irish language first publication) November 1984 (English version first in *Halloween Horrors* ed. Alan Ryan, Doubleday, USA, 1986
- "Aisling," *Weirdbook*, USA, Spring, 1985
- "The Pooka," *Shadows 8*, ed. Charles L. Grant, Doubleday, USA, 1985
- "The Singing Stone," *Fantasy Tales*, London, Winter 1986
- "Deathstone," *Winter Chills*, London, January 1987
- "Tavesher," *Shadows 9*, ed. Charles L. Grant, Doubleday, USA, 1986
- "Buggane," *Chillers for Christmas*, ed. Richard Dalby, O'Mara Books, London, October 1989
- "The Mongfind," *Weirdbook*, USA, Autumn, 1990
- "Fear a' Gorta," *Final Shadows*, ed. Charles L. Grant, Doubleday, USA, 1991
- "The Oath of the Saxon," *The Camelot Chronicles*, ed. Mike Ashley, Robinson, London, 1992

A PETER BERRESFORD ELLIS CHECKLIST

- "Daoine Domhain," *Weirdbook*, USA, Autumn 1993
- "The Dreeador," first published in *Aisling and other Irish Tales of Terror*, 1992
- "Amhrana," first published in *Aisling and other Irish Tales of Terror*, 1992
- "Marbh Beo," *The Mammoth Book of Zombies*, ed. Stephen Jones, Robinson, London, October 1993
- "The Foxes of Fascoumb," *The Mammoth Book of Werewolves*, ed. Stephen Jones, Robinson, London, 1994
- "The Last Warrior Quest," *Great Irish Tales of the Unimaginable*, ed. Peter Haining, Souvenir Press, London, 1994
- "Son of Dracula," *The Vampire Omnibus*, ed. Peter Haining, Orion Books, London, 1995
- "The Temptations of Merlin," *The Merlin Chronicles*, ed. Mike Ashley, Robinson Publishing, London, 1995
- "The Banquet of Death," *Classical Stories*, ed. Mike Ashley, Robinson, 1996
- "My Name Upon the Wind," *The Vampire Hunter's Casebook*, ed. Peter Haining Warner Books, London, 1996
- "The Magic Bowl," *The Chronicles of the Holy Grail*, ed. Mike Ashley, Robinson, 1996
- "The Way of the White Cow," *Great Irish Stories of Childhood*, ed. Peter Haining, Souvenir Press, London, 1997
- "The Family Curse," *Dancing With the Dark*, ed. Stephen Jones, Cassell, London, 1997
- "Knight of the Golden Collar," *The Chronicles of the Round Table*, ed. Mike Ashley, Robinson, 1997
- "An Ensuing Evil," *Shakespearean Whodunnits*, ed. Mike Ashley, Robinson, 1997
- "The Affray at the Kildare Street Club," *New Sherlock Holmes Adventures*, ed. Mike Ashley Robinson, 1997
- "Methought You Saw a Serpent," *Shakespearean Detectives*, ed. Mike Ashley, Robinson, London, 1998
- "Nights Black Angels," *Royal Whodunnits: Tales of Eight Royal Murder and Mystery*, ed. Mike Ashley, Robinson, London, 1999

- "Murder in the Air," *The Mammoth Book of Locked Room Mysteries and Impossible Crimes*, ed. Mike Ashley, Robinson, London, 2000
- "The Spectre of Tullyfane Abbey," *Villains Victorious*, ed. Martin H. Greenberg & John Helfers, DAW Books, USA, 2001
- "The Revenge of the Gunner's Daughter," *The Mammoth Book of Hearts of Oak*, ed. Mike Ashley, Robinson, London, 2000
- "The Siren of Sennen Cover," *Murder in Baker Street: New Tales of Sherlock Holmes*, ed. Martin H. Greenberg, Carroll & Graf, New York, 2001
- "The Bridge of Sighs," *Phantoms of Venice*, ed. David Sutton, Shadow Publishing, UK, 2001
- "Let the Game Begin," *Much Ado About Murder*, ed. Anne Perry, Berkley, New York, 2002
- "A Study in Orange," *My Sherlock Holmes, Untold Stories of the Great Detective*, ed. Michael Kurland, St Martins New York, 2003
- "The Kidnapping of Mycroft Holmes," *The Strand Magazine*, No 10, USA, 2003
- "The Passing Shadow," *Death by Dickens*, ed. Anne Perry, Berkley, New York, 2004
- "For the Blood is the Life," *Emerald Magic*, Andrew M. Greeley, Tor Books, New York, 2004
- "A Walking Shadow," *The Strand Magazine*, No 15, USA, 2005
- "Satan in the Star Chamber," *The Mammoth Book of Jacobean Whodunnnits*, ed. Mike Ashley, Robinson, London, 2006
- "The Stuart Sapphire," *The Mammoth Book of Perfect Crimes and Impossible Mysteries*, ed. Mike Ashley, Robinson, London, 2006
- "The Case of the Panicking Policeman," *The Strand Magazine*, No 20, 2006
- "The Fiery Devil," *The Mammoth Book of Dickensian Whodunnits*, ed. Mike Ashley, Robinson, London, 2007
- "Fear No More the Heat O' Sun," *Ellery Queen Mystery Magazine*, NYC, February 2010
- "The Case of the Reluctant Assassin," *Sherlock Holmes: The American Years*, ed. Michael Kurland, St Martins, NY, 2010

A PETER BERRESFORD ELLIS CHECKLIST

- "This Thing of Darkness," *Ellery Queen Mystery Magazine,* NYC, May 2011
- "Now Go We In Content," *Ellery Queen Mystery Magazine,* NYC, March/April, 2022

THRILLER NOVELS AS PETER MACALAN
He has also published eight thriller novels as Peter MacAlan. These are:

- *The Judas Battalion,* W.H. Allen, London, 1983
- *Airship,* W.H. Allen, London, 1984
- *The Confession,* W.H. Allen, London, 1985
- *Kitchener's Gold,* W.H. Allen, London, 1986
- *The Valkyrie Directive,* W.H. Allen, London, 1987
- *The Doomsday Decree,* W.H. Allen, London, 1988
- *Fireball,* Severn House, London, 1991
- *The Windsor Protocol,* Severn House, London, 1993

Overall, Ellis's works have appeared in 25 languages. His signed articles are almost too numerous to count and include several academic papers in the field of Celtic culture and history.

THE SISTER FIDELMA COMPENDIUM

CHE INTERNATIONAL SISTER FIDELMA SOCIETY

The International Sister Fidelma Society

I have known OF Peter Berresford Ellis for many years – mainly because I was a history major lo those many years ago in college. While my main field of study was Ancient Near Eastern history, I strayed during my graduate years into a broader spectrum of history, including medieval European literature. At the same time, I was investing more and more effort tracing my genealogical roots, which by happy occurrence, and through no real effort on my part, proved that I was a fortunate descendant of individuals of this fair island.

Years later, through our mutual membership in a now-defunct organization best left to the dust of memory, I became more aware of Peter's widely varied writing projects. Imagine my surprise to learn that the preeminent Celtic historian of our time was actually the pen behind recent incarnations of zombies, Dracula, a hound of Frankenstein, and more. Surely this was a different fellow – not the keen intellect behind the incredible wealth of Irish history on which I was weaned. But, a bit further studied showed that, not only was he a well-respected Irish historian, but a prolific author of fiction as well. For those who aren't aware of Peter's extensive output, I would recommend a review of our website for complete details.

In 2000 I worked up the courage to ask the permission (and cooperation) of Peter to set up a website devoted to the Sister Fidelma Mysteries. Now, let me say right from the beginning – I am NOT an avid fiction reader. I simply can't sit still through even the best of books. I am much more likely to be found PRODUCING than reading – though I am in no way a writer. My productivity falls in the realm of graphics – artwork for websites, creation and redesign of websites, production of marketing material for various clients, and the like. My other primary love is heraldry – something which piqued my interest while doing my aforementioned genealogical research, and a science and art form which has held my attention for over 3 decades, leading me to my current position as Executive Director of The American College of Heraldry.

So, if I am not an avid reader of fiction – though I can devour nonfiction – why would I have an interest in promoting some obscure 7th century nun and her author? Simply put – the Sister Fidelma mysteries held my attention like no other fiction I had come across before. While I don't live, breathe, eat and sleep the series – I don't wish to shock, but must be honest with you – I do appreciate the mix of the historical setting with stories that keep the mind enthralled and eager to watch the stories develop to their conclusion.

So, back to the website, for which I asked permission to develop. Originally it was intended merely as a reference site to "catalog" the works of Peter Berresford Ellis (and Peter Tremayne – I guess I HAD to include him). Within a few months of it being posted, an overwhelming number of people contacted the website to ask if some association or society for enthusiasts of the series could be formed. Hadn't thought of something like that – I was, and am, already involved in numerous other societies and organizations, usually handling the creation and/or editing of their publications, creating and maintaining their websites, etc. – but it didn't originally occur to me to develop any sort of Society. After all, I was not a rabid reader of Peter's fiction – but that's where the bulk of the inquiries were coming from.

So, again, I pestered Peter, who, though I was certain was becoming annoyed with this upstart American constantly badgering him, was de-lighted to become the official patron of such a Society.

Thus, in January 2001, The International Sister Fidelma Society was launched. The website was expanded to include a great deal more infor-mation on Peter, and his books, focusing primarily on Fidelma.

Almost immediately a modest print magazine, *The Brehon*, was launched and distributed to everyone in our small but die-hard circle of members throughout the world as part of their subscription. The magazine has appeared regularly ever since and we have attracted quite a number of distinguished contributors, from authors and anthology editors such as Peter Haining and Mike Ashley, to academics such as Professor Ed O'Rielly, Dr Michelle Klingfus, and Dr John Scaggs (who is graciously contributing his time to be here with us here this weekend). Likewise, we have published article from US attorney Wallace Johnson, as well as our highly prized regular contributor, Maurice McCann (also with us today), a founder member, who is also an author.

Peter himself has allowed us to publish some of his articles, and even given us rights on the first publication of two Fidelma short stories as a tribute to his fans – hopefully only the beginning of such a trend (hint hint).

It has been truly amazing to see the diversity of people who are united in their admiration of the books. The membership roster for the Society justifies the "International" part of our moniker – with members from the

ᏖᎻᎬ ᏆᏁᏖᎬᏒᏁᎪᏖᏆᎾᏁᎪᏞ ᏚᏆᏚᏖᎬᏒ ᎱᏆᎠᎬᏞᎷᎪ ᏚᎾᏟᏆᎬᏖᎩ

United States, Ireland, Great Britain, the Netherlands, Germany, Australia, Japan, South Africa, France, Canada, Brazil, Austria and Scotland. And those are strictly fans of Peter's one series of fiction works – we should also remember that he is widely admired for his scholastic non-fiction books written under his real name of Peter Berresford Ellis.

The praise that critics have showered on the Fidelma Mysteries continues to pour in. One recent critical review from G.V. Whelan (also known as the novelist O.R. Melling), writing in Books Ireland about *The Leper's Bell* and *Whispers of the Dead*, stated:

What a concept! A seventh century Irish Nancy Drew in the guise of a young female cleric who is a trained legal advocate in ancient Irish law ... Fidelma is an original and complex character; brilliant, analytical, emotionally withdrawn, touchy and testy, and conflicted over her relationship with the Irish-trained Saxon, Brother Eadulf. As with the other books in the series, this is a good read, well-paced and suspenseful, sprinkled with Old Irish terms and fascinating detail of early Irish life, food, habits, dress et cetera. I confess to being a fan of the intrepid Sister and this collection of fifteen short stories provides an excellent opportunity for any reader to discover if he or she, too, will succumb to Fidelmania. I'm not surprised there's talk of a television series. An Irish heroine for both the seventh and twenty-first centuries, here is a character more credible and captivating than Xena the Warrior Princess!'

In fact, Signet Books of New York summed up the general consensus of the reviews as being nothing less than "stellar."

As "Fidelmania" continues to grow, we continue to build new members across the world.

– David Robert Wooten
From several talks at Féile Fidelmas, updated for this volume

Feile Fidelma 2019

Attendees of Féile Fidelma 2017

Attendees of Féile Fidelma 2014

Attendees of Féile Fidelma 2012

THE INTERNATIONAL SISTER FIDELMA SOCIETY

Attendees of Féile Fidelma 2010

Attendees of Féile Fidelma 2008

Attendees of Féile Fidelma 2006

THE SISTER FIDELMA COMPENDIUM

SISTER FIDELMA'S TRAVELS
LOCATIONS BY TITLE

FIDELMA'S WORLD
ÉIRE
THE FIVE KINGDOMS
7TH CENTURY AD

1 ABSOLUTION BY MURDER
  (WHITBY, NORTHUMBRIA)
2 SHROUD FOR THE ARCHBISHOP
  (ROME, ITALY)
3 SUFFER LITTLE CHILDREN
4 THE SUBTLE SERPENT
5 THE SPIDER'S WEB
6 VALLEY OF THE SHADOW
7 THE MONK WHO VANISHED
8 ACT OF MERCY
  (VOYAGE TO SANTIAGO DE COMPOSTELLA)
9 HEMLOCK AT VESPERS
  (15 SHORT STORIES VARIOUS LOCATIONS)
10 OUR LADY OF DARKNESS
11 SMOKE IN THE WIND
  (DYFED, WALES)
12 THE HAUNTED ABBOT
  (SUFFOLK, EAST ANGLIA)
13 BADGER'S MOON

14 WHISPERS OF THE DEAD
  (15 SHORT STORIES VARIOUS LOCATIONS)
15 THE LEPER'S BELL
16 MASTER OF SOULS
17 A PRAYER FOR THE DAMNED
18 DANCING WITH DEMONS
19 THE COUNCIL OF THE CURSED
  (AUTUN, BURGUNDY)
20 THE DOVE OF DEATH
  (MOR BIHAN, BRITTANY)
21 THE CHALICE OF BLOOD
22 BEHOLD A PALE HORSE
  (BOBBIO, TREBBIA)
23 THE SEVENTH TRUMPET
24 ATONEMENT OF BLOOD
25 THE DEVIL'S SEAL
26 THE SECOND DEATH
27 PENANCE OF THE DAMNED

28 NIGHT OF THE LIGHTBRINGER
29 BLOODMOON
30 BLOOD IN EDEN
31 THE SHAPESHIFTER'S LAIR
32 THE HOUSE OF DEATH
33 DEATH OF A HERETIC

423

EADULF'S WORLD

BIBLIOGRAPHY OF BOOKS RELATING TO CASHEL

Towards A Bibliography Of Books Relating To Cashel And By Cashel People

- *Sanas Cormac* compiled by Cormac Ua Cuilennain, King-Bishop of Cashel in the 10th century, the first known Irish "dictionary".

- *Vision of Tnudgal* written by Brother Marcus of Cashel c. 1148-1150, which is an aisling saga about a Cashel warrior who journeys to Cork and has a vision of the Otherworld. The best English version is translated by Jean-Michel Picard and Yolande de Pontfarcy, Four Courts Press, Dublin, 1989.

- *Caithreim Cheallachain Chaisil* (The Battle-History of Ceallachain of Cashel) which was translated into English and published by Professor Alexander Bugge, University of Christiana, Det Norske Historishe Kilderkritford, 1905. It was written about AD 1127-1138 and Cellachán Caisil mac Buadacháin (died 954) was the Eóghanacht King who drove the Vikings out of Munster long before Brian Boru did his "thing" at Clontarf).

- *Leabhar Muimhneach* (Book of Munster) ed. Tadhg Ó Donnchadha, Irish Manuscript Commission, Dublin, 1940.

- *An Ecclesiastical History of Ireland in 4 Volumes* by Rev. John Lanigan, D.D. (Dublin 1822)

- *Forgotten by History: the life and times of John Lanigan, Priest, Professor and Historian* by J. Feehan in Tipperary Historical Journal (2005), pp. 43-60.

- *Historical and Legendary Recollections of the Rock of Cashel* by M. St. John Neville (Dublin 1873)

- *Cashel of the Kings* by J. Davis White (Cashel 1876)

- *A Guide to the Rock of Cashel* by J. Davis White (Cashel 1888)

- *Abstracts from the ancient records of the corporation of Cashel* by T. Laffan (JRSAI, 1904)

- *The Storming of the Rock of Cashel* by Lord Inchiquin in 1647 by Rev. St. John D. Seymour (English Historical Review, pp. 373-381, 1917)

THE SISTER FIDELMA COMPENDIUM

- *Illustrated Guide to Rock and Ruins of Cashel* by A Finn (Clonmel 1920)
- *Cashel of the Kings* by L. M. McCraith (Clonmel 1920)
- *Royal and Saintly Cashel* by A Finn (CTS 1929)
- *The Hermit on the Rock: A Tale of Cashel* by Mrs. J. Sadlier (Dublin 1921)
- *The Archbishops of Cashel* by Rev. M. Maher (Dublin 1927).
- *Cashel: The City of the Kings: Official Guide* (Cashel 1930?)
- *The Singing-Men at Cashel* by Austin Clarke (London 1936)
- *The Sack of Cashel, 1647* by John A. Murphy Cork Historical & Archaeological Society (lxx 1965, pp. 55-62)
- *Cashel and Its Abbeys* by Ada St. L. Hunt (Dublin 1960)
- *Cashel of The Kings: A History of the Ancient Capital of Munster from the date of its foundation until the present day*, Rev. John Gleeson 1927 (reprint De Burca, Dublin, 2001).
- *Irish Kings and High-Kings*, Francis John Byrne, B.T. Batsford, London, 1973. (section on Cashel is still standard reading)
- *St. Patrick's Rock* by Rev. A. O'Donnell (Cashel 1961)
- *The Rock of Cashel* by K. McGowan (Dublin 1973)
- *Historical & Pictorial Cashel* by Tom Wood (Cashel n.d.)
- *Cormac's Chapel Cashel* by A. Hill (Cork 1874)
- *Gleanings from Irish History*, W.F. Butler, Longman, Green & Co, London, 1925
- *A History of Medieval Ireland*, Edmund Curtis, Maunsel and Roberts, Dublin 1923 (still a good standard)
- *Early Medieval Munster: Archaeology, History and Society*, ed, Michael A. Monk and John Sheen, Cork University Press, 1988.
- *Armagh and the Royal Centres in Early Medieval Ireland*, N.B. Aitchinson, Cruithne Press & Boydell and Brewer, Suffolk, 1994
- *The Golden Vale of Ivowen: Land and people in the valley of the Suir*, Co. Tipperary, Col. Eóghan O'Neill, Dublin, 2001.
- *Royal and Saintly Cashel,* Andrew Finn, Dublin 1929
- *Cashel and its ancient Corporation* by A Finn (Dublin 1930)

BIBLIOGRAPHY OF BOOKS RELATING TO CASHEL

- *A Martyred Archbishop of Cashel: Dr. Dermot O'Hurley (1519-1584)* by Rev. Seósamh Ó Murthuile, S.J. (Dublin 1935)

- *Dermot of Cashel: Dermot O'Hurley, Archbishop of Cashel* by Michael O'Halloran (Dublin 1948)

- *St. Patrick's Rock, Cashel, Co. Tipperary: Official Handbook* by H. G. Leask (Dublin 1950?)

- *Vincent O'Brien: A Long Way from Tipperary* by Tim Fitzgeorge-Parker (London 1974). Sporting Prints Series.

- *Times to Cherish, Cashel and Rosegreen Parish History 1795-1995*, Bernie Moloney, Cashel, 1994

- *Rock of Cashel*, Karmac Publications, 1992

- *Parliamentary election results in Ireland 1801-1922*, Edited by B. M. Walker (Dublin 1978)

- *Parliamentary election results in Ireland 1918-1992*, edited by B. M. Walker (Dublin 1992)

- *More Irish Country Towns*, Edited by A. Simms & J.H. Andrews (chapter on Cashel by T O'Keeffe, pp. 156-167), (Dublin 1995

- *Our People are on the Rock: Gravestone Inscriptions from St. Patrick's Rock, Cashel, St. Dominic's Abbey, St. Mary's Abbey, Hore Abbey* compiled by Tom Wood and Cecile Huftier (Cashel ?)

- *John Davis White's Sixty Years in Cashel* by D. G. Marnane in Tipperary Historical Journal (2001) pp. 57-82, (2002) pp. 199-226, (2003) pp. 121-140, (2004) pp. 169-206.

- *Archbishop Charles Agar: Churchmanship and Politics in Ireland, 1760-1810* by A.P.W. Malcomson (Dublin 2002).

- *Rock of Cashel*, Conleth Manning, Heritage Service, 2008

- *The Rock of Cashel, Annual Report of the Commissioners of Public Works in Ireland*, Dublin 1908.

- *Sister Fidelma's Cashel: The Early Kings of Munster and their capital*, Peter Tremayne, International Sister Fidelma Society, 2008.

- *Cashel King Cormacs 1974: Celebration of a Great Year*, (Cashel 1974)

- *Dublin Historical Record Vol. XXIX, No. 4* (Dublin 1975) (Includes an article on a visit to the Rock of Cashel by the Old Dublin Society).

THE SISTER FIDELMA COMPENDIUM

- *Studies: An Irish Quarterly Review* (Dublin, Winter 1975) (Includes an article on the Wall Paintings in Cormac's Chapel at Cashel by Mary McGrath).
- *A History of Handball in Cashel* by Albert Carrie, (Cashel 1982)
- *G.A.A. History of Cashel & Rosegreen 1884-1984* by Seamus J. King (Cashel 1985).
- *A Tale of Two Cathedrals* by Rev. Barbara Fryday (Cashel n.d.)
- *Vincent O'Brien: The Master of Ballydoyle* by Raymond Smith (London 1990)
- *A Workhouse Story: A History of St. Patrick's Hospital, Cashel 1842-1992* by Eamonn Lonergan (Clonmel 1992)
- *Cashel & Emly Heritage* by Walter G. Skehan (Holycross 1993)
- *The Quatercentenary of the Death of King Donal IX MacCarthy Mór 1596-1996* (Cashel 1996)
- *Love and Growth: Poems by Tom Leamy* (Cashel 1997)
- *The Hurling & Football Heroes of Cashel King Cormacs 1974* by Séamus J. King (Cashel 1999).
- *The Cistercian Abbeys of Tipperary by Colmcille Ó Conbhuidhe, OCSO (Dublin 1999).* (This work includes a chapter on Hore Abbey, Cashel.)
- *Cashel Memories* by Francis Phillips compiled and edited by Martin O'Dwyer (Bob), (Cashel 2000)
- *A Brief History of the Sisters of Mercy in St. Patrick's Hospital, Cashel* by Eamonn Lonergan (Cashel 2001)
- *My Favourite Haunt: The Collected Poetry of Michael Luke Phillips* compiled by Thomas Wood & Marjorie Noonan (Cashel 2003)
- *Land and Settlement: A History of West Tipperary to 1660* by Denis G. Marnane (Tipperary 2003).
- *My Silent Voice* by Sally O'Dwyer Bob (Cashel 2004)
- *Sacred Breath* by Sally O'Dwyer Bob (Cashel 2005)
- *Cashel King Cormacs, County Junior Hurling Champions 1953, Golden Jubilee Celebrations* by Séamus J. King (Cashel 2004)
- *Cashel King Cormacs G.A.A. History 1985-2005* by Séamus J. King (Cashel 2006).

BIBLIOGRAPHY OF BOOKS RELATING TO CASHEL

- *The Ballad Collection of John Davis White* by Denis G. Marnane (Tipperary Historical Journal, 2005)

- *Ireland & Europe in the Twelfth Century: Reform and Renewal* edited by Damian Bracken & Dagmar Ó Riain-Raedel (Dublin 2006)

- *Cashel: History & Guide* by Denis G. Marnane (Dublin 2007)

- *Bolton Library County Tipperary: Heritage Conservation Plan* by the Heritage Council 2007

- *Archdiocese of Cashel & Emly: Pobal Ailbhe* by Christy O'Dwyer (Editions du Signe 2008)

- *27 Main Street* by Tom Wood (Listowel 2010)

- *Destination Cashel: 100 Things to See & Do in County Tipperary.* Compiled by Catherine Stapleton (Cashel 2011)

- *The Pauper Priest – The Story of Fr. John Barry* (first published 1890, republished by Martin O'Dwyer Bob (Cashel 2011)

- *Irish Gothic Architecture: Construction, Decay and Reinvention* edited by Roger Stalley (Dublin 2012) Includes a couple of important chapters on the architecture and construction of the buildings on the Rock of Cashel.

- *My Life & Times in Cashel* by Seán Ó Duibhir (Cashel 2012)

- *Cashel Rugby Football Club 1919-2012* by Séamus J. King (Cashel 2013)

- *The First 100: Talks on Tipperary's History* by Denis G. Marnane (Tipperary 2013)

- *Archbishop Miler Magrath: The Enigma of Cashel* by Patrick J. Ryan (Roscrea 2014).

- *Gift of Memory: Thoughts & Reminisences* by Marjorie Noonan (Cashel n.d.)

- *The Many Faces of Cashel Vol. 1* by Mark Fitzell (Cashel 2016)

- *Views to Amuse* by Joanie Browne (Lettertec 2016)

- *Yesteryears: A Photographic Trip Down Memory Lane in Tipperary* (Tipperary Star 2017)

- *Freeborn 100: The Freeborn Exchange Celebrating Ireland 2016* at Cashel Arts Festival (London 2017)

ƬHE SISƬER FIDELMA COMPENDIUM

- *The Many Faces of Cashel Vol. 2* by Mark Fitzell (Cashel 2017)
- *Cashel, Rhymes and Bygone Times* by Joanie Browne (Lettertec 2017)

– Peter Tremayne and Séamus J. King
Compiled for the 2017 Féile Fidelma

The Sister Fidelma Mysteries
Essays on the Historical Novels of Peter Tremayne
EDWARD J. RIELLY AND DAVID ROBERT WOOTEN, EDITORS
MCFARLAND, 2012

Review

The Sister Fidelma Mysteries took the world by storm during the 1990s, and the books have as devoted a following as one sees with Sherlock Holmes or Nero Wolfe. In particular, they have gained the attention of American mystery fans and feminist scholars. There is a society (The International Sister Fidelma Society) with a journal (*The Brehon*), two conferences,[‡] and other newsletters and Internet groups. All for good reason, as the historical mysteries are well researched and well written. Peter Tremayne, author of the series, is also known as Peter Berresford Ellis, an eminent Celtic Studies scholar.

The series is set in 7th century Ireland. For those unfamiliar with that era, Tremayne includes a helpful introductory essay as a preface to the novels. Readers may be surprised to learn that Ireland was quite progressive during this time period. In the novels, Fidelma has authority in her position in the Church, and she is also a trained legal investigator. She not only represents what was possible but what roles actually existed for women during this time and place. In the first novel, *Absolution by Murder* (1994), Fidelma travels to Kildare as part of the delegation to represent the Celtic Church at the debate held between the Celtic and Roman church leaders in 664 AD. Women do not have the same rights throughout the Anglo-Saxon world, and although she is not on her home turf, Fidelma still asserts her role and her rights. Tremayne addresses the resulting tensions, along with the religious ones, through his characters. *Absolution by Murder* is also a good mystery novel, with the true motive for the murder eventually revealed as having nothing to do with politics or religion, but with unrequited love.

[‡] *There have actually been a total of seven 3-day fan gatherings (not conferences) in Cashel from 2006 to 2019, with numerous academic speakers addressing those gathered on a variety of subjects related to the novels.*

THE SISTER FIDELMA COMPENDIUM

The essays in this collection touch on a wide variety of topics that will be of interest to many readers and scholars across a variety of fields. Edited by Edward J. Rielly and David Robert Wooten, the collection covers the historical backdrop of the series, places the work within current conventions of the genre, addresses pedagogical possibilities, and explores characters and themes.

Christine Kinealy's essay "Hidden from History: Fidelma of Cashel and Lost Female Values" explores women's rights in 20th century Ireland, contrasting more current events with the history depicted in the novels, while asserting that 7th century Ireland was probably not a "feminist paradise." Although not set in a feminist paradise, the series does provide ample food for thought about women's roles, as explored in M. E. Kemp's "Who Wears the Pants? Role Reversal in the Sister Fidelma Mysteries" and in Mitzi M. Brunsdale's "Fidelma of Cashel: The Plight of the Learned Lady."

Patrick O'Keefe delves into the Brehon Code, the legal system that existed at the time the novels are set. Other essays explore connections between Fidelma's world and the Druidic tradition and between Fidelma and the ancient Celts of Brittany, while Anna Heussaff addresses the role of the Irish language in the series and in modern Ireland.

John Scaggs contributes two pieces to the collection, the first essay places Fidelma at the beginning of the recent wave of Irish crime fiction while the second explores the dual historical contexts of the series. Scaggs notes that literary history is important for the study and understanding of Tremayne's work. By referring to Brother Eadulf as Fidelma's Doctor Watson, the Anglo-Saxon monk Fidelma meets and is forced to collaborate with in *Absolution by Murder*, Tremayne, in his introductory essay for readers, brings focus to both literary and social history.

Richard Dalby discusses "Fidelma's Position in the Female Detective Genre," drawing attention to female amateur sleuths who appeared as early as 1841. A great deal of attention has been paid to the genesis of the hard-boiled female private investigator genre and to fictional women in official police roles, but Dalby alerts readers to a wide array of female detectives, penned by both men and women, although the latter were often credited as anonymous or under a pseudonym.

The collection includes twenty-one essays in all, concluding with informative pieces about The International Sister Fidelma Society and

RECOMMENDED FURTHER READING

about the [gatherings] held in Ireland. Also included is the transcript of an interview with Tremayne conducted by Rielly via email and a complete bibliography of Tremayne's Fidelma novels and short stories.

— *Elizabeth Blakesley*
Associate Dean of Libraries
Washington State University
The Journal of American Culture, 36.2 (2013)

THE SISTER FIDELMA COMPENDIUM

ILLUSTRATIONS

ILLUSTRATIONS

THE SISTER FIDELMA COMPENDIUM

Acknowledgments

Acknowledgments

First, I would like to acknowledge two scholars who fostered an already-simmering love of all things history during my undergraduate and postgraduate studies at North Carolina State University. Dr. Gordon D. Newby, a specialist in Islamic, Jewish, and Comparative Studies and Professor Emeritus of Middle Eastern and South Asian Studies at Emory University, and Professor in the Graduate Program of West and South Asian Religions, served as my graduate advisor in Ancient Near Eastern Studies at North Carolina State, and nurtured my nascent love of poring over dusty tomes of obscure literature – a practice I maintain to this day. Likewise, I am indebted to Alumni Distinguished Professor Emeritus of History John M. Riddle, a specialist in pharmacological history particularly of the classical and mediæval periods, based on previously under-utilized ancient and medieval sources. I can think of no two learned individuals who made a greater positive impact on my early studies, and I would not have maintained a lifelong love of research in a wide variety of subjects were it not for their patient guidance.

Additional thanks are due to individual contributors who penned chapters to this compendium: the late Maurice McCann, Founder Member of The International Sister Fidelma Society, and a talented and generous contributor to the early publications of the Society; Hans van den Boom of De Leeskamer, Peter's Dutch translator and publisher, as well as the man who spearheaded bringing Sister Fidelma to graphic novel format – and one of the first members of the Society; Catherine Green, one of the earliest Féile Fidelma attendees and another longtime member of the Society; Norway-based longtime Society member Reidun Drange, without whose research work the article "Peter Tremayne: Murderer–Detective–Defendant–Judge–Jury–Executioner" would not have been possible; Professor Emeritus Edward J. Rielly of Saint Joseph's College of Maine, my co-editor on our previous collaboration, *The Sister Fidelma Mysteries: Essays on the Historical Novels of Peter Tremayne* (also a member of the Society – I'm sensing a pattern here...); Mike Ashley, Tom Dudley, Christy Gordon, Martin Doyle, and Rhys Williams, for the reprinting of their articles from the pages of *The Brehon*; Peter

ZHE SISZER FIDELMA COMPENDIUM

Breheny, whose research paper on Peter Tremayne (towards a BA Hons) is invaluable in its depth of detail; while not entirely devoted to Sister Fidelma, Philip Grosset's extensive – strike that, MASSIVE – website on every known fictional clerical detective includes his personal reviews on all of the Fidelma novels, as well as a quite "novel" listing of a "Who's Who" of the aforementioned Clerical Detectives in fiction, to include a "Best Of" and a thorough index of EVERY clerical sleuth, along with their authors – the relevant sections of his website are included (slightly abridged), with heartfelt gratitude for same; credit and thanks is also due to my friend Eric Müller for rendering an image of Fidelma PRECISELY to my specifications (based on a popular, appropriately-named Irish actress – you guess) as used both on the cover (as colored by another friend, artistic genius Franchesco!) and more than once in the interior; and finally, my sincere thanks to Cork-based photographer/artist Michael Walsh for the two renderings of The Rock of Cashel as appear on the front and back covers of this book – granted, Sister Fidelma's Rock of Cashel saw absolutely nothing akin to what currently sits on that rocky outcropping, but visitors to Cashel still envision the "modern" silhouette of that landmark as associated with Fidelma – Michael's brilliant digital "painting"/abstracting of his own fine art photographs hint at the current structures without reproducing yet another image we have all seen a thousand times before.

I am eternally indebted to all members of The International Sister Fidelma Society, past and present, many of whom I was fortunate to meet personally during our all-too-rare sojourns to Cashel, Co Tipperary, for the all-too-short Féile Fidelma weekends. Their encouragement and support kept the ever-growing and enthusiastic group of us Fidelmaniacs bound together by the common thread of love for Peter Tremayne's fiction, as well as his (very real in our own minds) titular sleuth, Sister Fidelma of Cashel. Likewise, the gatherings in Cashel known as Féile Fidelmas – which brought together geographically-disparate fans of Sister Fidelma and Peter Tremayne – would not have been possible without the unflagging efforts of The Cashel Arts Fest Committee; most specifically, I must applaud Seamus J. King (from whom I learned the intricacies of hurling, about which he is most-assuredly the world's leading authority) and Emily Kenneally for both tolerating my incessant nagging-aggravating-insistent communiqués prior to each of these events, as well as spearheading many of the preliminary tasks that actually made the Féiles happen in the first place.

ACKNOWLEDGMENTS

Ultimately, I must extend my most sincere thanks to someone I never imagined – while poring over those aforementioned dusty tomes in college (some of them his own non-fiction which I used in my research) – I would ever have cause to cross paths with. As I have detailed both previously and in this current publication, I contacted Peter Tremayne (or, as I knew of him LONG before he had ever begun gathering the literary "clay" to sculpt the character and figure of the premier detective of 7th century Ireland, Peter Berresford Ellis) only after learning of his "new" fictional character. I imagine I was a bit over-enthusiastic in my babbling fan-aticism for his work – and that was just the non-fiction!

As explained later in the pages of this book, we struck up a working relationship, as it were, which progressed into what I consider to be one of my most cherished friendships. Having lived long enough to know that you can usually count the TRUE friends you have in your life on the fingers of one hand (sometimes with digits left over), I do not toss out the word "friend" casually. Peter has gone above and beyond in supporting me in so many aspects of my life, not least of which is being tolerant enough to bear the whips and chains of the fartels of incessant letters, then emails, then phone calls, to the point that we speak now several times a week.

One thing that I have in common with both Peter and my own late father – we are/were insufferable punsters, playing on every possible twist of word or phrase until one of us finally throws up his hands in defeat. I mention this because I sorely miss that interplay with my father and sparring back and forth with Peter – well below my own ranking – is the whetstone that keeps the brain sharp and the tongue quick. A favorite quotation of mine is, "If you're the smartest person in the room, you're in the wrong room." When I'm in the room with Peter (or on the phone, or typing out horrific puns via email), I always know I'm in the right "room," and am delighted – and grateful – to have been allowed through the door.

Suffice it to say that none of that which precedes this would be possible without the abundant generosity of my dear friend, Peter Berresford Ellis (call him what you will).

– *David Robert Wooten*

THE SISTER FIDELMA COMPENDIUM

David Robert Wooten is the Founder and Director of The International Sister Fidelma Society and Editor of its thrice-yearly magazine, *The Brehon*. David took his degree in Ancient Near Eastern History at North Carolina State University. Before launching his business career, he worked in the North Carolina State Archives and remained interested in history and heraldry. He currently serves as the Executive Director, as well as a Distinguished Fellow and Head of the Board of Governors, of the American College of Heraldry. He is the author of *We All Become Forefathers* (1993) and was specialist editor (heraldry) for *The New Oxford Dictionary of American English* (Oxford University Press, 2001). He launched a small publishing house, Gryfons Publishers (later Phoenix Press), and became a website designer and graphics consultant, running his own 9august.com consultancy.

In 2000 David devised the first Sister Fidelma website, with Peter Tremayne's permission, and such was the response that he obtained the author's further approval to launch The International Sister Fidelma Society a year later, serving as Director and Editor of *The Brehon*. He is also co-editor, along with Prof. Edward J. Rielly, of *The Sister Fidelma Mysteries: Essays on the Historical Novels of Peter Tremayne* (McFarland, 2012), a collection of scholarly essays by noted academics on Peter Tremayne's Sister Fidelma novels.

He has one daughter – as a rule, she is far more perspicacious than he.

Made in the USA
Coppell, TX
20 February 2023